MEMORIES OF A HAPPY LIFE

William Lawrence

MEMORIES
OF A HAPPY LIFE

BY

WILLIAM LAWRENCE, D.D., LL.D.

Bishop of Massachusetts

BOSTON AND NEW YORK

HOUGHTON MIFFLIN COMPANY

The Riverside Press Cambridge

1926

The Riverside Press
CAMBRIDGE · MASSACHUSETTS
PRINTED IN THE U.S.A.

TO
MY WIFE
AND
CHILDREN
I INSCRIBE
THIS BOOK

PREFACE

THE pressure of my family and friends started me on this book: the fun of writing it has carried me through.

Was there ever such an interesting seventy-five years as this last? How can any one who has lived through them with eyes and ears open and friendliness all about him escape having memories that he enjoys sharing with others?

This is not a formal autobiography: it has not the required dignity: nor the solemnity that oppresses some examples of such literature. These pages are simply the jottings of one who has led rather an active life for over seventy-five years and who has been blessed beyond measure. During the writing my three bugbears have been egotism, dullness, and injustice to others. I hope that I have avoided them. At all events, I have tried to be myself.

Scores of loyal friends and fellow workers, too many to name, have been in the back of my mind as I have written. In turning these pages they will recognize the times and scenes wherein they have given me their guidance, cheer, and support.

To me the surprising feature of life is that it becomes more interesting as one grows older. And a lifelong Christian faith suffuses the later years with serenity and hope.

WILLIAM LAWRENCE

BAR HARBOR, MAINE
August, 1926

CONTENTS

ILLUSTRATIONS

MEMORIES OF A HAPPY LIFE

MEMORIES OF A HAPPY LIFE

• •

CHAPTER I

MY STOCK AND BOYHOOD

PEMBERTON SQUARE, Boston, in 1850 was a quiet pocket of the City's West End, where dwelt about thirty families of the well-to-do but not richer citizens. Here resided young couples who had fortunes ahead of them, and older people who had saved enough to live comfortably. Here I was born, May 30, 1850.

My ancestors on both sides, Lawrence and Appleton, were born on Massachusetts farms or in the villages. They tilled the soil, pastured the cattle, kept exact accounts of the farm and stock, were pious and careful to attend meeting on the Sabbath. On the Lawrence side, their farm at Groton sloped down from Farmers' Row almost a mile to the Nashua River, and, as they went to the barn to milk the cows, they looked across the valley and saw the sun set behind the hills between Wachusett and Monadnock. On the 19th of April, 1775, my great-grandfather, Samuel Lawrence, heard the voice of his neighbor, Colonel William Prescott and his command, 'Samuel, notify your men, the British are coming.' He mounted the Colonel's horse, notified his men, reported to the Colonel, marched with his company to Cambridge, and at Bunker Hill received through his beaver cap a British bullet which cut off a lock of his hair.

Both sides of my ancestry had a fair proportion of ministers. My great-grandfather Adams, minister of the First Church, Roxbury, died from exposure in preaching out-of-doors to the soldiers in the Revolution. My great-grandfather Appleton's grave is under the shadow of the

Meeting House at Brookfield, where he was pastor. Both my grandfathers came to Boston in their youth to seek their fortunes. Neither of them had more than a few dollars; but they brought character and talents, inherited and acquired, with them. These they adapted to city life, revealing exceptional ability in business and in making and keeping their fortunes, while still retaining their love of the country, economical habits, piety, and a habit of liking people. Amos Lawrence and William Appleton became known throughout Boston for integrity, ability, and public spirit. The latter served the country with distinction in Congress.

My father, Amos Adams Lawrence, who had been married eight years when I was born, had already responded to his ancestral love for the country by buying with his brother William some ninety acres of land two and one half miles west of Boston. My mother never cared for the country, but was persuaded that it would be better for the children. My grandfather, Amos Lawrence, lived on the corner of Tremont and West Streets, where the Lawrence Building now stands. From that corner towards Boylston Street was Colonnade Row — a block of the most dignified and comfortable houses in Boston, with colonnade porches and balconies from which we children saw the great processions. Behind the brick wall on West and Mason Streets was the fruit garden. Within the house were old-fashioned furniture, big four-posted beds, and for cooking an open fire with crane and a brick oven beside the fireplace. Sunday beef never tasted so good as that roasted before the fire, and the apple pies baked in the brick oven can never be forgotten. Across the Common, halfway down Beacon Hill, William Prescott, the historian, and my grandfather Appleton built adjoining houses, still standing. They also had a colonnade and balcony from which we children saw the soldiers marching to save the Union in '61.

It seemed a long drive from the Common to our house in Longwood, for just beyond Charles Street the blocks of houses stopped. The Public Garden was then a dirty waste, and at Arlington Street was the city dump, where ashes and other refuse were thrown by tipcarts into the Back Bay. In Revolutionary days there was no way except by ferry from Boston to Brookline, or to Cambridge, except over Boston Neck, through Roxbury, and across the bridge away up the river. The old milestone which used to stand in Harvard Square and is now in the corner of the near-by graveyard says, 'Eight miles to Boston, A.D. 1734.' In order that Paul Revere might ride direct to Lexington, he waited with his horse on the Charlestown side of the water and was signalled by lanterns from the Old North Church. Dawes rode his horse around over the Neck.

Some years before we moved out to Longwood, a causeway had been constructed running west from the dump at Arlington Street through the water to the marsh land where Beacon Street and Commonwealth Avenue now intersect. This was Beacon Street, but in those days was always called 'The Mill Dam.' On the south side was the Back Bay, and on the north the Charles River. A plank walk ran along the south side of the road and a line of poplar trees. Driving out from Boston on a winter day was a cold trip. The northwest wind swept down the Charles River valley unobstructed, and the great mass of snowy ice caused by the tides on the flats gave the scene an Arctic look, for Cambridgeport was well back of the river across water and marsh. To the south one's vision swept across the Back Bay to the Neck two miles away, and the Roxbury Meeting House stood out against the sky. Through holes cut in the ice men were spearing eels, and boys were skating. Halfway across the Dam was the tollgate, where every team and carriage stopped to pay toll: and just beyond, where at flood tide the Charles rushed in under a cut in the road to fill the Back Bay, and at ebb tide rushed out again, were the mill and the mill-wheel which ground corn hauled in from Brookline and Newton by the farmers. At the fork the 'Brighton Road' ran out where

Commonwealth Avenue now is, and the 'Punch Bowl Road' to the left, leading to the Punch Bowl Tavern in Brookline. Straight out Beacon Street, we drove over the marshes, crossing the Boston and Worcester — now the Albany — Railroad tracks. Over the road was a great sign, 'Railroad Crossing: Look out for the Engine while the bell rings.' On reaching the solid land we turned up to the right to 'Cottage Farm' where my father built our house. There was but one cottage in that whole district: hence the name. Houses in those days were built of wood, and the air-tight stove had succeeded the ancient open fireplaces. Mr. George M. Dexter, the architect of our house, had made a study of English country houses; he had taste, but little experience on the financial side of building. The result was that my father built what was for those days a beautiful English house of Roxbury pudding-stone, with large open fireplaces and a great hall, really unique in its time. In front was an open lawn, behind, a large grove of oaks. When, however, the extra bills came in, my father protested, then yielded; paid them, and threw them all, receipted, into the fire.

The neighborhood is now closely built up, and is almost a part of the city. Our grove, lawn, and garden are gone: the stone house has been lifted and turned on its axis: but from 1851 we, my father and mother and seven children, lived there. From it went the brides, and to-day the children, grandchildren, and great-grandchildren play in the hall; but the oak burning in the great fireplaces comes from the grove no longer. Suburban life had hardly begun then. Although less than three miles from the State House, we were really in the country. My father rode his horse every day into the city. Mother drove in when necessary. Our carriage, drawn by a pair of big gray horses, was a large English coach with C springs, a great brocaded coachman's box, massive lamps heavily mounted with silver, and with platform and straps at the back for the footman. We drove out from Boston on Christmas evenings, as is described in my father's diary: 'At ten we left for home; nine inside the carriage, and myself riding as footman behind.'

We attended a little school in a one-storied shanty at the corner of Beacon and Carlton Streets; and later my brother Amory and I walked to the Brookline public schools, across the fields over two miles away. Cut off as we were in our early years from the advantages of the city, our life had its compensations; and our habits and education were independent of city customs. Early hours, country games, and habits of industry were natural.

Breakfast was at seven o'clock, by candlelight, for we had no gas. Before that, however, my brother and I had blacked the family boots in the cellar, for which we were paid five cents a pair; for my father believed that the best way to set a right value on money was to earn it; and in many forms of labor we added to our savings bank account. Occasionally an extra dividend came in. When, for instance, a heifer calf was born, father claimed it; but when a bull calf, we claimed it, and sold it to the butcher for five dollars. My brother Amory and I had ponies, but only so long as we fed and cleaned them; and this was no slight work before school, for in spring and autumn the grammar school in Brookline began at eight o'clock. Most of the boys at school were of New England stock; the rest were Irish — no other race was represented. One of my most intimate friends was Dan Miley, the son of a day laborer.

Boys and girls were whipped at school in those days. I never saw that it did much good, for the same four or five were always whipped, made stubborn, and put in a temper which in time brought another licking. How still the whole room was as the teacher picked up his heavy ruler from the desk, took the disobedient boy into the side room, and shut the door! Then we could hear him say, 'Hold out your hand,' and down came the ruler — one, two, three; sometimes a howl, sometimes stubborn silence — four, five, up to twenty and thirty; and out came the boy crying or simply sullen. If cries would not come, then the

hand was turned over, and the blows fell on the back of
the hand, and even then John Griggs's stubborn endurance could not be broken. Sometimes the women teachers
did the whipping. A thrill went through the room one day
when a pretty new teacher called into the side room a
popular but stubborn girl who refused to hold out her
hand, and the teacher beat her across the eyes. We missed
the teacher from her desk the next day. The School
Committee had acted.

The only real physical discipline that I had was from my
brother Amory. He was two years older than I, strong
and fat. My temper was hot and quick, and I struck out
in a second. He would then push me down, sit on me,
pinion my arms under him while I wriggled and turned and
fought. But there he sat quietly and for what seemed to
me an eternity, getting up only after I had cooled off and
promised humbly not to do it again.

When we were not riding over the country or playing
games in the afternoons, we were with the men on the
place, or the carpenters and masons. Unconsciously we
gained information, friendship, a spirit of democracy, and
a liking of people as such. Our own carpenter's bench and
tools made us 'handy,' so that through life I have had
a real interest in the details of carpentry, plumbing, and
house building. I believe that some of the present conditions of education, the private boarding-school, and the
concentration of boys' interests on certain sports have
very great disadvantages. Boys do not have the chance
to meet, like, and respect all sorts of people, or gain that
handicraft, faculty of observation, and general intelligence
which come only by experience.

Our fruit garden was a constant source of interest. Old
Maloney, the gardener, who was always smoking his clay
pipe, taught us to prune and graft. As the grapes did not
flourish, father thought of a unique way of enriching the
soil. Being a lover of horses, and a persistent rider, he was
stirred with anger and pity at the cruel treatment of many
working horses. The Society for the Prevention of Cruelty

to Animals had not been thought of in those days, and it was difficult to get a man arrested for cruelty; so father bought many a worn-out horse and shot him. At the Brighton Cattle Market every Thursday there were usually decrepit horses for sale. One day he told Maloney to dig a deep and large trench the whole length of the grapevine trellis: then he rode to Brighton, bought nine horses at from $2.50 to $10 apiece, and had the limping, sore-covered beasts driven to the garden. Maloney led one and another and another on the edge of the trench: father shot him and Maloney covered him in. Thus the soil was in time enriched and the crops of grapes increased while the horses were released from suffering.

In 1856, the North was deeply angered by the cowardly blow of Preston Brooks, Congressman from South Carolina, upon the back of Senator Sumner's head. The issue of slavery was rising fast. My father was a conservative and not a supporter of Sumner. This, however, was a national issue. Hence, when Sumner, partially recovered, came on his triumphal tour to Boston, he was taken from the train at Cottage Farm Station and rested over Sunday at our house. On Monday he drove over the Roxbury Neck to Boston amidst the cheers of the people.

The Prince of Wales made a tour of the country in 1860. We in these days are so accustomed to the reception of distinguished foreigners, even of royalty, that we have no conception of the interest and enthusiasm aroused throughout the country by the Prince. He too stopped at Cottage Farm, and I remember well the attractive young man as he drove through our avenue.

The Revolution was only twenty years farther away from us than the Civil War is from the boys of to-day. In our grove we found remains of earthworks, soldiers' buttons, and Indian graves; across the Charles River was a fort where cannon still stood for the defense of Boston; and at church, Colonel Aspinwall, who had lost his arm in the war of 1812, made the history of our country very real.

I wonder if the boys of 1914 to '18 have as vivid a

memory of the World War as I still have of the years of
the Civil War.

In politics my father was a conservative, a Whig, a
strictly Union man who believed that the Union could be
preserved and slavery gradually abolished by peaceful
means. In 1856–'58 Kansas was the center of the struggle. Would her people vote for slavery or freedom? The
South poured in a horde of men; the New England Emi-
grant Aid Company recruited families and sent them to
Kansas to settle and vote for a free State. My father, as
treasurer, advanced and begged money for the cause and
threw himself into the fray with such vigor that later,
when Kansas was organized, its capital was named 'Lawrence,' and Lawrence University, to which he gave the
first endowment, was afterwards made the State University. He worked in order that in legal ways and by a
majority vote Kansas should be free. He deplored the
savage methods of the Abolitionist John Brown; and yet
he could not help admiring the fanatic. I remember that
as he sat down to dinner one day he said, 'John Brown
came into my office to-day and I told him to go to Whipple's to have his daguerreotype taken; he may be famous
some day.' Later he joined a few others in paying for
counsel for John Brown, that he might have a fair trial.

The nomination of Abraham Lincoln threw everybody,
schoolboys as well as voters, into parties. Father, as a
Whig, supported the Union Party, not the Republican,
and indeed allowed himself to be nominated for Governor,
sure, however, of defeat. The majority of the boys at
school backed 'Abe the rail-splitter,' and had on their
jackets a pin with a little hatchet and three rails: at all
games they stood the rest of the school and always beat.
Torchlight parades were at their best in those days, for
with street lamps of oil, or feeble gas, the torches and lanterns shone out gloriously; the 'Wide Awakes' with white
rubber capes were Republicans. We, of the conservative
minority, lived a disappointed life, although one Bell and
Everett procession did pass through our avenue, stop at

WILLIAM APPLETON
Crayon drawing by Cheney in 1843

the front porch, and salute my father, as candidate for Governor. From Lincoln's election to his inauguration were more anxious days than we youngsters knew. Very few anticipated war; but no one dared prophesy. After the inauguration events moved fast, and when, on April 6th, Fort Sumter was fired upon, the whole North awoke to the danger. Even then, however, few realized what was coming. My grandfather Appleton, who had lately retired from Congress, had started south by sea, and, happening to be entering Charleston Harbor, he heard the guns and then saw the surrender of Fort Sumter. By the courtesy of General Beauregard he visited the fort, then in Confederate hands, and, continuing his trip through the country, was entertained by Southern friends and came home. He and others could not believe that the South was really committed to rebellion. The shot of Sumter sounded, however, in the ear of every man and boy in the North, and on the moment political differences were wiped out. The Union was in danger, and every loyal man sprang to action. Colonel Salignac's Zouaves with blue uniforms and red caps drilled in our grove and where the Braves' Ball Field now is; my father, twenty years older than the rest, marched and drilled with them, and we boys, setting a barrel on our pony wagon filled with lemonade, served as sutlers. The Boston Cadets guarded the magazine across the river in Cambridgeport at the end of Magazine Street, and we carried them green vegetables and fruit. The Militia gathered on the Common and in the halls of Boston and were quickly shipped to Washington that Massachusetts might be first in the field. We children stood on the bank of the Worcester, now the Albany, Railroad, just behind our grove, and cheered the Sixth, as they went their journey through Baltimore to spill their blood on Lexington Day, the 19th of April. We walked into Boston to see the first volunteer regiment, of which my cousin, Sam Green, was assistant surgeon, and Company A, mostly from Brookline. When after review they came to 'rest,' the crowd burst through the ropes, and embraced every soldier of the regiment. Our blood boiled with anger at the death of Colonel Ellsworth, of the New York Zouaves, shot by a tavern-keeper as Ellsworth was hauling down a rebel flag: and we thrilled with patriotism at the order of General Dix, 'If any man hauls down the Union flag, shoot him on the spot.'

The Brookline Rifles was organized, made up of boys armed with real but miniature rifles. Captain Moore of the Army was drill-master, and Moses Williams, captain. School drill was unheard of then. We went to various towns to show the school committees what boys could do. A committee from the Legislature, appointed to study the question of drilling in public schools, came out to the Brookline Town Hall to inspect us. I was twelve years old at the time, one of the drummer boys.

At the Brookline Town Meeting, father presented the committee's report putting the Town on a war footing, and in the evening he drilled the townspeople. In the mornings, after an early breakfast, he mounted his horse and rode over to Harvard College, of which he was treasurer, to drill the students. He taught some of them single-stick and broadsword. With Colonel Henry Lee he recruited the Second Cavalry. How vividly I remember looking through the crack of the dining-room door and seeing Colonel Lowell and his staff, Major Caspar Crowninshield, Henry Russell, and others, who were then, and always remained to us, heroes! Bull Run sent a shock through the hearts of boys and men; we all scraped lint; and on the news of Gettysburg, as we came out of Sunday morning service, every man, woman, and child set to work tearing sheets, tablecloths and napkins, making bandages and sending them to the front. The battle of the Monitor and the Merrimac was as if that of David and Goliath had taken place at Hampton Roads. Censors were unknown then. The country did not have to wait long days and weeks before getting news of the battle. But the very next day the papers were filled with reports and personal experiences. Lists of killed and wounded direct from the field were scanned by every man and woman of the land. Fathers took train and went to the battle-field to find their boys. The story of Oliver Wendell Holmes, 'My Hunt after "The Captain,"' is a bit of true history, very real to us boys; the 'Captain' is now an Associate Justice of the Supreme Court in Washington.

In the winter of '62, father took Amory and myself to Washington. We passed a Sunday in Philadelphia, and heard the young preacher, Phillips Brooks, who was stirring the city. After service, his tall figure stood over us, as my father talked of the six Brooks boys in Saint Paul's Church, Boston, and claimed him as one of his Sunday-School class.

In the station at Baltimore we heard cheers, and then saw the first squad of exchanged prisoners just arriving from Libby Prison, some of the Twentieth Massachusetts, emaciated, ragged, holding up pieces of maggoty bread which they had brought as evidence of their treatment. The low ceilings of all the cars were pierced with bayonet holes. Tired soldiers lay in the aisles, while the closed stoves at both ends of the cars sent forth a headaching heat.

Our rooms in Washington looked out on Pennsylvania Avenue. In the morning began a six-hour long procession of army wagons, each drawn by six mules or four horses, covered with Virginia and Maryland mud, going to the storehouses for supplies, and back they passed in the afternoon. Washington was knee-deep in mud, and the few Government buildings stood in the midst of a squalid city, magnificent then only in plan and distances. Willie, the President's favorite son, had died the day before we arrived, so that we missed seeing Mr. Lincoln, a loss which I have always regretted. Colonel Lee and Major Revere, of the Twentieth Massachusetts, just from Libby Prison, were being welcomed by their friends. Confusion seemed to reign; officers and orderlies galloped here and there, throwing mud in every direction; office-seekers and ne'er-do-weels from every part of the country jostled modest heroes, and anxious and mourning parents who had come to learn about their boys.

System makes for efficiency, but shuts out much personal experience. To-day boys are roped a hundred yards away from a house on fire; in my day we rushed into the house, helped save the stuff, and then watched the roof fall in. In the World War the people worked at a distance and through great organizations; in the Civil War we were in the midst of things.

In the sixties Harvard College and the public schools, except the Boston Latin, had but little relation to each other. Hence in '63 Amory and I, leaving the Brookline Grammar School, after some tutoring in Latin, went to Mr. Dixwell's in Boylston Place, Boston, which was then the best fitting-school for Harvard. The boys presented Huntington Wolcott, who left his desk for the War, with a sword, and within a few weeks we gathered at his bier. He was, like thousands on thousands of others, a victim to typhoid fever. He left Roger at the school to live to be the Governor of Massachusetts during the Spanish War. We studied our Latin and Greek grammar, learned interminable lists of exceptions to rules, and in spite, no doubt, of the best teaching of that time, those of us who were of only average ability got a distaste for the classical authors for whose enjoyment we had struggled through the grammar. In the spring of '65 the sound of drum and music warned Mr. Dixwell and the school that a returning regiment was passing and we ran out to Boylston Street, saw the bronzed and thin faces of the officers and men, their stained and worn uniforms, and cheered the tattered flags which now stand in the State House. The news of Lincoln's death is so vivid to me now that I recall just where I stood and the voice of the man, a stranger to me, who told me.

During my early childhood our summer cottage at Lynn stood on the bank where our view had the sweep of Long Beach, Nahant, Egg Rock, and the open Atlantic. William Prescott, the historian, John Lowell, who founded the

Lowell Institute Lectures, Benjamin R. Curtis, a leader at the bar, and merchants like Nathan Appleton and Benjamin T. Reed had estates whose lawns sloped down to the ocean. Later, my father bought Clark's Point at Nahant where Amory and I sailed our boat and rode our horses. At Cupid's Rock all Nahant boys and men in the garb of nature bathed and dived. Cabot Lodge's father had bought the old hotel estate on East Point, and to the indignation of his neighbors gradually closed what they felt was a public right of way.

As the bowling-alleys and stables of the old hotel were still standing, we boys, Cabot Lodge, Frank Chadwick, Sturgis Bigelow, and Frank Amory, amused ourselves smashing the windows and were chased over fence after fence by Cabot's gardener. Smashing windows was, I am inclined to think, a favorite amusement; for it was our custom in riding over the Mill Dam on the bus to and from Dixwell's School to break the street lamps with our catapults: a harmless amusement in our minds until we saw posters upon fences offering twenty-five dollars reward for the arrest of lamp-glass breakers. Though still conscious that it was a harmless amusement, we thought it advisable to stop. In the sailing races, a Beverly boy, a schoolmate and friend, always beat the rest of us— Edward Burgess, who through boyhood and college was deeply interested in the study of bugs, moths, and butterflies; drawing sketches, figuring their speed and the curves of their wings. He also studied the models of his boats and improved them each summer. It was he who in later years modelled the Puritan, the Mayflower, and the Volunteer, and thus set this country to the fore in international yachting.

A New York boy, Seth Low, sometimes made visits with us at Nahant. His father's firm of shipping merchants, A. and A. Low, had business relations with father. Seth, who was our age, about fifteen, used to sit and talk solemnly with father of business and politics. When he left, we shouted with relief, for we had not got to be polite to him any longer: at which father used to say, 'Boys, Seth will amount to something one of these days and you won't.' Seth did. He was a most successful Mayor of Brooklyn, President of Columbia University, to which he gave the great Library, and first Mayor of the City of Greater New York, organizing the departments and setting the huge civic machine going. He had other broad interests and duties, and was one of the most useful and esteemed citizens of his generation. During the last thirty years of his life a warm friendship bound us together.

To us at Nahant neighbors were simply neighbors, not men of distinction. Next to our cottage was Mr. Longfellow's. With his beautiful white hair and beard, his gracious manner, he looked the poet; but he never recited 'Evangeline' to us, nor did he ask us to recite 'The Village Blacksmith.' It was simply, 'Hullo, Mr. Longfellow,' and we passed on. For several years Dr. Holmes lived next us on the other side. His talk was like the running of a mountain brook, fresh and inexhaustible. He dropped in upon the piazza and talked and talked. My father listened, my mother slipped away, and we caught stray sentences. At supper, however, there were always quotations of the bright things the Doctor had said. Nothing remains to me now of his talk except a discussion as to why a donkey standing upon a rough field is more picturesque than a well-groomed horse. Agassiz, too, lived at Nahant; he was kindly, but we stood at a distance from him. He was to us a man of whom it was said that if you should give him one bone of a fish, he could tell you what kind of fish it was and draw a picture of it. Charles Sumner, too, made visits at Nahant, and his salt-and-pepper suit, his pompous manner, and deep voice impressed us. When Lincoln was nominated for a second term, Mr. Sumner opposed his election. One evening father came back from taking supper with him at Mr. Longfellow's, and said with some tartness, 'Charles Sumner wants to elect a President with brains; one who can make a plan and carry it through.' Lothrop Motley was often at Nahant. On Sundays we had

AMOS A. LAWRENCE AT NAHANT

'Over fifty years of horseback'

in the Union Church the leading preachers of the country and some of their sermons thrilled us. But our chief companions were Luscomb, the painter, who was the modest possessor of medals for life-saving and who taught us to sail, and Kemp, who was skipper of the Foam, the fishing smack.

In making connection between the Brookline Grammar School and Dixwell's, I found myself a year behind the boys of my age, my best friends, and I have always thought it a mark of confidence in me that my father acceded to my wish to skip a year. He engaged a tutor at Harvard to coach me. Between October and May I did the equivalent of two years' schooling and entered the freshman class in the autumn with only one condition. Possibly I was aided by this singular incident. Two or three days before the examination my tutor asked me to read certain passages in, I think, the Anabasis. I went over them carefully. He, it so happened, was my examiner in Greek. To my surprise and gratification, he called me up to read the identical passages!

In May, 1867, my father and mother, having seven children, two of whom were married, and who had not broken away from business and home cares since their marriage in 1842, decided to take the family to Europe from May until September. This stopped my tutoring. How much rest they gained from the trip I question. We made up when travelling a party of twelve, of all ages down to a baby grandchild; also a courier who appeared in the morning on two or three occasions penniless, having gambled away what money of father's he had had in hand. We made the usual summer tour of Americans, rarely stopping two nights in the same place, except for Sundays. Paris, where we were for ten days, was at the height of its imperial glory. Napoleon III and his beautiful Empress Eugénie, drove by our apartments through the Champs Elysées to the Arc de Triomphe, little reckoning on the Germans and what was to happen there three years later.

The Great Exposition was open, and the whole gay world was its gayest. Father's cousin, George Richards, partner of the bankers, John Munroe and Company, in Paris, had married a beautiful Boston girl a number of years before. We children met our Paris cousins for the first time. One of them, a most attractive girl, Élise, later married a young man in the French Foreign Office and some thirty years after came to the country of her mother's birth for the first time as the wife of the French Ambassador. Élise Jusserand and her husband, in the more than twenty years of their residence in Washington through the administrations of Roosevelt, Taft, Wilson, Harding, and Coolidge, gained the affection and respect of the Nation.

Father with his simple New England traditions abhorred the Paris of the Empire, its flash, noise, and immorality. I have often heard him say that he would rather see his son in his grave than have him pass a year in Paris; hence, when we took a train for Switzerland he felt as if he were fleeing from 'Sodom,' as he often called Paris. Arriving at Dijon for a night, we were put into a musty hotel with windows opening upon the courtyard, where horses, cows, and dogs swarmed. The familiar noises and the reeking smells brought father's memory back to the barn at Groton and Longwood, and he would have liked to go directly home. But my mother was not the wife of a farmer, nor was she fond of cows and farmyards; so we continued our journey through Switzerland, down the Rhine, and to England and Scotland. Returning, I crammed for ten days, took my Harvard entrance examinations, and on the afternoon of the second day stood in line before the Dean in his office and was told that I had passed.

CHAPTER II
COLLEGE
1867–1871

MIDWAY in the course of the Class of '71, Harvard crossed the line from a college to an American university. Charles W. Eliot was inaugurated President October 19, 1869, at the opening of our junior year. As undergraduates it was our duty to be there; but the tall, thin form, and rather severe face of the young President aroused no enthusiasm from the students.

There must have been grave fears and great expectations among the doubters and supporters as the young President laid down his radical platform, so familiar to us now. 'This University recognizes no real antagonism between literature and science, and consents to no such narrow alternatives as mathematics or classics, science or metaphysics. We would have them all and at their best.' 'A University must be indigenous: it must be rich, but above all it must be free. The winnowing breeze of freedom must blow through all its chambers.' 'A University is built not by a sect but by a Nation.'

From my earliest boyhood Harvard College, which was about two miles away from Longwood, across the Charles River, had been familiar. The westerly air wafted the chimes of old Christ Church to our house. We drove over as children to the Longfellows', and I remember well Mrs. Longfellow, whose tragic death by burning shocked the whole community. The dancing around the Tree by the Seniors on Class Day was the great social event of the college year. It was a modest scene viewed at this distance. The Class Day Tree, standing in the centre of the Quad created by Holden Chapel, Hollis, Harvard Hall, and the two-bar open fence on the street, had encircling its trunk at about nine feet high a broad band of flowers:

no seats were constructed, but parents and friends of the students stood near the buildings, the public at the fence while the seniors marched in, cheered, sang, and danced around the tree; at a signal they leaped for the flowers and after a sharp struggle brought their tokens of victory to their favored ladies. I remember well the War Class Day of 1862. Standing on the fence we boys saw General Frank Bartlett, a young graduate, with one leg lost in action, watching the fray. A short time afterwards he led his new regiment down Broadway, New York, while the people cheered and cheered as they saw the young hero, strapped to his saddle with his crutch across his back, as it was later when he led a charge against the enemy.

We knew the names of the professors and instructors, but their personality did not always impress us. It was in the sophomore year, after I had studied Latin for five or six years, that I first caught, through the teaching of Professor Lane, a glimpse of the beauty of Virgil and of the charm of the Odes of Horace. Professor Child taught me more English style in one lecture than the instructor in English did in a month: indeed, Harvard did not pretend to teach English to the body of students. Professor Shaler was, I believe, reckoned by experts as unreliable in statements of facts; but Shaler had imagination and kindled an interest in geology in hundreds on hundreds of students whom a literal and exact teacher would never have touched. Agassiz as a lecturer was a genius. He was one of the few teachers who had charm. So had Jeffries Wyman, whose style was as lucid as crystal. Professor Goodwin, author of 'Greek Moods and Tenses,' who was a bashful and nervous man when teaching, was in later years my neighbor and warm friend. He was a striking illustration of that large class of men who reveal their human qualities only when they are not in the professor's chair. Dear old Asa Gray was a wonderful botanist and a teacher too when he had half a dozen sympathetic students; but a division of fifty boys played havoc with his specimens and rolled his log of California redwood down the stairs, but they rarely disturbed his equanimity.

My father, who was a horseback rider for over fifty years, sometimes happened upon accidents on the road; hence he thought it important that young men should be so accustomed to blood and surgery as to be able to lend a hand. A few of us, therefore, went with Sturgis Bigelow to the Harvard Medical School to see his father, Dr. Henry J. Bigelow, operate. No more deft, skilful, and rapid operator was ever seen in this country, so experts say. He was dressed in a dark blue broadcloth frock coat and gray trousers, both spattered with the blood of operations for months back. Shades of Lister and Pasteur! What marvels have been wrought since those days.

The one professor who was known and beloved by every undergraduate was the Reverend Andrew Peabody — 'Old Pebo' — the college pastor. Awkward, homely, absent-minded, yet withal wise and human, he represented to the students all that was guileless and charitable — so guileless that no one would think of doing or saying anything wrong in his presence, so charitable that every one felt that he could be guilty of almost any student prank or wickedness and be confident of 'Old Pebo's' appeal for pardon at the Faculty Judgment Throne. At prayers he always took off his spectacles to read the Scriptures and put them on to pray; but the hardiest student would not have dared to suggest that this was in order to keep his eye on the unruly members of the congregation. Although his Chair was that of Plummer Professor of Christian Morals, he told me that he had taught from time to time in every subject offered by the College, and it was his habit to serve as President between the presidential resignations and elections. In walking he lurched from side to side upon the sidewalk, and occasionally took to the street; yet he could walk long distances, for he once told me that, when he was to preach at Winchester or Salem, he had started very early Sunday morning and walked to these towns from his house in Cambridge. In his meanderings he must have covered double the distance. Being very near-sighted and always careful to touch his hat to every student, he kept his left hand well up toward the brim of his hat as he passed through Harvard Square. In the past generation almost every college had such a character, beloved by all.

From earliest boyhood I used to run across the Worcester Railroad to the river to see the class races; and passed many afternoons with legs hanging over the Cottage Farm drawbridge waiting for the boats to go under. The shell had hardly taken the place of the lapstreak; there was no steam launch in those days. The crew was of six and no coxswain, for the bow oarsman steered with his feet upon a tiller near his stretcher, watching the course by frequently turning his head. I remember well, when I was eight years old, the race in which Charles Eliot and Alexander Agassiz, wearing for the first time in history the crimson handkerchiefs, brought the Lawrence Scientific Crew in the lead to the line. At Lake Quinsigamond, too, the great crew stroked by Caspar Crowninshield beat Yale, and on that same day, July 24, 1860, the sophomore and freshman crews left Eli behind. In our junior year the Harvard Crew went to England for the first International Collegiate race with Oxford. The crews were of four men with coxswain. Loring, Simmons, Bass, and Rice, and Coxswain Burnham went across; and had the rare privilege of being entertained at the house of the idol of our fathers, Jenny Lind. Harvard sent a second crew to New Haven and beat Yale. Two of them, Fay and Lyman, took ship the next day for England and being found in condition stepped into the boat in place of Bass and Rice. The excitement was far greater than the boys of these days realize. After a handsome struggle Oxford won. On hearing the news, I threw myself on the sofa in despair; the joy of life was gone; the universe had dropped out.

Hasty Pudding plays were not the ambitious exhibitions of the present. Occasionally an *opéra bouffe* was put on the stage. 'Alonzo the Brave' or 'Faust' and the 'Fair

Imogen,' the latter being most successfully impersonated by Cabot Lodge; while a modest farce like 'Poor Pillicoddy' with myself as Mrs. O'Skuttle was the curtain-raiser. The University nine had five men from our class, and in touring the country beat every amateur nine and most of the professional teams; though it is fair to say that professional baseball was then in its infancy. What a game it was, however, when the runs mounted up to thirty and forty, with two and three on bases!

When we entered Harvard the Athletic Field was The Delta on which Memorial Hall now stands. Colonel Henry Lee, my father, and others had solicited funds for the proposed Memorial Hall; their first great effort, not entirely successful, was to get twenty five-thousand-dollar subscriptions, for that figure was the largest sum that could be expected from the richest and most generous. At the laying of the corner-stone there was a great gathering of the alumni.

The thrill of the Civil War again passed through us young men as we heard the voice of Dr. Holmes ring out the words:

> Hushed are the battle-fields, ended their marches,
> Deaf are their ears to the drumbeat of morn —
> Rise from the sod, ye fair columns and arches!
> Tell the bright deeds to the ages unborn.

Of the one hundred and fifty-nine members of my class who graduated, I recall only three or four who took high rank because they loved literature, the classics, or mathematics for their own sake. The very large proportion of those who took excellent or high rank were impelled by the necessity of earning scholarships. The rank and file of men, some of whom had excellent ability and latent intellectual ambitions, either loafed away much of their time, or read and studied in lines outside the college curriculum. I represented the average in ability; but there was only one subject in my whole course, history, which really aroused my ambition.

Toward the close of the senior year a sense of duty spurred me to hard work, and I made what was for a Lawrence a creditable rank. This, however, was largely due to a classmate and friend — Samuel Brearley — who had the faculty of sensing what sort of questions each professor would ask. He kindly offered to study with me for the final examination and the results were as if I had had a private coach. I mention this because Sam Brearley, whom we called 'Bob' Brearley, the name of the hero in 'The Ticket-of-Leave Man,' became an exceptionally successful coach, thrusting the dullest boys into college. A few years later the Brearley School for Girls in New York sprang into prominence. He was a most reserved, exact, and dignified character, with no sense of humor, high-minded, and a gentleman. His success in founding and carrying on a school for girls was, however, a source of surprise and amusement to his classmates. In referring to Brearley School I must mention a later head master, James Croswell, whose memory is dear to hundreds of New York matrons to-day. Croswell, too, as a young man was *gauche*, retiring, high-shouldered, and homely. One rarely meets a man, however, with more charm, affection, and a keener sense of humor. A very small bit of bread once cast upon the waters of Croswell's kindness returned to me. When I came to Cambridge to live in '84, Croswell was an assistant professor in Greek. When we first met in the Square, he said, 'Mr. Lawrence, you do not know me, but I know you. You were the first junior who spoke to me when I was a freshman: and a freshman never forgets that.' We struck up a warm friendship and in a year or two I received to my surprise election as an honorary member of the Phi Beta Kappa, an honor which I never could have earned, but which was, I am sure, due to the kindness of Croswell, then Secretary of the Harvard Chapter.

During the last half of the college course, an influence entered my life which has never weakened, the leadership of Phillips Brooks. He came to Trinity Church, Boston, in 1869. Those of us who had a dutiful but never enthusiastic interest in the Saint Paul's Society asked him to address us, which he did again and again in the South Basement Room of University Hall, Floyd Tomkins accompanying the hymns on the piano exercising the super-energy which he has thrown into his sermons at Holy Trinity, Philadelphia, and over the country to this day. Three of us, as a committee of the Saint Paul's Society, asked Phillips Brooks to preach one Sunday evening in a course of sermons at Saint John's Memorial Chapel. Anticipating a crowd, we bought one hundred camp chairs, and to our gratification the chapel was jammed. This was the beginning of his preaching in Cambridge and of his great service to the University. I heard Phillips Brooks preach from time to time in Boston, Cambridge, my own parish in Lawrence, Yale University, New York, and Westminster Abbey, London, for over thirty years; and from this first sermon in Cambridge to the end I have never known the time when the church was not packed with people. I shall say more of Phillips Brooks later.

An address given in Upper Massachusetts stands out in my memory. I cannot recall any other than this one occasion when we students were reminded of our duty to our country and the responsibility of educated men for loyal public service. Singularly enough, this one address was by an Englishman, Tom Hughes, the author of 'Tom Brown at Rugby.' James Russell Lowell, with whom Mr. Hughes was staying, introduced him, and his direct appeal as an Englishman to American youth stuck.

In the winter vacation of my junior year, Amory and I, Frank, now General Appleton, and Ignatius Sargent, with Dr. Sam Green, made a short trip to Cuba. It was in the days of their many revolutions: one of our fellow passengers standing beside us was captured and held for a while in Moro Castle. Havana was a Spanish-negro city saturated with romance and filth; we stayed upon a sugar plantation and saw slavery on its own soil. We ate pineapples, bananas, and oranges fresh from the trees, thereby spoiling forever our taste for those fruits as we have them in the North, weeks after the picking.

Returning by New Orleans, we saw the Legislature of Reconstructed Louisiana, composed almost entirely of negroes, elected to legislate for the proud white people. By good fortune General Sherman and his daughter were our fellow travellers north. It was the first time that he had passed through that country since the siege of Vicksburg, and he pointed out to us the salient points of the campaign. One day, as we went by boat up the Mississippi, the General was standing on the forward deck, and I near by happened to be watching him. The breeze was strong, and Sherman took off his old army hat. It uncovered a forehead and dome which amazed me. I mention this because never before had I consciously noticed any man's head. Saint-Gaudens, who was a great admirer of noble heads, has revealed Sherman's in his equestrian statue at Central Park Gate; but the impression was more vivid to one standing immediately before him.

In the next winter vacation, Amory and I went with mother to Washington, where we and a number of classmates went into society. Those were days of simplicity. The families of military and civil officers on Government salaries were society leaders: there were afternoon receptions and early hours at evening parties with very simple repasts. No person who, having made a fortune and built a big house, would have been recognized had he not merit of his own.

The receptions at the White House were even duller than in later years. As we passed President Grant and our names were mentioned, he, without a spark of intelligence or recognition, put out his hand and said, 'I am pleased to meet you, Mr. Lawrence,' and we passed on. By contrast, I met General Sherman at a reception, who immediately recognized me, recalled the incidents of our trip, and said, 'Come to my house to-morrow night; all the girls will be there; we'll all dance and hit up the ball for a fine time'; and he did it.

During our stay in Washington we passed a day at the Naval Academy at Annapolis. Admiral Worden was then Commandant. It was he who commanded the Monitor in its fight with the Merrimac; and in looking through a sight-hole he lost his eye by a splinter from the enemy's shot. He put Amory and myself in charge of a young lieutenant named Dewey, who was so courteous and friendly that my brother Amory, who was older, kept up an occasional correspondence with him, visiting him later in Washington. I did not see him again until as the hero of Manila Bay he received that wonderful welcome in this country. At the dinner given him in Boston by Governor Wolcott, we recalled the day at Annapolis.

With the dancing around the Tree, and the Class Day spreads, the college course of the Class of '71 ended. Rural Cambridge, with its elm in Harvard Square, its broad open spaces, its tinkling horse-car bells, and ancient manners, was abandoned for the stress of life. It has, however, been my happy fortune to have had a part in Harvard's life for half a century.

My father used to say that no man was ever more blessed in life than he. I can say the same of my life and the blessings began early. When he built Lawrence Hall, Cambridge, he had this inscription cut in the stone over the door:

IN MEMORIAM; SUMMAE DEI BENEVOLENTIAE

Our home life, unbroken for many years, full of health, prosperity, and comfort, was enough to spoil parents and seven children for active, strenuous, and useful lives. But we were brought up to feel that gratitude, not necessity or distress, was the strongest and finest motive of character and service, and every one of the seven children, two sons and five daughters, all married later, tried throughout life to do their part by hard work, home care, and public service.

The wellspring of the home was, as it should be, in our mother; she was a woman of rare dignity of person, erect of body, of handsome face, clear-eyed, of exceptionally fresh complexion to the end, and in her self-restraint a happy complement to my father's rather nervous and emotional temperament. Dr. Jackson used to say that she had one of the three backs in Boston; and I have seen her lift a sideboard which two men refused to touch. Mr. B. C. Porter, who painted portraits of all five daughters, said that he would rather paint their mother than any one, but she refused. After her death, Mr. Porter once described her as she stood watching him paint, her stately figure set off by her black velvet dress with a magnificent Russian sable cape brought from Pekin by Mr. Gordon Dexter after the sacking of the Emperor's palace, thrown back from her shoulders. Upon our commission he painted her portrait dressed as he had described her. Those who did not know her well thought her somewhat distant and cold; it was bashfulness, but the children never suspected it. Inheriting from her father exceptional administrative ability, she handled the household and the coming and going to Boston, Nahant, Longwood, and elsewhere with ease. I can hear her say near the end of breakfast, 'Now what is the order of performances to-day?' — and the order was made out. Father used to remark during the war that, if President Lincoln would make her Quartermaster General, the army would be able to move on to Richmond. Dr. Francis said that he answered the call in our sicknesses just to find out 'what medicine Mrs. Lawrence would advise him to give, and he gave it.' Anxiety was never revealed in her face or action, only in a sick headache. She did not receive her cultivation from books — indeed, I have never seen her read a book of standard literature; nor had she a taste for music or art. Her cultivation and intelligence were inborn or gained through association with cultivated people. My father's interest in music began and ended with the hymn tunes which we, our children and children's children, have sung on Sunday evenings. He, however, had, especially in his earlier years, an interest in literature, and like his father had a terse and vigorous style in writing.

MRS. AMOS A. LAWRENCE
Painted by B. C. Porter

Neither parents nor children had the theatre habit, and I have never known father and mother to go to the opera. We were a busy, happy, and big family three miles from the city, with plenty of work and pleasure to occupy us; and a seven-o'clock breakfast demanded early hours.

Soon after they were married, my father and mother were confirmed in Saint Paul's Church, Boston, now the Cathedral. I was baptized there. Later we all went to Saint Paul's Church, Brookline, and as the neighborhood about us increased — for father built a number of houses and took pains to have an agreeable set of neighbors — he and his brother William erected the Church of Our Saviour, Longwood, in memory of their father. Later my mother built the rectory; and later still we children added the choir and adjoining rooms in their memory.

Every morning we went to father's or mother's dressing-room to say our prayers; then came breakfast and family prayers which the servants, who were always Protestants, attended. After breakfast we were off for school, and father on his horse for Harvard College, or Boston. On Sundays we started at quarter before nine for Sunday School. Mother followed in the big coach and we met at church, filling two pews, and then came home to cold roast beef, baked potatoes, and a cold pie or pudding; for the servants were given a day of rest. And in the afternoon father drove the older of us to church while mother stayed at home to read to the younger children.

It is a habit of some men and women to try to justify their non-attendance at church in later years by the excuse that they had so much in youth. I believe that everything depends upon sympathetic leadership. Father did not tell us to go to church; he went, and we went with him. Our parents never asked us to do what they did not do gladly themselves. Prayer and religion at home were as natural as meals and sleep.

I am sure that one of the most potent influences in the development of young people's character is the confidence placed in them by their parents. We children were always trusted, and thus we developed in self-restraint and healthy self-confidence. It was understood that we would not tell other children the semi-confidential and family table talk, hence conversation was free and personal. They believed that we would not abuse our liberties. Wine was always on the table for meals — never on the sideboard for use between meals. Father always had his sherry or claret; we too as we grew older, if we wanted it; but we did not happen to want it often. Father took a box of wine over to our college rooms when Amory and I entered college and told us that he would supply us with all that we needed. It was not good form to serve wine in college rooms, and we brought back the boxes unopened.

Good example is not always reliable, at all events in the Lawrence family. My Uncle William, who had three sons, gave up smoking as an example to his boys. They all smoked. Father kept on smoking and neither of his sons did. When we were boys he offered each a horse and chaise if we would not use tobacco until we were twenty-one: that helped to carry us through the cigarette age. At twenty-one we received $1200 apiece in place of our horse and chaise, and I have always put off smoking until to-morrow. Moderate smoking may be of no harm, in fact to some temperaments of benefit; but since I have been in the ministry, I have seen good reason not to smoke. Clergymen working in their studies are freer to smoke than business men; and many of them do smoke too much and thus weaken their influence. Again, in visiting in homes and upon sick people of delicate sensibilities, it is not fair to bring into the room the odor of tobacco.

Father gave us a larger allowance than we could reasonably spend, expecting us to save as well as give away a certain proportion. Parents are largely to blame for the extravagance of their sons and daughters. They have doled out money as the children asked for it, and have never trusted them with systematic and liberal allowances requiring always, however, an accounting. It is in my judgment a part of a boy's liberal education, to create in him the ability to go downtown with a dollar in his pocket, spend part of it sensibly, and keep the rest until another time. As we came of age, father cut deeply into his capital and gave each one of us a modest capital of our own, making us responsible for investment, saving, giving, and expenditure of income. We had been educated to it; and he had the pleasure of seeing his children not dependent upon his death for their financial independence.

Father and mother too gave us the best of their time and wisdom. In driving or on horseback I have learned more than I could have learned elsewhere about business, horses, morals, politics, and especially about people. His practical philosophy has been of untold service to me. Children are receptive of their parents' best wisdom. It is thus that family traditions are handed down through the generations.

CHAPTER III
STUDYING FOR THE MINISTRY
1871–1875

BUSINESS was the career which was open to me. Both my grandfathers had been men of exceptional business ability and success. My father, not entering the firm of A. and A. Lawrence, started on his own account, and as merchant and manufacturer built up a business which before his death had, besides his own enterprises, absorbed most of the business which the firm of A. and A. Lawrence, then dissolved, had enjoyed. My brother Amory, who upon graduation a year before me had entered the office of Lawrence and Company, naturally expected that I should join him, and within a few years earn a large income, amass a goodly property, while remaining in our delightful social and family associations. What first turned my thoughts to the ministry, I do not know — probably the life and preaching of Phillips Brooks. When college was over, I had no plans or definite future. Classmates asked me to pass a year with them in Europe; a cousin urged me to go up the Nile; but such a year would, it seemed to me, lead nowhere. I wanted time to think things out. Under the guidance of Professor Torrey of Harvard, I read history, which was the one subject that interested me in college; I went frequently to Cambridge for lessons in German, and I am recorded as a member of the first class of the Harvard Graduate School. Friends and parents were good enough to let me alone in my doubts and questionings. My only adviser was Phillips Brooks, who, entirely open-minded as to my future, in response to my questions put clearly the opportunity as well as the romance of the ministry.

Gradually my line of thought worked along this line. What am I here for? Why has God given me my bless-

WILLIAM LAWRENCE AT FOURTEEN AND AT TWENTY-THREE

ings? I have everything that a man could ask; most people have very few things; so far as I have faith and character, why is it not for me, as a bit of gratitude and honor, to put at God's service for others myself and all that I have? The ministry is simply a life of grateful service. There had been no personal appeal to me in definite form, when one day I received a letter from my friend, Frank Peabody, later Plummer Professor of Christian Morals at Harvard, who had just then entered the Unitarian ministry, putting the opportunity in a more direct way, and I had to think out my future in definite terms. Would business and the usual social life satisfy me as a life career? Was there not a call to something larger, finer, and more satisfying in the ministry?

One evening I told my father and mother, with whom I had never passed a word on the subject, that I hoped to be a minister. They were gratified; no doubt it had been an object in their hopes and prayers; and that was over. It never occurred to me to ask myself whether I should be successful in the calling. I knew that I always received zero in speech-making in school; I could therefore never preach, but I might talk a little. I had never visited a sick person, and I tried without success to teach a class of boys in Sunday School. My cousin Arthur, a man of great charm, the Chief Marshal of his class, had just become rector of a country parish; perhaps some country parish or mission in the West might have me. But the future did not count much. I did not think of that; my life-work was the ministry, and my first duty was to get ready.

There are few things of which intelligent people are so ignorant as they are of the methods of the preparation of young men to be their spiritual pastors and moral leaders. The common conception of a theological seminary is that of an institution where young men are stuffed with a theology much like the stuffing given their predecessors. The truth is that the changes in theological thought and in methods of study have been almost as radical as the changes in the study of medicine.

Largely through Phillips Brooks's advice, I decided to go to the Andover Theological Seminary for a year or two. Having lived within two miles of Boston and Cambridge all my life, I wanted to get into another atmosphere. I had been brought up in the Episcopal Church: I wished to gain the point of view of the Orthodox Congregational Church, which had been at the foundation of New England thought, philosophy, and theology. Andover had been and was thought to be the leading seminary in the country. Neither Phillips Brooks nor I knew that it had passed its zenith. Andover was a beautiful village well apart from the pressure of social and commercial life. The Seminary was in its way a New England Protestant Monastery. We were able to concentrate upon our studies; we ate, drank, walked, and slept, talking and thinking theology.

One September morning I left our cottage at Nahant upon what was for me a rather stiff venture of faith. From childhood I had lived in most comfortable if not luxurious surroundings, in a large family and delightful social circle. I was now starting off alone to prepare for my life-work at Andover Seminary, which at that time seemed a hundred miles away, and to live in intimate relations with young men from small colleges, rural missions, and foreign missionary fields, to take up studies of which I knew absolutely nothing, under professors who in their theological interests and traditions were to me as the monks of old. The students were compelled to chum. The only person whom I knew was a Harvard classmate by the name of Harry Nichols, whom I had seen something of at college, but had not been intimate with. Frankly, I dreaded the experience and shrank from chumming. However, Harry Nichols turned out the best of chums. He got up early, lighted the fire in the Franklin stove, cleaned the study lamp, dusted the room, and kept everything in perfect order. All that I had to do was to make my bed. He was a scholar of ability; I was not. Nichols was therefore a stimulating chum, as he has been a stimulating parson in

New Haven, Minneapolis, and New York. He has been a mountain-climber, and while I write this is walking in the Canadian Rockies at seventy-five years of age.

Dr. Mark Hopkins, President of Williams College, the great educator and philosopher of his generation, the man of whom President Garfield said that to him a college was a log with himself at one end and Dr. Hopkins at the other, was staying with us at Nahant. He closed the door of my carriage, and, as I drove off, said, 'Don't think that you have begun to settle your doubts and questions; they are yet to come.' I wondered what he meant: I had supposed that doubts and questions came in college, and certainties in the theological seminary. I soon learned what Dr. Hopkins meant. Doubts and questions sprang up the first month: how could it be otherwise?

When I entered college in 1867, the great mass of intelligent Christian people believed, or thought that they believed, that this world was created in six days of twenty-four hours each, and that that event happened in 4004 B.C., for was it not so written in the margin of the first page of the King James Bible? Of course every word in the Old and New Testaments was inspired, and those sceptics who said that the story of the flood was a tradition, or that the whale did not swallow Jonah, or that Joshua did not make the sun stand still, were unbelievers or atheists. This is no exaggeration; these were truths vital to the faith. A system of theology founded by Saint Augustine and, passing through Calvin, was with some modifications the dominant faith of Protestant Christendom. Andover Theological Seminary had been founded upon this theology, and its name was known through the great work of the missionaries of New England in India, Africa, and the Sandwich Islands. Children of these missionaries were being educated in the Andover Academies to go back to convert the heathen. One of the first native Japanese missionaries, Joseph Neesima, who later founded one of the great Christian colleges in Japan, was getting his education in Phillips Academy the year that I came. Business men, statesmen, scholars, doctors, and lawyers of prominence scoffed at these missionary enterprises; and now, fifty years later, leaders in these subjects are pressing their interests into these very countries to which the missionaries first carried the elements of Christian civilization. The Medical School in China, founded and administered by the Rockefeller Foundation, is an illustration.

Darwin's 'Origin of Species,' the milestone of modern thought, was published in 1859. Dr. Edwards A. Park, a descendant of Jonathan Edwards, was Professor in Theology at Andover. In his younger days he had broken away from the extreme Calvinism of his ancestor and had admitted into his system, so far as they could be received without cracking it, some modifications. Indeed the Arian, or Unitarian, uprising had compelled some adjustments; but the attitude of mind expressed by Darwin and the path of discovery opened by him could not possibly be adjusted to Professor Park's system; it would smash it. The issues were radical and had to be fought out, and herein were the keen and exciting discussions and conclusions of our day. When Professor Park gave us the subject for a thesis, 'Is the theory of evolution consistent with the Christian Faith?' I took the affirmative. My arguments were no doubt weak and illogical, for I was not free from the old methods of thought; but my instincts and traditions told me that I was right. Professor Park, however, insisted that I was wrong, that a man could not believe in evolution and remain a Christian. The present generation has no conception of the leap which science, philosophy, theology, and every phase of thought have taken in the last fifty years. Asa Gray, John Fiske, and others introduced what was popularly called Darwinism into this country; it takes years for such a radical change to seep through the leaders of thought and into the minds of the people; even Agassiz did not yield to the pressure. Professor Park had taught his system for twenty-five or thirty years; he was over fifty in 1859 and sixty-four when I was at Andover. Just across the entry from his lecture room, however, we entered that of Professor J. Henry Thayer, a younger man, fresh from Germany, full of enthusiasm for the newer attitude and interpretation of Christian thought and faith. Under his guidance we gained from the study of the New Testament conclusions directly opposite to those of Dr. Park. I went into Professor Park's lecture, and came out with the feeling that he had a system of theology to defend. I went into Professor Thayer's room with the feeling that his high purpose was to guide us to the truth. 'Gentlemen,' he said, 'it is not for me to defend the Faith. A true faith will defend itself. It is my duty to guide you with open mind, humble spirit, and a pure heart to the Truth, the Truth alone, wherever it may lead you: and be ye sure that it will always lead you to a fuller knowledge of Christ, who is the Truth. Hold as for your life to that attitude of mind. Seek the Truth and the Truth shall make you free.'

Such an attitude brought the lives of some of us to a crisis. The class divided into two camps, and with the minority I stood for Dr. Thayer's method, and have ever since. The issue is broader than that of Darwinism or the entrance of modern thought. It is to my mind the issue of one's attitude to the truth; it touches every department of life and thought. Can the truth of science, philosophy, or of religion be compacted into a theory or a system, kept there and withstand the coming thought? Men and women who think so stand on the defensive as fresh truth comes, and so far as they can, adjust it, or fit it into their system or creed; but to them the fresh truth is a source of annoyance. It disturbs people's minds and leads many away from the old faith, or the old system. Or, on the other hand, is truth a living thing? A living creed expresses the fundamental faith of a people of one age. With the revelation of fresh truth, the faithful, gladly welcoming it, breathe into the language of the creed fresh interpretations, which continue to enrich and make more vital the faith from generation to generation. The same process brings enlargement of faith, and a firmer conviction to each person. Only in this way can we follow Him Who leads us into all Truth.

I have written thus at length because in this half-century of active life since Andover days, I have seen system after system crack and fall to pieces, while the Orthodox in science, philosophy, or religion bemoan the overthrow of the faith; whereas new thought, so far as it has been found to be true, has, if welcomed, added to the strength and glory of the faith.

We students at Andover did not realize that at that very time these two principles were fighting for the control of Andover. Park and Thayer stood for the past and the future. A few years later certain professors at Andover refused to sign the Andover Creed in its original intent, and the 'Andover Case' was soon being tried before the Supreme Court of Massachusetts.

The coming generation won, as it always must win, in the issue of the evasion or suppression, or, on the other hand, the reception, of the coming truth.

But I have wandered from our life at Andover. I went to this Congregational Seminary with the cordial consent of Bishop Eastburn. He died, and Bishop Paddock came, who questioned the wisdom of his candidates studying at Andover; but he did not disturb us. With full appreciation of Congregationalism and with many warm friendships gained there, we were stimulated to study the deep things of God, and of the human heart, the Atonement, and the relation of man to Christ. We tried to master 'Edwards on the Freedom of the Will,' and gained a fair conception of the history and development of New England theology.

It was customary for the students to preach in distant village churches and missions on Sundays. This practice in preaching was good for the young man, though hard on the people. My first experience is vivid to me. One Saturday I took train for a little hamlet in New Hampshire near Lake Winnipesaukee. It was late autumn; I arrived after dark and was received at a small farmhouse. The family life was rather primitive and the food badly cooked. It was a new experience to me, and I was lonely and homesick. On the Sabbath morning, however, I got through the Scripture reading, the hymns, and the long prayer, but, as I opened my manuscript and gave out my text, my host, the deacon, in the front pew was fast asleep. It was disconcerting; I rallied, however, with the thought that he had not gone to sleep under my preaching, but had been enwrapped long before, and that it was my part so to preach as to wake him up. In this I did not succeed. I did not then know that a hard-worked farmer will almost always fall asleep when he sits down and cannot talk. People do not go to sleep in church as they used to. I never see an adult asleep in church in these days. I doubt if all the credit for this can be given to the clergy. Our population and congregations are made up of people of the towns and cities. These do not fall asleep when relaxed for a few minutes; our services have more movement, and the heating system is not that of the hot-air closed stove. Early Monday morning the deacon saw me to the train and handed me a somewhat mutilated and well-worn five-dollar bill—my first wage for preaching. It went into the inner pocket of my pocketbook, for it could not be spent as ordinary five-dollar bills are spent; and there it remained. The next summer I took a swim one day off the rocks at Nahant, and two or three hours later missed my pocketbook. Could I have left it on the rocks? There were four fresh ten-dollar bills, some postage stamps, and the five dollars in the inner pocket. I ran back; the tide had risen, a heavy chop was striking the rock; but well down beneath the surface I caught sight of fractions of the melted pocketbook. I stripped and dove again and again, bringing in a stamp, a ten-dollar bill, until all were landed but the five dollars: finally, I reached it near the bottom; and soon put it in a new pocketbook, awaiting an appropriate use which came in the following spring: for with it I bought a wedding ring which I placed upon the finger of my wife, Julia Cunningham, in Emmanuel Church, Boston, on May 19, 1874, where Phillips Brooks married us, for Trinity Church was then building.

Taking Parker's 'Handbook of Gothic Architecture,' we passed the summer studying the cathedrals and castles of England; for there is no better way of studying English history. One Saturday, as we were at our hotel in London, Phillips Brooks suddenly appeared, saying that Dean Stanley had asked him to preach in Westminster Abbey the next evening and handing us cards for two seats. It was not the custom in those days to invite Americans to preach in the Abbey, and Phillips Brooks must have thought it an exceptional occasion, for I never knew him before so to overcome his modesty as to suggest that any one would want to hear him preach. On Sunday evening the nave was packed. His sermon was one that I had heard him preach in Boston, Cambridge, and at Yale University, 'Walk in the Spirit and ye shall not fulfil the lusts of the flesh' — The Positiveness of the Spiritual Life. For the first ten minutes I never knew an English congregation so attentive; even choir men and boys seemed to be enthralled; then suddenly his voice broke, as it sometimes did, this time worse than I ever knew it, and for perhaps five minutes, which seemed an eternity, he rushed on with his speed and volume of thought and words but in a whisper: then his voice came back; but the mighty grip upon the people was loosened. It was a great disappointment to his friends, but he never seemed to realize it. A few years later he so preached in the cathedrals and churches of England and at Windsor Castle as to win the devotion of masses of people. The next morning Dean Stanley showed us over the Abbey; George Bancroft, then on his way as Minister of the United States to Berlin, joined us; and, as the Dean moved from memorial to memorial, from Pitt and Canning to the modest stone inscribed 'Jane Lister, Dear Child,' we caught his enthusiasm for the shrine of all English-speaking peoples. On returning home I entered the Seminary at Philadelphia; for again I wanted to get into another atmosphere and into the vigorous church life of the city.

Philadelphia before the Centennial Exposition was a

1924

1874

W. L. AND J. L.

very different Philadelphia from that of to-day. The long
blocks of red-brick houses, with white marble trimmings
and steps and solid wooden shutters, were practically
unbroken by the present modern and often obtrusive
façades. Where a member of the family had died, all the
shutters on the front were closed and tied with crêpe for
thirty to ninety days or longer. Each house was exactly
like the other within as well as outside. Much of the house
drainage was on the surface, flowing along the street
gutter. The city water pipes were laid so near the surface
that a cold snap froze them. The winter of '74 and '75 was
an exceptionally cold one. Hence bonfires were burning in
the streets throughout the city thawing out pipes under
the pavements. We rented a house which fortunately had
two bathrooms: for the furnace was so small and the house
so cold that one Sunday morning, before one of the bath-
tubs could be emptied, the frost had nipped the waste;
the water in the tub froze, and remained until a few weeks
later I flung it out the window, a block of ice.

The warmth of hospitality of the Philadelphia people
more than compensated, however — memories of terrapin
and Augustin's croquettes are still fresh.

I was fortunate in having a practical training in reading
the service and preaching which I commend to candidates
for the ministry. John Brooks, Phillips Brooks's youngest
brother, who also came to Philadelphia via Andover, and I
were placed by Bishop Stevens as lay readers in charge of
the little stone church at Tacony, at that time a suburban
hamlet, now a part of the city. We took turns reading the
service and preaching Sunday mornings and afternoons;
then on our way home and after supper we criticized each
other unmercifully. There is wisdom in our Saviour's
system 'two by two': mutual sympathy and cheer, mutual
criticism. Our congregations numbered from nine to
thirty-five only, but we got the practice, whatever they
may have gotten. How cold that little church could be!
I well remember one morning when, with heavy overcoat
under my cotta, I read those cynical words of the prophet,

'Yea, he warmeth himself, and saith, Aha I am warm.'
However, the little congregation gave us each for our
winter's work twenty-five dollars in addition to their
patient endurance of our sermons; and with this second
wage I bought and gave an appropriately inscribed clock
to my father and mother.

The professors in the Theological School, Drs. Goodwin,
Hare and Butler, had been able men in their day, but they
were about seventy years old, and of course saturated with
the evangelical system and methods of thought. While I
gained something from them, I received a greater stimulus
from observing the practical work and enthusiasm of the
people of the Episcopal Church in Philadelphia. I watched
the great Sunday School, created and carried on by the rising young banker, George C. Thomas, who, never flag-
ging in his interest in this local work, became the leading
layman of the whole Church. Thirty-five years later we
worked together on the Board of Missions.

We came back to Boston at Easter and for the next
three months I attended lectures at the Episcopal Theological School in Cambridge.

It would be unfair to the professors and theological
seminaries of those days to stop here. What I have said
applies in large degree to the medical and law schools of
the same era. Graduate and professional study has taken
a great leap in forty years and the schools have responded
in new methods and younger teachers. It was not until
1870 that Professor Langdell, of the Harvard Law School,
introduced the 'Case System' of teaching law; and in 1875
Dr. Gilman gathered the great and youthful faculty of the
new Johns Hopkins Medical School. Since then legal and
medical schools have entered upon a new era. Theological
schools have not moved so radically, for an organization
like the Church moves slowly; but the movement for a
better preparation of young men for the ministry of the
next generation is going steadily forward.

During the four years from college to ordination, Phillips
Brooks was my friend and adviser. When entangled with

the reasoning or sophistry of Professor Park, I went to him; and his fresh and sympathetic spirit, his deep spiritual insight, and his instinct for truth were like the opening of shutters to the light. When I reported his conclusions to Professor Park, the Professor lost all interest in me, wondering how Phillips Brooks, whom he admired, could so err from the orthodox faith. John Brooks and I accompanied him on his preaching trips to Yale and elsewhere. There was no topic connected with preparation for the ministry, from the argument for the existence of God to the manner of preparation of his sermons, even to the tying-up the manuscript, which he did not share with us. During my ministry of fifty years I have used for my sermons and addresses form and index exactly like those of Phillips Brooks — alas, without the results!

Upon June 20, 1875, I was ordained deacon by Bishop Paddock in Saint John's Memorial Chapel, Cambridge. He offered me the choice of two or three missions in Massachusetts; but my thoughts were for the West. Bishop Morris, a noble missionary, had lately gone to the almost unknown Territory of Oregon, and Mrs. Lawrence and I were considering throwing in our lot with him, when a call came from the city of Lawrence which seemed to be more pressing, and I accepted to take up work September 1st.

Forty years ago typhoid fever was a commonly expected feature of summer life; every August and September brought cases into thousands of homes. The cause was unknown, but was commonly connected with drainage: its relation to drinking-water was undiscovered. I passed one night in the Profile House, White Mountains, and, upon reaching home, came down with typhoid. Sixty-three cases were, as I remember, traced to the same place that summer. It was some months before I could take up work, and then I became the assistant of the Reverend Doctor Packard of Grace Church, Lawrence, who had kindly waited for me.

CHAPTER IV
LIFE IN LAWRENCE
1876–1883

Just after the South African War I lunched at Eton College, having as a fellow guest General Lord Methuen, lame from a wound. Mr. Donaldson, the Master of the House, having asked me to speak to the boys, introduced me somewhat as follows, 'Boys, the Bishop of Massachusetts [the Englishman often puts the accent on the last syllable], is going to speak to you. You probably have no idea where Massachusetts is, but the Bishop is a warm friend of mine and I hope that you will listen.' I said, 'Boys, Massachusetts is in the northeastern part of the United States; it is an Indian name and savage Indians wandered through the forests two and a half centuries ago while Eton boys studied and played here. But it is an Indian country no longer, and is not so far away as you think. For instance, I have two homes three miles apart, one in Boston and the other in Cambridge. That sounds rather homelike to an English boy. Between Boston and Cambridge runs the river Charles, named after King Charles I. That sounds familiar. About twenty-five miles from Cambridge is a village called Methuen [the English put the accent on the first syllable], named over one hundred and fifty years ago after an ancestor of Lord Methuen who is beside me. About sixty years ago, some Boston manufacturers found in Methuen a broad and deep river, with an Indian name, the Merrimac, with falls running to waste; they constructed a big dam, created a great water power, cut a tract of fields out of Methuen, and built a city on it; that city they named after my grandfather and great-uncles, Lawrence. So in our country Methuen and Lawrence have been beside each other for seventy years.'

When, in 1845, the dam was building and several hundred men were housed or in camp upon the fields, Bishop Griswold asked the Reverend Doctor George Packard to go there and hold services. Dr. Packard, having been for several years a physician in Saco, Maine, had taken orders and was a diocesan missionary. He gathered the men of all denominations in a hall, and soon after moved into a wooden chapel opposite the proposed Common. Later a stone church was built. In 1876, when I became his assistant, he had served the people of Lawrence as Rector of Grace Church for over thirty years: the population had grown to thirty-five thousand, and no citizen was more respected or better known than he — a strong character, reserved, of evangelical piety, a typical New Englander. His brother, Alpheus Packard, was a professor at Bowdoin College for over fifty years, and was commemorated by Longfellow in his poem, 'Morituri Salutamus,' read by him upon the fiftieth anniversary of his graduation.

Many persons assume that a young man entering business in a large city has thereby opportunities for a broad outlook, development in character and experience, whereas a clergyman going to a smaller town or provincial city leads thereby a rather narrowing life. My purpose here is simply to record my own experience in the first years of my ministry. Had I gone into business, I should have remained in the same social circle and have moved with capitalists or those who lived in comfort. I should have had the business support of my father and influential friends. In going to Lawrence, I did not know a person in the city except Dr. Packard, whom I had met only three or four times. I was undertaking a job of which I knew practically nothing; and while, of course, because of my name and of Dr. Packard, I had a favorable start, I had got to make my way as pastor, preacher, administrator, and citizen by my own efforts. No influence or pull can make men listen to a preacher who does not help and hold them. As for any social connection with Boston, Lawrence was practically a thousand miles away. Such a situation puts a man on his mettle, especially if he have in him the one motive that he is there to serve and help the people and bring Christ to them.

Dr. Packard never gave me advice but once: he expected me to learn by experience and by watching him, if I wanted to. I remember well my first pastoral visit with him. It was upon a dying sailor at a sudden call to a little cottage outside the city. The man had lived a hard and roving life, and was anxious to confess his sins and make his peace with God: he cried through it all. Dr. Packard prayed with him. I was deeply moved. It was my first call on a sick person. As we went out the door, the west was aglow with the sunset and the stone tower of the Methuen Church dominated the village a mile away. Dr. Packard stood on the step and said, 'Do look at that sunset.' I was shocked at the sudden change of thought and said to myself, 'You hardened hypocrite, how could you feel as you did a minute ago and talk as you did to that sailor, and now exclaim at the beauty of the sunset!' I soon learned that the secret of true pastoral work, as of medical or any other, is to throw one's whole self into the immediate need, give the keenest personal attention, the most sympathetic help, and then put that instance out of mind and go on to the next duty.

A few weeks after my arrival, when escorting Bishop Paddock from Boston to Lawrence for a confirmation, I started to pay for his railroad ticket. He, however, drew from his pocketbook a card which gave him clerical half-fare. It was the first time that I had ever heard of 'clerical discount.' Just behind him a working-woman was waiting with her hard-earned money to pay her full fare to Lawrence; and as she watched the Bishop's half-fare and then put down her money, I seemed to feel her sense of injustice. When Dr. Packard later offered me a clerical half-fare card, which he had been at pains to get for me, I looked upon the back and saw that it was given 'on the condition that the person using it would make no claim against the road for injury or death.' I returned it to him, saying with Irish logic, 'Thank you, Doctor, if I am killed, I would rather collect the damages.'

On our first Fourth of July in Lawrence, a day of terrific heat, I went at Mrs. Lawrence's bidding to the apothecary's, who happened to be a vestryman, to buy some fans. Upon asking the price, the clerk said, 'Three for a quarter; four for a quarter for ministers and school-teachers.' 'Why on earth should ministers and school-teachers fan themselves cheaper than the working men and women?' I asked. 'I don't know,' he said, 'but that is our custom.' I took three fans, and said, 'You tell Mr. Whitney that I have taken three fans for a quarter and I expect him to pay his pew rent promptly.'

In a village or provincial city, society is divided into religious denominations. The Roman Catholics, the Congregationalists, the Baptists, the Episcopalians, the Methodists, each patronize their own people, the butcher, grocer, and doctor; and when the new minister comes, it is assumed that he will fall into line. Dr. Packard would not hesitate a moment in any question of right or wrong, but he had lived so long under this parochial system that he was unwilling to tell Mrs. Lawrence which was the best butcher in town, lest the Episcopal butcher be offended; and she had to go to a disinterested neighbor to find out.

The one bit of advice given me by Dr. Packard was when he was near his death. It was not easy for me, a young man, to make a pastoral call on the venerable saint. As I rose to go, I timidly suggested that I offer a prayer, when he said, 'You are just beginning your work, and I want to tell you that you will never find a person, sick, in trouble, or dying, who would not be grateful for a prayer.'

At Dr. Packard's death I found myself with less than a year's experience, in temporary charge, until another rector came, of a parish of nearly a thousand souls. The future, immediate or distant, did not occur to me. I simply did the work.

One day, however, the leading physician of the parish

called me into his office, and said, 'Mr. Lawrence, have you noticed that there is a call posted on the church door for a parish meeting to elect a rector; you must know that your name will come up?' I said that I had noticed the call, but had not thought anything more about it. He then went on, 'When you came here, I had a right to think that you would have me as your physician. You have engaged a physician from the Congregationalists. It will hurt my practice. You cannot expect me to support you or vote for you.' I was naturally a little hot. However, my answer came, though I am afraid in a shaky voice, 'Doctor, you have been frank with me, I will be frank with you. When I came to this city a total stranger, I had the names of three physicians given me by my Boston doctor; yours was among them. I inquired of three or four disinterested persons, who told me that you were an excellent doctor, but that since you have come back from the war you drink too much. Now I am not going to put my wife and baby into the hands of a physician who drinks.' He then said that I was altogether too independent, and I told him that I fortunately could afford to be. I learned afterwards that his was one of two votes cast against me at the parish meeting. Some months after, a young man came running to my door saying that his sister was dying. I ran over to the house and the girl was reviving from a collapse; the same doctor was there. Later, the mother came to me with the bill saying that, when probing her daughter's wound, the doctor was partly drunk. 'It was he that almost killed her; shall I pay the bill?' she asked. I advised her to return the bill to the physician unpaid, saying that he knew why. No protest came back to her. Although this incident may be exceptional, I have told it that laymen and women may learn the sort of experience which ministers have to meet sometimes in our towns and villages. Later, the doctor became my warm friend and gained my respect for his better life.

The other negative vote was thrown by a young man named Charles G. Saunders, a high churchman; Dr.

Packard, the vestry, and most of the parish were low church; hence Mr. Saunders had been kept off the vestry and there was increasing friction. I have always shrunk from and have hated to waste time and strength in party strife. Lawrence was full of sin and needed the Gospel. The text of my first sermon after ordination to the priesthood in Grace Church was, 'We preach not ourselves but Christ Jesus the Lord.' When, therefore, a group of young men asked me before the Easter parish meeting if I had any objection to the election of Mr. Saunders to the vestry, I told them that that was the business of the parish: I should only insist on churchmen of good character. Mr. Saunders was elected. For years he gave his services as choir master and afterwards became senior warden. When I was Bishop, and he upon the Standing Committee, I turned continually to him for advice. Later he became in the General Convention one of the most trusted leaders of the Church. We were not of the same opinion in some ecclesiastical matters, but he was from first to last as loyal to me as I was to him. Had he been met by me with distrust, we should have drifted apart into partisan groups.

Until I came to Lawrence, I knew only the point of view of the capitalist; my relatives were owners of mill stocks and manufacturers. On the other hand Lawrence was a city of wage-earners and people of small incomes, dependent upon five or six large mills whose stock was owned in Boston and elsewhere. Within a week of my arrival I was going from tenement to tenement, sitting in the kitchens, talking to the women at the tub and cook stove, or in the evenings meeting the men. In a short time I had learned much and thought more. Robert Russell, a friend and college mate, son of a Boston manufacturer, was working as a hand in the mill, learning manufacturing: he, too, was learning fast, and we talked things over, and reached such conclusions as any fair-minded man would come to. The Monday Evening Club, composed of about twenty-five leading citizens — mill-agents, lawyers, doctors, shopkeepers — had elected me a member. I was by fifteen or twenty years the youngest. One Monday evening, after a hard afternoon at calling in the tenements, I broke out in the hour given to discussion, and, turning to the agent of the Pacific Mills, said to him, 'You have in your big spinning rooms some three hundred children who are growing up in ignorance, sapping their strength, and in associations which harden them.' He gave the answer which almost any good and conscientious mill-agent would have given, 'The children like it better than going to school; the parents need their earnings and it doesn't seem to do them any harm.' 'But,' I protested, 'the labor unions are moving for legislation to protect child labor; they are right, and the corporations are wrong. Why do you wait for compulsory legislation? Why do you oppose it? Why not take the lead and show the working people that their best interests are your interests too?' There was no answer.

I turned to the paymaster of the Pacific, and said, 'The mills of this city pay their help monthly; if a family comes to town without money, they have to work five, six, and seven weeks before they get a dollar; they go into debt to the grocer, the landlord, and the butcher; the trades-people are saddled with debt; they have to ask higher prices. Why don't you pay your help every week?' 'Why, Mr. Lawrence,' was the answer, 'we have five thousand hands, and it is impossible to pay them weekly.' 'Very good,' was my answer, 'the unions and the Legislature will make you do the impossible within a very few years.' And they did.

Mills have been built in the South by Northern capitalists, and there again many of their officers have carried on the fight against the protection of women and child labor. It has been passing strange to me why many of the administrators of mills and other industrial corporations have been so blind to their best interests and to humanity.

My uncle was treasurer of the Pacific Mills, a man of large experience. I was inexperienced and only twenty-

seven years old when I had the temerity to write him that,
if he continued to handle the help of the mill as he did
then, there would be a bad strike within a few months;
that I knew the help and their temper. Nothing was done;
the strike came, engendering bad blood, sending many of
the best workmen and women out of the city and laying
the foundation for a mutual distrust which hampered
work for years. Foreigners have come into our mills by the
hundreds of thousands. They do not understand English,
and yet until very lately our English-speaking manufacturers and industrial leaders have gone on as if the for-
eigner understood everything. Hence, when a bill was
passed in Massachusetts shortening the hours and the
manufacturers assumed that wages would be reduced in
proportion, the help were told in their foreign languages
by their leaders that the pay would remain the same;
then, when on payday the help tore open their envelopes
and found a reduced pay, they rose up in anger; they felt
they had been cheated, and a strike followed bringing
militia, death, and the spirit of hatred.

Conditions have improved much: we are learning that
men and women, even though they speak a foreign
language and seem dull, are men and women. We are discovering that the real industrial leaders are men who,
while skilful organizers, *are* leaders of men, are human, and
care for a man because he is a man.

The clergy are often criticized because they are socialistic or too sympathetic with the masses. The clergy, a
very large proportion of them, fortunately live and work
among the working people, they see their point of view
and to their credit stand for it. All this I say as one who
believes in the present system, at all events until a better
be found, but who is sure that a finer spirit, a better understanding of the mind of the worker, a juster administration and increasing recognition and representation of the
workers must come steadily on, or the system will be
smashed. A younger group of administrators and industrial leaders is arriving, some of them are already in respon-

sible positions, who will set forward with rapidity and power the spirit of justice, humanity, and coöperation. The signs of the times are hopeful.

Drink was the curse of Lawrence in my day. Young people whose memories do not go back beyond the beginning of War Prohibition can have no conception of the power of liquor under the license system in a city like Lawrence. Thousands of men and some women wasted a large fraction of their wages in drink; hundreds if not thousands were 'beery' a good deal of the time. The waste of child life, the privation of wives, and the personal degradation were unspeakable. But the influence of liquor was pervasive; it represented big money. The patrons of grocers, butchers, and banks, the clients of lawyers and doctors, had some relation with drink or its finances; the City Hall was a centre of liquor and its political influence. Men have got to support their families, and when a man, be he tradesman, banker, or of a profession, sees that by active opposition to the liquor interest he loses his trade, clients, or patients, and his income which feeds his children falls off, he, being human, has not the courage to stand up in the fight for temperance or the enforcement of law; for law under the license system was never thoroughly enforced. Whatever the police might be ready to do, there were influences higher up that forbade. I mention these things because in these days some people assume that evasions and infractions of the law did not exist under the license system. They were rife, and bribery was frequent.

When I moved from Lawrence to Cambridge, I found a body of men of independent income who without fear for their children's bread could stand firm. Cambridge became a no-license city in 1887. But in Lawrence aggressive action took tenfold courage. A very few men and women dared to act, but of many of the high-minded citizens it was too much to expect. Hence a vigorous, healthy public sentiment against the power of liquor could not be marshalled.

The temperance crusades were left to earnest women.

I had been brought up to a moderate use of wine, and believed in local option. Soon after my coming to Lawrence, a temperance revival took place. Halls were crowded to hear the orators: then came the campaign for pledges, and an earnest, white-faced woman approached me in an office, saying, 'Mr. Lawrence, I have here a pledge which I am getting the ministers to sign, and then I am going out to get the poor drunkards to sign after them. Will you please sign?' The method seemed to me so preposterous, and the woman looked so guileless, that I reacted and said, 'Unfortunately, madam, I am a drinking man, I cannot sign.' Seeing her dismay, I explained my position, but it was of no use. She said she 'would not tell on me.' I then said, 'My dear madam, I have in my pocket a pledge signed by a man a month ago. In a drunken frenzy he tore a fistful of hair from his wife's scalp. When sobered, I got him to sign the pledge for thirty days. I have kept an eye on him, and now I am going to get him to renew it. He will not care whether I sign the pledge or not; it would not affect him.'

The question of wine-drinking did not exist in Lawrence; nobody could afford wine. The only issue of temperance was drinking whiskey or beer at the bar or drinking not at all. The most disappointing feature of my eight years in Lawrence was the slight impression that those who stood for high standards could make in the drink problem in a mill city. Of personal work, helping the wife to keep her man from drink, or the husband his wife, to hold together the families of well-meaning drinking people, there was no end, and amidst many failures there were occasional redemptions which paid for all the time and strength.

Since those days I have lived in Cambridge and Boston and have watched a generation of men pass through college and beyond middle life. The great majority of them have, of course, been temperate. I have, however, seen many enter college alert, fresh, and vigorous; then gradually become full-faced and later bloated; some of them dying twenty and thirty years before their time, others heavy and soggy in body and character. I have sometimes been appalled at the moral and physical waste and the apparent indifference of those closest to them. The cocktail habit, which has come in since my day, champagne, then whiskey, strike at the mental and physical vitality of some of our most promising young men. Starting life I believe without prejudice, and a moderate drinker of wine and beer, I have been driven by facts to think things through; and although I have never signed a pledge, I gradually ceased taking even a little wine, and for some fifteen or twenty years have touched nothing. It made me uneasy to feel that my slight example should give any man the excuse for abusing his liberty.

Hospitals and charities must be supported in a mill city, but the mass of the people are wage-earners. I recall with the greatest admiration the way in which thousands of women and men of small salaries or wages supported the civic institutions: a dollar in Lawrence seemed to serve the purpose of ten dollars in Boston.

A clergyman's chief work lies, however, in his parish, and for eight years my time and thought were centred there.

The Sunday School had outgrown the wooden chapel. Teachers, workers, and scholars were asking for a parish house. But the vestry, like many other vestries, knew very little about the activities of the parish, and they thought me young and over-enthusiastic as I urged the enterprise. They gave me permission, however, to have a plan drawn, and to test out the interest of the people. This was my second experiment in money-raising. In college, when the Hasty Pudding Club was allowed by the Harvard Corporation to break down partitions and take in two additional rooms on the upper floor of Stoughton Hall, I was appointed on the committee to raise the money among graduate members. Cabot Lodge and I trod the bricks of Boston and called on our fathers' friends for cash; and Caleb Loring, later Justice of the Supreme

Court, and I gathered in four hundred dollars in one after-noon. But this parish subscription of small pledges running for months from wage-earners was a different matter. A man who has moved among the rich does not learn what generosity is until he has tried the poor. Within a short time I brought to the vestry such a long list of monthly pledges that they were amazed and asked who these people were. I replied, 'You think that the parish is made up of people whom you know on the centre aisle. The real parish is on the side aisles, in the gallery and Sunday School and the tenements.' The vestry took hold, gave strong support, and the parish house was built. This is the history of many a similar parish enterprise.

Personal work, services, and preaching are the backbone of a rector's life.

Of the first there was infinite variety, offering play for sympathy and humor. How well I remember calling upon a woman who as a child in Scotland worked as a spinner beside the boy David Livingstone. She had been bed-ridden sixteen years when I first called on her. On her bed were strewn newspapers and two or three story books. 'What do you read, Mrs. Grant?' I asked. 'Oh,' said she, feeling that she must make a good impression on the young minister, 'I read good books, the Bible and sermons.' 'Yes,' I replied, 'but if I were you I should read a newspaper or a story once in a while.' 'Oh, yes,' she answered, 'I do read something cheerful sometimes.' Mrs. Riley, a Lancashire weaver, was a noble woman with many children and a 'beery' husband: always cheerful and full of courage, refined, too. She had triplets who had died. A year or two later I knocked at the door of her tenement and walked in, finding her in bed. I said, 'What is it this time, Mrs. Riley?' She pulled the counterpane aside, and with a smile answered, 'Only twins.' We kept up our friendship with Mrs. Riley for many years after leaving Lawrence, until her death.

The Reverend Doctor Donald of New York and later of Trinity, Boston, who used to take my services in the summer, once said to me, 'I would give a great deal to have in my congregation such an attentive listener as an old gentleman who sits always just under the pulpit on the left.' I replied, 'That is old Franklin. He is an English spinner, crippled with rheumatism, and earning eighty cents a day. He is the most attentive and one of the most intelligent members of the congregation.' If there was any merit in my preaching, much was due to the face of Franklin as it was before me in the preparation of my sermon.

Many people have the impression that the day for pastoral calling has gone by. Rectors say that they have not time to go from house to house; that the people also' are too busy, and that they must devote themselves to preaching and administration; parishioners can see them at their office. During the eight years of my rectorship I was continually in and out of the tenements and houses of the people. Most afternoons and many evenings were devoted to calling; for it is as important to meet the men as the women and children. Calls are of all kinds. If the rector be human, and of reasonable tact, he will meet conditions as he finds them; sometimes an earnest talk, sometimes a prayer, sometimes simply a cheerful friendly greeting. I remember that at a meeting of clergy years ago the subject of pastoral calling was discussed and one man after another spoke of its futility. 'Far better,' said they, 'to give the time to the preparation of the sermon.' Finally the chairman turned to Phillips Brooks, who had been silent, and asked his opinion. He said, 'I wish that I could devote every hour of the day to calling on my people. I know of no happier or more helpful work that a pastor can do; and I call as much as I can. How is it possible for one to preach to his people if he does not know them, their doubts, sorrows, and ambitions?'

If the parson is not associated with the home when there is health as well as sickness, he will be associated in his people's minds with the undertaker — in at the deaths and funerals. My firm conviction is that even in these hard-pressed days a house-going parson makes a church-going people. Lawrence people had no skilled nurses or servants to hold the minister at a distance. I knocked at the tenement door and walked directly in to the kitchen or bedroom.

Speaking of illness, no doubt some clergymen are unwise and tactless in the sick-room, and it has been the habit of many, perhaps most, doctors to shut them out. There is a new day coming in the treatment of the sick. Men, women, and children are not merely physical mechanisms, but are living persons subject to the interplay of physical, mental, and spiritual forces; physicians as well as clergy are realizing this more and more, each from his own point of view. It is a fortunate parish where the physician and minister so understand each other that they join together in the care and recovery of the sick whether it be of body or mind. The two great and merciful callings have under modern conditions and by coöperation a future of untold beneficence. My life in Lawrence was before the days of antitoxins and people did not protect themselves against contagion as they do now. I sometimes found one or two children or most of a family down with diphtheria: then followed two or three funerals. One funeral I remember of a physician's only child who died of malignant scarlet fever; the coffin was tightly closed, but the room was crowded with friends and neighbors.

Intimate pastoral relations created keen interest in each and all the people and personal affection, too. I recall as if it were yesterday the blow and the stop of my heart-beat when word came that a young man of the parish, a bank clerk, had been arrested for stealing.

The Sunday School, which was a very large one for those days, was a perpetual joy. Children kindle one's imagination; they have a future. I remember one family, good but uninteresting, apparently destined to be mill hands for generations. Over thirty years later the mayor of a large city introduced himself as a Lawrence Sunday-School boy; he was one of that family. I meet the people of

Grace Church or their children all over the country to the
Pacific Slope. This friendly spirit makes the ministry full
of happy surprises and keeps one human and sympathetic,
and there are few experiences more humanizing, strenuous, or happy than a parish picnic of hundreds of men,
women, and children, the most democratic institution in
the world.

I doubt if any one ever entered the ministry less fitted
for its public functions, the services and preaching than I.
And I can honestly say that such moderate success as I
have had has come through persistent, dogged, and systematic hard work.

When I first decided to enter the ministry, I went to a
singing master to learn if I had a speaking voice, for it
cracked frequently. He tested it and said that, in using
my voice badly in cheering and shouting in college, I had
ruined it; that I could never be a public speaker. However,
I put hours on hours for months into building up my
voice. Then when I came to read the service, bashfulness
overwhelmed me so that by the time I reached the General
Thanksgiving my voice was trembling, and once or twice
it gave out entirely. During the first fifteen years of my
ministry I took lessons from time to time in voice culture
and in reading. When Dean of the Episcopal Theological
School, I continued the lessons for my own sake and as an
example to the professors and students; for I believe it to
be the bounden duty of every clergyman to read the service
well; it is an essential part of his ministry. To Mr. Hayes,
late Instructor of Elocution at Harvard, I owe a great debt;
full of mannerisms himself, he taught his pupils to read
and speak naturally, distinctly, and in a way fitting to the
occasion. With a keen sense of mimicry, he burlesqued
the rotund and artificial voice and taught me to throw my
voice naturally to the farthest end of the hall or church.
It was my habit for years before going to the church to
read aloud in my study every word of the service and so
familiarize myself with the notices, their order and sub-
stance, that there would be no hesitation or correction·

That there might be no hitch in the service, I found the lessons beforehand, for a nightmare which has agonized many clergymen tortured me for years, that of standing at the lectern and turning the pages of the Bible forward and back, forward and back, unable to find the place, while the eyes of the congregation grew ever larger and more piercing.

As to preaching and public speaking, it was a source of dismay, horror, and remorse for many long years. My disgust with myself, especially after speaking without notes, was such that I had to walk it off, and to gain the habit of forgetting as soon as possible the text and sermon so that by Monday I could not recall the texts or topics of the day before. Nothing could exceed the kindness of Phillips Brooks in his advice and encouragement. But he was so unique that it was sometimes oppressive. However, the fact that a young man has a high conception of the sermon, and a determination to put his best work into it, is of the greatest value. In spite of pressure in other directions, the best part of five mornings each week was given to study and sermon work. Written sermons were then almost mandatory; everybody preached them; and in preaching without notes I was hopeless. However, the Friday evening lecture compelled speaking without notes, and gradually I came to it on Sunday evenings and then on the first Sundays of the month; but the latter effort usually knocked me out with a sick headache. I always rehearsed my sermons without notes once or twice to the unresponsive walls of my study. To my wife I owe almost everything as a sympathetic and merciless critic. I always read my written sermons to her and slashed them afterwards. I remember one Saturday morning in Cambridge, after I had been preaching ten years, I told her that I was going to preach without notes, and she quickly said, 'I wish that you could hear yourself preach without notes once — you would never do it again.' An hour after, I met Phillips Brooks in Harvard Square, and told him what she had said, adding that I wanted to get a stenographer for Sunday morning who would take down every word, that I might know exactly what I said, how much I stuttered and repeated. His quick comment was, 'I would get a divorce first.'

How vividly I recall one of my first Sunday evening sermons without notes. I held fast the sides of the pulpit to keep my brain steady. One girl only was in the gallery. I knew her: she was subject to fits: and the thought came, 'What if she should have one!' Nervously my brain began to reel: when suddenly there was a groan: she had fallen to the floor. The congregation turned their backs to me, while the groans continued. It was hopeless. I stopped and said in a hard voice, 'It is only a girl in a fit; I know her; we will all sing "Nearer, my God, to Thee"!' . The organist struck up; people joined in, and by the time the hymn was over the girl had been carried out; all was quiet and I had caught again the lost thread of my address. That hymn, so familiar as to be quickly taken up by a congregation, has served me well on several similar occasions.

The adjoining town of North Andover gave opportunity for a mission and soon a parish. This led me to ask my cousin, the Reverend Augustine Amory, to be my assistant: a perfect gentleman and a saint if there ever was one, tireless in work, with a strong digestion enabling him to take supper every night with a different parishioner. By his efforts a lovely church was built, in the west end of which is a memorial window given by Phillips Brooks in memory of his mother who, born in the Phillips mansion near by, grew up to womanhood in the village.

We had never thought of any other home than Lawrence. It was a busy, happy life: four children had been born in the eight years. Rosamond, the youngest, with her angelic face was here only a few weeks. Having moved from house to house, we had finally built one of our own, and had little more than settled when on almost the same day I received two calls — the only calls I ever had except that to Lawrence and later to the Episcopate. Bishop Henry Potter, who had been recently consecrated

Assistant Bishop of New York, asked me to become Vicar of Grace Chapel, William Huntington having just entered upon the rectorship of Grace Church. The offer was attractive, the work at that time was a large one, and both men, though older, were my warm friends. Huntington was a Lowell boy, the poet of his class at Harvard, and had entered upon his ministry in Boston. During his rectorship in Worcester, I saw him often, and in any question of parish work or administration turned to him for advice. Bishop Potter's father, Alonzo Potter, later the Bishop of Pennsylvania, was Rector of Saint Paul's Church, Boston, from 1826 to 1831, and became a lifelong friend of my grandfather Appleton. Hence, when Henry Potter came, a young man, to Boston as Assistant Minister of Trinity Church, my father induced him to rent a house opposite our gate in Longwood, and he and his young family lived in closest intimacy with us. Years after, when he was Rector of Grace Church, New York, and Bishop Eastburn had died, many of the clergy and laity of Massachusetts hoped to elect him Bishop. Henry Potter, who was at heart a deeply religious man, was also a man of the world, of great charm. His summer cottage was at Newport, and he was to be seen in his dogcart on Bellevue Avenue in a white flannel suit, bright tie, and white beaver hat. This was too much for some of the conservative brethren, and they hesitated about voting for him. He too was averse to having his name presented, for he was right in thinking that his lot was cast in New York; for with his exceptionally popular gifts, his charm and wit, his administrative ability, and his prophetic leadership of the Church in her relation to social questions and the rights of the working people, he belonged to the metropolis and thereby exerted vast influence for good through the Church and whole country. I have always felt that his open letter to Mayor Van Wyck upon the degradation of the city government, the police, and the city was a great philippic. It started a lasting reform movement. Some months after writing it, he gave me a characteristic retort. I told him that his letter was one of the best pieces of English style that I had ever read. He said, 'You remind me of the professor of English at Yale who wrote me the same thing, and I answered asking him if that was all he found in the letter.'

The other call was in the form of a letter from Mr. James S. Amory, Secretary of the Trustees of the Episcopal Theological School, Cambridge, asking me to take the Chair of Homiletics and Pastoral Care, divide with the Dean the Reverend Doctor G. Zabriskie Gray, the preaching in Saint John's Memorial Chapel, and have pastoral care of the Harvard students attending the chapel: with the intimation also that, as Dean Gray expected to retire within a few years, I should succeed the Dean. Totally unprepared as I was to teach homiletics, I felt that there was a work for me in giving the theological students the benefit of my personal experience and in meeting Harvard students. Hence I accepted, and on the first day of January, 1884, bade good-bye to the people of Grace Church, Lawrence, who had given us eight happy years. The parish was left in good hands. Doctor Packard was rector over thirty years; I took his place: Augustine Amory, my assistant, followed. Later Arthur Moulton, his curate, followed him, and Malcolm Peabody, his curate, followed him. Thus for seventy-five years the parish was not a day without a resident rector. It was a happy event that on April 29, 1920, at the consecration in Grace Church of Arthur Moulton as Missionary Bishop of Utah, Bishop Tuttle presided upon the fifty-first anniversary (lacking one day) of his consecration as Bishop of the Continental District of Utah, Wyoming, and Idaho.

It was a source of great gratification to me when the president of the leading bank of Lawrence, a deacon in the Congregational Church, in bidding me good-bye said, 'I thank you for having lived here these eight years, for you have shown us that there are no classes, that we and the mill workers, the workers and we, are one community with common interests, hopes, and sympathies.'

CHAPTER V
CAMBRIDGE
1884–1893

THE founders of the Episcopal Theological School showed courage, good sense, and prophetic judgment in placing the school in Cambridge and near the University where the students would, under scholarly guidance and spiritual leaders, prepare for the ministry in the atmosphere of modern thought and life.

In so doing they laid the school open to the suspicion of disloyalty to the faith on the part of many Bishops and others of influence in the Church. When I came as a professor, only Bishop Clark, of Rhode Island, set the school as his first preference for his candidates. Men like Bishops Potter and Whipple sympathized with it. Bishop Paddock, of Massachusetts, feared for the faith and pressed his candidates to go to other, safer schools.

There has, however, been built up during these fifty years a body of alumni, loyal and consecrated, who are strong bishops, missionaries, pastors and teachers throughout the Church.

The faculty was small. Dr. George Zabriskie Gray, the Dean, holding the Chair of Theology, was a wide reader and positive though open-minded teacher who stimulated the men to work and to come to their own conclusions. Professor Steenstra, who held the Chair of Old Testament, was a ripe scholar. Old Testament interpretation was moving fast in those days. He never could publish, because by the time his manuscript was ready, new discoveries compelled him to rewrite. His intellectual honesty, clear style, and determination to find the truth, gained, as such qualities always do, the loyalty of young men.

Dr. A. V. G. Allen, Professor of Ecclesiastical History, was unsurpassed in all Cambridge as a lecturer. Of rich imagination, gathering his knowledge from every source, from the Greek and Latin fathers to Sir Walter Scott, he carried his class along by the charm of his manner and diction, his mastery of the subject, and his ability to bring the thought, action, and faith of the Church throughout the ages into touch with the thought and life of to-day. One book of his has wrought a great change in the attitude of scholars, ecclesiastics, and religious people. To a generation which had been educated to think that the Latin, Augustinian, Calvinistic interpretations of the Christian faith were final, he revealed in his 'Continuity of Christian Thought' the fact that throughout the Church's history there had run a continuous stream of Greek interpretation: through history the principles and methods for which Coleridge, Maurice, and Bushnell stood, heretics in their day, were justified. Since his book was published, those principles have entered wonderfully into the thought of the Church.

Henry Nash, just out of the university and seminary, an omnivorous reader and brilliant scholar, was beginning his remarkable career of over thirty years as a teacher. His character and spiritual attitude were consonant with his great ability. In humility and saintliness he was as deep and fine as in his scholarship. He was a striking and moving preacher; and in spite of a difficult style, an original and stimulating author.

My duties were with Homiletics and Pastoral Care, preaching also in the chapel, and having responsibility for Harvard students attending it. Thrust without preparation into a professor's chair, I could not assume the air of scholar and professor, but simply that of a practical and sympathetic teacher; and of the many imperfect bits of work that I have done, I count Homiletics the most imperfect. I wish that I could try it again. From Professor Phelps at Andover I had gained a sense of the worth of strong preaching, a high estimate of the value of careful work, good method, and logical form. But his whole system was limited to the topical sermon. In Phillips

Brooks I had seen the practical application of these principles; for no preacher was ever more careful of the construction of his sermon. Then his spiritual power and eloquence drove his sermon home with power.

We make a mistake, however, in assuming that a sermon is something entirely different and apart from other forms of speech and oratory. Its purpose is different: its object is to move men to God and the higher life; but the sources of its power come, as does all true eloquence, from the preacher himself. What he was as a boy, his faith and character, his education, his moral and spiritual experiences, his consecration to the ministry, all form the background of the preacher. The effort of the teacher in Homiletics is so to guide the young man as to enable him to throw all these forces into the persuasion of men to follow Christ. In the seminary the student gains a strong grasp upon the faith, a deeper knowledge of God and spiritual truth, a fuller confidence in his mission. Through ordination he receives new spiritual power. Through contact with men and women from year to year he gains a closer knowledge of them, their needs, ambitions, temptations, and ideals; and impelled by a love of Christ and his fellow men, he brings the combined force of these experiences to bear in his sermons.

Looked at in this way, preaching is the most natural thing in the world; whereas by our special methods, our expectation of a certain form and manner, our thrusting a young man up into a conventional pulpit, we do all that we can to make him, and his sermon, unnatural and conventional.

One of my most difficult problems was to lead the young men to be themselves, their best selves, in chancel and pulpit; but early associations and memories of the mannerisms of the pastor of their boyhood unconsciously overwhelmed them. How to train men while they are in the seminary to express themselves in preaching is most difficult. The custom of sending students up into the pulpit to preach to their schoolmates is a method of necessity, but artificial, and sometimes leads to unexpected results. One day a young man of extremely oratorical manner, after mounting the pulpit, waxed warm with eloquence, and reached a climax in his appeal to his class-mates below him, 'Mothers, have you any children?' If they were mothers, they probably had; but being only a dozen young men, the reaction was boisterous beyond the anticipations of the preacher.

I have watched laymen, lawyers, and business men give addresses from pulpits, and it is a rare man who does not un-consciously speak in an affected pulpit voice and manner. The difficulty is too that many people enjoy the pulpit tone: it makes them feel religious.

I believe that one great reason for the unreadiness of men and women to listen to sermons is due, not to the dullness of the thought, but to the pulpit language. Again and again I have compelled men to rewrite their sermons, translating every abstract, philosophical, theological, trite, and conventional word and phrase into language which the average man and woman understands. It is strange how we neglect the one great preacher, his method and style as well as his spirit: but 'the common people heard him gladly.'

I have run on, for the subject, uninteresting as it seems, is really of the deepest interest and importance to the laity as well as the clergy.

No professor can make preachers: he can help. God's spirit working through the warp and woof of young men's education, experience, and character is the vital element. These, however, also need something now lacking, but within the power of the Church, and that is a real conviction on the part of the people that strong preachers of Christ can and must be raised up in these days. Men and women throughout this land, bewildered, without faith but yearn-ing for it, estranged from Christ and His Church, as well as men and women of faith within the Church, are waiting for straight, true and sympathetic preachers.

In coming from my parish in Lawrence, which had in

it only one college graduate, to preach to professors, scholars, and students, as well as other Cambridge people, the contrast was very sharp. The fact is, however, that while one has to be even more careful in thought, form, and literary style, people are at bottom very much the same — glad to listen to the interpretation of the Christian faith, if it is put to them in a simple, sincere, and a reasonably interesting way. And of course, unless a man is stupid, he unconsciously adapts himself to the needs and characteristics of his people.

How well I remember my fright when I gave out my first text in Saint John's Chapel and saw before me Professor Bowen, who used to try to teach me philosophy. I learned later that his religious faith was as simple as a child's. Under the pulpit was a transept full of Harvard students, who were there under the compulsory system of college prayers and Sunday service in some church. Within a year or two after coming to Cambridge, I was convinced that in a university which had a full elective system, thus making each subject a choice and privilege, religion was placed at a disadvantage where students were driven to chapel and church by compulsion. Hence, when the question arose as to the adoption by the University of a voluntary religious system, I supported it: granted all the losses, the gains have been greater. I was, for instance, immediately placed in more natural and easy relations with the students. The University, too, immediately put in force the system of preachers, whereby leading men of various churches from over the country came into residence for several weeks at a time; and in a room in the College Yard any student could and still can find every morning a clergyman of large experience, sympathetic and open-minded, for counsel.

During several years, and even after I became Bishop, I was a University Preacher, an office of great happiness and of high challenge. And now, after almost forty years of work among students I feel even more strongly than ever the greatness of the field and the crudeness of our work. The fact is my ambitions are high, and neither parents, the young men's pastors, nor our colleges begin to realize the need and the opportunity.

Tens of thousands of the ablest youth of the country when entering college are plunged into problems of philosophy, economics, and morals, into athletics and social activities. The confusion is great, the growth in thought and experience rapid. Meanwhile the boyhood grasp on the Christian faith remains dormant, without growth or guidance. Within a year or two many find themselves either wrestling with an impossible situation, that of making an undeveloped faith keep step with the rapid strides in intellectual and social experience, or they drop the faith with indifference and easy carelessness as to results. Parents, clergy, the Church, and the universities have got to study and work much harder than they have done in the past at the problem of the synchronous development of faith and intellectual life. The opportunities are equalled only by the difficulties of the problem. Whatever is done will be done by personal leadership. Students care little for institutions; they care much for and will follow the right men.

Soon after I came to Cambridge, an older Harvard graduate said to me, 'How are you going to see the students?' 'I am going to call on them,' I replied. 'Why,' said he, 'if a minister had come into my room when I was a student, I should have gone out the window. I thought that they were a different kind of creature from the rest of us.' 'Well,' I answered, 'if I can make them feel that I am about the same kind of a creature they are, it may be worth while.' 'It will be worth your stay in Cambridge, even if you do nothing else,' was his answer.

One never knows what he accomplishes by a call. Dean Briggs has said that the lonely boy has special temptations. I remember calling on a freshman who received me with rude indifference — indeed the only rudeness I ever experienced from a student; and as I left, I said to myself, 'That is the last I want to see of you.' Over three years later a senior called at my house saying that he was in the worst kind of a mess. It was several days before he would let me write the facts to his parents, and when I did, a telegram came from a well-known physician in a distant city, saying, 'Hold on to my boy until I can get there.' As he left the house one day, I asked him why he came to me. He answered, 'You called on me when I was a freshman; you are the only person who has gone out of his way to show an interest in me.' It was the same boy: his *gaucherie* and bashfulness were the cause of his own undoing. He is now a physician of excellent standing.

Many an afternoon I ran up and down scores of flights of stairs, knocking at doors, slipping in cards, and occasionally meeting students. Of course I kept in touch with the schools and academies which sent boys to Harvard, getting from the masters and pastors the names of the Church boys. The number ran into the hundreds; to-day Harvard has the largest body of Episcopal Church students in the country.

My cards and calls led many students to come to my house. Once a year I gave an evening reception having a public man — Theodore Roosevelt, who was then Police Commissioner of New York; William Russell, Governor, and the most popular man in Massachusetts; Henry Drummond, of Scotland, whose addresses to students, and whose little book, 'The Greatest Thing in the World,' were making a great impression in this country; Seth Low, Roger Wolcott, Sir Lyon Playfair — as a lodestone to attract. I had a Bible class of students every Sunday in a room in the College Yard, my one purpose being to meet the questions and problems in the minds of the young men at the moment.

In the summer of 1884 I passed a few weeks in England in company with my cousin, the Reverend Arthur Lawrence, Rector of Stockbridge, who was an enthusiast about English life, a seasoned traveller, and of such charm that doors opened to him everywhere.

Driving by stage and dogcart along the cliffs of North

Devon — through Lynton and Clovelly, we explored the scenes of 'Westward Ho' and 'Lorna Doone.' We stopped at quaint old Morwenstow where ships went ashore, and the inhabitants reaped the treasures thereof, and, going through Truro, we stood on the very last rock of Land's End. Surfeited with chops and tomato sauce, gooseberry tart, ale, and cheese, we went back to London and sampled the old chophouses of the Strand and the cosy French restaurants. Out again we fared forth to Kingsley's parish at Eversley and Julius Hare's at Hurstmonceaux, which overlooked the moors and the Channel; slipping into a cathedral here and there, browsing over the meadows, lying on our backs listening to the skylarks, we absorbed rural England. Then back in London, we heard Gladstone in the House of Commons answer Lord Randolph Churchill; it was as a bulldog and a snapping terrier. Out to Harrow Prize Day, when Doctor Montagu Butler, later Master of Trinity College, Cambridge, and my warm friend, gave more prizes to one boy than had been given to any one boy since the Doctor himself graduated.

The evening before I left home, Asa Gray had come stumbling into my study with a letter to Dean Church, saying that I must not leave England without meeting his dear friend. In simplicity, self-forgetfulness, scholarly refinement, and saintliness, Dr. Gray and Dr. Church were as twins. The Dean was most gracious; we heard him preach, and Liddon too, in the nave of Saint Paul's, packed with people.

For two Sundays we took the services in the noble Norman Church in Smithfield, London, Saint Bartholomew the Great, to give the vicar a rest. Unaccustomed to intoning the service, Arthur was so intent upon keeping the right pitch that he forgot how old was the Prayer Book from which he was reading, and suddenly found himself praying for Queen Anne and all the Royal Family. In his confusion and effort to substitute Queen Victoria, he lost the note entirely.

As we were walking across the city with the Vicar of

Saint Bartholomew's to Saint Paul's Cathedral, a peal of bells from a church tower crashed out above our heads in magnificent tones. The vicar stopped, and in anger exclaimed, 'It's an outrage that those bells should be in that tower; they belong to Saint Bartholomew's; they used to hang in our tower, but the vestry sold them for a paltry sum.' 'When did they do that?' I asked, thinking that it might have been a year or so ago. 'In Queen Elizabeth's time,' he answered; and strode on in righteous anger.

I remember vividly one night that we passed in Windsor. It was in a tiny inn on the Eton side of the Thames. The river ran close under my window, and in the middle of the night the moon streaming in waked me up. I went to the window, and before me loomed up in a magnificent mass, with the full moon behind it, Windsor Castle: the great round tower dominated all, and above it floated the Union Jack, showing that Her Majesty was in residence. And then it came over me: the little old lady sound asleep, the Queen, the Empress of the greatest Empire the world has ever seen: her word, her command, and even her personal influence go into the deepest valleys of India, up the rivers of Africa, across the steppes of Australia, and into the mountain ranges of Canada. The stillness, broken only by an occasional footstep on the bridge was complete; and as the moon swept slowly over from east to west, and the dawn began to break, I could almost hear the reveille and the drumbeat around the world, as soldier, sailor, and subjects of the Empire awaked and went to their day's duty.

England is our mother country; but with her conservatism and radicalism, her monarchy and democracy, her smug self-satisfaction and her magnificent self-sacrifice, is always interesting, always an enigma.

In the senior class, when I came to the Cambridge school, was a boyhood friend of mine, several years younger than myself, Endicott Peabody. As his father had been for several years a member of the London firm of J. S. Morgan and Company, his boys were educated in English schools and at Trinity College, Cambridge. The family came back to Salem, and Endicott became a clerk in the office of Lee, Higginson and Company in Boston, but in a few months decided that his life-work should be in the ministry. He entered the School, and after a year's study, wishing to have some practical missionary experience, responded to the appeal of the Bishop of New Mexico and Arizona to start a mission at Tombstone, Arizona. The arrival of the young layman from the East was soon announced in the 'Tombstone Weekly Epitaph.' Having given the mission a good start and gotten his experience, he returned to his studies. His observation of American life and education had led him to think that there was room for a boarding-school for boys, which, while genuinely American, would have some of the features of the English schools familiar to him. Having taken into his confidence his father, Phillips Brooks, myself, and three or four others he began to plan for a school of thirty boys. About one hundred acres of land on Farmer's Row, Groton, were given by James and Prescott Lawrence. While Endicott Peabody was still a senior, he raised the necessary amount: the trustees whom he had selected voted to build: the school-house was dedicated October 5, 1884, and in a few days the boys arrived.

His classmate, Sherrard Billings, and his cousin, Amory Gardner, were in the enterprise from the start. At the opening of the school, Mrs. Peabody threw in her lot; and every one knows how under the leadership of Endicott Peabody Groton School has taken a high place in the educational and spiritual forces of the country. In peace and war the graduates have revealed the character of Groton. It was a fine venture of faith, for Endicott Peabody and his two first masters were all under twenty-six years of age. Phillips Brooks was Chairman of the Board of Trustees, and I was Secretary. Since his death I have been Chairman. Endicott Peabody and I are the only ones living of the original Board. My associations with the school in planning and watching the construction, in playing baseball with the boys, in companionship with the mas-

ters, in confirmation services, and in handing the boys
their prizes, have given me great pleasure these forty
years. In walking across the grounds from Hall to Hall
and looking over the Nashua Valley, I have had before
me the same view of Wachusett and Monadnock which my
ancestors had as they went from house to barn to care for
the stock.

On August 25, 1886, my father died. Almost to the end
he rode his horse as he had done for over fifty years; but his
strength was declining. After an active Sunday at church
and in visiting friends, he went upstairs, and, while lighting his candle, dropped to the floor, dying instantly, as his
father died, and as he had hoped to. A father's death
thrusts one forward a generation to new responsibilities.
Two years later I wrote the 'Life of Amos A. Lawrence,'
believing that the record of such a character was due his
descendants and friends.

In the summer of 1888, Dean Gray died. We had
worked together in complete accord; he was my loyal
friend and counsellor. Although a good part of the administration of the school had been upon me for some two
years, I now entered definitely upon the full responsibilities
of Dean. The congregation of Saint John's Chapel, quite a
parish, came under my charge. I had, however, the assistance of the Reverend Edward Drown, then Instructor
in Theology.

My first aim was to unite in even closer sympathy than
before the teachers and students as one family, each and
all joining in building up the character of the School, and
therefore the personal character of the students; for while
each teacher has his own work and influence, the best
results are in my judgment gained by team play. Hence I
stayed 'on the job,' believing as I do that the public character of an educational institution is not made by the
speeches of its deans or president moving about the country, but by the graduates. A large fraction of my thought
and time was, of course, that of building up with the co-

operation of the faculty higher standards of scholarship and character, instilling in the students a deeper spirit of devotion and a finer conception of the calling of the ministry.

The presence of the Dean in chapel morning and evening, the fact that he is at the service of the students every day in the week, and his personal leadership in the routine are vital to the welfare of a school. It was my business to know every student, his ideals and weaknesses, his general character and idiosyncrasies. Many of them were working under heavy financial handicaps, or had home anxieties. The problem of the financial aid of young men, especially theological students, is a very difficult one, and I am after forty years' experience as much at sea as to the best methods as ever.

A few things are clear to me. Financial aid given mechanically and without consideration of each case is bad. I am sure that aid given to young men in college, certainly in the early years of college, with the understanding that they are to enter the ministry, is dangerous. Any method which leads young men towards the ministry along the lines of least resistance fills the clergy list with indifferent men, of whom there is too large a number now. As Bishop I have never given or loaned a dollar of aid to any candidate; as his Father in God I will not be in financial relations with him. I doubt the advisability of so-called scholarships or stipends for work done, unless the money is earned according to market values. Better give the help outright, trust the young man, and demand of him his very best in scholarly work and practical service. With all this said, no uniform rules or methods stand; intimate personal knowledge of each young man by a wise counsellor is essential.

When I became Dean, there were practically no elective subjects in the theological seminaries. We then began an elective system which has continued and developed in Cambridge and other seminaries. To-day the School has entered into such a mutual affiliation with Harvard that practically all the courses of the University are open to the theological students. Hence every man can plan his whole three years of essential and secondary studies, drawing upon the curricula both of the School and the University.

As the endowment of the School from its founder, Benjamin T. Reed, had certain life interests, and had not therefore been fully paid in, there was an annual deficit of from fifteen to twenty thousand dollars, which the Trustees gathered from generous patrons. The Dean, however, had his share in that work, which was at times very heavy. I gained thereby, however, much experience which served me well in later financial campaigns.

The orderly routine of chapel prayers and communion is a most helpful way of building up the spiritual life of the students; but there is always danger of listlessness and formalism. How so to vary the routine and pour into it fresh spiritual force is a perpetual problem of the faculty of a theological seminary. One principle, however, I pressed home continually, which is that the student and later the clergyman must have the habit of so connecting his higher spiritual moods and his prayers and worship with his routine work that the latter will continually feed and support his spiritual life and character.

So we lived on happily together, teachers and students. The young men are now missionaries, bishops, rectors, masters, and pastors in quiet as well as conspicuous places; and no satisfaction is greater than that of a teacher who watches the development, work, and success of his scholars.

On March 9, 1891, Bishop Paddock died. On April 30 Phillips Brooks was elected Bishop and on October 14 was consecrated. Always a warm friend of the School, he now gave it his strong official support, commending it to the Church in his first and only address to the Diocesan Convention. The students increased in number, so that Lawrence Hall was overcrowded. One night the thought came to me that in the building of a new dormitory, we could take care of our overflow, and gain income by renting rooms to Harvard law students, who were already taking meals in the refectory. This comradeship of law and theological students was helpful to both.

The Honorable Robert C. Winthrop was then, and had been for many years, President of the Trustees. Half a century before, he had been a leading figure in political life, and was the youngest man ever elected Speaker of the House of Representatives. The youth of our Nation is suggested in a remark which he made to me as late as 1893, that he had met personally every President of the United States except Washington. With the generous support of members of his family, of his personal friends, and patrons of the School, I gathered some ninety thousand dollars, with which the handsome Winthrop Hall was built and paid for.

Happy in the growing work, planning Winthrop Hall, and just publishing by the advice of Bishop Brooks a little pamphlet for young men called, 'After College, What?' I had no thought but that many such years would pass — when the great calamity fell.

On the morning of January 23, 1893, I went into Boston and upon the bulletin boards of the newspapers saw staring out in big letters the words, 'Phillips Brooks is dead.' The people on the street seemed stunned, and it was as if the city stood still. I went to his house, the crêpe was on the door; and then wandered about the streets and finally drifted into Leighton Parks's study, where Allen and Percy Browne, intimate friends, soon came, and we four talked of Brooks.

Here at the close of his life I record something of his education and development which enabled him to become so great a spiritual leader. One Sunday back in October, 1839, Phillips Brooks's father and mother went up the steps of Saint Paul's Church, Tremont Street, to make that parish their home. Their boy Phillips was then four years old. She was a Phillips, of the strongest, most religious, and most orthodox of Massachusetts. He was a conservative Unitarian. Following the custom of those

WILLIAM LAWRENCE AND PHILLIPS BROOKS
Boston Common, 1892

days, when the husband was head of the family, the young couple attended Mr. Brooks's parish of which the Reverend O. B. Frothingham was pastor. His teachings offended Mrs. Brooks, and became more and more irksome to Mr. Brooks. Hence one Sunday after service they agreed that they must find another parish. They decided upon Saint Paul's Episcopal Church, of which the Reverend Doctor John S. Stone was Rector. Here their six boys were brought up, four of them becoming clergymen of marked power and influence.

This incident is a parable of New England's religious experience; and because Phillips Brooks's spiritual experience was so representative, he understood that of the people of his day. The Puritans were dogmatic and mystic, of deep religious experience. Their descendants, weakening on the spiritual side, had broken into two parties, both over-rationalistic, one dogmatic, the other discarding all dogma. The people were yearning for spiritual food, but husks were plenty. In the simpler creed and spiritual traditions of the Episcopal Church was the foundation of a revival of faith, but the spiritual element for which the people hungered was often lacking. From Coleridge, Wordsworth, Maurice, Robertson, Tennyson, and Bushnell, a fresh light had broken; and the young preacher of New England, Phillips Brooks, first in Philadelphia, then in Boston, and later throughout the country, gathering in his great personality the mysticism and spiritual experiences of his forbears, and interpreting history and the creeds through the living power of Christ, brought to the people a fresh and living gospel.

The discoveries of science, the theory of evolution, opposed by many ecclesiastics, were seized by him as fresh revelations of God's truth. Reacting from the Puritan dogma of original sin, he preached that all men are the sons of God, redeemed by their grateful recognition of the life, sacrifice, and resurrection of Jesus Christ. Of course he, like all forerunners, was distrusted by the conservatives, and deemed a heretic by those who thought and talked in the ways of the fathers; but the people of his own generation, the young men and women, understood him, gathered about him, and followed him. No artifice of sensationalism, no mechanics of eloquence were his. He spoke naturally, with rapid, rushing eloquence, out of the abundance of his heart and experience.

When, however, the Diocese of Massachusetts elected him Bishop, these conservative and hostile elements were focussed in opposition to his confirmation by the Dioceses and Bishops of the Church. Those were anxious and unhappy months. To all charges of heresy he kept silence. Finally the approval of the Church was certified, and on October 14, 1891, in Trinity Church, where for over twenty years the people had heard him gladly, he was consecrated. Happening to be so placed in the chancel, I faced him; and when in response to the questions of the Presiding Bishop, he said, 'I will so do, by the help of God,' 'I am ready, the Lord being my helper,' his voice and countenance were as Saint Stephen's.

The fifteen months of his great episcopate had flown, and now in a moment he had passed out of sight. I kept no diary then, but I happen to find this memorandum in an engagement book on the day of his death, 'The Light is gone out of life.' The next morning in chapel I selected the Beatitudes for the Lesson, so expressive of him; and as I began to read, 'Blessed are ye when men shall revile you and persecute you,' the memory of two years back and of the unjust accusations swept over me, and for the first and only time in a service I broke down completely. Nash stepped forward and continued the Lesson and prayers.

Knowing intimately his work at Harvard, I determined that his body should be carried upon the shoulders of students. Mr. Sowden, in charge of the funeral, refused my request as involving too much risk. The brothers finally yielded, if I would take full responsibility. He had weighed in his prime over three hundred pounds, and stood over six feet four. Enlisting eight of the strongest Harvard students, most of them members of the crew, and placing three hundredweight of iron in a coffin which I had ordered over from East Cambridge, Mr. Sargent, the Physical Director, and I drilled them in the Gymnasium, up and down, turning and lifting, until all fear of risk passed. Up the aisle of Trinity Church they bore the body high; the church packed with officials of State, City, and Church, and the people, all personal mourners. Then the procession moved out into Copley Square, which was massed with people, for the city shops were closed. Facing the body lifted high on a platform, the whole multitude sang, 'O God, Our Help in Ages Past.' The procession crossed the river and passed through the College Yard, while the bell tolled and the students lined the avenue. In Mount Auburn the body was laid to rest.

We came back to the School and its routine. Cambridge with its associations and work seemed dearer than ever. Here was to be my life-work.

Three months later, two or three weeks before the Diocesan Convention, Dr. Steenstra left at my house a letter saying that he thought I ought to know that my name was being mentioned in connection with the election of Bishop. I was panic-stricken. Being in an official position, I had kept away from conferences, but upon my own responsibility had gone to New York to try to induce William Huntington to allow his name to be presented to the Convention, but he refused. I wrote to the Doctor that under no circumstances would I allow my name to be presented; and sent for my cousin Arthur Lawrence to come to Boston and head off whatever movement there might be. I was where I knew that I was doing useful work, and under most happy conditions. The duties of a Bishop, as I saw them, were most irksome; and to step into Phillips Brooks's place was unthinkable: I was sure too that I should soon break under the strain.

As I was at work in my study a few days afterwards, Leighton Parks called and asked me if I would come down to the Harvard Preachers' room in Wadsworth House for a talk. We walked to the College, and when Parks threw open the door to the room, I found there a number of the leading laymen and clergymen of the Diocese.

Almost immediately their spokesman, Robert Treat Paine, said, 'Dean Lawrence, we know that you do not wish to allow your name to be presented to the Diocesan Convention; and that you shrink from and do not want the office of Bishop. We have come out simply to say to you that these are questions for the Convention to decide. If it should come to pass that you are elected, it is for you then after full deliberation to make your decision as to whether you will accept or not. Meanwhile your duty, as we see it, is to be silent and wait until the question comes before you.'

They were right. It seemed presumptuous in me to protest that I would not consider accepting an office which had not been offered me. I could do nothing but wait.

May 4, 1893, I was elected Bishop. I immediately discovered how the situation is changed when the solemn decision is laid upon one to refuse or to accept so sacred and weighty an office.

A glance back at the election is interesting. During the latter part of Bishop Paddock's régime the Diocese, as represented in its officers, administration, and the personnel of its committees, had moved along in a quiet, conservative way. Under the lethargy of habit practically the same persons were elected to the various offices year after year. When, however, the Diocese came to the election of a Bishop, the clergy and laity put their best thought upon the subject: Phillips Brooks, up to the time of his election, had almost no recognition in the diocesan administration; preacher as he was, it was ten years after he came to Massachusetts before he was selected to preach to the Convention.

Even his election as Bishop did not stir the official diocesan waters. Practically the same persons succeeded each other upon the Standing Committee, the Deputation to the General Convention, and the Examining Chaplains. I had been a member of the Diocesan Convention for eighteen years, and had never been elected, hardly considered, for any office or committee in the Diocese. It was therefore rather a bold experiment for certain clergy and laymen to present my name (I was only forty-three years old) to the Diocesan Convention.

I was not present, of course. Three men were nominated. The Reverend A. C. A. Hall (now Bishop of Vermont), of the Society of Saint John the Evangelist, had been recalled to Cowley soon after the election of Bishop Brooks, because, so it was commonly understood, though not voting for the election of Dr. Brooks, he had signed his testimonials. This recall had aroused much indignation and he had left many loyal friends in the Diocese.

Bishop Hare was one of the most heroic and chivalrous missionaries of the Christian Church, a man of the utmost refinement and culture, and of exceptional eloquence. He was giving his life in behalf of the Indians of South Dakota.

I was nominated by the Reverend John C. Brooks, youngest brother of Phillips Brooks, Rector of Christ Church, Springfield, and seconded by Colonel Charles R. Codman. On the first ballot there was no election, as I failed by a few votes of a majority of the clergy; it has always been a source of gratification to me that the laity gave me their support from the first, and registered a majority: on the second ballot I was elected by both orders.

I immediately realized that, keenly as I dreaded the office and shrank from it, the burden of proof was now upon my side. The Church through the Convention having chosen me, it was my duty to accept, unless I showed valid reason to the contrary. Choice, home life, a happy work in Cambridge, did not count in the issue. One thing did count. From younger manhood I have been subject to conditions of nerves which very few persons suspect, and almost nobody knows. My fight has been lifelong. The dread of the conditions of the work of the Episcopate almost overwhelmed me. I was sure that I should break down under them before a year was over.

My first thought, therefore, was to seek the advice of

my family physician, Dr. Wyman, and a nerve specialist, Dr. Folsom, confident that they would advise against acceptance. But after consideration they advised me that, in the meeting of the conditions one by one, I should with care gain strength and confidence to meet the next; and so it has been — but the struggle has been a long one. Fortunately I have had a very strong heart, that has enabled me to bear the extra strain.

Within a few days, therefore, my decision was made, and in my little engagement book I find the record, 'So go behind the happiest years of my life; God's will be done. I will set my face forward with glad faith.'

Before breaking away from my happy life at the Cambridge School and my comradeship with the students and teachers of Harvard, as well as the neighborly people, I must call to memory familiar scenes.

Old Cambridge in 1884 and for a few years after retained much of the beauty, spaciousness, and charm of the past. The quadrangle of the Episcopal Theological School on Brattle Street, built of Roxbury pudding-stone, of English academic style, fell into harmony with the neighborhood. Over the Gothic Chapel towered a great walnut tree. Of this Mr. Longfellow had written: .

> I stand beneath the tree whose branches shade
> Thy western windows, Chapel of Saint John,
> And hear its leaves repeat their benison,
> On him whose hands thy stones memorial laid.
>
> Not only tongues of the Apostles teach
> Lessons of love and light, but these expanding
> And sheltering boughs with all their leaves implore,
> And say in accents clear as human speech:
> 'The peace of God that passeth understanding
> Be and abide with you forevermore.'

Just around the corner stood the elm under which Washington unsheathed his sword in command of the American Army, which was marshalled on the Common. Facing

HOUSE AT CAMBRIDGE
(Craigie House on left)

EPISCOPAL THEOLOGICAL SCHOOL, CAMBRIDGE
(Lawrence Hall on left)

the Common were the ancient halls of Harvard, old Christ Church, where Washington worshipped, and the Manse where Oliver Wendell Holmes was born. On Appian Way lived John Holmes, most bashful bachelor, but reputed to have greater wit than his brother. Under the shadow of the Washington Elm stood the comfortable old Fay House then called the Harvard Annex, now Radcliffe College.

After living three years in Ernest Longfellow's house, we had the good fortune to buy the Hastings estate between the Theological School and Craigie House, headquarters of Washington, the home of Mr. Longfellow. Our house, with colonnade porch and terraced lawn facing Brattle Street, had, as did Craigie House, a clear view across the Longfellow Field, the Charles River and marshes to the Brighton Hills. Sitting at my study desk, I could watch the masts of the schooners slipping up the river, as if it were Holland. Nearly opposite us lived John Fiske, the historian; next was the ancient Vassal House; and a few yards nearer the river stood 'The Willows' of Lowell, still massive trees. Brattle Street, curving down to the Square, had been widened some years before, in spite of the protest of the neighborhood, but 'the spreading chestnut tree' was still standing, although the smith and his shop were gone.

One day as I stood with Mr. Longfellow at his gate, he pointed down the street and said, 'Mr. Brewer the butcher, whose shop is in Brattle Square, was an alderman when the street was widened, and after my protest he said, "Why, Mr. Longfellow, if we can only widen and straighten Brattle Street, you can stand at your front gate and see into my shop." Mr. Brewer seemed to think,' continued Mr. Longfellow, 'that my greatest satisfaction would be in seeing his meat hanging in the window.'

During Mr. Longfellow's life and for years after his death, it was a rare hour when some one from a distant part of the country was not standing at the gate, gazing upon Craigie House. In the near neighborhood lived

Howells and Scudder, editors of the 'Atlantic'; Justin Winsor, the great librarian; Charles F. Choate, as able a financier as his brother Joseph was a lawyer, but unlike Joseph, most reserved and silent in company. Just behind us were Professors Jeremiah Smith, and James B. Thayer of the Law School, also William Roscoe Thayer, interpreter of modern Italy. Up the street lived William E. Russell, the popular Governor of the Commonwealth, and Thomas Wentworth Higginson, foremost in the anti-slavery movement and in equal rights for women.

The provincialism of Old Cambridge was one of its pleasantest features. The Misses Palfrey, full of intelligence and wit, were typical. One autumn upon their return to Cambridge, Dean Gray said, 'Have you had a good summer, Miss Palfrey, and where have you been?' 'We have had a delightful summer. We stayed at a great hotel in Magnolia, and met a number of really intelligent and agreeable people of whom we had never before heard.'

Dr. Morrill Wyman was the Nestor of physicians, a genius in diagnosis. He once told me this pretty story. 'I had completed a very critical operation upon a delicate woman. She had come out of the ether and lay there very white and gentle. Well satisfied with my work, I had put aside my instruments, when she, evidently conscious of my self-satisfaction, said with the New-Englander's desire to speak the cold truth, "Doctor, we are all nothing but instruments in the sight of God," and then after a pause she turned towards me and added, "But there is great choice in the instruments." '

Brattle Street was a favorite walk of Professor Norton. While I was dressing for breakfast soon after seven, President and Mrs. Eliot on their morning bicycle ride passed by. And immediately after breakfast, Dean Le Baron Briggs, loaded with a bag full of themes, hurried on a jog-trot that he might slip into chapel before old Jones gave his last pull at the bell-rope. Then the college bell in the cupola of Harvard Hall, whose sharp, clear voice rings in the memory of every Harvard man, came slowly to rest and silence, while the chapel organ, with Warren Locke at the keyboard, caught up the sound, and the preacher entered the pulpit.

Walking up Brattle Street by colonial houses, one came to Elmwood, where James Russell Lowell was born, lived, and died. Every bit of Old Cambridge was dear to him and every vista. Standing with him once on Mount Auburn Street and looking across the river and the meadows with great stacks of salt hay, I said, 'How beautiful this will be when it becomes the college playground!' He cast a look at me as much as to say, 'You poor fool,' and quietly responded, 'Do you think it can be any more beautiful than it is now?' And it could not; the color, curve, and sweep of the meadow have all gone.

One of the last times that I met Mr. Lowell was at a small dinner which he gave for Leslie Stephen, of England. There were besides Mr. Lowell and Leslie Stephen, Professor Norton, Phillips Brooks, John Holmes, and two or three others. Mr. Stephen was a silent man, and Mr. Lowell was not well. Conversation halted. Phillips Brooks had a rather unjust prejudice against Professor Norton, who often struck a pessimistic note which offended the optimism of Brooks. The next morning as I met Brooks in Harvard Square, he said, 'Dull dinner last night.' 'Yes,' I answered, 'Mr. Lowell evidently was not well, but Mr. Norton did what he could to brighten the talk.' In a second he replied, 'Norton says that art is dead, patriotism is dead, religion is dead. What are you going to do with a man like that?' Sometime later, when Phillips Brooks and I were at Bar Harbor, I received a telegram calling us both down to Mr. Lowell's funeral. We laid his body in Mount Auburn under a weeping willow; but his spirit, that of a sound and true American, lives in literature and the heart of the Nation.

At the end of our ten years in Cambridge most of these men had died, and new houses were crowding in between the old; another era was setting in.

CHAPTER VI

CONSECRATION AS BISHOP AND TAKING UP THE WORK

1893–1896

UNTIL I was consecrated I kept only an engagement book, but as a bishop is required by canon to keep a record of his official acts, I began a diary which usually fills only a few lines each day; sometimes when travelling or for the record of special events I have written more.

The diary opens:

October 5, 1893. Consecrated Bishop in the Church of God in the Diocese of Massachusetts — and may God give me strength for His work. A lovely October day. I gave Julia a watch and each of the children a gold or silver memento. We all went to town in the morning. I went direct to Trinity Church which was filling up with a great congregation.

The whole service was beautiful and everything so ordered that I could take full part in it without distraction.

Bishop Williams presided with great dignity and sympathy. Bishop Whipple preached a sermon of fine large spirit and alluded to me beautifully at the close. Bishops Potter and Clark presented me. Arthur Lawrence and Gus Amory were my attending Presbyters. Bishops Doane and Courtney my consecrators; Bishops Neely, Niles, Randolph, and Huntington also present. The Archbishop of Zante in most elaborate costume also present and read an address after the sermon. About 250 clergy. The Theological students as a body in caps and gowns. A large body of my friends and classmates there; and almost all my relations. How much gratification it would have given father and mother to be there! I trust they were in spirit. Baby (Appleton, three years old) stayed through the Consecration and drew pictures of Bishops in the sermon. The Governor and his aides in the front pew interested him. The music was very good and the congregational singing fine. The Church very full and all impressed with the beauty of the service; a

WILLIAM LAWRENCE AT FORTY-THREE
When he was consecrated Bishop

most gratifying, sad, and happy day. The spirit of all, clergy and laity, so united and pleasant.

After the service Amory gave a lunch to clergy and invited guests (about 400) at the Vendôme. I am surprised at the general interest taken, e.g., three professors from the Andover Seminary there; also college presidents, judges, etc. Drove out with Julia and baby to our lovely and happy home at Cambridge. We shall always consider it our home, hailing from Cambridge, I hope, but living in Boston four months of the winter.

I hate the thought of leaving dear Julia and the children so much and of losing so much happy home life. But much as I dreaded it and refused it, the call seems to have come clearly as duty. So one 'must walk to-day and to-morrow.' The peaceful, happy part of life is in the past.

This was the last consecration by Bishop Williams of Connecticut, who for over a generation had been a great and interesting personality in the Church. As he, the Presiding Bishop by seniority, took me, the Junior Bishop, by the arm and led me down the broad aisle at the head of the great procession, I realized as never before the continuing life of the Church from generation to generation.

Bishop Whipple, the 'Apostle to the Indians,' of tall, spare figure, swarthy complexion, high cheek-bones and long hair, who lacked only the blanket and feathers to be taken for an Indian, was a national figure, a hero and one of my youthful ideals. Bishops Clark and Potter were friends of my boyhood; frequent guests of my father and mother. Bishop Courtney had been Rector of Saint Paul's Church, Boston, and a fellow worker in the Diocese. Of Bishop Doane I shall write later.

As we were taking off our robes, Bishop Whipple came to me, and with assumed solemnity said, 'My dear brother, let me give you a word of counsel which an aged bishop gave to me at my Consecration, "Don't get separated from your baggage."' Alas! I heeded it not that very week.

My first visitation I decided to make in the northwest corner of the State, the most distant point; and, as the routine of that first Sunday was typical of hundreds to follow, I give it in some detail.

On Saturday evening the rector at North Adams met me at the station, but the trunk which I had packed for a ten days' absence came not. Suddenly the thought swept over me that I was 'separated from my baggage,' for in that trunk were my sermons and all my notes; and as I preached from manuscript in those days a sense of helplessness followed. A bishop's first confirmation is an event to him; as critical as the first sermon of a deacon. Ahead of me on the next day were five services, three sermons and four addresses. Through the night sleep alternated with nightmares of the piercing eyes of the people looking at me, dumb in the pulpit. Happily after the early service and just before the confirmation, the trunk arrived. After the confirmation at North Adams, I drove to Adams; and there found a German-American congregation; baptized the rector's son, and had one other service with an American congregation; then by carriage to Williamstown where in the evening the decayed mission chapel was so crowded with people that during the second lesson the whole structure dropped an inch or two, to the fright of the congregation.

So easily does one adjust himself to new conditions that I find this record written that night: 'My first Sunday; full of work but beautiful. It seemed most natural, as if I had been at it all my life.'

It was the week of the Centennial of the Founding of Williams College. The setting of the scene amidst the Berkshire Hills was beautiful. Graduates from over the world had come to do honor to their Alma Mater: college presidents, the Governor, and national officers were there. Mark Hopkins, the great President of the former generation, had been a warm friend of my grandfather Lawrence, who had erected the College Library. It was my good fortune to be the guest at 'Buxton Farm' of Colonel Amos Lawrence Hopkins, who had married my cousin Theresa Dodge.

In the procession I walked with the Oriental scholar Professor Briggs, who at that time was the centre of such hot theological controversy as churches of those days were capable. Driven from the Baptist Church for his heterodoxy, he had been recently confirmed and ordained in the Episcopal Church. He was a professor in the Union Seminary, at that time in close relations with the Presbyterian Church. Such a career in those days was of national interest.

From Williamstown I made the visitation of Berkshire. Colonel Hopkins, with his coach and four-in-hand, drove me down to Lenox, stopping for an hour's service at the quaint hamlet of Lanesboro. Then farther south I held visitations in the Berkshire churches, each having its own individuality in the elm-shaded villages with the Housatonic River slipping through the meadows and around the hills. How well I remember the tiny church at Sheffield with a robing-room so small that when Phillips Brooks vested there, the rector had to step outside and wait in the chancel!

I was again amazed at the interest of the people; the whole country seemed to want to catch a glimpse of the young successor of Bishop Brooks. At Lenox began a warm friendship between the young rector William M. Grosvenor and myself. He had aroused among the people a keen interest in the spiritual and moral welfare of the surrounding villages and hill towns. Charles Lanier, William Sloane, John E. Parsons, Morris K. Jesup, and others, Churchmen and Presbyterians, were of the vestry and strong supporters of his work. Called a few years later to the Church of the Incarnation, New York, he there built up a vigorous congregation with Lynde Stetson as warden, and became a force in the Diocese. Years after, Bishop Greer made him Dean of the Cathedral of Saint John the Divine. By his complete forgetfulness of self, his direct, vigorous preaching, and his genius for friendship, he set the Cathedral before the people of New York and was at the same time at the service of any one who needed his help.

The sympathetic support which he gave me years after, when I came to New York for the Church Pension Fund, was of untold value. Thoughtless of his health and a weakened heart, he dropped dead in the apparent fulness of his strength and left to the Diocese of New York and its Cathedral the heritage of a gentleman and a saint.

In the lovely village of Stockbridge my cousin Arthur Lawrence had been rector for well-nigh a generation. The most popular man in the class of '63 at Harvard, he had marched through Georgia with Sherman and after the war entered the ministry. He was beloved by every person in Stockbridge and the surrounding towns, an intimate friend of Joseph Choate and of the humblest wage-earner in South Lee. His delightful rectory under the elms, with the open lawn behind overlooking the meadows of the Housatonic, suggested the England of George Herbert and Keble.

Upon my return to Cambridge from my first visitation, I took up the routine of work, and as it changed but little in the first ten years I may here say something of my daily life, methods of work, and varied interests.

We had hoped to make our home in Cambridge our real centre, but the demands of the Diocese compelled us to have a house in Boston. With, therefore, the Bishop's House Fund and the gift of ten thousand dollars from my brother and sisters, our winter house, 122 Commonwealth Avenue, was acquired. For eighteen years we passed our springs and autumns in Cambridge: while the two summer months were spent at Bar Harbor.

Behind all detail, talk, correspondence, and other duties, lay two supporting sentiments. First, the great Consecration Service in which I received my commission and the strengthening of the Holy Spirit was not of my doing. The Church was responsible; she had appointed me and commanded my service; my first, last, and only duty was to give my whole strength to the work; and second, the spiritual atmosphere created by the great but short Episcopate of Phillips Brooks, only fifteen months, gave buoyancy to the whole Diocese. Clergy and laity alike were determined that his spirit should 'carry on,' and they gathered in support of his successor.

Instead of finding a bishop's duties monotonous or narrow, I was increasingly amazed — indeed my amazement still continues — at the wonderful variety of interests and subjects coming before him. Each day brings fresh personalities, new problems, broader interests, religious, social, commercial, political, personal. I can think of a hundred paths of service which I should like to have followed through to the end: and the various callings of doctor, prison reformer, financier, publicity writer, social worker, detective, and plumber have beckoned to me. But life, even though it be very full of activity, is too short to fulfil in a very imperfect way even one calling, one so great and inspiring as that of a bishop.

I started with no theories as to methods, distribution of time and work. Perhaps I should have been wiser to have had definite methods and have stood by them. I know that I ought to have been studying at times when I was talking, praying when I was telephoning, and thinking instead of skating. But each man stands or falls in his own way — and my way has been to be always open to everybody. This involves the chopping-up of one's time, ability to break away from a subject and quickly concentrate again, the faculty of forgetting each problem in taking up the next. Deep thinkers, scholars, mystics, and philosophers cannot so work, nor can great preachers or administrators. But being a plain, practical man set to administer a Diocese, I have had my own methods. For seventeen years I have had the comfort of a congenial and efficient Secretary, Miss Marguerite Kimball. Through a large part of my Episcopate, my study has been my dressing-room, and the telephone on my desk has been free to call me at any time from eight in the morning until ten at night seven days in the week. There is something invigorating in the thought that two hundred and fifty clergymen as well as church officers and workers, who look to me for counsel, help, and leadership, have me, as it were, in their very houses and offices all the time; and while there has been active use of the privilege, there has been but little abuse; men and women have usually, been considerate.

How well I remember one of my first official telephone messages from the warden of a parish composed of Irish Protestants and English high churchmen. It was on a Monday morning and a voice, as unmistakably Protestant as it was Irish, shouted in hot excitement, 'There's trouble broke out in the parish between high Church and low Church — what'll we do?' 'Turn on the hose,' was my immediate answer. 'What do you say?' replied the warden. 'Turn on the hose: cool off; and come and talk to me to-morrow.'

I once said to a bishop who had no sense of humor that in my opinion a sense of humor was more essential in a bishop than piety; he looked sadly at me and thought that I meant it. Nevertheless, there is much truth in the thought; for the pathetic, tragic, and commonplace enter one's life almost every hour; a mother to ask about her wayward son, a widow with a mortgage on her house about to be foreclosed; prisoners just released from the 'Institution,' wanting a job; presidents of Southern schools, black and white; inventors and cranks; men and women of forward vision seeking counsel, tactless vestrymen and tactless rectors; persons in trouble of such sort that they cannot go to their rector or any one in their own locality. I have, however, always been very careful not to assume the duties of a rector; otherwise my personal work would be endless. The very last letter that I received yesterday was from a bride elect asking if her bridesmaids at an evening wedding should wear hats!

Few people realize the obligation upon the clergyman to be very fine, not only in his morals and observance of conventionalities, but also in the slightest courtesy. I remember an early warning. One Monday morning I stepped into a downtown elevator; the boy was stupid in handling it, and I was just going to speak sharply but held myself in, fortunately, for he turned to me and said, 'Good-morning,

Bishop: you confirmed me last evening!' In a New York trolley car a young woman entered with golf clubs. Holding my seat I said to myself, 'If she can play golf, she can stand.' However, my manners getting the better of me, I stood, and as she took my seat she said, 'Thank you, Bishop, I believe that we are bound for the same place out of town.' Sure enough, we were bound to the same house for a visit. Some fifty or sixty thousand people upon whose heads I have laid hands in confirmation are scattered over the country. I meet them everywhere, on the Pacific Coast, in the South, in Canada, even in Europe and Egypt. The association is delightful. They greet me on the street, in hotels and churches, and they have their eye on me and my manners. A business man can turn a book agent or a life insurance bore out of his office; but what of the bishop who discovers the next Sunday that the man is a vestryman of the parish he is visiting?

A popular conception of a bishop is that of a pious conventional man standing at a distance from the people and their everyday interests. A conception as incorrect and grotesque as most of the impersonations of clergymen upon the stage. The bishops of to-day are as far removed from those of Trollope's time as are Ford cars from the bishop's coaches of old. My desire, like that of every worthy bishop, has been to keep in personal touch with all the people; my pleasure has been to shake hands after service with all. Parish sociables and receptions, suppers of vestries and societies, I have been obliged to avoid. The work was too heavy and I drew the line there.

When a rector exchanges pulpits with another rector, he is preaching to the other man's people; he cannot speak to them as to his own people. A bishop finds his own people in every parish and mission in the Diocese and he has a special care and affection for each and every one. That the Confirmation candidates might realize this, I have sent to every one through the rector at the time of my visitation a small, attractive confirmation card especially designed by Berkeley Updike and signed by myself.

A true bishop will never allow himself to be so over-whelmed with administration as to cut himself off from occasional personal ministrations among the lowliest of the people; only thus can he understand the patience, faith, and cheer with which his clergy are carrying through that work week in and week out.

For thirty years I have kept in touch with my corre-spondence summer and winter except for three or four short trips abroad. During one of these my brother Amory opened my mail, and on my return said, 'You seem to keep an intelligence office.' It was true, and is true of every bishop. I have had some two hundred parishes and missions to keep continually supplied with rectors and missionaries. For, although a bishop of our Church has no power of appointment of a rector, the vestry, if they have confidence in his judgment, turn to him for advice, for names and information; and some vestries are as ambitious to get a great preacher and pastor for a small parish on a meagre salary as are some housewives to get a capable cook on the smallest wage. Hence there is never a day, year in and year out, when there are not from one to ten parishes seeking men; and it must also be said that there is an equal number of men seeking parishes. The problem, however, is to fit the man for the place; for where a misfit occurs, the trouble is liable to come back on the bishop. As other bishops are at the same work, seeking information about clergymen in the Diocese, I have written hundreds, thousands of letters descriptive of men, their abilities, and characters. It is sensitive and difficult work, that of so de-scribing a man and his limitations as well as his talents as to do him justice and tell the full truth to your correspond-ent. My effort has always been to write with perfect frank-ness the truth about a man, and at the same time never write a letter which I cannot show to the man himself; so that when, as has sometimes happened, a clergyman feels aggrieved that I have not treated him justly, I have shown him copies of the whole correspondence, saying, 'If there is anything untrue or unjust to you, show it to me and I will recall it.' The uniform answer has been, 'Bishop, I have to say that you are right.' A bishop may be a great preacher or a spiritual leader in meetings and retreats, but if his clergy be weak or unworthy, his Diocese is disintegrating. Having observed bishops and dioceses for a generation, I am convinced that the most essential talent of a bishop, next to high character and personal piety, is that of assizing the abilities and character of other men. Of course, this is the essential talent of every administrator.

Throughout my Episcopate I have acknowledged or answered every letter coming to me and with rare exceptions have signed all my letters with my own hand. I have no use for a rubber-stamped signature unless a man's hand is palsied; and of course manifolded letters, no matter how skilfully wrought out, are not letters. Who can measure the possible harm done by the neglect of an unknown correspondent or by a discourteous answer? And the humbler the writer, the more careful the response should be.

In questions of health, exercise, sleep, and food, no wise man will attempt to lay down general rules for others based upon his personal experience. On the other hand, a man who has observed a generation may have gained some general impressions.

I have known great college athletes to go to pieces physically in a few years and die early. I have also known some of their fellow athletes to live useful, strenuous, and long lives. From either group I could with a fair amount of prejudice prove college athletics to be either bad or good. I have seen men work hard in some semi-sedentary occupation in office or study, and once a week put one or two whole days into strenuous golf or mountain-climbing, coming home stimulated and fit — so they think. As a matter of fact, however, their professional brain work has drawn on heart and nerve; and their occasional over-strenuous exercise has drawn upon the same. Some day they suddenly drop helpless or dead. Had they distributed their exercise more widely over the week, they would, it seems to me, have been wiser. One of the ablest and most useful professors of Harvard, an athlete in his day, on arriving at my house at dinner one evening said that he had run the last half-mile; that he had the habit of concentrating his exercise in that way. I said, 'You look out.' A few years later he had dropped.

A man must have rare and all-round strength to do his best work under the somewhat artificial conditions of modern professional and industrial life and at the same time excel in any line of athletics. On the other hand, good and continued work under these artificial conditions require that a man habitually get a fair amount of exercise, fresh air, and mental relaxation. Mr. Joseph Chamberlain once told me that he never consciously exercised for his health, a rare statement for an Englishman to make — and he was an habitual cigarette smoker. But his interest in orchids kept him in touch with nature, and who knows how many years his pathetic breakdown might have been postponed had he conserved his health?

I once said to Sir George Trevelyan, 'How is it that statesmen of the Georgian period, Fox and others, were able to drink hard, gamble through the night, and live to a good old age?' 'They did not,' was his quick answer; 'Fox died at fifty-eight and the others shortened their lives.' But there are exceptions to all rules, and each of us is liable to take pride in being an exception. There is no continued pleasure like that of hard, steady, useful work whose results are seen or are anticipated by prophetic imagination. Worry, excess, or some other form of foolishness does the killing, not work.

For few things have I been more grateful than that I have had over fifty years of steady work under the happiest of conditions. Physically and in all other respects I was an average boy. My brother Amory was much stronger, and in play, caring for the pony, or sailing, he was always captain and I mate; it is fair to say that he did three quarters of the hard work. I rode horseback for years, making the roads dangerous and the old ladies of

Brookline uncomfortable as Frank Amory and I scampered through the village and byroads armed with riding-whips and long lashes for the dogs. At Nahant we lived in our sailboat. Later, in 1874, I played upon the first lawn tennis court in the country, with a tennis set which had been brought from England and set out upon the lawn of my Aunt Emily Appleton. Here Richard Sears, national champion, and Jim Dwight played and outplayed the rest of us. When in the Brookline Country Club a short time ago, my attention was called to a very old-fashioned racquet to which was attached this inscription: 'Racquet used by Bishop Lawrence in the first lawn tennis game in this country.'

As the priority of lawn tennis sets in this country has been much discussed by experts, I make this note. Richard Sears writes: 'Arthur Beebe brought out a set for Mrs. William Appleton in 1874 which was immediately set out by Jim Dwight at Nahant and used. The same autumn a set was sent to Mr. Sherman at Newport, but not used until the spring of 1875. In that spring Mr. E. K. Outerbridge, of New York, also got permission to set his set out in a corner of the Staten Island Cricket Club and Baseball Grounds. So the game was actually played first at Nahant on private grounds, while the Staten Island Club was the first club to try it out.' Theodore Frothingham has told me that he saw the game played on grounds of the Germantown Cricket Club by officers of the Sixth Rifles in September, 1875.

Sparring and fencing I tried, but they had no charms for me. In baseball I played an average game, but never made a team; modern football was not discovered in my day; and golf came too late to enable me to do more than get some good exercise. My father rode regularly for over fifty years, taking pleasure in stubborn and high-strung horses. He skated when over sixty, and I have done the same: indeed, even now with each winter I expect to take it up again. During these fifty years of steady and sometimes heavy work I have consistently clung to a few habits. I have always and at regular hours had three meals a day, besides at times a raw egg or other bit of lunch, and in later years afternoon tea; from eight to ten hours' sleep in the twenty-four, including in later years an after-lunch nap; some exercise in the fresh air almost every day, if nothing more strenuous than a walk of one, two, or three miles, or a drive. Theoretically, I have during the past thirty years stayed in bed one day a month to catch up physically, reading and loafing. Practically, I compromise by staying in bed for a morning.

It was popularly assumed that Phillips Brooks died of overwork and that my first step would be to ask for a division of the Diocese or other relief. But it seemed to me best to try out the conditions. When my first list of visitations was published in the 'Transcript,' I received from that Prince of Old Bostonians, Colonel Henry Lee, a copy of the list with a letter like this, 'My dear Willy, Phillips Brooks killed himself in trying to do this. You must stop now. I have run a red-ink line through every other engagement and I expect you to cancel them. Your father's and your friend, Henry Lee.'

My constant wonder has been that my digestion, which was never strong, has stood the strain; for the excitement of speaking after meals is the worst kind of a digester. In the first twenty years of my Episcopate, every evening except Saturday was engaged weeks or months ahead, often with a public dinner: and what is worse for digestion than such a dinner, bad air, and a speech? One thing this after-dinner speaking did for me — it gave me more ease and freedom of expression, and that was reflected in my sermons; they came easier, and were less academic. For an instrument in conventionalizing a speaker give me the box pulpit, and a congregation of men and women whose taste or orthodoxy is easily offended. They would have killed the eloquence of Demosthenes, Cicero, or Pitt.

Two, three, or more evenings in the week I took a train or trolley car to some city, suburban town, or village, had supper or dinner at the rectory, went directly to service, preached, confirmed, and gave an address to the class; and then took train or trolley, arriving home at half-past ten or so. On Sundays I had services, sermons, and confirmations in three, sometimes four different churches, usually in different towns. While the food offered was varied, and often not according to my notions of digestion, it was almost invariably good. In the thirty years I remember only one really inedible meal, a breakfast. The rector, poor man, was a widower, and of his two daughters one was an artist and the other a musician. Parsons' wives, at all events in Massachusetts, are to me a marvel. Women of refinement and education in rectory or tenement, with one or two children, usually without servants except an occasional helper for the heavy work, have provided me with comfort, food, and cheer for thirty years. The cooking was good, for they cooked: the service was good, for they served: and the conversation was good and on a high plane, for they talked. I have occasionally met a parson's wife who would have done better in some other sphere; but as a whole I do not believe that there is a finer, more economical, capable, cheerful, and self-sacrificing body of women than the wives of ministers and missionaries of the Christian Churches. At all events, I can speak for Massachusetts with first-hand knowledge. And be it remembered that the parson's wife, who must be well clothed and have her children well clothed, is often the most efficient parish worker in guilds, Sunday Schools, or at the organ.

At our wedding reception, when Phillips Brooks, who had officiated at the church, came to greet us, he turned to Mrs. Lawrence and said, 'Don't let them think they hired you.' Many parishes in engaging the pastor seem to assume that his wife is a fellow laborer without wage!

As for the hospitality of people and parsons, I have in thirty years of Massachusetts visitations passed only two nights in a hotel, and then only because it was thought I would be more comfortable.

As Massachusetts is an industrial and railroad community, the people have the habit of punctuality. Of scores of thousands of engagements, I have been late to, or broken, only four by fault of the railroads, and not more than four or five by other delays or my own neglect.

I believe in short services. In old days we looked for a two-hour service when the Bishop came for confirmation. In these days of rapid action few souls are saved after the first hour.

At the end of the first eight months of my Episcopate, I looked back over my engagement book, feeling that the pace of work had been rather high and noted that in 268 days I had had 217 services, including 190 confirmations. I had delivered 252 formal addresses, speeches, and sermons, besides 241 short addresses. Curiosity led me to study the confirmations of other bishops of our larger dioceses, and I discovered that Phillips Brooks, who had made 184 visitations in his first year, had exceeded the number of any American bishop. And inasmuch as we make more visitations than English or Continental bishops, it seems that he had exceeded all others up to that date. Hence in my 190 visitations I have the satisfaction of having made the record, since Saint Peter! What humbles one is to think of the thinness and superficiality of the work and talk.

My experience as Dean and friendship with many theological students affected my relations as Bishop to candidates for the ministry and incidentally got me into trouble.

I believe in youth and in having the greatest possible confidence in youth; I believe also in giving youth large freedom of thought and action.

It has not been my habit to receive and record young men as postulants until they are well through their college course; for it seemed to me wiser that they, intending to prepare for the ministry, should in the testing experience of college be unhampered by the thought that they have formally committed themselves to a definite life-work and would be looked upon somewhat askance if their names should be erased from the Bishop's list.

When after the testing process of college, they are clear as to their calling, they should in my judgment be made to feel the responsibility of their decision. Hence, while I expect a young candidate to turn to me for advice, I have never exercised my canonical power to direct him to any particular theological school. A young man who has made his great decision for the ministry, should in my judgment be trusted after getting the advice of his bishop, rector, and friends to decide as to his place and course of study. He will do better work under conditions for which he alone is responsible. This assumes, of course, that candidates are young men of some maturity of character and judgment; immature young men or men who will never be mature had better wait or be refused.

The three years testing as candidates are of the greatest value, if bishops do their duty. Indeed, I know of no Church which in theory has better laws and methods for the safeguarding her ministry than our canon for candidates. A bishop who is sympathetic with young men, who follows with interest the life, study, and thought of his candidates, has a knowledge of them far beyond that which examinations of a few weeks' common residence can give.

Canonical examinations for Holy Orders are tests of men's knowledge of the faithfulness and ability with which they have studied and of their beliefs and the proportions of their beliefs on the day of their examinations. But any one intimate with theological students and the intellectual, doctrinal, and spiritual experiences through which they are passing cannot expect them to have on a certain date fixed and definite convictions on many questions of the faith which will require years to mature and solidify. And so far as my experience is concerned, a number of the strongest and most adventurous of the men will take doctrinal positions and deny certain received doctrines either because they have not thought them through, or because in their moral integrity they lean over backwards in their desire to be frank. When I recall the number of strong young men, held up by examiners or bishops for heresy, some of whom have done great work for the Church since, I am moved to go slow in refusal. William Huntington's examination, for instance, was postponed because he believed in the annihilation of the wicked; and it was his Bishop, not he, who finally yielded. I have, however, known weak and docile young men to pass their doctrinal examinations easily, while men of real moral strength have been delayed or have been passed with hesitation. My policy has been, therefore, to depend upon the examining chaplains, who should be in sympathy with the problems and intellectual processes of young men, to test their abilities as well as their knowledge and grasp of the fundamentals of the faith, and to depend upon my own knowledge of the men, their character, record in their school, and their answers to a few fundamental questions, to decide as to their fitness for ordination.

It so happened that at the very first examination for Holy Orders, I had to meet an issue which advertised me in some of the Church papers and throughout the Church as a supporter of heresy.

Two candidates were reported to me by the examining chaplains as denying the Virgin Birth and of being unsound upon the inspiration of the Bible. This, be it remembered, was over thirty years ago, before the first question had come to public notice. Consideration of the facts convinced me that the young men had been misinterpreted by an unsympathetic examiner, an aged and very conservative man. Notice was served upon me that if I ordained them, which I had no intention of doing until all the facts had been sifted, a public protest would be made in the service. Feeling ran high. The conservative Standing Committee, of which this examiner was a member, took up the case, and I had a sharp debate with them lasting most of a year on the rights of a bishop in the doctrinal tests of candidates. The result as to these two candidates was that one who held firmly to his original statement, which had been misinterpreted, was finally passed by the

Examining Board and was ordained; while the other felt
— I believe wisely — that he was not enough in sympathy
with the temper of the Church to be happy in the ministry.
I mention this episode, 'The Massachusetts Case,' because
it was a critical experience for a young bishop and because
I entered the House of Bishops, touched, many of them
believed, by the taint of heresy. At the next meeting of
the House of Bishops the desire to put down such heresy
was the chief motive for the appointment of a Committee
of the Bishops in Council to prepare and publish to the
Church a Pastoral Letter in which occurred the expression,
'Fixity of interpretation is of the essence of the Creeds,'
which roused great hostility in many quarters of the
Church. Since then the Bishops have never trusted a
committee to issue a Pastoral Letter.

Another young man named Parsons, was ordained by
me, whose career suggests that the test of fitness for the
ministry is in character, temper, and a sense of honor
rather than in exact orthodoxy at examinations. After
graduating from Yale, this young man completed his
course for the Presbyterian ministry at the Union Theological Seminary, but in his examination for Presbyterian
Orders had been refused because of unsoundness in the
faith. The Seminary had given him a travelling fellowship, and in Europe he had met a young clergyman who
told him of the Massachusetts incident and the temper in
which it was being met. Upon landing, he came directly to
me with the request that I receive him as a candidate for
the ministry of our Church. As he was from New York, I
insisted that he get permission from Bishop Potter, who
gave it gladly. Studying at the Cambridge School for a
while, he was ordained and then became a curate of Dr.
Huntington at Grace Church, New York. From there he
went to California, and is to-day the Bishop of the Diocese. At two General Conventions, first in the House
of Deputies and then in the House of Bishops, he has
represented the Prayer Book Commission in their important work. Bishop Parsons is but one of many strong

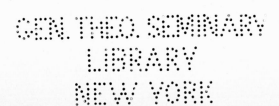

and loyal men whom I know in the ministry to-day who are in it because they, their intelligence, and sense of honor have, even though their opinions at the time have been thought by some to be unsound or radical, responded to the confidence placed in them by their bishops.

Few people realize how little legal power a bishop of our Church has to require of the clergy conformity to any given line of teaching or of ritual — a fortunate condition, I believe. Every clergyman is under the obligation of loyalty to the Church's doctrine and ritual as is the bishop, and each clergyman has the right to interpret them. The strength of a bishop among his clergy is to a large degree spiritual; he is their Father in God, their leader; and in spiritual things mutual confidence is the binding force. During these thirty years I have become more and more clear that spiritual unity in a diocese, loyalty, and happy and effective work are dependent upon the confidence which the bishop places in his clergy and the clergy in him.

The testing came early in my Episcopate. A certain clergyman was reported to have preached doctrines which others of the clergy felt were heretical, and a committee called upon me asking that I should do something about it. 'What shall I do?' I asked. 'Cannot you publicly express your disapproval of these heretical teachings?' they said. 'Suppose that I do so, and the clergyman publicly proclaims that his teachings are consistent with the doctrine of the Church and continues to preach them; and that other clergymen support him, what has been gained? Would you want me to bring him to trial?' 'No, hardly that.' 'Then how are we better off? I shall have put myself on record for a certain interpretation and have set my interpretation in opposition to that of others of the clergy; I practically proclaim him a heretic, and do not bring him to trial, and he goes on preaching. Am I not placing myself as Bishop in a weak position, asserting much and doing nothing but crystallizing diverse interpretations of doctrine which are already patent to every one? More-

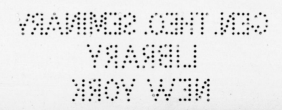

over, am I not, in stating publicly an opinion that a certain clergyman teaches heresy, making it impossible for me to have as Bishop of the Diocese any part in his trial, for in case it should take place, how can I be both prosecutor and judge?' And then I turned to them with this, 'I do not fancy this man's teachings any more than you do; but you are in the habit of administering the Sacraments in ways that some clergymen believe are contrary to the law of the Church. Several have complained to me. Now, if I call this other clergyman to order, how can I help calling you to order; and, this done, how can I help insisting upon my own interpretation of the doctrine, law, and ritual of the Church as the only standard for this Diocese: and thus the Church in this Diocese will be no bigger in its teaching and ritual than the Bishop himself?'

This, of course, was not acceptable. And from that day I have become more and more clear that, unless it be for some very extreme and exceptional condition, the real ecclesiastical court and judge of doctrine and ritual is consecrated public opinion. In the creation and guiding of that opinion, the Bishop has influence in proportion to the confidence placed in him as an intelligent, fair-minded, and loyal man in a responsible and sacred office.

Again and again have I been faulted for allowing this doctrine to be taught or that ceremonial to be exercised. It is easy for churchmen to say that the Bishop ought to stop it: but how? And many of the critics are the last ones who would want to be stopped in their teachings or actions. Liberty creates a sense of responsibility, and through liberty and reasonable variety the Church is led into larger fields of thought and action and appeals to a greater variety of men and women.

We belong to a Church and not a sect. Our historic background gives sanction to this variety and keeps us restrained in the use of our liberty.

At the same time bishops, because they are bishops, are restrained in the expressions of their opinion in matters of disputed doctrine and ritual, for by such moderation they can best serve the Church as administrators and leaders. A wise statesman leads by keeping well in the van of the best thought, being careful also to keep in touch with the mass of the people. I rejoice in statements and writings of high-minded clergy, radical and conservative; they stimulate thought. I have listened to men give utterance to views which I have held for years and which I would have given much to express, but it is well that these expressions should come from those who are freer from administrative responsibilities.

It is not easy for a bishop to keep a true balance; much depends upon his temperament and special abilities. This restraint of expression is largely responsible for the idea that men of intellectual leadership abdicate their leadership when they become bishops. As a matter of fact, their leadership is unconsciously expressed for them by those who are sympathetic with their thought and purpose.

The bishop of a diocese holds a life office, and may therefore make his plans for diocesan development with the expectation that he will carry many of them through. I am sure, too, that a man can do his best life-work by concentrating on his job, at all events, until he is compelled to broaden his field of service. He who thinks his job too small to consume his whole time and strength, and who spreads himself out early, will usually keep his job small; it may disintegrate. He, however, who concentrates on his job, using his best abilities to build it up, will be likely so to succeed as to be needed in wider service. At all events, my policy through life, whether as Rector at Lawrence, Dean at Cambridge, or as Bishop, has been to 'stick to my last.' As time has gone on, calls to other lines of service have been so imperative that I have felt in duty bound to respond; and even then, as for instance in the Church Pension Fund campaign, or in the War, I have kept in close touch with the Diocese, shooting between my offices in New York and Boston like a shuttle.

Responding to the popular impression that Phillips Brooks had been killed by overwork, and that the Diocese, being next in strength to New York and Pennsylvania, was too great for one man to administer, I set about to study all the conditions, and what was almost as important, to prepare the whole Diocese to accept my conclusions in such a spirit as would ensure a vigorous future. No one knew what was in my mind, and it was eight years before I recommended definite action. These years were full of happy service, the beginnings of many friendships, and the enjoyment of the variety of human interests as well as the physical beauties of Massachusetts. Indeed, I have ever since the division of the Diocese in 1901 regretted my official exile from the spring and autumn glories of the western part of the State, and my loss of touch with the people, the colleges, and the county towns.

A vivid impression sweeps over me now of the wealth of character, and ability hidden in our communities as suggested in this illustration. As I went through the Connecticut Valley preaching to the students at Amherst College and the people of Northampton, there was among the students and afterwards in the town a Vermont farmer's son, quietly making his way to learning law, and public office, Calvin Coolidge. And this impression is enhanced as I recall that somewhat later there was hidden among the audience of townspeople at the Smith College Vesper services a young woman from the University of Vermont, the teacher of a humble group of deaf mute children in the Clark School, who is now mistress of the White House.

From the beginning of those eight years I had one great asset, a sympathetic knowledge of the spirit and traditions of the people of Massachusetts, and personal associations with many of the parishes and clergy. At my first visitation I was able in a few words to link myself up with most of the parishes by a story of personal associations or an incident of parish history. And when personal connections are made, half the problem of leadership has been met.

I recall one interview which has resulted in more than thirty years of friendship and service.

One cold January afternoon in my first year, Mr. Joseph Burnett, who in 1865 had founded Saint Mark's School, Southborough, and who had watched over it with devotion, came to see me, and in much anxiety told me that there was division of feeling on certain important issues in the School and the Board of Trustees, that the School was suffering and liable to suffer very seriously. He added, 'Bishop, if you will allow yourself to be elected a trustee and will give your thought to the situation, I will support every recommendation that you make.' He fulfilled his promise to the end. Although the head master and trustees were all wise men, there were traditions and conditions with parish and school which made coöperation impossible. Within a few months the head master resigned and founded another excellent Church school. Through the influence and self-sacrifice of Mr. Burnett the local conditions were smoothed out, and although no one of the trustees knew William G. Thayer, they accepted my nomination of him as head master. Thayer had prepared for the Presbyterian ministry, but, inclining towards the ministry of the Episcopal Church, had by the advice of Endicott Peabody and myself tested out his frame of mind by a year's teaching at Groton and a year at the Cambridge School. Returning to Groton as teacher and vicar of the little church at Ayer, he had in four or five years shown such qualifications that I could commend him for the head mastership of Saint Mark's. Taking the School with numbers depleted, and with a majority of the masters new men, he welded them together and for over thirty years he, with Mrs. Thayer, beloved by every boy, has led the School without a ripple of friction to its present high estate. I count it one of the happiest incidents in my Episcopate that at Groton and Saint Mark's two outstanding head masters, intimate friends of each other and of myself, have been spared to work together. The great days of the school year have been to me events of great emotional satisfaction and of glad response to the romantic ideals of boyhood. Friendship won with boys sustains one's youth as the years pass.

At my first General Convention, in giving a dinner to the Bishops, who like myself had been consecrated in the past three years, I began friendships with my contemporaries in the House. With the passing of years I have realized that in all legislative assemblies, clubs, and organizations, the older members do not fully appreciate the sense of loneliness and awe on the part of the new members. At the General Convention of 1922, in Portland, Oregon, I again gave a dinner to all the Bishops who had been consecrated in the previous triennium, and seated among them the four Bishops who had been Chairmen of the House. Later in the session one of the young bishops was heard to say that that dinner was the most human thing in the whole Convention. Hence I gave a similar dinner last autumn at the New Orleans Convention.

The General Convention of 1895 in Minneapolis was the first time that the Church had crossed the Mississippi; and as Bishop Whipple of Minnesota, the Apostle to the Indians, was the host, there was an historic note to the session. In Faribault the East and West met; for in that Western city, where only sixty years before the Indians had held their war dance, stood the best of educational institutions facing the State asylums, which housed hundreds of the derelicts of the older civilization of Europe; while in their midst was the rude chapel where the savages of the wilderness first heard the Gospel.

One act of the Convention is worthy of record. Alaska, that great empire of untold wealth and opportunity, was hardly touched by missionary effort; a few heroic souls were there to minister to the Eskimos and the gold-seekers. After long discussion as to whether the Church should send a bishop to lead in the work, the decision had been almost reached that the three thousand dollars for salary could not be spared and that postponement was advisable, when Bishop Potter, who was staying with Mr. J. Pierpont Morgan, rose and said that a layman had agreed to pay the salary of a bishop for three years. Then Peter Trimble Rowe was elected and sent to travel with sled and dogs, on river and snowshoe, ministering by word, hospital, and school to that scattered people; and ever since then, now thirty years, he has been upon the outpost, one of the heroes of Christian history.

CHAPTER VII
TRIPS TO EUROPE
1896–1897

In the summer of 1896, Mrs. Lawrence and I undertook an enterprise which, I claim, called for courage and physical strength. We then had six children of from two to twenty years of age, and other domestic responsibilities. One duty had loomed before us for several years, that of giving our older children a glimpse of Europe. How to accomplish this without committing ourselves to a caravan of babies was a problem. Fortunately, I had the most helpful, resourceful, and affectionate mother-in-law ever known.

From girlhood Mrs. Cunningham had been popular for her wit, and alertness of mind and body, as well as beautiful character. She was one of an exceptional group of Boston women of the middle nineteenth century. Her husband, Frederic Cunningham, had died suddenly in the prime of life, leaving three small children, — Julia, Frederic, and Stanley, — a house on Chestnut Street, and life insurance of eleven thousand dollars. Soon came the notorious Boylston Bank robbery, where the robbers cut through the walls of the adjoining building and of the safes, and with other plunder carried off the securities of eleven thousand dollars.

Her parents joined forces with her by coming to live with her, while Mr. Cunningham's parents gave their assistance, and the widow faced the future with cheerful courage.

Julia, the oldest, was, of course, brought up to do her share of the work, and to have an eye to the boys. She made most of her own dresses, hats, and bonnets, and later planned and cut out her own bridal dress, with its long and graceful train, which was the dignified fashion of those days; she was a great favorite at Papanti's and the Germans of the season.

I mention these things that her descendants may know that, through practical work and some hardship, my dear wife, their mother and grandmother, learned by necessity how to carry responsibility.

Added to the care of her family, Mrs. Cunningham was one of the active workers in Emmanuel Church under Dr. F. D. Huntington (afterwards Bishop of Central New York) and later she was the leader of women's work and the Sunday School of the Church of the Good Shepherd. From the days of our marriage she always had time to help in our increasing household, coming to Lawrence, or Cambridge, in every domestic emergency, and filling every gap.

As years passed, her three children presented her with twenty grandchildren. At Thanksgiving and Christmas parties she, even in her old age, was the centre of the games and dance, playing the piano or leading in the Virginia Reel. The climax of the evening came when after a ring at the front doorbell a strange woman dressed in the costume of fifty years back, with a great calash, carrying an ancient ample bag, walked into the parlor. In the voice and accent of a Down-East country woman, she told a pathetic story and asked for food to fill her bag. When, however, the children tremblingly stepped forward, they found the bag filled with presents, and amidst great shouts and shrieks Grandma was discovered.

I well recall two typical retorts of her old age. She was a granddaughter of Bishop Parker, second Bishop of Massachusetts, who, though a worthy rector of Trinity Church, Boston, during the Revolution, died so soon after his consecration as Bishop that he never performed an episcopal act — a fact that I never allowed her to forget. In the 'Transcript' one evening was the notice of the death of her cousin, the Reverend Doctor Samuel Parker, of Stockbridge, who was described simply as 'a nephew of the late Bishop Parker.' I protested that this was not fair to Dr.

Parker, who had done a good work in the ministry, to be known only as 'a nephew of the late Bishop Parker,' to which she quickly replied, 'When you die, the "Evening Transcript" will simply say, "he married a great-grand-daughter of the late Bishop Parker."'

She had a great aversion to electric cars in their early days, and, insisting that every passenger would be shocked by electricity, did not enter one until they had been well tried out. At the coming of automobiles, her aversion to them was intensified, and, although I went to the extrava-gance of buying a limousine, partly for her comfort, she, although over eighty, would walk, not drive, until one day, after women had received the right to vote for the School Committee, a reform for which she was very keen, she jumped into a shaky, one-cylinder Cadillac which had been sent for her, and drove to the polls.

One evening, when the Bishop of Southwark, later of Winchester, England, our dear friend, Dr. Talbot, and his daughter were staying with us, and we had motored down to Plymouth, where the Bishop had laid the corner-stone of the Church, Miss Talbot, who had dropped into Mrs. Cunningham's house, remarked to her that we had run rather fast. 'Yes!' replied Mrs. Cunningham, 'that is what these automobiles all do; they destroy character, humane feelings, and everything; they run over chickens, dogs, children, anything.' 'But, Mrs. Cunningham,' pro-tested Miss Talbot, 'the Bishop would not run over a child.' 'Oh,' was her answer, 'William, of course, is a care-ful man; he would never run over one of his *own* children.'

One of the happy incidents in our married life was that, some years before she died, she was enabled to live in the house next to us, with doors cut through. The children always found joy, wit, and a piano there.

To Mrs. Cunningham's care, therefore, we confided the baby Elsie, and her older sister, little Ruth, who cried her-self to sleep for a week after our departure. They boarded at Bar Harbor at The Belmont, where presided the typical Yankee, Mr. Manchester, who as hotel manager enjoyed

Bar Harbor summers, and, like other thrifty Bar Harbor-ites, used his profits in enjoying a balmy winter in Southern California, while his guests remained in Northern climes.

The caravan of which I was the leader was composed of Julia, four children, Marian, Julie, Sallie, and Appleton, a companion, Miss Payson, and a Norwegian nurse, Kareen. Those who have travelled with young children well know the difficulty on arrival at hotels at the end of the day of so arranging beds, cots, or cribs as to enable them to get into bed betimes; and when a cot and mattress have been found and set up, no one knows where they have come from, and what sort of company may dwell within them.

Just before we sailed, Julia made a great discovery at Jordan Marsh's — a trunk half the size of a steamer trunk, within which were folded a cot, mattress, pillow, blanket, and sheets, which could be set out in five minutes. She was told that it was a sample which had stood there a year unsold. I doubt myself if another was ever made; I like to think of it as unique in the line of trunks and cots. Everything happened as promised. By the time that we were dressed to go down to table d'hôte, which in those days was at a definite hour, with all the guests, English, Austrian, German, American, French, Russian, sitting beside each other, wondering what language the next person talked, Kareen had opened the trunk, set up the delicate trestle-work, made the bed, and tucked Appleton under the sheets. The one difficulty was that upon our return from dinner Appleton, who was always in our room, was awake, and slept only at intervals during the night, intervals frequently broken by nightmares. He was always pleasant in his night vigils, but such refreshment as was needed for the next day's sight-seeing was not vouchsafed. Whether this was due to the spring of the trestle, the thin mattress, or the excitement of lying on a unique bed, we never discovered. But so we continued to the end of the trip. For years that trunk, which we could neither sell nor give away, stayed with us. But in some removal it vanished.

On the ship was a great company of Yale graduates headed by that unique humorist and barrister, Judge Howland, who were bound for Henley where their exceptionally fast crew was to race. We all went to Henley and cheered for Yale as loudly as we dared amidst the solemn 'Well done,' 'Well rowed,' of Englishmen. Unfortunately, Leander put up a faster crew. Through London and its sights, Westminster, guard-mounting, the Tower, Saint Paul's, the National Museum, Madame Tussand's, and a host of other sights we blithely tripped. English friends entertained us. And then we made the Grand Tour through Oxford, Warwick, Chatsworth, and the Peacock Inn and Canterbury. Brussels and Holland, the Rhine and Heidelberg passed us on to Lucerne, where we were drenched with rain for a week, while a German physician came twice a day to see Appleton and to receive his fees for medical advice which did no good.

Cheered by a lovely day in the Italian Lakes and Milan, and two glorious days in Venice, we returned through Geneva and Chamounix. We risked our lives with a half-drunken driver over the Tête Noire, and then to Paris, where we tramped through the Louvre, Hôtel Cluny, Le Bon Marché, Versailles, and every place that has sounded to the tread of American feet. Fontainebleau Forest and Barbizon detained us for three hours. Finally through London we took ship for home, found all well, and caught our breath with the glad consciousness that we had seen Europe.

Immediately I was in All Saints' Church, Worcester, ordaining Henry Washburn, now Dean of the Episcopal Theological School, and was immersed in the routine of visitations, meetings, office calls by all sorts of people with all sorts of questions, and happy fellowship with the parsons and their wives.

In the summer of 1897 came the Jubilee of Queen Victoria. For sixty years she had reigned with wisdom while England passed through peaceful revolutions in every department of life, thought, and administration. She was now the Empress of India, the ruler of a world-wide Empire. Passing through phases of unpopularity, she was acclaimed as Queen and woman in a way unsurpassed in history. The thought and sympathy of the world centred in London. At the same time the Bishops of the Anglican Communion were invited to Lambeth Palace for conference.

Sailing with my cousin, the Reverend Augustine H. Amory, as my chaplain, we caught the first note of the Jubilee in a special service on the Teutonic on the 20th of June, the Queen's accession day. No sooner had the ship touched the dock at Liverpool on Monday than men with tools, timber, and later cannons, trooped on board to transform her into an armed cruiser which was to carry a distinguished company to the naval review at the Solent on Friday. All England was keen in expectation. London when we arrived was almost a camp: along Piccadilly and the Strand, wherever the procession was to go, tiers of seats or bleachers had taken the place of show windows; shops on the side streets were barricaded against the crush of the crowds — a form of preparation hitherto unknown in the history of London. All the night through the people were collecting from every part of Great Britain and the Colonies; and as morning broke, the streets were alive with incoming regiments of soldiers and platoons of police. From Hyde Park Corner to Saint Paul's Cathedral, usually so crowded with carriages and buses, none but official carriages passed for two days and nights.

The great procession was the climax of the Victorian Era. I jotted down notes as it passed us, sitting under the Duke of York Column in Pall Mall:

The weather is pleasant: overcast. Here go some cheers while veterans with crutches and Chelsea pensioners in their scarlet uniforms take their seats in a stand in the square. Now a company of Horse Guards passes. Now a magnificent carriage with two coachmen and two footmen standing behind, red coats, white and gold chapeaux, and white stockings. Six nurses march by on their way to duty on the streets. Uniformed men with a stretcher and hospital nurse stand here.

10 A.M. For twenty minutes there has been passing the advance of the procession, the Colonials, a contingent from every part of the world. First the Royal Horse Guard Band in cloth of gold coats; men from South Wales in picturesque brown and yellow, with broad-brimmed hats; negroes from Africa, each company in different uniform and each setting off their black skins better than the other; Chinamen with queues in Chinese military dress, Japanese, Indians, etc. Color and picturesqueness are the features. Interspersed are bands of trumpeters with the drummer leading, mounted always on a calico-colored horse, a kettle drum slung on each side of his saddle, hung in yellow, gold, and red, playing both drums with flourishes and with a vitality and decision to awake the dead. General Wolseley, the Commander of the whole Army, on a white charger; barouches with Colonial Governors; footmen in scarlet, four horses, and postillions; Life Guards on magnificent black horses, brass helmets, plumes, lances, flags, beautiful saddle cloths, artillery, blue uniforms, then red and yellow, all moving in magnificent form. The military procession follows: they halt and dismount for rest. A band strikes up, and the crowd whistles with it. A fainting woman is helped away; another lies in a dead faint, carried by two soldiers; police and soldiers jam back the crowd.

11.05. Guns in the distance show that the Queen is starting from Buckingham Palace, sixty guns, one for each year of her reign. The first man to take the crowd off its feet is Bobs, General Roberts, on his little Arabian charger. Cheers are drowned by the screams of bagpipes, with the Scotch in kilts, the Irish in green, and again the bray of trumpets and the sharp stroke of kettle drums. The sound of the steady military tramp of horses is now broken into the irregular hoof-step of unserried ranks; for nearly one hundred princes, each in his rich military uniform, ride by, not in line, but as a group of comrades.

At last come sixteen barouches, rich to the last point, with members of the Royal Family, bowing to right and left; the children on their spring seats, the small son of the Duke of Connaught touching his hat many times a minute like an automaton. Here comes the Queen in her great barouche, with her eight cream-colored horses, with postillions and outriders; dressed in black and white with lace parasol — the only parasol in the procession — she bows to this side and that with great dignity. Alexandra, Princess of Wales, lovely and adored by the people, is with her. The Prince of Wales and the Duke of York ride one each side of the carriage: the roar as they pass is as that of a mighty ocean.

It was an acclaim which went with the Queen for three hours as she passed from West, to East, to South of London. The old Queen, who in lineaments and figure defied all conventional conceptions of royalty, so carried herself and so acknowledged the homage of her people that to every man, woman, and child she was indeed Her Gracious Majesty the Queen.

Towards evening, when the illuminations at the West End burst forth into glory, the whole East End rolled up by Saint Paul's, through the Strand and Trafalgar Square like a tidal wave. Bishop Potter and I tried to go eastward, but were overwhelmed and lost each other entirely. Up swept families by the thousands, husband, wife, four and six children, baby in the mother's arms, the next one on the father's shoulders with legs dangling in front, the rest hanging on to parents' hands, jacket, or dress; sturdy and dirty, boys and girls, men and women tramping in groups, blowing horns in your ears, shrieking, screaming, tramping and still tramping. The ginshops filled with men, women, children, and babies, all drinking beer, tens of thousands boozy, thousands drunk later: by early morning the City itself seemed to reel with drink: Londoners, East Londoners of the Victorian Era, there has been no race like them.

Great Britain never felt so big: perhaps no such crowd ever was: and no woman ever had such homage. The great reviews of the Army at Aldershot and the Navy in the Solent impressed the contingents from every corner of the world with the power of the Empire.

The Jubilee was over. Ship and rail began to carry the guests back East, West, North, and South, while a pervasive satisfaction swept through the heart of every Englishman — 'Great and glorious is the British Empire.'

On Monday the people of England on opening their Morning 'Times' read for the first time Kipling's 'Recessional,' printed in bold type on the front page, 'Lest we forget, lest we forget.' Seldom, perhaps never, has a hymn written for an occasion so vitally expressed the deeper, sober thoughts of all.

The Sunday after the Jubilee was passed by me in old Boston, where from the pulpit of John Cotton in the great old Parish Church, Saint Botolph, packed with townspeople, aldermen, and mayor, I reminded them of our common lineage and faith.

Returning, I had my first taste of London life. Through the kindness of friends, I was at home in the Athenæum Club. As the Secretary showed me about, he pointed to the favorite armchair of this or that bishop. 'You take your bishops very seriously here, do you not?' I said. 'Oh, very, very,' was his subdued reply. Dean Bradley of Westminster took me under his wing; and there was never a man more unassuming, kindly, and hospitable. I read a paper in the Jerusalem Chamber to a small company of the Christian Social Union, Canon Scott Holland, perhaps the leading preacher of the Church at that day, presiding; 'the Christian Anarchists,' Dean Bradley called them. Cards came to me from Mr. and Mrs. Chamberlain to an evening reception on Piccadilly to the Prince and Princess of Wales and the Duke and Duchess of York; multitudes of distinguished strangers still lingered in London; and the crush on the street and indoors was indescribable. However, it was a satisfaction to see even at a distance the great head and shoulders of the Marquis of Salisbury, the huge bulk of Sir Vernon Harcourt, and a host of others. Mrs. Chamberlain, whom we all knew and admired as Mary Endicott of Salem, was unique in her beauty, charm, and simplicity. 'The little Puritan,' the Prince of Wales was said to call her. The crush was so great that even London police could not cope with it, and word came that the Prince and Princess of Wales were unable to get in. The Duke and Duchess of York (the present King and

Queen), however, served to give a centre to the reception. My slight experience is that the presence of royalty is always sufficient to spoil a party as a social function, for almost every one, even those with long experience, stops intelligent talk to push towards and gaze at the face and figure of royalty.

My chief duty was, however, with the Lambeth Conference of Bishops of the Anglican Communion which met by invitation of Doctor Temple, Archbishop of Canterbury. Three events at the beginning stand out in my memory.

In the chapel of Lambeth Palace, crowded with historic associations, some two hundred bishops met to pray and meditate together for a day under the leadership of the saintly Bishop King of Lincoln. To be sure, he had been under trial for some extreme form of ritual; but even bishops reach below these incidents when the question of saintliness and spiritual leadership arise. In the silence of the chapel and the peace of the garden of the palace the great issues of life and thought come to the surface, and men are prepared for conference.

Westminster Abbey reveals to me its most impressive beauty when the setting sun sends its rays, made more glorious by the west windows, sweeping through the nave, past the screen, and to the very topmost arches over the altar. What is rude and tawdry in memorial sculpture falls into the background: history, memories, faith are revealed in the beauty of the great church. Here and at that hour the Bishops met for their first formal service: as they moved up the nave, and then around the whole interior with their scarlet robes and hoods, men from China, Japan, and Australia, from India and the wilds and morasses of Africa, from Madagascar and Ceylon, from the Arctic belt and Equator, all consecrated to devoted service in Christ's name, singing hymns of praise and adoration, one's heart was lifted towards the vision of a world conquered to Christ.

In Canterbury Cathedral, the chief seat and centre of the Church of England, the Bishops met to hear the allocution of the Archbishop, speaking from the chair of Saint

Augustine before the altar. Chancel, choir, and nave were filled with bishops, high officials, and Canterbury pilgrims from all parts of the world. As the arches rang with the Te Deum, English history seemed to be suffused with a spiritual glow and Christian chivalry. Our host in the Deanery was Dean Farrar, who when Canon of Westminster had by his 'Life of Christ' brought the Master's personality before millions of English-speaking people as never before: and by his 'Eternal Hope' freed multitudes from the depressing bonds of a Calvinistic theology. He was of course a heretic to the conventional churchman.

The next morning at Canterbury, Sunday, the rich voice and diction of the old Archbishop of Armagh, Dr. Alexander, charmed and held the people. He had stayed with me at Cambridge a few years before, and never was an Irishman more Irish in his voice, brogue, humor, poetic temper, and saintly gentleness.

To a nave full of men the Bishop of Christ Church, New Zealand, spoke in the afternoon in the virile language of the New World. And in the evening I heard for the first time that consummate preacher, the Bishop of Ripon, Dr. Boyd Carpenter, charm and lift a multitude. Bishops, soldiers from the barracks, visitors from everywhere, the whole city of Canterbury pressed into the nave and stood at every available point. Beginning, as I heard him many times in later years, in a gentle voice which reached from nave to altar (to quote from my diary), 'For sixty-two minutes he held the congregation, and no person took their eyes off of him; he had not a note to look at; thoughtful, strong, well planned, he led us on step by step, uplifting.' For years after I had the privilege of his close and warm friendship here and in England.

As I was one of the youngest of the Bishops, I enjoyed a good deal of freedom during the days of the Conference in which the older and more influential Bishops were sitting in committee. Of this freedom I made full use.

Through the kindness of my friends, Lord and Lady Playfair, Augustine Amory and I were during most of the

Conference the guests of Lord and Lady Ashcombe, who lived in a handsome house in Prince's Gate facing Hyde Park.

They were representative of the late Victorian Era. Lord Ashcombe was of the family of Cubitt, who had made a large fortune in the development of London, a gentleman of intelligence, courtesy, and devotion to the Church. Lady Ashcombe was a typical matron of the period, kind, conservative, and truly British. From the first moment one felt himself to be a member of the family, but a young American also had to realize that he was in an English household.

For instance, I remember well coming downstairs to the first dinner. I had taken pains to be fitted out at a clerical tailor's with an English Bishop's dress-coat enriched with silk frogs and silk-thread buttons; but, following the habit of almost all the other American Bishops, I had neither apron nor shorts. I thought myself to be rather elaborately and appropriately dressed, but it was a singular make-up for an English churchwoman to behold: and, as I stepped into the drawing-room, I noticed that Lady Ashcombe looked me up and down, finally fixing her eyes upon my legs, but said nothing. The next evening, however, we were dressed to go to the Lord Mayor's dinner, and that is a function where the fullest dress is expected. As I met Lady Ashcombe in the drawing-room, she again looked me up and down, and said, 'What, no short clothes, even for the Lord Mayor?' I answered, 'Why, Lady Ashcombe, if it should be reported in the "Boston Evening Transcript" of Boston that I had appeared in shorts, silk stockings, pumps and buckles, they would not let me come up the harbor.' It was a form of humor that she did not understand, for the situation was a serious one. However, the Lord Mayor made no objection.

In later years, and especially when received at Court, I have so far risked American conventionality as to own and very occasionally to wear apron, shorts, and shoes with silver buckles.

I remember well how at the next Conference the Bishop of Virginia, a very simple and retiring man, who happened to be staying with Lady Astor, appeared at the Conference with full English Episcopal dress, leggings, apron, and all. As a shout went up from his brethren, he protested that he was staying with Lady Astor, a Virginian, and that she herself had taken him to the clerical tailor's and fitted him out, so that he could not escape. This, however, was the last time that he was seen in that dress.

The butlers and servants of the English are, or used to be, a very interesting study — so dignified, formal, and awful on duty, so simple and kindly off duty. To the Ashcombes' butler I unconsciously gave a shock from which I think he never recovered. The Archbishop of Ontario was also a guest, and we were expected at Lambeth at a service for which the carriage was ordered at half-past ten. When in my room, I suddenly recalled the engagement, looked at my watch, seized my robe-case, rushed downstairs, and there stood the butler at the door, stiffly watching the rear of the carriage as it was driving out the avenue to the street. 'Has the carriage gone?' I said quickly. 'Yes, milord.' 'Call it back,' I said. 'I cannot, milord, it is too late.'

I dropped my robe-case on the floor, put four fingers into my mouth, and gave a shrill whistle which caused coachman and footman to turn quickly round. I waved my hand to them; the carriage swept out on the street and around back again to the door. I stepped in and joined the Archbishop, who never knew what called him back. What thoughts went through the butler's mind, if he had any thought, I do not know; but he looked very pale.

During the two or three weeks following the Jubilee, Her Majesty the Queen was engrossed in receiving delegations from the Colonies over the world and from the towns and cities of England. The Bishops of the Conference were also invited to Windsor. A special train was furnished us, and after evensong in Saint George's Chapel, we went into the castle and wandered about the state rooms and library.

In the banqueting-hall we were given a handsome afternoon luncheon, including, even though it was only five o'clock in the afternoon, champagne.

Servants in scarlet coats and white stockings gazed at us pantalooned bishops; gentlemen-in-waiting in black dress-suits, colored cuffs, and brass buttons, looking like servants, were most courteous in receiving us. We were then all guided to the back of the castle, where we stood on both sides of a broad path, awaiting the Queen, who because of her age had adopted this form of reception.

First came a white horse and rider, followed by the barouche drawn by a pair of white horses: upon the box were a coachman and the famous Scotch bodyservant, John Brown, in bonnet and kilts: within were the Queen and Princess Henry of Battenberg. The barouche stopped, while Archbishops and a few Bishops were presented to the Queen. They bowed, and so did she. The barouche moved on, turned back, and again she and we bowed. Homely as she was, her manner was so gracious as to make us all feel that Her Majesty had really received each one of us.

At a garden party given by the Archbishop and Mrs. Temple in Lambeth Garden, the Prince and Princess of Wales and the Duke and Duchess of York received the Bishops and a large company.

Mrs. Temple presented me to a group of three or four ladies. To one who stood in front and who, as I shook hands with her, appeared very tired, I volunteered some commonplace remark. She evidently did not hear me, and the thought shot through my dull head, 'The Princess Alexandra is deaf: this is she,' and I bowed and stepped back in confusion, to be presented immediately to the Prince of Wales, later King Edward VII, who of the whole group seemed really to enjoy himself. No doubt he was amused, if not refreshed, at the informality of two or three of the older American Bishops, who, without waiting for an introduction, stepped up to him, and shook hands, saying, 'Prince, I am glad to see you again: I have not met you since as a boy in 1860 you made a visit to our city.'

One of the ablest and most individual of the officials of England and of the Lambeth Conference was the then Bishop of London, Dr. Creighton. In speaking of his relations to the clergy, he said to me, 'I expect my clergy to obey me.' 'But what if you appoint a man to a living and he refuses to leave his present living and go?' I asked. 'If I have plainly told him that it is his duty to go, and that it is my will that he shall go, I taking the responsibility, and he will not,' he replied, 'I then tell his present congregation that he has disobeyed his Bishop: I refuse to visit his parish, and do not invite him to any ecclesiastical conferences. This age needs to break from its excessive individualism and to have obedience.'

At Mrs. Creighton's invitation I undertook to talk to a company of typically English women on the lawn of the Palace upon the typically English subject, 'The Additional Curates' Fund.' In response to my question as to what I should say, Mrs. Creighton remarked that they usually expected amusing stories from American Bishops. Even Bishop Talbot, then of Wyoming, who had captured the English people by his account of the Wild West, would, I think, have found it difficult to extract anything amusing out of 'The Additional Curates' Fund.'

To go from Fulham Palace to the Deanery of Saint Paul's Cathedral is a journey across the city, and a translation from a moat-surrounded palace with garden and great trees to the still deeper quiet of the very heart of London; for the Deanery is shut in by a high wall, and one feels rather than hears the rumble of the traffic.

Years before, I had been received there by Dean Church, and now by Dean Gregory, who, though apparently unpractical, ecclesiastical, and absent-minded, was a remarkable administrator. He told me that he remembered when there were often only six at a Sunday morning service at Saint Paul's, sometimes he and the choir alone. Now the nave is filled three times every Sunday with thousands of worshippers.

Such reading as I had done of Stubbs's English history had given me the expectation of finding in the author a dignified and rather dry scholar. Our fellow guest in the Deanery, this same Dr. Stubbs, then Bishop of Oxford, was the most informal and most childlike of men, filled with anecdotes more suited to children than to his elders. He had a kindly humor that was irrepressible. He told me that, on his arrival at a station for a visitation, the porter, after failing to find all his luggage, came back and touching his hat, said, 'How many articles are there, milord?' 'Thirty-nine Articles, of course, you dunce,' was the answer. And the porter went off in his vain search.

The Conference was held in the Guard Chamber, which is the great dining-hall of Lambeth Palace. Its size may be inferred from the fact that two hundred Bishops were seated there, while a dais held the Archbishops and Metropolitans. The roof is lofty and timbered. On the walls hang the portraits of the Archbishops from 1533, Wareham by Holbein, Laud by Van Dyke, Herring by Hogarth, Seeker by Sir Joshua Reynolds, and others.

The centre of the Conference was the Archbishop, Dr. Temple. When Head Master of Rugby he had edited and written one article in 'Essays and Reviews,' which to-day seems to be a very harmless volume, but which at that time created a storm of disapproval from evangelicals, Puseyites, and all the conservatives. Upon his appointment as Bishop of Exeter the storm reached its height. Bishop Wilberforce, Lord Shaftsbury, Dr. Pusey, and an army of religious leaders protested, but Mr. Gladstone, the Prime Minister, stood his ground, and Dr. Temple refused to be dragooned.

Translated later to the See of London, he had, upon the death of Archbishop Benson in 1896, succeeded him. He was now seventy-six years of age, three fourths blind, and a personality of such marked force, kindliness, and unconventionality as had made him the centre of many traditions and anecdotes.

Through the five weeks of the Lambeth Conference,

scores of guests stayed with him and Mrs. Temple, and each day at luncheon two hundred Bishops were entertained. At breakfast, Mrs. Temple, who was a gracious English lady, of Victorian manner and a delightful voice, always sat at the head of the table, with the Archbishop on her left, that they might talk together. Sitting opposite him and on her right, I noticed his teacup, which was the size of a porridge bowl, whereon was printed in large gilt letters, 'I am not greedy, but I want a lot.' It was a Christmas present from his two boys, he explained. One of those boys is now Bishop of Manchester and a leader of the Church. Turning from the person next him, he said to me, 'We have been discussing whether it is better to have good manners or no manners. I say "no manners," for the man is then always himself.'

Happening one day to drop into the sitting-room of Parker, the porter, in the arch at the gate of the Palace, I caught sight of a picture which immediately made me feel at home. It was a portrait in oil painted by Miss Benson, the daughter of the late Archbishop, of a splendid great cat: at the foot of the portrait was printed, 'Massachusetts.' 'Where did you get that name?' I asked the porter. 'Why, you see, milord, my boys always called the cat Esau, but one day at school they heard in their class the strangest word, so strange that when they came home they changed the name from Esau to Massachusetts: and Massachusetts he was until he died.' As long as my friend Parker lived, a photograph of the Bishop of Massachusetts was fixed in the corner of the frame. Every visitor to Lambeth from this Diocese received a warm welcome from Parker, and was shown the portrait in the sitting-room. I miss his greeting as at the approach of my hansom he threw open the heavy gates, touched his rusty beaver hat, with a cheery 'Good-morning, milord.'

Of the eleven subjects before the Conference, the discussion of three or four stands out clear in my memory, not so clear, however, as the voice, face, and personality of the Archbishop. An English Bishop presiding over a Church assembly is more than a moderator, as with us: he may take part in the discussion, support motions, and speak in such a way as practically to affect or decide legislation; Archbishop Temple, a great and authoritative school-master, made full use of this liberty. We American Bishops were startled at the vigorous way in which he presided, and it seemed to us at first as if the Conference were to be merely the Archbishop's mouthpiece. We soon felt the signifi-cance of the Rugby boy's remark, 'Temple is a brute; but he is a just brute.' To us nothing of the brute was discov-ered. When, however, his strong face lighted, his broad mouth betokened both decision and a smile, and his Cornish enunciation was emphatic, the Bishops knew that, while his word was authoritative, his mind was open to conviction.

His zeal for foreign missions burned with such heat that he would brook no mild appeal, but, in most emphatic Cornish English, said, 'When a man thinks strong, he speaks strong; on this I think strong.' At the close of a warm discussion he expressed his convictions and added, 'I have given my opinion: the Conference may vote against it, but they know my opinion.' There was no doubt about that, and he did not take it ill if the Conference voted against him.

The Bishop of London, who had become restive at the length of a discussion, suggested that there was too much time wasted in talking; when the Archbishop retorted, with a force and smile at which no man could sulk, 'The best way to stop the talk, Bishop of London, is to hold your tongue.'

'Can I explain why I do not vote on this subject?' asked the Bishop of Springfield. 'I don't think it worth while; you had better sit down,' was the answer.

The discussion of 'The Critical Study of the Bible' gave the English Bishops and a few Colonial Bishops educated in England their opportunity, for in scholarship and hence in intellectual courage they were far ahead of most of their brethren.

The burning question of the Conference was 'The Or-

ganization of the Anglican Communion.' The creation of
the British Empire and the Jubilee of the Queen had so
solidified Britain and her Colonies that there was some
hope in the minds of influential English Bishops that all
branches of the Anglican Communion might enter into
some sort of organic unity. The Bishops from the Church
in the United States were clear that their Church could not
enter into such relations. The problem was as to how their
inability might be expressed in decided but courteous
terms. Bishop Doane of Albany never did a finer piece of
work than his expression of the mind of the Church in the
United States, its reverence for the Mother Church, its
loyalty to the Faith, and its determination to remain
organically independent. At the close of the debate
he turned to the archbishop and said, 'I thank your Grace
for having dealt so generously with my suggestions.' To
which the Archbishop responded in his broad Cornish
accent, 'It wasn't generosity, but simple justice. A Chairman who can't be just isn't worth his salt.'

Indeed, I do not recall a finer instance of self-restraint
and patience than that of this strong, determined, and
masterful old man reading his draft of the Encyclical
paragraph by paragraph for criticisms, important and
trivial, for a whole day, accepting them or justifying his
language. It was as if he were a Rugby boy before two
hundred masters. At evening and into the early morning
he worked over the phrases and brought them in again for
criticism or approval.

The Bishops staying at Lambeth Palace passed their
evenings talking about the Old Man and the discussions,
up in the Water Tower, the only place in the Palace where
smoking was then allowed. Just above was the dungeon
where the Earl of Essex, Lovelace, and others were imprisoned, and where the large iron rings and inscriptions
of imprisoned heretics still remain. At midnight we crept
down the narrow, echoing, circular steps; and each one,
taking his candle from the hall table, sought the chamber
assigned to him as told by a card on his door.

The best results of the Lambeth Conference are often not in the printed reports, but in the intimate contact of men from all parts of the world, who, having similar problems, varied conditions, and differing opinions, are trying to lead their churches to bring Christ closer to the people.

Another noble service, this time in Saint Paul's Cathedral, closed the Conference. The glory of the Te Deum echoing through the nave, choir, and lantern could not drown a note of pathos as we realized the words of the good old Archbishop that we should never meet again in this world.

Of the many scenes and incidents which dwell in my memory, I mention only one.

Farnham Castle, Surrey, built in the thirteenth century, was the residence of the Prince Bishops of Winchester, and has been longer in the hands of the Bishop of Winchester than any official or family dwelling in all England. Set well above the town upon a bold terrace, its massive, half-ruined keep and huge tower, its stately dining-hall and quaint chapel, harbor ghosts of the Prince Bishops. The fireplace of the lofty kitchen I myself measured, nineteen feet across. A labyrinth of rooms and chambers opens from the winding stairs. My room, well at the top, was marked 'Paradise.' Outside the wall is a park with great oaks. Here lived the then Bishop of Winchester, Randall Davidson, with his charming wife, who later became our very dear friends. In his early ministry he was the Secretary of Archbishop Tait, and at Lambeth won the Archbishop's daughter Edith. Later, as Dean of Windsor he had the full confidence of Queen Victoria and was called to her side in personal sorrow or crises. First appointed Bishop of Rochester, then Bishop of Winchester, he was still the Clerk of the Chamber, the personal adviser of the Queen, as, for instance, in the appointment of Bishops; for which valuable services he received a salary of something like seven guineas.

Coming down for the week-end, we entered through the ancient gate, and before us was spread this typically Eng-

lish scene — the sward of the terrace lawn, broken into
the deepest and most brilliant greens by the flashing of the
sun through the branches of an ancient cedar of Lebanon;
the town of Farnham a mile away, with the tower of its
parish church; the face of the castle itself with bright flowers against the gray walls; Mrs. Davidson presiding at
the tea-table with the large urn, the inevitable thin slices
of buttered bread, and the round loaf cake. Mr. and Mrs.
Bryce were there; and he had already captured big Bishop
Kinsolving of Texas, who could give him information of
the South which Mr. Bryce coveted. Bishop Talbot from
Wyoming in the great West; other English guests; Miss
Lucy Tait and Mrs. Benson, the mother of Arthur, E. F.
('Dodo'), and Hugh — an archiepiscopal company. Tradition has it that Mr. Gladstone called her the most agreeable woman in England. Her first request of me on learning that I was from Boston was to tell her all about Christian Science! Talk on the terrace and in the Castle,
prayers in the chapel with Mrs. Davidson at the organ,
walks through the hop fields to the village church, and
again talk; a full moon shining through the cedar of
Lebanon; its shadows on the sundial; and the quiet of an
ancient castle. It was Old England. Alas! the expense
of upkeep, the movements of population, and changes in
diocesan administration may soon compel the abandon-
ment of Farnham as the Bishop's residence. Indeed, the
Bishops of England are moving from palaces to plain
houses, as they have exchanged their coach and four for a
bus or a taxi. The picturesque is departing; but the change
may lead to a closer sympathy with the whole people and
more helpful service. If this transpires, the Bishops are
glad to have it so.

CHAPTER VIII

WAR WITH SPAIN

1897–1898

On Memorial Day, 1897, Boston felt a thrill of patriotism that cast her thoughts back to the Civil War before entering upon the war with Spain. For almost a generation the people had waited for the completion by Saint-Gaudens of the memorial to Colonel Shaw. The story of his command of the Massachusetts Fifty-Fourth, the negro regiment, the march of the regiment through the city to take ship for the South, and of his leading the regiment in the charge upon Fort Wagner was familiar to those of us who were boys in the war as well as to our elders. Boston was moved with deep emotion. I quote from my diary.

Sunday, May 30. Memorial Day, P.M.: Sanders Theatre, Cambridge: to hear Henry Higginson on Col. Robert G. Shaw, very touching and inspiring. Went home and got some bunting to decorate Shaw's picture in Memorial Hall: the colored waiters were glad to do it.

Monday, May 31. Overcast and light rain. To town with the family to see the procession at the unveiling of Shaw's statue. A first-rate procession. Frank Appleton, Chief Marshal. U.S. troops and Navy, Militia, 7th New York regiment and the Cadets. Then the old 54th colored, with tattered flag; Col. Hallowell at head. Very touching. We cheered and they bowed. Governor and Henry Lee, Booker Washington, etc. Before procession started I dropped in at Dr. O. W. Holmes': the Judge, buckling on his sword, reminded one of 'My Hunt after the Captain,' for he was the Captain; old John Holmes too: four negroes singing negro songs in the hall. It brought one back to the war. Went up to Union Club and saw unveiling of statue. Then to Music Hall: sat on platform in midst of Loyal Legion, O. W. Holmes, Jr., Henry Higginson, Lewis Stackpole, Charles Peirson, Arnold Rand, Bob Clark, R. Stevenson, Col. Livermore, John Gray, etc., all of them men who had seen hard service.

Each winter I tried, not always successfully, to break away from routine for two or three days, sometimes a week.

In February, 1898, Mrs. Lawrence and I struck for the South for rest and warmth. We visited New York, Jekyl Island, Georgia, and Saint Augustine, and were at home in just one week — hardly restful. As for warmth, how well I recall the chill of the sleeper as we passed through a South Carolina snowstorm! But in the morning every passenger was hot with surprise and anger as, on opening the newspaper, he saw in great headlines, 'Battleship Maine blown up in Havana Harbor,' with suggestions of foul play on the part of the Spaniards.

On the morning of the 1st of May, in Manila Bay, the quiet command of Admiral Dewey to the captain, 'You may fire when you are ready, Gridley,' and the guns of the Olympia marked the beginning of the end of Spanish misrule in the New World and beyond. With peace came the dispute between the supporters of Admirals Sampson and Schley as to who won the victory at Santiago. Behind the clash were the sentimental prejudices of North and South. Admiral Schley had the warmth, cordiality, and enthusiasm of a typical Southerner — informal and often thoughtless of rule or conventions. I remember one summer afternoon rowing under the stern of his flagship at anchor in Bar Harbor, when from the quarter-deck a cheerful voice called, 'Hello, Bishop, how are you? I have not seen you for a long time: come aboard.' I looked up, and there was Admiral Schley leaning over the rail, and pointing to the gangway for us to mount. Flattered and pleased, I came aboard and found him as genial and confident as if no abuse or trouble had ever touched him.

On the other hand, two or three years before the Spanish War I was with an officer on a cruiser in Bar Harbor, when he said, 'I want you to meet the man who will come to the front, if this country has trouble in the next ten years, Captain Sampson.' I shook hands with a slight man of quiet reserve, who stood courteous and silent while I did the talking. During the controversy he was silent, and self-obliterating. After the war he came to Boston, and was given a dinner. I recall how when the toastmaster, Mr. Olney, called on me to speak, I took for my first word, 'Better is he that ruleth his spirit than he that taketh a city.' I felt the large eyes of the Admiral looking through me with a fixedness which has made me think since then that the trouble which killed him had begun its work. The day after the dinner I had him to luncheon with Governor Wolcott, Messrs. Olney, Charles Francis Adams, John C. Ropes, Henry Higginson, Augustus Lowell, Professor Hollis, Reverend Doctor Parks, my brother Amory, and myself. After it I jotted down: 'The Admiral, a delicately built, refined, and academic-looking man; worn and tired from campaign; modest; talking only when questions were addressed to him; but he talked the last hour, telling much of the Santiago campaign, destruction of Cervera's fleet, etc.'

Upon the question of the disposal of the Philippines, the strife of tongues was almost as sharp as the rattling of guns. That this Nation should consider expansion and the taking of other lands was unthinkable. Even the flag was to some men a token of Imperialism. During the war the Stars and Stripes were unfurled on houses, office buildings, and some churches. Noticing that the Unitarian and Congregational Houses had staffs and flags, I innocently suggested to Mr. A. J. C. Sowdon, the President of the Episcopal Church Association, which owns the Diocesan House, that a flag upon the House might express our loyalty to the country in this time of war. He broke forth with a burst of indignation and said that, if the Stars and Stripes were flung out from the Diocesan House, he and all his directors would resign. Thinking it hardly wise to make the display of the flag of our country the subject of public debate, I dropped the matter. Mr. Sowdon was a most loyal and enthusiastic patriot, but he, as did some others, associated the flag with a policy which they believed to be un-American.

Boston was more identified with Anti-Imperialism than any other part of the country. In February, 1899, soon after the purchase for $20,000,000 and ceding of the Philippines by Spain to this country was announced, President McKinley and several of his Cabinet visited Boston and were given a luncheon at the Algonquin Club. During the luncheon, Mr. Charles F. Choate, who presided, kindly asked me to take his place beside the President. He talked very freely upon the subject of the Philippines and his dilemma. I remarked that he must feel a little strange in a city which was supposed to repudiate his policy. 'But,' I added, 'Boston like other financial centres is conservative, and we have perhaps a few men who are able to talk with more force than have some other cities.' He answered: 'Not at all. I feel very much at home here; and if I did not have the responsibility of decision, I should probably be thinking and talking as these men do. But unfortunately I had to do more than talk: I had to act. I did not want the Philippines; you did not want them; the country did not want them; but when our Commission which went to Paris gained information besides that which we had here, we had to decide. We could not in decency hand the islands back to Spain's misrule; we could not leave the people to cut each other's throats. We knew the intentions of Germany; and Japan was near. The Administration found itself by the Treaty of Paris in honor bound to hold them. The responsibility now is ours; our first duty is to make the people ready for self-government; and as to their future, the Nation will decide when the right time comes.'

The generation which had been born since the Civil War had never seen a war hero. Hence, when Admiral Dewey came home, he had a triumphal reception throughout the country which exceeded anything that has followed the World War. As he went from city to city, the whole people arose, and met him with overwhelming and almost ludicrous adulation. Fortunately, he received his welcome modestly and with few words.

His coming to Boston was made the occasion for the

delivery to the State of the flags of the Spanish War. I
quote from my 'Life of Governor Roger Wolcott.'

It was a brilliant day. The population from all parts of the
State had poured into Boston, for it was the day on which the
Commonwealth and the city gave their welcome to Admiral
Dewey, the hero of Manila. The morning was given up to the
procession. The whole state militia was in line. Later the officers
and sailors of the flagship Olympia led the column through the
gates of the Common to the parade ground. The Governor took
his position on the slope of the hill just below the soldiers' and
sailors' monument. Two hundred trumpeters gave the call to
colors, and seventeen sergeants with their colors stood before the
Governor. The commanding officers took their positions in
front; and one by one the officers turned the colors over to the
Governor, who, in accepting them, said: 'On behalf of the
Commonwealth of Massachusetts and in her name, I receive
into perpetual custody these flags borne by Massachusetts men
in a righteous and triumphant cause, and emblematic of the
power of the Nation and of the fortitude and valor of her sons.'

Alas! The handsome and chivalric Governor who led
the Commonwealth through the Spanish War, and who
laid down his office amidst the applause and affection of
the people, was cut off in his prime, and, like his brother
Huntington in the Civil War, died, December 21, 1900, a
victim of typhoid fever. Both of them had been boyhood
friends of Amory and myself. Later, I counted it a privilege to write his 'Life,'[1] that his spirit might enter the
next generation.

[1] *Roger Wolcott* by William Lawrence, p. 202. Houghton Mifflin Company,
Boston, 1902.

CHAPTER IX
WASHINGTON AND JAMESTOWN
1898

In October, 1898, the General Convention met in Washington. One morning, as I was sitting at my desk in the House of Bishops, Bishop Randolph came across and whispered, 'Will you speak on Virginia and Massachusetts next Saturday at Jamestown?' My first emotion was one of fright, for I knew but little of Virginia, and the Jamestown excursion meant much to the Virginians. Then the subject gripped me, and I said, 'Yes.'

On Saturday morning the members of the Convention who had come to Richmond the evening before, accompanied by Virginia citizens, filled two river steamboats for a trip down the James River. It was a perfect autumn day. The genial owner and editor of the Richmond 'Times,' Joseph Bryan, pointed out to the company on our boat the historic spots, and interpreted Virginia's history. As we passed the stately Colonial mansions with their negro quarters, Shirley, Westover, and Brandon, and slipped down towards the Virginia Tidewater country, the charm of Virginia's early history took possession of us New-Englanders. Plymouth Rock, set in the middle of the town, with the landing of the Pilgrims in 1620, fell into the background as we came near the quiet, solitary Isle of Jamestown, whereon the Royalists had landed in 1607, where they nailed a board between two trees for a reading-desk, and where under a stretched canvas their chaplain, Robert Hunt, the first clergyman of English America, read the service.

Here were gathered hundreds of churchmen from Maine to California to pay homage to the loyalty and faith of the founders and leaders of the Commonwealth of Virginia. In the company were members of the families of Washington, Randolph, and Pocahontas; their rightful pride of lineage and achievement pervaded the atmosphere. There was a touch of chivalry and romance in their Royalist blood to which we sons of the Plymouth Pilgrims could not lay claim. Alas, however! In coming down the river we had passed battle-fields of the Civil War: below were Hampton Roads and Fortress Monroe. The very soil beneath had felt the tramp of Northern troops, and, in the victory of the North, Virginia had been humbled to the dust. Until that morning I had no idea that the tragedy of the defeat of a generation past still lingered, a living, burning memory, in the hearts of Virginians. But as good old Bishop Randolph spoke, and then Dr. McKim, who was an officer in the Confederate Army followed, I seemed to feel that the Virginians were waiting, hungering, for a word of comradeship from the North.

When called upon, I sketched in a few words the story of the two sister companies at Jamestown and Plymouth; of the like spirit and love of constitutional liberty in the two Colonies; of the fact that John Adams nominated Washington to be Commander-in-Chief, and that in Cambridge, Massachusetts, Washington first unsheathed his sword. I reminded them that in the great tragedy of the Civil War we each fought as sons of Englishmen in America would fight for what we believed the right; that Massachusetts had mingled her blood with the soil of Virginia, and had left her sons beneath Virginian sod; to the tender care of Virginia we commended them. The only two Commonwealths of the Nation, Virginia and Massachusetts, pledged to each other their loyalty to the faith of their fathers.

I spoke only twelve or fifteen minutes. I do not know that I ever made an eloquent speech, but if so, this was it. And the response from the Virginians then and for years after was to me grateful evidence that my words had helped.

As three or four of us were driving across country from Jamestown to Williamsburg, one, a Massachusetts man, said, 'Bishop, you spoke more truly than· you knew. I have a brother lying somewhere near this very spot. He was killed here and we never found his body.'

The next day, Sunday, a number of us passed at the Hampton Institute, near Old Point Comfort. Hampton has always been to me a notable illustration of the way in which the missionary output of a country may come back to enrich it. General Armstrong as a boy watched his father, a missionary from this country, teaching the Sandwich Island savages the rudiments of industrial skill as an integral part of his Christian work in their development. Coming back to the United States, young Armstrong entered the Northern Army, rose to be a general, and at the close of the war was given by the Government the great responsibility of training the leaders of the five million black freemen. Recalling his father's method in Hawaii, he gave an object lesson to the world as to the true method of building up the character and civilization of a backward race. And I know of no more touching illustration of the spirit which moved this great man than that of his simple gravestone standing in line with those of his students, once slaves or the children of slaves, according to his own request that he should 'be buried with his boys.'

An occasional visit to Washington is, I believe, a part of the liberal education of every citizen. I have by such visits watched its growth from a morass and unkempt settlement of shiftless whites and negroes, broken by an occasional public building or fine or modest residences, to its present great beauty, enhanced by one's imagination of the more beautiful city to come. For many years I used to go to the Patent Office, and later to the Congressional Library, to study the two models of the city, one as it was in about 1890, the other laid out under Act of Congress by the great Architectural Commission. The young people of to-day visiting Washington have no conception of its growth in dignity and beauty.

The movement through the city of interesting persons,

the ever-changing guests at the dinners and receptions, and at Mr. Putnam's Round Table in the Congressional Library, to which I was first introduced by my friend the Reverend Doctor Roland Cotton Smith, were a constant source of pleasure and enlightenment. Through the hospitality of Justice and Mrs. Gray I met many distinguished men of that day. Justice Horace Gray was a family friend. As Chief Justice of the Supreme Court of Massachusetts, and Associate Justice for many years of the Federal Supreme Court, he left his impress on the decisions of both courts. Genial and massive in figure, a comrade of Phillips Brooks, Richardson the architect, and Bishop McVickar, each of whom stood six feet, two to five inches, and weighed three hundred pounds, the Judge was well known for his legal lore, his reverence for tradition, and his punctiliousness in little matters bearing upon the dignity of the Court. Advocates who appeared before him were wise to be careful in their dress, and observant of all forms of judicial courtesy.

I recall, however, one lapse on his own part. Happening to be in the Supreme Court one morning, I listened to an argument by a bombastic attorney, who was followed by one who in clearness of thought, grace of expression, and modulation of voice charmed all. As I listened and watched his face, I recognized James C. Carter, of New York, a great lawyer and a loyal Harvard man. Deeply interested, I was interrupted by a messenger who gave me Mr. Justice Gray's card and directed me to go behind the mysterious curtain at the back of the Justices. On starting and looking at the Justices, I saw them sitting with half-closed eyes in all solemnity; but upon coming behind the curtain, I was met by the massive figure of Mr. Justice Gray and his cheery voice, 'So Bishop Paddock is dead, and they tell me that Brooks may be made Bishop! Will he take it? What are the chances? It is too good to be true.' I learned that Justices may be able to carry on two lines of thought at the same time.

Early one morning I received a telephone message from

Dr. Henry Bowditch urging me to appear with some surgeons before a Joint Committee of Congress upon Vivisection, for an effort was being made to pass an anti-vivisection law for the District of Columbia, which would have great influence in the legislation of the different States. At the request of physicians and others, I had spoken at various hearings on the subject at the State House in Boston; I have always felt that the agitation of the subject has done good in leading investigators and vivisectors to be more careful and humane in their work than was the case many years ago. When, however, we realize what animal vivisection has accomplished in eliminating suffering and the saving of human life, as well as in the avoidance of human vivisection, and know how humane and practically universally painless experiments are to-day, I find it difficult to listen patiently to the propagandists of anti-vivisection.

At the Congressional hearing were Drs. Bowditch, Osler, Keen, Hare, and others. Being brought in to represent a lay point of view, and as one of the clergy, I spoke very briefly. On my return home to Boston, I was summoned away from my luncheon by a telephone call from Mrs. Ward (Elizabeth Stuart Phelps), who was a leading anti-vivisectionist, who asked me what I had said at the Washington hearing, as she was writing a letter to a New York newspaper. I answered that it was the doctors who gave the important testimony, and that I had said nothing worth reporting; at which she took up the argument against vivisection. After several efforts on my part to check her, she finally said, 'I feel with a well-known English surgeon that if my happiness or life depended upon the wounding or death of any living thing, I would rather die.' At which I said, 'My dear Mrs. Ward, some chicken has been cooling on my plate for ten minutes: I must go back to my lunch and eat it.' There was no response from the other end of the wire.

As I sat beside Dr. Pritchett, who was then President of the Institute of Technology, at a dinner at which both of us were to speak, he said, 'Some of us laymen are doing as much preaching as you do, Bishop, but we stand behind the dinner-table for our pulpit.' My answer was that bishops and other clergymen were using the same pulpit, and that I counted after-dinner speaking as one of the large opportunities for preaching the gospel of righteousness and of public spirit, and at times of the deepest elements of the Christian Faith. One often finds an audience and a response which he may not find in church.

At one of the great annual dinners of the Chamber of Commerce in New York, that of 1900, I spoke upon 'The Relation of the Material Prosperity of a People to their Morality,' illustrating the theme by the influence of the commercial forces in the City of New York upon the character of the people. A few days later I was much gratified to receive a letter from Walter Hines Page, saying that he would like the speech in the form of an article for the first number of a new magazine which he was starting, 'The World's Work.' The article appeared under the title of 'The Relation of Wealth to Morals,' but my gratification received some mitigation from the fact that he never asked for another article.

CHAPTER X

A FAMILY DIGRESSION

1899

A FEW days ago I received a letter from which I quote, 'Mr. John D. Rockefeller said at Pocantico Hills in November, 1917, "How clearly I remember reading when I was a boy the Life of Amos Lawrence, the philanthropist. My employer gave me the book. I was sixteen years old. Mr. Lawrence was a great philanthropist who did big things in his time. He gave away more than one hundred thousand dollars to help mankind. I remember how fascinated I was with his letters. I can see as if the type were before my eyes now, how he gave away the crisp bills. Crisp bills! I could see and hear them. I made up my mind that, if I could manage it, some day I would give away crisp bills, too. The Life of Amos Lawrence was a great inspiration to me." '

Taking up 'The Diary and Correspondence of Amos Lawrence,' which was published by my Uncle William in 1855, and which had a very large circulation, I find on page 178 this letter to one of his partners. '... I am housed, and denied the sight of most of those who call, but not the privilege of reading the papers, and spending money. In short, I have more use for money when in the house than when able to be abroad. If you will tell Brother Sharp [teller of the Massachusetts Bank] his beautiful bills find an exceedingly ready use, I shall be glad of one hundred in ones and twos, two hundred in fives, and three hundred in tens and twenties; say six hundred dollars, just to keep me along till the end of the month. ¡The calls are frequent and striking.'

Amos Lawrence, my grandfather, was the farmer's boy who came down from Groton to Boston, started in business, and then sent for his young brother Abbott, who joined him in the firm of A. and A. Lawrence, later perhaps the leading firm of merchants in Boston. Abbott became an able and widely known business man and statesman, also Minister at the Court of Saint James's. He was the grandfather of Abbott Lawrence Lowell, President of Harvard University. Amos, after making a goodly fortune, retired an invalid, and devoted himself to what used to be called philanthropy and to giving the Boston boys rides on his big sleigh.

My father, Amos A. Lawrence, of whom I wrote in an earlier chapter, became more and more beloved by every one as years passed. Starting in the early morning on his horse, he rode through Brookline, up to his farm at Chestnut Hill, or over to the College in Cambridge, stopping here and there to knock with his riding-whip on a window where friends were still at breakfast. During the Civil War, when gold was at a high premium, he always managed to have a few gold dollars — no longer minted, alas! — to give to the children as he passed through the Punch Bowl district where the Irish lived. He carried around subscription papers for good and patriotic causes, and paid high for the privilege. At the same time his business increased to large proportions. He was cautious and wise. He also had courage, and at a moment's decision would clear off a mass of goods at a heavy loss; for he is a successful business man who knows when to take his losses as well as how to make his profits.

In addition to her brood of seven children, my mother took in her little nephew, Frank Dexter, whose mother died when he was born. Our house was large, also our appetites; we had a number of servants; and we entertained. It was no sinecure to provide and keep house for such a company with Boston and Brookline at arm's length. Hence the carriage and gray pair travelled across the Mill Dam every day. Sometimes mother walked one way, and we must remember that from our house across the marshes to the fork and over the Mill Dam to Charles Street there were no other buildings than the Mill and the

AMOS LAWRENCE
Painted by Chester Harding

tollhouse. The plank sidewalks, however, gave an elastic tread. She was, of course, indispensable to each one of us in every problem, trouble, or illness. She never gave way to her emotions, but was ever strong and dependable, showing her sympathy in loving care and firm action.

The children grew up, married, and had children. Here is the record written by father and by his request cut into a tablet in Lawrence Hall after his death.

'In remembrance of God's great goodness.'

This sentence refers to the blessings of my past life: but particularly of the past thirty years, since my marriage. At this time my good wife and my seven children (with three grandchildren) are all living and in good health. And not one of them has ever caused me an hour's pain by any misconduct.

As I have refused to name the hall during my life, so I shall be pleased to know that it will be for a memorial after I am dead: and that it shall be called 'Lawrence Hall,' as now proposed.

AMOS A. LAWRENCE

Mar. 31st, 1872, the anniversary of our marriage. 1

This record stood until 1882, when the first break came in the death of my oldest sister, Mary Anne, the wife of Dr. Robert Amory. On August 25, 1886, father died suddenly at Nahant, and mother, who lived at Cottage Farm with my sister Hetty and her family, died May 27, 1892. In 1895, Emily Silsbee, the wife of Amory, died.

On our silver wedding day, May 19, 1899, there were six of the seven children living, the youngest being forty-one years of age. Sarah, the wife of Peter Chardon Brooks, a gentleman farmer; Amory, who succeeded father as the head of Lawrence and Company; myself; Susan, the wife of Justice William Caleb Loring, of the Supreme Court; Hetty, who married Frederic Cunningham, Julia's brother, a lawyer; and Harriet, the wife of Augustus Hemenway, also a gentleman farmer, who at his graduation from Harvard gave the Hemenway Gymnasium. The grandchildren

1 *Life of Amos A. Lawrence*, by William Lawrence. Houghton Mifflin Company, 1888.

at this time made a company, broken only by the death of our little Rosamond, of twenty-four. Each and all, elders and the younger, were in sound health. We were and still are a grateful, happy, and united family.

Julia and I had resolved to say nothing about the silver wedding, and the morning passed quietly. Our lawn and terrace on Brattle Street were of a brilliant green. On the north side was Mr. Longfellow's Craigie House, with the great lilac bushes coming to bloom. In the rear and to the south were Winthrop Hall and Lawrence Hall, filled with law and theological students. At one o'clock a wagon drove up to the door and began to unload baskets of provender, while the sisters and brothers, reënforced by a very few cousins and intimate friends, came trooping across the rear lawn, loaded with affectionate greetings, a beautiful oil painting, and a modest supply of champagne.

It was a happy surprise party. The third day after, May 22d, we gave them a surprise party, for early that morning was born the last of the grandchildren, Frederic Cunningham; and by noon a delegation had arrived to inspect and report if it could really be true. Thus our house was filled with the standard number of seven children, and, as with our parents, five girls and two boys.

A word about our moves. We were a family of six and later seven children, servants, John Herlihy the coachman, carriages, and three or four horses. John, when he came to us in Lawrence, was the most Hibernian Irishman that I ever knew, big, awkward, ignorant. He did his work as coachman, stableman, and choreman; went to evening school; and married the pretty parlor maid of Dean Gray, Mary Ann. They had an indefinite number of children. After years of devoted service, John entered into the larger sphere of choreman and gardener for the neighborhood; bought a house, horse and wagon, and is still living to see his children grow up to be self-respecting, useful citizens. Our debt is great to his loyal service and his herculean strength.

We made four moves each year — in June, from Cambridge to Bar Harbor, returning to Cambridge in September; to Boston in November, returning to Cambridge in April. This generation of motors does not know what it was to pack and handle eighteen trunks by wagon, to send horses and carriages by boat, and to care for children and servants.

In February, 1901, Julia and I, undismayed by the strenuous activity of our former trip to Europe, steamed through the floating ice in New York Harbor on the Fürst Bismarck, to give our four daughters a glimpse of Italy. We left the three little ones to the care of Mrs. Cunningham, the youngest taking, as usual, such an occasion to be quite ill.

Can one ever forget the first sight of Gibraltar, with the sun flooding its cliff? It was the twenty-second of February; and after an arduous day upon and around the Rock, the evening was given to a ship's concert and speeches, at which I presided. Mr. Peter Dunne (Mr. Dooley), who was a fellow passenger, sat patiently in the audience, but, as I reached a pitch of eloquence prompted by the English associations of the day, Mr. Dunne went out. Finding him on deck, I asked if he felt faint. 'No!' was his answer, 'but when you proclaimed that Washington was an Englishman before he was an American, it was more than an Irishman could stand.'

We passed seventeen days in Rome, every hour of which was booked for a gallery, a palace, a garden, Saint Peter's, the Catacombs, Coliseum, Campagna, the Appian Way, or something. The sudden contrasts of modern and ancient Rome startled us as they have thousands of tourists. As we drove along Appian Way with memories of classic days and the entrance of Saint Paul, we were met by a group of scarlet-coated huntsmen, George Meyer among them, returning from a hunt on the Campagna. Rome has been visited for many centuries, but I doubt if among the millions of tourists there has been a more conscientious, weary, or bewildered group than was the Lawrence family as we took train for Florence. To be sure, I preached and confirmed at our own church, Saint Paul's. We dined with our cousins, George and Alice Meyer, who were then moving into the magnificent Palazzo Brancaccio, which was theirs during his very successful term as American Ambassador. We had seen Rome, and I have never had time to see it since.

From Florence, through Paris, confirming and preaching in both American churches, we swept on through London, and in a few weeks were in Boston, where I jumped into the usual routine of work, services, and confirmations, as if Rome had never been. Intelligent Americans really ought to bask in the ancient glories of Europe, but what is one going to do if he has the New England conscience that there is more to be done for people here than he can do in a long lifetime? I have weakly yielded to conscience, and have never left my work except for an absence just long enough to catch my breath.

CHAPTER XI
THE DIOCESE DIVIDED
1899–1902

ONE might infer from recent chapters that during the first years of my Episcopate my life was given to diversions in Europe, the General Conventions, or family affairs. The fact is, the bulk of my time, strength, and thought was given to the Diocese. From parish to parish, rectory to rectory, service to service, committee to committee, caller to caller, and problem to problem, I went morning, noon, and night, seven days in the week. Although the routine was heavy, it was happy and exhilarating work. When the question of relief of the Bishop came up in the Diocesan Convention of 1900, I said, 'During these seven years I have been blessed with health and strength. In the summer the work ceases, though the mail still comes and goes. During the seven years I have not lost half a dozen days' work through illness, nor, as far as I can remember, one public engagement. I have been obliged by indisposition to postpone at the last minute five visitations; but neglected visitations, like a schoolboy's lessons, have to be made up.'

Conscious that the Diocese upon the death of Bishop Brooks was expecting some sort of action for the relief of the Bishop, I was studying the problem, and without a word to others was preparing for it. Bishop Paddock had increased the spread of the Diocese in starting many parishes and missions; Bishop Brooks in the fifteen months of his great Episcopate had by his personality fused the churches in Massachusetts into a stronger spiritual organism; my work was so to build up a public sentiment and an organization as would enable the different parts of the Diocese, whatever might come, to stand upon their own feet with self-government and self-respect — not an easy task, for all parts of the Church in Massachusetts had been in the habit of looking to Boston for financial and spiritual support. The women of the Diocese by their missionary and other organizations had done much to develop and sustain a spirit of diocesan loyalty. My personal obligation to them throughout my Episcopate is very great. By the division of the Diocese into five archdeaconries, and the appointment of leading rectors in each as archdeacon, there were created five bodies with certain powers of legislation and administration. The Archdeaconries of Worcester County and of Berkshire, including the Connecticut Valley, were of special value in creating in them a spirit of self-reliance and independence.

Realizing how little the different parts and interests of the Diocese knew about each other, I enlisted the Reverend Edward T. Sullivan in the creation and publication of 'The Church Militant,' which, under his editorship, and with the aid of others, was an excellent and interesting diocesan paper — the only diocesan paper at the time which limited its circulation to paying subscribers, on the ground that the free circulation of religious reading is usually unread and unappreciated.

Meanwhile the Diocesan Convention considered the subject almost every year, appointing committees, who conferred with me and who reported plan after plan with the statement that action was 'not expedient at the present time.'

To the recommendation of the election of a Coadjutor I answered that it was not fair to the Diocese of the next generation to elect the Bishop's probable successor now. Suffragan Bishops were not then allowed by the Church. Instead of the phrase, 'the relief of the Bishop,' I gradually introduced the phrase, 'the welfare of the Church in Massachusetts.' Both of course went together, but the latter was the prime consideration. It was clear that division must come; but no Massachusetts man wants to be cut off from a part of Massachusetts, least of all the Boston part. The strength of the Church was so great comparatively in the east that every sort of a gerrymandering plan was suggested to make two equal dioceses.

After a careful study of the situation from all points of view by competent committees, I was sure that there was going to be a deadlock until I should throw in the weight of my word; and this I was very slow to do until it was clear that whatever division was made would be cordially accepted by all. In time the Convention came to what was really the only possible conclusion: a division, when division should come, along the eastern line of Worcester County. There would clearly be diocesan integrity in the Eastern Diocese; and although the churches in the western counties had not much in common with each other, they could be welded together into a working unit in time. By this division the State would be divided roughly into halves geographically; but in point of population and the strength of our Church the ratio was as one to three or four. Even with this handicap, the Western Diocese would be stronger than a majority of dioceses in the Church. Something had to be done; for the Diocese in eight years had increased in strength by just about the amount of the proposed Western Diocese, and its administration under one Bishop was bound to be less and less effective.

Two obstacles stood stubbornly in the way. The churches in central and western Massachusetts did not want to be set off; and they refused to accede until every other resource was tried. Moreover, the financial strength of the Church was in the east; and if they were to be set off as the stronger dioceses have usually set off the weaker, with a mere pittance, they could not live; the Western Diocese would be perpetually anæmic; therefore in behalf of the welfare and dignity of the churches, they objected.

The Convention in May, 1901, upon the report of a committee of twenty-four, voted in favor of the division under certain general conditions. As the approval of the General Convention, which was to meet in October, was necessary, the terms of the division of the Diocese had to be completed soon; hence the Convention adjourned to meet in

June. I dreaded the session, for it was impossible to guess what explosive results might follow. A committee reported in favor of division along the Worcester County line (except Southborough, which contained Saint Mark's School), recommending also that from one quarter to one third of the charitable and missionary funds be transferred to the Western Diocese, and that an outright gift of one hundred thousand dollars in cash for the support of the Bishop be presented to the new Diocese. By the enterprise and generosity of Mr. Francis W. Hunnewell and two other laymen forty-six thousand dollars was already pledged. I then read to the Convention a short address, written in anticipation of this report, approving the plan, and asking for its immediate adoption.

The reaction was fine: those who had strenuously objected and had led in protecting what they felt the safety of the churches in western Massachusetts heartily supported the division, and unanimous action followed. Mr. Hunnewell was over sixty years of age, a man of wealth and leisure, director of large corporations, highly esteemed downtown, senior warden of the Church of the Advent. He undertook what was for anybody, and for him especially, a most irksome task, the raising of the one hundred thousand dollars to be presented to the Western Diocese, which included cities like Worcester, Springfield, and Pittsfield, as well as the village of Lenox. During that summer he sat on the piazza of the hotel at Bethlehem, New Hampshire, writing personal letters in his own hand to those whose names I sent him. 'The paint of the piazza under Uncle Frank's feet is worn through to the board,' wrote his niece. Mrs. Auchmuty of Lenox generously sent me a check for five thousand dollars, which I returned to her with warm thanks, saying that eastern Massachusetts proposed to make a gift of one hundred thousand dollars to western Massachusetts, and that she could use her five thousand dollars for something else.

In September a popular contribution from all the parishes completed the amount. Favorable action by the

General Convention in San Francisco would consummate the division. I have been proud of the Diocese again and again, as I shall show later, but this great gift carried through by the devotion of Mr. Hunnewell was something that had never been attempted in the division of dioceses, nor has it been approached since.

At the Primary Convention of the new Diocese of western Massachusetts in Springfield on November 19th, over which I presided, Dr. David H. Greer was unanimously elected Bishop. Upon his declination, Dr. Alexander H. Vinton was elected at a later Convention, and consecrated Bishop in All Saints', Worcester.

Thus my official connections with western Massachusetts were severed. I resigned as Trustee of Smith College, over which that sagacious and kindly man, Dr. Seelye, served as President for thirty-seven years from its foundation.

I now had a very compact Diocese; two hours took me to almost every point in it. The population was urban, suburban, or industrial; there was not one rural parish. Hence a marshalling of forces, a concentration of spiritual interests, and an intimacy of life were possible. The Diocese was capable of becoming a family; and my purpose — imperfectly, very imperfectly carried out — has been to make the clergy and laity each and all realize these close and sympathetic bonds. One little token caught from a custom of Harvard suggests my idea. Upon the death of a clergyman of the Diocese, a black-edged note with the time of the funeral is sent by me to every clergyman in the Diocese; it is as if one of the family had gone.

Time has shown that the division of the Diocese was for the welfare of the Church. Within seven years this Diocese had regained its full strength and numbers. In certain ways it has brought relief to the Bishop, although the speed and intensity of the work have increased. While concentrating the standing organizations, I was able to enter upon new enterprises. Alas! Much that I had hoped to do has been left undone for lack of time or of skill in throwing responsibility upon others. But every one knows that voluntary service is not always reliable, and putting one's shoulder to the wheel is sometimes easier than waiting for some one else to start the team.

November 30, 1902, marked an epoch in my life and work, for on that day I first rode in an automobile. After a service in Swampscott I was due in Salem, some six miles away. An adventurous business man said that he could make the trip faster than a horse; so I entered the noisy, one-cylinder Cadillac, and held on tight while we speeded at the rate of fifteen miles an hour, making the corners at what seemed a furious pace, but arriving safely at the house of my friend, James P. Franks, for forty-six years rector of Grace Church, Salem. Among the millions of people to whom the automobile has brought better service, bishops may be included. To be sure, life has speeded up; one does more, and perhaps accomplishes less. I know well that in the multiplied engagements I am cut off far more than I like from the intimacy of the rectories, a distinct loss. As I start off some lovely Sunday morning for four visitations and a hundred-mile run, my New England conscience often protests, 'Have I a right to enjoy myself so much in doing my work? Is not my duty in the stuffy railroads and trolleys where it used to be?' — for discomfort often satisfies the sense of duty. Experience, however, leads me to believe that bishops, clergymen, and especially missionaries, should make not less but more use of motors. Laymen are poor economists who allow their ministers to waste time and shoe leather in covering distances. Recurring to my first ride, I recall all the rough and dusty roads of twenty-five years ago. I wonder if the younger generation realize what clouds of dust used to settle on one in a summer's drive, and what loads of earth, laden with all sorts of bacteria, were carried for miles by the March winds. While motors have come to kill, they have also come to make alive.

On the 19th of December, 1901, Charles H. Brent was

consecrated Bishop in Emmanuel Church, Boston; Bishop Doane presided, I serving as a presenter and co-conse-crator. When he first came to Boston, I recall him as a rather unimpressive Canadian youth, dressed, if I remem-ber aright, in the habit of a postulant of the Cowley Fathers. When Father Hall was recalled to Cowley, England, Brent was appointed by Bishop Brooks to min-ister in Saint Stephen's Church at the South End, where he showed himself to be such a leader that he was ap-pointed Missionary Bishop of the Philippine Islands.

The visit of Prince Henry of Prussia in March, 1902, suggests memories of the evident desire of the Kaiser to gain the good will of the country, and of our readiness to reciprocate. The inauguration of the Germanic Museum, followed later by the gifts of casts illustrating German art and history, was an incident in this programme. My short record runs:

At 12.30, meeting of Overseers at Memorial Hall to vote LL.D. to Prince Henry. 1.30: Sanders Theatre: visit of Prince Henry: music: President Eliot read address and gave degree. Theatre crowded: students standing in pit, and galleries crowded: dignified and enthusiastic. Lunch at University. Presented to Prince and short talk. He alert, interested, vigorous, fine face and figure. Later to Harvard Union. Great enthusiasm. Speech by Henry Higginson: excellent speech and poem by two students: short speech from the Prince: songs and cheers: cable from the Emperor.

How little we can see into the future! The sagacity and reserve of President Eliot were evident, for to the amuse-ment of some and satisfaction of others, in presenting the degree he laid emphasis, not only upon the Teutonic sources transmitted through England of many of our democratic institutions, upon the contribution of Protes-tant faith, of literature and of citizens, but he made this expression the climax of his address: 'Forty years ago the American Union was in deadly peril, and thousands of its young men were bleeding and dying for it. It is credibly reported that at a very critical moment the Queen of England said to her Prime Minister: "My lord, you must understand that I shall sign no paper which means war with the United States." The grandson of that illustrious woman is sitting with us here.'

A very different and more interesting occasion was a dinner given by about fifty citizens of Boston to General Wood and his staff on their return from rehabilitating Cuba; for while Henry Higginson, who presided, said that there were to be no speeches, General Wood at his request called upon one after another of the members of his staff to tell the part that they had taken in the work. The entrance of our army into Cuba, its possession, and its retirement is one of the fairest pages in the history of this country; and those of us who were at the dinner realized what honor these men did to the Nation and their service by the manner, ability, and skill of their administration. Colonels Scott and Bliss and others of the Staff described in the most modest and straightforward way how each one without preparation had by order taken charge of the customs, the education, the health, the policing, and other departments of administration, while Major Walter Reed told the wonderful story of the heroism of his volunteers, who by his experimentation and their deaths demonstrated the fact that a mosquito was the carrier of yellow fever.

The next morning I hurried down to Henry Higginson's office to make sure that the talks had been fully taken down or would be written out; for they made a story of which the Nation and the Army might be proud, a story wherein educated men trained to military service transformed through the arts of peace a mediæval colony into a self-governing nation. Alas! the story as told that evening was never recorded.

In November, 1902, a disagreement had arisen between the National Newspaper Association and the International Typographical Union on a new scale of wages between the publishers of Boston and the Mailers' Union No. 1. The number of men immediately concerned was not large, but the issue was a national one, as this was the first instance in which the agreement which admitted conciliation, local arbitration, and national arbitration had been tested out, and the result would be a precedent for all others.

I was asked to be an arbitrator, together with a representative of each party; which, of course, meant that the two official representatives, one from Chicago, the other from New York, would each press his case in the strongest way, and that my decision would be final. Although it was a strange business for me, I took the risk of blundering, for it was an interesting problem. For a week, therefore, I haunted the newspaper offices at every hour of the day and night, studying their mailing system and the conditions of work. I learned also how the department stores handled their mail, compared the relative cost of living in different cities, listened to testimony, and finally considered the arguments of the two representatives. My decision met with approval on both sides. As a matter of fact, I judge that if in such a case both parties have confidence in the good sense, fairness, and intelligence of the arbiter, they are content, even if things do not go altogether as they wish.

Massachusetts has now and again the good fortune to have for its Chief Executive a typical Yankee, and such a man was Mr. Crane. One hot July day, as I was going up Park Street in one of those queer hacks called 'herdics,' I caught sight of a very spare man, his straw hat cocked over one eye, his thumb in his vest armscye, wandering slowly up the hill to the State House. It was the Governor on his way to the Executive Chamber.

The Yankee cropped out in his nasal voice, dry humor, and kindly smile. Quaint and unimpressive in manner, he had innate dignity. His first remark to me, made immediately after his first visitation of the State's almhouses, revealed his kind heart and loyalty to family life. 'Bishop, I am shocked at the number of old people in our public in-

stitutions whose children ought to and could support them:
I cannot understand how a son can allow the State to support his mother; there is something lacking in our bringing
up of young people.'

He was very bashful and dreaded making a speech. At
his last Commencement visitation at Harvard, I happened
to sit beside him. He was as nervous as a witch, talked
about his dislike of speaking, lighted cigarette after cigarette, and when called upon, got off what he had to say
in a *gauche* but attractive way. As he sat down with immense relief, I said, 'Governor, that was excellent, and the
longest speech I ever heard you make. I timed you: it was
just two and a half minutes.'

Governor Crane was a man of quiet determination. He
knew what he wanted: he was generous and sympathetic
almost to a fault; and when in a quiet mood, his voice lost
its nasality and was very sweet and winning. In recognition of his work, Harvard gave him an LL.D. after his
retirement as Governor.

In October, 1902, the whole North was in a critical situation due to the great coal strike since May. Bins were
empty, cold weather was approaching, and there was no
sign of conciliation from either side. President Roosevelt
took hold, and by the combined use of suasion and the
'club' finally appointed a commission whose report opened
the mines and started the coal trains. Hearing that Governor Crane had been in Washington, I asked him a few
weeks later what part he had in the President's action.
'Well,' he said, 'since you ask me, I will tell you. There
were of course lots of people and things that led up to it.
But you ask about myself. Well! I had not been able to
sleep for worry; for I had made up my mind that when
people are dying of the cold, they are not particular as to
what is their property and what is the other man's. And I
could see the time was pretty near when the barns, houses,
mills, or anything might go for anybody's firewood. So
one evening, when I could not stand it any longer, instead
of going to bed, I packed my bag and took the train for

Washington. I left my bag at the station and went straight to the White House and the President. I told him how we stood in New England, and what was going to happen if we did not have coal. He said, "You are right, Governor, you stay right in this town and near me, and give me your advice." So I stayed, and I suppose that that among other things may have helped.'

The mention of Roosevelt's name reminds me of an incident. It was at the time of the political excitement in 1907, due to the way in which the President was handling the situation in connection with the shooting-up of Brownsville, Texas, by some negro regulars. A number of the Republican Senators, led by Senator Foraker, were taking the opportunity to hit back at the President. One morning, having opened the Senate with prayer by invitation of Dr. Edward Everett Hale, its Chaplain, I was sitting with him on a sofa watching Senator Crane moving about from desk to desk as if he had some special mission in hand, when he came and sat beside us, and immediately broke out, 'I am worried; I hoped that we would come to a vote to-day on that Brownsville matter, but we can't. If the President keeps pressing his action, we are likely to have a split in the party and Foraker and his crowd will go off.'

An hour later, I was lunching at the White House. It was a larger company than usual, the Tafts, Robert Bacons, and some twelve or so others, when some one raised the question of Brownsville. As I had just told Mrs. Roosevelt of my talk with Mr. Crane, she called across the round table to the President, and asked me to repeat it. The company was silent as I said, 'Mr. President, Senator Crane has just told me that if you insist on your policy about those negro companies, there is likely to be a split in the Republican Party, and Senator Foraker will go off.'

The President paused a moment, and in his falsetto voice and characteristic manner announced to the whole table, 'The Senator told me the same thing yesterday, and I said to him, "Senator, if there is to be a split in the

Republican Party and Foraker goes off, I call that a splinter." '

Of course, Senator Foraker heard of it before the sun set, but the President was a free lance in such rallies; every one understood him and was amused, except perhaps Senator Foraker.

I cannot recall any private citizen whose hold upon the interest of the people has endured as has that of Phillips Brooks. Even now, after almost a generation has passed, his is a name to conjure with.

Soon after his death a committee of citizens of Boston gave an opportunity to the people to subscribe for a memorial to him; and the money poured in, over one hundred thousand dollars, until the committee had to call a halt. This memorial took the form of the Saint-Gaudens statue, and the overflow is used as an endowment for the charities of Boston. Later, Phillips Brooks House at Cambridge was built by the gifts of Harvard men from over the world. Memorials sprang up in various parts of the country. The 'Life of Phillips Brooks,' by Professor A. V. G. Allen, published in 1900 in two large volumes, had a remarkable sale, as did the editions of his sermons and addresses.

January 23, 1903, was the tenth anniversary of his death. To make a popular occasion of such an event is usually to invite failure; yet on that Friday morning, for a communion service and address,[1] Trinity Church was crowded — indeed many were turned away, and the city was full of the thought of him.

[1] *Phillips Brooks: A Study*, by Bishop Lawrence.

CHAPTER XII
A JUNE IN ENGLAND
1903

In the spring of 1903 I broke away to England for six weeks, taking Marian and Sallie with me. My friend, Stuart Donaldson, whom I first met in 1884 when he and Mr. Littleton, afterwards Head Master, were living together as young masters in a queer gabled house at Eton by Barnes Pool, had now one of the best houses and coached the Eton eight. Since my last visitation there in 1897, he had married: Lady Albinia, with her delightful Irish humor and occasional inconsequential ways, was a happy complement to the matter-of-fact temperament of her husband. In his 'Memories and Friends,' Arthur Benson, who was also a master and lived with Donaldson nearly thirty years, has written a delightful description of their Eton and Cambridge life, saying, 'I have never known so crystal-clear and so unclouded a nature.'

The service in chapel on Sunday morning, which with its hundreds of boys is always moving, was more than ever touching, for in the week before two boys had been burned to death in one of the houses, imprisoned by fire in the upper floor by windows barred with iron to prevent the boys from stealing out in the night. The social compactness of England was felt in the expressions of grief from every part of the Kingdom.

Sunday afternoon vespers in Saint George's Chapel, Windsor, just across the river, was well known as one of the most beautiful services in England, for Sir Walter Parratt was at the organ, and led a finely trained choir. As I walked back towards Eton with Sir Walter, I spoke of the beauty of the singing, when he said, 'Not as good as it ought to have been; there were too many people in the nave; the resonance was not right.' Was this an unconscious confession of an ideal service — no one in the nave? Sir Walter, however, was a devout worshipper.

Can anything be more delightful than a few days living in a master's house and in comradeship with the English boys? England's history, her scholars and heroes, form the background. To come suddenly upon a class of twenty or thirty boys lounging under a great oak, with the master in the centre teaching them to construe Virgil, with the gray walls of the college and chapel behind them, is a scene which one cannot forget.

Within, the house on the master's side is substantial, of solid comfort: on the boys' side, unbreakable desks and chairs carved, cut, and hewn on the edges by boys of earlier ages; and conveniences, or lack of conveniences, which American boys would spurn. But tradition and a healthy view of the fitness of things on the part of the boys endear these primitive conditions to them; and old Eton boys, bringing their sons, glory in the story of the austerities of their day.

On the cricket field, the deep green of the wicket, the spotless white of the players, the sharp click of the bat, and the quiet movement of it all is a refreshing contrast to some of our baseball games. The river, too, crowded with crews getting away in the afternoon, with Windsor Castle looming up behind, is the same river that fetched the barons to Runnymede, not far away. To accompany masters and boys to Henley Week, to lunch on the lawn, sit in the punts, watch the succession of races, and hear the talk of the river and the crews is a delight.

In response to a letter saying that I was in England, dear old Dr. Butler, Master of Trinity College, Cambridge, the primate of England's Dons, wrote me in his humorous way, 'This is the time of our official visitation by the Chancellor; the Duke of Connaught and the Duke of Devonshire will be here until Friday or Saturday; but you come Saturday, at all events, and we will push them out!'

We arrived on Saturday for luncheon, to find that the Duke of Connaught had just gone, while the Duke of

Devonshire, with his heavy but gracious manner, left after lunch; and we took their rooms in the Master's Lodge, rooms which are unique among university quarters, for here the judges have a right to sleep when in Cambridge to hold court, and here royalty and chancellors have slept on occasion for centuries. Everything was as it should be: great spaces, high ceiling, heavy furniture, a lofty four-post bedstead, with curtains, a stepladder on which to climb in, and a bed of untold depth; as the weather and house were cold, the process of warming the bed before falling asleep was a long one.

A fellow guest was Mr. Francis Galton, a most interesting man, best known, however, for an incidental discovery, the individuality of finger prints and their use in detecting criminals. I preached in Great Saint Mary's for Archdeacon Cunningham; dined in hall at the upper table; then to the combination room where wines, cakes, and snuff were pushed along the rich mahogany table, but no smoking was allowed.

Dr. Butler was inimitable and indescribable. Large physically, a profound and brilliant scholar, overflowing with kindness and anecdotes, he was courtesy itself to every one from royalty to the humblest woman in the college scullery. When I visited him in 1897, just before the Lambeth Conference, he said, 'You have never met any of the English Bishops. Sit down and let me tell you what I think of each one of them.' As his admiration of bishops in general was discriminating, and of some bishops much mitigated, he gave full play to his insight, humor, and kindliness. Would that I had taken down his talk; it would have often refreshed me as I came to know the men!

An American is wise who takes with him to England for use in June his thickest winter clothing. A long, cold storm was on. The Master's house was spacious, and the fire of coals smouldered. As we went down to luncheon or dinner, he said to Mrs. Butler, who was also a brilliant classical scholar, 'Should not the windows be thrown open, my dear, that the drawing-room may be fresh when we come back?' Hence, on our arrival at Canon Mason's, the Master of Pembroke, to stay for a few days, I excused myself from a dinner-party at Professor Darwin's and, when the house was quiet, rang for the butler and asked him to bring hot water enough for two hot-water bags and a tumbler, and two boxes of coals, also a little sugar. Fortified by the use of these and a little brandy, I passed the next day in bed and wrote home that I was the only warm person in Great Britain.

To Oxford we went for Commemoration Week. Louis Dyer, who had been an Assistant Professor of Greek at Harvard, and had later married Miss MacMillan, lived in Oxford and made it his joy and business to welcome his friends and all Americans. We saw everything and met everybody. Dr. Sanday I called upon early. To be sure, it was a very busy week, and perhaps I should have known better. However, he entered the room in the nervous academic manner of many scholars, looking much worried at being interrupted. I immediately assured him that I called to tell him how we valued his writings in America, that I regretted coming at such a busy time. At which he replied again nervously, 'Yes, I am very busy, but — but — ' adding a few polite sentences, and I departed. Dr. Driver, being younger and perhaps less busy, gave me a pleasant and interesting call.

One wonders sometimes if Oxford does not yawn at its centuries-old habit of hospitality. There was no sign of weariness among them as I went from the hospitable board of the Master and Mrs. Caird at Balliol to that of the Master of New College and Mrs. Spooner. Dr. Spooner, the creator of Spoonerisms, was the kindest and most thoughtful person possible. Then there were Dons and Fellows of College after College, as well as Mrs. Temple, who now lived in Oxford while her son William was Fellow at Queen's. I recall a breakfast at Oriel; the table was furnished with the silver plate of Edward III. There was interesting talk of Oriel tradition, the Tractarian days, and of Generals Sherman and Lee.

Commemoration in the Sheldonian and the giving of degrees followed. The usual noisy interruptions from the undergraduates took place, and the gibes at the Vice-Chancellor and orator, 'Take off your hat!' 'Shut up!'; but there was no wit, and the custom then waning has now ceased.

We left Oxford and the Magdalen Meadows swamped in rain, the Thames higher than it had been for many, many years, nothing like it ever seen — at least so the loyal Oxonians said.

Finally we went up to London and to Lambeth Palace. Archbishop Temple had gone, also Archbishop Benson, and our hosts at Farnham of 1897, now Archbishop and Mrs. Davidson, received us. Let me say once and for all, that since June, 1902, we have counted them as of our dearest, most hospitable, and generous friends. Lambeth has been a London home to us, as indeed it has been to hundreds of others from all parts of the world.

From the gray walls and subdued colors of Oxford colleges to the trooping of the colors on Whitehall Parade Grounds was a contrast, indeed: The King, Princes, and Generals mounted, the Queen and Princesses also present, detachments drilled to the last point, a band of two hundred and fifty pieces. Later we called at 10 Downing Street, the house of the Prime Minister, then Mr. Balfour. This room, with red royal dispatch boxes piled up in the corner, is the same in which Lord North and the rest planned and fought our War of the Revolution. Later, Mr. Balfour received me, and had apparently all the leisure which scholars at Oxford are supposed to enjoy. He would not let me go until he was called out to a committee. Self-discipline in making one's guest feel at home is the grace of a statesman.

A dinner at the Stationers' Guild with Herkomer, Rider Haggard, and other guests, found me by the side of Lord Kelvin, a most modest, quiet, approachable man, ready to talk. He reminded me much of Asa Gray, another modest leader in science.

At a dinner at Lambeth to Prince and Princess Christian, I was presented to one of the ladies-in-waiting, a charming woman, widow of a brave officer killed in the Boer War. Thinking that she would be puzzled at the mention of my title when introduced by Mrs. Davidson, 'The Bishop of Massachusetts,' and knowing from experience that Boston is more familiar to the English, I said, 'You may know nothing of Massachusetts, but Boston is my See city.' 'Ah, yes,' she said, 'I know, for hearing that you were to be among the guests, I looked it up. But this morning on telling a friend that I was to meet the Bishop of Massachusetts at dinner, she exclaimed, "How delightful: and he will be black!"' At this same dinner one guest, Mr. Goldschmidt, the husband of Jenny Lind, was fairly delighted to meet some one from Boston, of which he had very happy memories.

The Choates' house on Carlton Terrace was a delightful centre for Americans and English, as was that of Mrs. Joseph Chamberlain. Dean Robinson, Canons Henson and Beeching of Westminster, our old friends the Archbishop of Armagh and the Bishop of Ripon, with many others, enabled us to make other friends.

In the early part of our visit, before Mr. Choate's return from America, Mr. White kindly asked if I cared to be presented at His Majesty King Edward's levee; and as it was the first since his coronation, all the leaders of the realm would be there. Mentioning this at Lambeth, I added that Mr. White was to learn from the Lord Chamberlain the proper dress of a bishop. The Archbishop, however, said that in Queen Victoria's day bishops at presentation wore a black gown, but that King Edward, wishing more color, had decided upon convocation robes, which are bishops' robes with scarlet in the place of black; and of course shorts, silk stockings, shoes and buckles. As I had none of these, the Archbishop kindly offered to lend me his, which turned out to be a perfect fit. When, however, Lamb, the valet, brought them to dress me for the occasion, he brought no shorts. 'It is all right, milord,' he said, and taking some strings from his pocket, he rolled up my trousers to above the knees, and tied them there. Thus was I presented to His Majesty.

On arriving at Buckingham Palace, I found Mr. J. P. Morgan, Mr. H. H. Hanna, of Indianapolis, who did so much to bring this country to a gold standard, and two or three other Americans in velvet, silver buttons, silk stockings and pumps, armed with silver-hilted swords over which they were in constant fear that they would stumble. The dignified and orderly way in which the presentations were made, the name of each person announced by, I think, the Duke of Norfolk, the gracious manner of the King, who sat during the ceremony, and the promptness were admirable. Remaining in the presentation room, we were enabled to see the presentations following us, while Mr. White noted for us the most important or interesting personages. It was all over in sixty minutes.

At Fulham Palace the Creightons, by the death of the Bishop, had given place to Dr. Ingram, the Bishop of London. As he came home at eleven o'clock at night, his personality shed a glow and warmth in every room and corner of the palace. Was there ever a more friendly, vital, popular, and truly pious Bishop than he? 'Well, here I am. I left at nine; have driven through thirty miles of London streets, talked, prayed, and met committees. How glad, very glad I am that you have come.'

As we drove with him, six of us, in his big barouche the next morning, his secretary read his letters to him. Tearing off a signature, he gave it to Marian, saying, 'That is from a royalty who wants me to enter another bishop's diocese and do what the diocesan bishop should do. Royalty ought to know better than to ask such a thing.' Then he went on, 'The vicar of this church that is to be consecrated is very fond of mediæval services, and a few days ago he sent me the proofs of an endless consecration, such an one as has not been used for centuries. I put a blue pencil through much of it, but there was one phrase which I could not omit, though I am sure the vicar has not humor enough to see why I let it stand. The procession arrives at the door and we have document after document read to a most tiresome length; and this is the phrase that I let stand, "In the Name of God, let us begin." '

As the service opened, and the procession entered the church, we watched the Bishop as he moved up the aisle, his head covered, almost extinguished by a great and heavily embroidered mitre, his hands decorated with gloves far too long, of an ecclesiastical red, suggesting Mephistopheles; and his whole body ornately decorated with proper garments.

May he not represent England to-day — modern, very modern in certain ways, with features of mediævalism cropping out, sometimes where least expected?

CHAPTER XIII
VARIED INTERESTS
1903–1904

On the 3d of October, 1903, the clergy and representative laity of both Massachusetts Dioceses filled Trinity Church in recognition of the tenth anniversary of my consecration. A luncheon with addresses followed. In the evening I held a service which is one of the happiest memories of my Episcopate.

The relation between a bishop and those whom he has confirmed is full of spiritual significance. Whether a bishop has laid hands upon hundreds or thousands of persons, each one has been touched and blessed by him at one of the critical moments of his life; and for each one the true bishop has a tender regard. In the ten years I had confirmed over twenty thousand, and had it been possible for me to say a word to each and every one that day, I should have been gratified. Failing that, I asked as many as could get into Trinity Church to meet me there on that evening. Of course, only a fraction of those wishing to come could receive the entrance cards. I claimed the privilege of being alone in the chancel with that great company, and in simple words I tried to remind them of their vows and to wish them Godspeed. As I went about the parishes that year I arranged that those whom I had confirmed should sit together that I might speak to them as a body. I often wonder if the scores of thousands whom I have confirmed, now scattered over the land and throughout the world, recall the laying on of hands with the same tenderness that I do.

From this time my work broadened in scope and became more intense. Hence more thorough organization became necessary. The missionary work in Boston had thriven under the leadership of the Reverend Frederick B. Allen, and was safe in his hands and those of his faithful workers. Stanton King, that unique inspirer of sailors and people, was at his post at the Sailors' Haven, now rebuilt, and to my daughter Marian the success of the campaign for its reconstruction was largely due.

The Theological School at Cambridge was in the competent charge of Dr. George Hodges, who had entered upon the office of Dean soon after my consecration. He had been the beloved rector of Calvary Parish, Pittsburgh, and as a leading citizen opened up to the people visions of social service.

A very modest man, inconspicuous in person, deeply religious, of breadth of mind and charity, he had also such a delightful and original style that his books and published sermons were read by tens of thousands. The sermons, short, crisp, direct, constructive, and spiritual, were peculiarly adapted for the use of lay readers; and in this way I doubt if any sermons ever reached a larger number of people. In purity of motive, sincerity, and industry, he was the right man to lead young men towards the ministry. And he had what is essential in such a position, a keen and refined sense of humor. At an alumni dinner upon his twenty-fifth anniversary as Dean, I said that among other rich contributions that he had made to the ministry and the School was his complete transparency of character. To which he quickly responded that through life a dread had followed him lest people should some day see through him.

Persistent and hard work as Dean, professor, preacher, writer, and speaker finally wore him out, and soon after the close of twenty-five years at Cambridge he fell asleep, beloved by all.

Archdeacon Babcock resigned his rectorship in order to devote his whole time to the missionary work of the Diocese. Those entrusted with other duties, gaining experience, assumed more responsibility. I was thus given more freedom, and, as the freedom came, fresh responsibilities opened at a much faster pace than I expected or wished for.

In the same October, I became a member of the Board of Missions, and later of its Executive Committee, which involved a day a month in New York for thirteen years, until I resigned to inaugurate the Church Pension Fund. Intimate knowledge of the work of the men and women in the mission fields, of their cheerful endurance and loyal service, of their love for their people, stimulates one's own spirit and deepens one's sense of humility. Bishop Doane was then the Chairman of the Board; George C. Thomas, the treasurer, was, through his experience as a successful banker and his generosity, a tower of strength; I found myself continually with him in supporting a conservative policy of finance.

Until I became Bishop, I had taken no special interest in the financial methods of the Church or its business administration beyond the obvious duties of Rector and Dean. Occasional lapses on the part of some officer of a parish guild had disturbed me, but I had assumed that Church finances were on the whole systematically and honestly conducted; as all Church people were, of course, of honest intention.

In the first few years I had several rude awakenings. No sooner had I looked into the management of one of the important diocesan organizations than I discovered that the treasurer had so mixed the several accounts that even an expert accountant could not unravel them. The treasurer, who had grown old in the service, who had never received any emolument, and who had probably dropped a fraction of his own property into the mixture, was now somewhat feeble mentally and could not clear up the difficulty. He made every restitution in his power and resigned. I raised from a few loyal friends over twenty thousand dollars and with expert advice we opened up fresh accounts with estimated credits to each fund.

It was clear to me that such looseness of methods was not only unworthy of the Church, but would naturally check contributions. I began to insist upon the expert auditing of diocesan funds.

One Sunday over twenty years ago, as I was waiting in a robing-room of a city church for the service to begin, I saw in a drawer a few handfuls of small change. In response to my question as to what the money was, the warden said that he supposed it was the offering of the Sunday before, or perhaps the Sunday School offering of a Sunday or two ago which the treasurer had overlooked. I wrote a sharp letter to the vestry, making clear to them their abuse of trust, and there was evidently a reform; for a year or two ago I found a treasurer there who had not missed taking charge of the offering any Sunday for some twenty years.

A few years after these incidents, an officer of a Boston bank told me confidentially that the treasurer of Saint Luke's Home for Convalescents had borrowed money upon collateral and the vote of the Trustees signed by himself as clerk; for he held both offices of treasurer and clerk, a situation which no Society should allow. Upon inquiry, I discovered a similar loan from another bank. This treasurer was the head of the Boston office of one of the large surety companies of the country, and was therefore of excellent standing in the business community. He was also treasurer of a large Boston parish. I had no right, therefore, to suspect him of dishonesty without great reason; and even less right to speak freely of my suspicions. Yet the matter had to be cleared up. Under the by-laws of Saint Luke's Home the finance committee had no power to demand entrance to the securities. Finally, upon taking into my confidence the president of a trust company and the vice-president of a leading bank, both of them parish treasurers, we evolved this plan. It was clear that the time had come for better financial methods and stricter accounting throughout the whole Diocese. We therefore drew up two lists of rules, clear and simple, one as to the care and handling of trust funds and the other of parish contributions. I then called a meeting of some twenty of the leading Church treasurers, in the office of the Massachusetts Hospital Life Insurance Company, read these rules, and asked their advice as to their adoption. The discussion brought out some differences of opinion, and the treasurer whom I suspected and watched closely, hesitated over the rule giving the finance committee of a society power to demand entrance at any time to the securities, but was strong in his support of bonding treasurers. The rules were recommended by these men as a diocesan standard.

Having gotten this informal authority, I called a meeting of the Trustees of Saint Luke's a few days later to consider the adoption of the rules. No objection to them was made, even to that which gave power to the finance committee to open in the presence of the treasurer the security box at any time. In response to my questions, the treasurer said that he had not borrowed money at any bank on vote of the Trustees. The meeting having adjourned, I detained the finance committee and told them that the treasurer had lied, and was probably a defaulter, and insisted that they go with him to the vaults the next morning early and examine the securities. The next afternoon I telephoned the chairman of the finance committee, a kindly old gentleman, as to the result of their visit. He answered that the treasurer was so busy, he had asked them to wait two or three days. I then told the old gentleman with some directness that I would meet him and the treasurer at the opening of the vaults the next morning. As I was putting on my coat early the next day, the telephone rang and the message came that the treasurer had just been arrested by his own company for the defalcation of over one hundred thousand dollars.

The loss to Saint Luke's was some forty or fifty thousand dollars. The amount would have been larger except for the fact that, so the treasurer told me later, he had passed that last day in returning to our box bonds which he had used as collateral for other purposes. And he added, 'Bishop, I do not understand what all this fuss is about. I have tried to do my duty by the Church, and did what I could to put back the bonds, and here I am arrested!'

Human nature is a mysterious thing. Some men seem to have no moral sense at certain definite points. How it was that this man, who held such an office, could have been peculating for some twenty years, and have remained unsuspected by a surety company, is testimony to the fact that even the best accounting systems of those days were quite imperfect. It was a pathetic case: the man was in the State's Prison several years and came out to die.

Why should I tell these stories? Not because of their sensational, pathetic interest; much less to advertise a seamy side of the Church; but that I may bring out, with such vividness as I can, the conditions which have moved me to work for over thirty years for better financial methods and higher standards of administration.

It is to me a constant source of wonder that so many men of high standards seem to assume that in Church matters these standards need not be upheld. For instance, of the two men, both treasurers of large parishes, who helped me in making up those rules, which, by the way, have since become the standard rules throughout the Church, one, the president of a trust company, had hundreds or thousands of dollars — no one ever knew how much — stolen by an under-sexton from the plates because the treasurer did not observe his own rule of counting the money immediately: and the second persistently broke the rule by carrying home in a bag thousands of dollars to be counted by his clerks at the bank on Monday. In response to my question as to whether he handled his bank's money in that way, he said, 'Certainly not, but I cannot without great inconvenience handle the Sunday contribution of the Church in any other way.' Yet he was one of the most high-minded, religious, and respected laymen in the Diocese.

It is only fair to those who have the care of Church funds and contributions for the Church to set about them the safeguards which banks demand. There are in the Episcopal Church probably thirty or forty thousand treasurers of funds, parishes, societies, guilds, and other organizations, handling scores of millions of dollars. Practically all of these treasurers are honest, conscientious, and responsible: some have had but little experience in accounting; some are careless; a very few may be easily tempted to use money wrongfully; it is very, very seldom that one is wilfully dishonest. These latter groups bring the Church and the Christian faith into disrepute and check the flow of gifts. The experience of a long and active life has shown me that as a rule reasonable publicity is the true way to arouse public opinion and to correct evils.

The temper of my business forbears was roused by what I saw and heard, and at the risk of being thought a 'business bishop,' I have pressed for reform. The time was ripe. The issue is more than that of money and contributions: it is of the morale of the Church and the moral character of the youth.

'The moment that a dime drops from the hand of a working woman into the contribution plate, the Church becomes its trustee, bound to see that it is used for the purpose given in the most prompt and efficient way. Multiply that contribution by a thousand and everybody will recognize the obligation.' 'The very fact that the dime is of insignificant value makes the danger of its loss or misuse all the greater. There are more careless than dishonest people.' Thus I began a Church Congress address on Parish Finance which was afterwards distributed widely through the Church. In 1912, at my request, the Diocesan Convention took definite steps towards a better financial system and auditing.

A number of the bishops, clergy, and laity, realizing the conditions, entered actively into the campaign, and groups of men here and there pressed for reform. Only eleven years ago but one half of the eighty-eight dioceses had a good system of accounting for their parishes, and very few had any kind of an audit standard or system.

In 1913, the General Convention, upon the initiative of Robert C. Pruyn, of Albany, appointed a committee of five, one bishop, two clergymen, and three laymen, which has since been made a permanent board to promote better financial methods in the Church. It has been a source of satisfaction to me to serve as chairman upon a board of such men as have formed its membership. With the support of friends we have been at no charge for expenses to the Church, and have with the aid of the secretary carried on a strong and pervasive campaign of education. By diocesan financial commissions, by canon and practical activities, the Church is now approaching in her financial and statistical methods the best nation-wide organizations, secular or religious; and by her unified system of reports the Church is beginning to know so far as figures can suggest where she stands in spiritual, financial, and administrative strength. The fact is that officers and people were unconsciously waiting for such a movement.

At about this time I took up by way of avocation, the study of certain problems coming under my personal observation.[1]

As I ordained men, questions arose in my mind as to where they came from. Were they the spiritual product of our own Church or of other Churches? What had been their background and their education? I therefore undertook the study of the first hundred deacons whom I ordained, and published the results. Of the one hundred, only forty-two were brought up in the Church. The Episcopal Church was not, therefore, so far as this group showed, supplying one half its own ministry. Was it for lack of spiritual vitality in the Church or other conditions? Was this immigration from other Christian bodies liable to bring with it sectarian spirit? Would the solid historic traditions of the Church be upheld?

Of these one hundred, eighty-three per cent had received a full college and theological education, seven years: and practically all had received some collegiate training and substantial theological education. These figures, quoted by me to a Lambeth Conference Committee in London,

[1] *One Hundred Deacons*, printed in 1904.

surprised the English Bishops, who were accustomed to a much lower standard.

In discussions about ministers' salaries, no one seemed to have any reliable figures. I determined therefore to learn what the salaries of the clergy of the Diocese were. So secretive were the parishes and clergy in those days that I could get the figures only by promising to keep them confidential and to destroy the answers to my questionnaire as soon as I had made up my report.[1] In this way I received answers from all except three, and reported the results to the Diocesan Convention showing that the average salary of our one hundred and fifty-seven clergy in active work in Massachusetts was then, including all sources of income, about eighteen hundred dollars; but that the average salary of seventy-four per cent was only twelve hundred dollars, including the rental value of the rectory or its equivalent.

It was this study that started me thinking upon the larger subject of pensions.

Being much disturbed at the number of notices received by me from bishops of depositions of the clergy, I made a confidential study of the facts, obtaining from each bishop by personal letters written by myself the record and causes of each man's deposition in the preceding decade. The facts being given me with the names, I destroyed all the original papers after I had made up the figures. No assistant or secretary ever saw these lists. At a meeting of Bishops in Council I read the facts as classified. They caused deep searchings of heart. A decade later, I repeated the work, summing up for twenty years. There were more heart searchings and questions as to how the Church and her bishops can sustain higher standards of character and loyalty in the ministry. Of course, the great body of the clergy are of sound character; but even one fall prompts serious thought.

It is suggestive, if not ominous, that of every one hundred of our clergy, one is on the list of pensioners on the

[1] Address to the Diocesan Convention, May, 1906.

ground of 'total and permanent disability'; and this does not include those receiving old-age pensions or those temporarily disabled.

I mention the fact of these studies, not for their value in themselves, but to stimulate others to think. Every organization in these days should know where it stands, and its knowledge must be based, not on impressions or guesses, but upon facts and the skilful interpretation of facts.

For instance, it is the opinion of some of the leaders in our universities and other higher educational institutions that one chief cause why more young men of superior ability and fine ambition do not enter the ministry is due to the amount of financial aid that is given to theological students; and that this also partly accounts for the meagre salaries and the comparatively low financial esteem in which the ministry is held by many parishes which could well afford to pay more. Other educators think just the opposite.

The more I have studied the question in practice and theory, the more bewildered I am; because there has been so little serious, comprehensive study of the whole problem in its social and spiritual relations. It is time that men skilled in research study such problems and throw light upon this and a dozen other subjects to which the Church assumes too readily that she now has answers.

As my memory runs back over those earlier years of my Episcopate, various incidents come to mind.

In October, 1903, Bishop Satterlee called a Pan-Anglican Conference of Bishops at Washington. The Bishop, who was brought up a Presbyterian, was enamoured, as are many who come from other Churches, with the Anglican Church idea. He was an enthusiast about the Lambeth Conference, of which he was a very helpful member, of English ecclesiastical ways, of the Cathedrals and every detail of English life. He was at the same time a most loyal American. Of large frame and deep voice, warmhearted and absent-minded, he went his way, sometimes blundering, but never for a moment relaxing in his fine character, spirit of joyful sacrifice, and sympathy. I have known no man who gave the impression of deeper and fuller consecration; and while his friends smiled at his foibles, we all loved and revered him. He was a visionary, and the Washington Cathedral was his great vision and that for which he literally gave his life. On one of his hard, money-raising trips he returned one night from Providence to Washington. The ferry which in those days carried the sleeping-cars around New York City from Harlem to Jersey City got caught and held overnight in the ice; the cars had no steam connection, and the Bishop, chilled and exhausted by such work and disregard of health as would have killed two or three other men, arrived in Washington to die of pneumonia on Washington's Birthday, 1908.

As Bishop of Washington he felt a certain responsibility for the Anglican Communion in this hemisphere: and, perhaps with the example of the Lambeth Conference in mind, he invited the Bishops of the Church in Canada and the English Colonial Bishops south of the United States to meet with the Bishops of our Church in conference. The Bishop of Quebec and I read papers on the relation of the different branches of the Anglican Communion in America to each other. While little came of the conference in practical results, there was real gain in the fellowship and common sympathy and understanding.

My most vivid recollection of that visit is, however, a luncheon at the White House. I doubt if ever in the history of the world a more interesting procession of men and women has sat at a table than those which President Roosevelt gathered at luncheon during his administration. His formal dinners were of necessity more conventional. Even these, however, felt the force and charm of his personality. He and Mrs. Roosevelt kindly invited Mrs. Lawrence and myself to the first diplomatic dinner after his great election. All the formalities, gold lace, and variety of languages could not suppress the President, and laughter rippled about the fifty guests in a way that seldom happens at state dinners.

As to the luncheons, if an interesting person from any part of the world passed through Washington, he called upon the President, of course, who was quite sure to say, 'I hope that you will join us at luncheon to-day or to-morrow.' Then, turning to the secretary, he would add, 'Send word to Mrs. Roosevelt that so and so is coming to lunch.' There might be two guests: there might be twenty; but all were interesting and his personality gathered them into a veritable Round Table with general conversation, he taking much the larger part; and that was what the guests wanted.

October is an off season: hence I found that there were at the table only the President and Mrs. Roosevelt, Wayne MacVeagh, President Butler of Columbia, and myself. Mrs. Roosevelt had a headache, and the shouts of laughter evidently hit her hard, but she kept smiling. Wayne Mac-Veagh was in his most brilliant and witty form — and no man in the country could excel him. The President was in high feather and in his most boisterous mood, while Dr. Butler responded with wit and laughter. What became of me or what part I took, I forget. For over an hour the President held forth upon the Alaskan award, labor questions, his answer to union leaders, and ex-Secretary John D. Long's criticism of him; he read from Abraham Lincoln's message on labor; was perpetually interrupted and pierced by the witty shafts of Mr. MacVeagh. Then, taking us to his office, he read aloud a letter in his most racy style, correcting it as he read and then signing it, to a distinguished citizen who had asked for the appointment to office of a man clearly unfit. The amount of physical and nervous energy that Roosevelt sent forth in an hour is beyond description.

On the 5th of January, 1904, I married Robert Erskine Childers and Mary Osgood in Trinity Church, Boston. It is a far cry from serene Mount Vernon Place, under the shadow of the State House, where the wedding reception was held, to the prison yard in Dublin.

Childers's career is one of the inscrutable tragedies of the

Great War and Irish Rebellion. A brilliant young man, graduate of Trinity College, Cambridge, later a clerk in the House of Commons, skilled in the preparation of bills to be presented, he fought in the Boer War, was wounded, then wrote for the London 'Times.' Studying the working of the German spy system, he wrote 'The Riddle of the Sands,' an attempt to expose an alleged plan for a German invasion of England. Becoming interested in the Irish Coöperative Movement, he wrote the 'Framework of Home Rule.' Throwing in his lot with the Sinn Fein leaders, he nevertheless entered the English Intelligence Service in the Great War, and after experiences at Gallipoli, the Red Sea, and the North Sea Squadron, received a D.S.C., and was appointed by the King on the Irish Peace Convention. Then with his wife he threw himself into the propaganda and 'gun-running' for the cause of Valera, whose chief lieutenant he became. Uncorruptible, able, and fertile in resources, fanatically opposed to the Free State, he was finally captured and executed as a traitor to England at Dublin, November 24, 1922.

After several annual invitations from Robert C. Ogden to join one of his trips to the South, I was finally able to get away in April, 1904. Mr. Ogden's execution of these trips was to my mind a piece of original statesmanship. Ever since the Civil War the North had learned but little of the South, and the South, after enduring the reconstruction agony, was suspicious of the North.

Mr. Ogden, who was the New York partner of the Wanamaker Company, and had built up their great store, had become keenly interested in efforts to coöperate with the Southern people without seeming to patronize them, as Northern philanthropists had often done, in creating better systems of education, multiplying schools, and especially in stimulating the people of the South, who were beginning to prosper, to tax themselves increasingly for the education of the coming generation, both white and black. He was the President of the Southern Education Board, which had this subject in hand.

Mr. Ogden realized that the vital need was to educate leaders of the North in Southern conditions. Hence he chartered for two weeks each year the finest train, with two dining-cars, that the Pennsylvania Railroad could provide, and filled the staterooms with college presidents, professors, head masters of schools, and other educators, legislators, business men, publishers, clergymen, and other leading citizens, women and men; and as their host he carried them from city to village, from Hampton to Tulane University, from Tuskegee to the University of North Carolina, from Calhoun School to the University of Virginia, revealing to them what the North had done by its voluntary associations and gifts, what the South was doing in the building up of a new South, and thus blending the whole Nation together in one common purpose. His train was like a shuttle shooting from East to West and West to East below Mason's and Dixon's line, weaving a fabric of national integrity.

How well I recall waking up one beautiful Sunday morning near Calhoun and, looking out the windows, I caught sight of a great company of negro men, women, and children in wagons, on horse and muleback, many barefoot and walking, yellow bandannas and red flannel petticoats flashing in the sunlight. The whole countryside, of which eleven out of every twelve of the population were pure black, had been touched for a generation in their homes and churches by Calhoun School, conducted by chivalrous men and women from the North. I remember well one smart Yankee girl, a physician, who in that black and lonely country rode or walked unattended day or night. The whole trainful alighted and joined the negroes in the march up the hill to the school. A massive black woman, with brilliant bandanna and skirt, slipped off her mule and gave me a 'leg up' onto her saddle; others the same; and on that beautiful Sabbath we caught one unforgettable glimpse of the South.

Elsewhere at normal schools girls from the best families of the South, headed by their teachers, came to greet us;

and so the days passed. The genius of a great administrator touched every detail. As on our return we stepped
off the train at Jersey City, every one of us had seen a
vision and heard a voice of National Unity, of brotherhood and sympathy nigh to a real spiritual conversion.
Those Ogden trips marked the beginning of a new era in
the sympathetic relations of North and South.

To show how stupid we Northerners can be, I will tell a
story of how by one sentence I came near breaking up
the whole trip. It was at Tuskegee. The chapel was filled
with hundreds of whites and negroes. Booker Washington
called me unexpectedly to the platform to say a few
words. In order to give myself time to think what to say, I
began, 'When Dr. Washington comes to Boston, my children always want to have him come to lunch or dinner; it
is a pleasure, therefore, to me to be entertained by him
here.' Then I began a short address, but felt that something — I did not know what — had dropped with a thud;
and after a few feeble sentences I sat down. The reporters
had immediately caught at those words and were about to
send through the South the headlines that the Ogden party
had come to instruct the South how to entertain Booker
Washington. But Mr. Ogden jumped to the rescue and
induced them to cut out the copy. I suspected nothing of
this until the next day, as a few of us were sitting on the
piazza at Calhoun, Mrs. Montague, the wife of the Governor of Virginia, said to me, 'Bishop, if you lived in the
South, would you entertain Booker Washington?' I looked
at her, and the truth dawned on me as I said, 'I did make a
fool of myself yesterday: I had no idea' — 'Oh,' she interrupted, 'I did not mean that. I want to know.' 'If I lived
in the South, Mrs. Montague, I am sure that I should do
as Southern gentlemen do and should not entertain him.
But living in the North, I feel as a Northern gentleman
at liberty to do so.' Then, turning to Dr. Buttrick, who
was a pure Yankee, but sensed the South as few Northerners have, I said, 'Doctor, suppose a Southern gentleman should entertain Booker Washington, what would

happen; what would he do?' 'Why,' replied the Doctor in his dry way, 'he would entertain Booker Washington.' 'But what else would happen?' I persisted. 'What would he do?' 'Oh,' answered the Doctor, 'he would never do anything else.'

Human nature and race antipathies are much the same the world over. We in Boston have prided ourselves on being free from those things, but there is a good deal of ignorance of facts, or rather of inconsistency in our attitude. I notice that when the negroes increase to approaching twenty per cent of the population in church, shop, or factory, a sense of restlessness creeps in, and the whites say, 'They may be excellent people, but if more come, we go.' The problem of such segregation as will enable the two races so to live as to work out each its best civilization is, of course, one of the great problems of this country. Mr. Ogden's theory, which is, I believe, that of almost every intelligent student and leader, was that it will be solved only by giving each race, black and white, the best opportunity possible to work out its own state of life and civilization.

Such a policy involves self-restraint, character, and mutual confidence. Booker Washington was a shining illustration of this spirit. Meeting that Ogden train both at Hampton and Tuskegee, he would not join the party where we of North and South were of one racial group, but took a common train across the country. We know how irksome it is to wait for our meals on a crowded dining-car. Booker Washington, who was entertained by the rich, cultivated, and public-spirited people of the North, told me in response to my question that he never entered a dining-car until every white person was out, and then he took his meal, often with the waiters; and sometimes missed them altogether. Northern hotels from which all colored people were barred were ready to entertain him, but he invariably declined, and went to those where other colored people were received.

When I became Bishop, there was one feeble mission for

colored people ministered to by Father Field. It was assumed that the white and colored people should, of course, worship together. As, however, the colored population has increased in Greater Boston, they themselves have taken the initiative in building up their own parishes. In Cambridge and Boston we have two large parishes of colored people, strong in self-respect, self-support, intelligence, and loyalty. Few visitations give me greater satisfaction than those with these congregations.

At the Commencement of 1904, Princeton University did me the high honor of giving me the honorary degree of Doctor of Laws. As President Woodrow Wilson presented it, we little thought what the future had in store for him.

Before entering upon another and broader phase of my life's work, I must, though with some reluctance, describe one limitation and struggle which has accompanied me through manhood, and which I mentioned in telling of my doubts about accepting my election as bishop.

Fifty-seven years ago, when a student at Harvard, as I was walking home to Longwood across the vacant fields then lying between Cambridgeport and the river, I suddenly felt as if I were falling. I can remember as if it were yesterday, the sudden start and fear. I righted myself, stiffened, and walked on, having one or two more turns before reaching home. Soon these feelings grew upon me so that I was afraid to be alone in a room with the door locked: I shrank from crowds lest I faint or go out of my head. I never travelled alone if I could help it. When in a strange city, if compelled to go on the street alone, I braced myself for it; and even then I seemed to stagger and I watched the passing people to see if they thought me drunk. For weeks before crossing the ocean I was inwardly depressed lest in some moment alone on deck I should suddenly find myself leaping overboard. For the same reason I dreaded heights, and shrank with utmost fear from going up lofty buildings. For years I swayed or seemed to sway in the pulpit, and clutched both sides to keep my body and brain steady, fighting the thing through, and wondering if the congregation observed it. Standing near the edge of a cliff or at some high window, I have shrunk back with fear, almost terror, while a kind friend, entirely unconscious of my suffering, discoursed upon the view. Again and again I have thanked God for a strong heart. It has stood the racket for many years, often beating like a trip-hammer under the fear and strain. In time I found myself hampered in my work, excusing myself from situations which might be uncomfortable, evading going alone or by night where it was my duty to go. I recall with remorse definite duties which I have shirked and evaded. There was danger lest I yield entirely and become a hypochondriac. Time and again I almost decided to put myself in the hands of Dr. Weir Mitchell in Philadelphia; and then the conviction mastered me that it was for me to fight it through: he might be only a temporary support.

My devoted wife suspected rather than knew it from me, and she has often made conditions easier. Nothing, however, had been said, for talk might exaggerate the mania, if it were a mania. When a boy I have heard my mother say after walking home from Boston across the Mill Dam, 'I believe I shall throw myself into the Back Bay some day.' And I have seen my father violently protest at being left alone in a crowd. I did not know what it meant then. They had fought it through: so ought I.

Who knows the number of men and women going through life under some such conditions? I have no right to suggest these dreads to others unless I have some help to give them: indeed, that is my only purpose in thus revealing a personal limitation.

The line of action which has led me out into comparative freedom has been something like this. The simplest and most natural step has been by a definite effort to turn the direction of my thoughts. Many a time when I have felt the dread of falling or loneliness, I have quickly taken my engagement book out of my pocket and have set my thoughts upon the details of what I had to do the rest of the day or the coming week; or I have pulled out a newspaper or a book and have read intently; or with determination I have studied every face that passed me or every shrub and tree near by. The power to turn and control one's thoughts increases with exercise.

Sometimes the fear would rise, 'Perhaps I cannot master this: my brain may give way.' Then with steely resolve came the answer, 'If it does, I cannot help it. If God destroys my mind and will, then let Him. I am going to fight this thing through. Here is my line of duty.'

While these thoughts were whirling and the struggle was on, passers-by seemed to note nothing strange about me: friends stopped and talked as if life never had a care. They would tell me how well and vigorous I looked and sometimes express envy that I never suffered from nervousness as they did. How little they knew!

Life at Cambridge with its delightful and friendly associations was easy. When, however, the suggestion of my election as Bishop first came, I was panic-stricken; for apart from my distaste for the duties, how could I possibly go through life, travelling alone, away from home, in strange cities? I might carry through the fight, but my heart would give way under the strain. I felt that under the circumstances I had no right to take the office: but I could not make public my reason.

When, however, the election came, I had to face the question. My physicians advised me that if I would avoid all unnecessary strain, I could go ahead, and that I would in time overcome the difficulty. It was then that a sense of duty reënforced my will power. 'Here,' I said to myself, 'is my life-work. I did not seek it, but I have no right to shirk it. I *must* walk to-day and to-morrow.'

If a man or woman hampered as I was is living an aimless life, he or she has not the great stimulating and driving power of a sense of duty. But if one has a purpose in life, no matter how humble—it may be the doing of a good day's work, or the support of a family — the carrying through of that purpose is his duty: and the sense of duty keeps his mind steady and enforces his will power.

There is, however, an even greater secret of power: it is such a complete and simple faith in God that one is perfectly sure that, come what will, God will take care of him and see the thing through. Such a faith in the first place minimizes the first flutterings of fear, quiets the mind, and prevents a panic. It enables one to take the events as they come, and quietly live and walk on. 'Underneath are the everlasting arms.' Alienists and physicians are, of course, essential in the treatment of mind and nerve diseases, and we cannot be too grateful for the wonderful work they are doing; but I believe that there are thousands of people who claim to be Christians, who are running here and there to charlatans and warped forms of religion, and getting real help too, because in them they find a confidence and support which the Christian faith can give more fully and naturally, but which, although they have lived in formal Christianity all their lives, they have never appropriated. So far as Christian Science has helped thousands on thousands to this quiet confidence in God, it is Christian and doing the work which the historic Churches have sometimes neglected to do.

When one has caught the secret of 'the peace of God which passeth all understanding,' he has a source of power which is quieting, represses dreads and panics, and gives complete serenity. Such a secret may take years to gain, but the exercise of faith increases faith.

I believe, therefore, that the elemental force in the character of an alienist, a psychopathic physician, a mental healer, or any one who hopes to lead people from dreads and panics is a simple faith in God, which can best be aroused through the comradeship of Christ. This has real power and enables people to do things and to win personal victories. So long as we live, we shall most of us have some kinds of limitations or untoward conditions to fight through. I know that I still have them ahead, and I know of no more helpful and final support than the Christian faith.

CHAPTER XIV

FIFTY-FIVE YEARS OF MOUNT DESERT

On the 20th of July, 1870, Francis G. Peabody (now Plummer Professor Emeritus of Christian Morals at Harvard) and I, having shipped at Portland on the steamer Lewiston for Bar Harbor, found the whole summer population, perhaps seventy-five in all, gathered at the wharf, as was the custom on the arrival of the Lewiston, to welcome us and other guests. As the steamer warped up to the wharf we shouted out the news that France had declared war on Germany, the opening of the Franco-Prussian War.

To the new cottage, with plaster still damp, of my friend and classmate George Minot, I went, while Frank Peabody went to the Welds. Those were primitive days for Mount Desert. As we had steamed along the south of the island, touching at South-West Harbor, there were only farms and forests where the hotels and cottages of North-East and Seal Harbor now stand. The mountains responded to the French title, Mont Désert, for frequent fires had swept the trees from their rocky tops and sides. They were grim and rugged as compared with their present appearance, since care against fire has covered them with birch and spruce. Great Head and Schooner Head were bold and barren of all else than bush. As we skirted along the shore, thick masses of short spruce ran down close to the water, and there was no sign of human life. As we approached the wharf, the brown fields, innocent of lawnmower or water, were backed by a few white or unpainted native cottages and boarding-houses. The white spire of the Union Church was conspicuous. Near the wharf a boarding-house lately built by Captain Tobias Roberts had a sign running its whole length, 'The Agamont,' and the old bowling-alley was occupied by 'roomers.' West of Main Street there was, except for the Meeting House, the schoolhouse, and half a dozen other buildings, nothing but scattered farms and forests back to Hull's Cove and Somesville. Captain James Hamor's farm included everything north of the village, and where are now Cottage and West Streets were rough field and bog, brilliant in July with wild roses. From the plain one could see the whole sweep of the mountains, a view now shut off by shade trees and houses. Indeed the growth of trees has done much to hide the beauties of the sea and mountain. Skilfully swung axes are needed at many points to open up the vistas. There were no fences, no lawns, no gardens, or estates. The whole island was ours, and we a company of hardy boys and girls, with enough older people to keep us in order, owned it all.

We slept in the two cottages or wherever we could, and all took our meals at some boarding-house. Ours was the Ocean House: Rodick's came later. We were 'mealers.' Those who in later years slept in more distant places were 'hauled mealers.' We carried empty pails up to our meals, and, filling them at the pump, brought back the water for our pitchers and tubs. Comforts indoors were so rare that we lived out of doors. Starting in the morning and taking our luncheons, we walked along the dusty Schooner Head, Seal Harbor, or Eagle Lake Road, and struck up Newport, Green Mountain, or Dry Mountain, then practically pathless; or, more lazily inclined, we passed the day on the shelf under Great Head or on Sand Beach; or we clambered along the rocks to Otter Cliffs, for there was no Ocean Drive then. Des Isles general store was the post-office, and any one near at hand sorted the mail. So little known was Bar Harbor, however, that most of our letters were addressed simply to 'Mount Desert,' which was Somesville, and there they waited until some picnic party gathered them in and brought them across the island to Bar Harbor.

Of green vegetables there were practically none, but lobsters were two cents a pound. As but little ice was cut, the meat was cooked and eaten soon after the killing. If

one wanted a tender steak, he hung it deep down in a
cool well for a few days. Nothing but flannels were worn
by either sex; although calico dresses appeared on hot
days. Two or three years later, a young woman essayed a
black silk skirt, but she was taboo. The enthusiasm of the
Bar Harbor group the following winter was so great as to
irritate all our friends in Boston; and many of them, especially the elder, thought it a vulgar and rowdy place
because young men and women walked the mountains un-
chaperoned, and young women swung their arms when
they walked; for in the city in those days ladies held
their hands before them in walking.

For several years I passed two or three weeks with the
Minots — a holiday worth six weeks anywhere else, for the
combination of sea and mountain air, the freedom and informality, were then and have been ever since most stimulating, though freedom and informality have been much
hemmed in. I doubt if any seashore place in this country
has harbored a greater variety of interesting people during
these fifty years than Mount Desert.

Among those in our little group at the Minots was Anna
Roosevelt, who was soon followed by her father, Theodore,
who was in energy, patriotism, and enthusiasm the worthy
forerunner of his son. After a hard day and a light supper
before bedtime to fill the spaces left vacant by the boarding-house meals, we left him reading, to find him in the
morning up before us ready for the next day's tramp. He
accompanied me to Nahant and after a short stay was off
to New York; alas, to die a few months later in the prime
of life.

James Russell Lowell enjoyed the talk of the village
people, for there were individuals in those days, Yankees
whose characters and idiosyncracies had not been
smoothed out by the conventionalities of city people.
Captain Hamor, the postmaster, was a strong character
and quaint. Stephen Higgins, too. Stephen had a religious note to his conversation. On arrival one summer
at his cottage of which Stephen had charge through the

winter, Mr. Minot could not find a bottle of whiskey which he had carefully concealed in the autumn. In response to inquiries, Stephen acknowledged that he had found the bottle, and added, 'I don't calculate it made my starry crown any less: my wife and I needed it.'

Winters in such a village must have been long and hard in those days. Snow was deep: even the bodies of the dead had to be buried near the house; family graves and lots are a familiar and touching sight throughout New England, as in other northern countries.

Mountain wagons were the vehicles of those days, except the stage-coach which ran between Bangor and Bar Harbor. The roads were as they had been from the first, rough, steep and dusty. 'Corkscrew Hill' and 'Breakneck Road' meant what they said. In later years buckboards came in and held the road; in them we often made the twenty-two mile drive, or, climbing over the Eagle Lake Road, passed by Pretty Marsh, High Head, Salisbury Cove and the Ovens; or a full day would be given to Beech Hill, one of the most beautiful views in New England. These were all day drives then, and involved much uphill walking, until the cut-under, Victoria, and other city teams came in, all of which offended the eyes of us early settlers: and so great was the opposition to motors that they did not enter the island until 1913. The buckboard was a most fitting 'rig': to be sure, its length made it heavy to haul, and three on each seat of four seats was a killing load, even for four horses. The running-board was so low, however, that the whole party stepped off onto the road without checking the horses, and walked up the hills, each passenger being in doubt as to whether to fall behind and take the dust, walk beside the buckboard, bruised by the stones and bushes, or ahead of the team, which with the well-blown horses pressed him hard up the hill.

Francis Parkman, who was one of the company of those days, was of course familiar with the earlier history of Mount Desert, but we young explorers and discoverers had no more interest in it than had the conquering Spaniards for the early civilization of Mexico. As years have passed, however, the romance of French traditions has caught the interest of later comers, as is seen in the names now given the National Park and the mountains, such as Sieur de Monts and Lafayette.

The only church in early years was the Union Meeting House where itinerant preachers came. Bishop Neely began to make annual visitations and held services there. He was a very large man, rigid in theology and churchmanship, kindly and very human. He was accustomed to untoward events in a service. I recall his coming down the aisle in the midst of the Communion Service looking under each bench, and finally saying, 'Where is that bottle of wine? There is not enough on the Lord's Table.'

After three or four years, however, the summer population became so large that, as the Union Church would not accommodate all, the Bishop held his service in Rodick's parlor one Sunday. For the next Sunday my friends and the Bishop urged me to preach. Having preached only two or three times since my ordination, I was so scared that I positively refused, but finally yielded if some one would read the service, for I did not dare to take it all alone. I always recall Bishop Neely with gratitude, for in the most brotherly way he read the service, while I, a timid deacon, was the preacher. Simple as I was, but courageous when supported by him, knowing well the amount of gossip in the place, I had the hardihood to preach on the use and abuse of the tongue.

In 1878 the Church of Saint Saviour was built under the leadership of Gouverneur Morris Ogden, and later was doubled in size. As hotels rose up in the village, the church was packed morning and evening, and for twenty years had as its rector the Reverend Christopher Starr Leffingwell, a man of such quaintness, humble spirit, and individuality of manner as to be worthy of a biography: had he lived in England, Trollope would have immortalized him. In his modesty he shrank from preaching to the summer congregation; so there was an understanding between us that I should help in case of need. Hence he frequently gave this notice with his peculiar cadence of voice: 'Next Sunday a sermon may be expected from the Reverend Doctor Lawrence, provided I can obtain no one else meanwhile.'

A visitor preached a sermon which Mr. Leffingwell disapproved. Consequently, before the blessing he came forward to the chancel steps and said, 'This evening a *sermon* may be expected from the Reverend Doctor ——' [naming another preacher]; and as we parted he said, 'Did you notice my emphasis on the word "sermon"?'

In talking of his winter's work, he told me that he tried to be helpful, and was often gratified when called for. 'This year, for instance, one of the wickedest men in the village, when about to die sent for me.' 'I know that you must have helped him,' I said. 'I trust so,' he answered, 'but of course, considering his open hostility to religion, I did not think it tactful to mention that subject.' And he was probably right: the presence of the old saint with his snowy white hair and long beard, his innocence and faith, were more likely to suggest penitence and the spiritual life than exhortations to repentance.

With the passing of years, the panorama of life moved. Soon came the great barracks called summer hotels, where people of wealth and refinement from the large cities brought their daughters, or their daughters brought them, and Rodick's piazza and broad steps with scores of young people answered well to its popular title, 'The Fish Pond.'

There followed thousands of tourists who, coming by train and ferry, filled large four-horse barges, drove to Eagle Lake, which they crossed in a stern-wheeler, took the cog railway to the top of Green Mountain, and camped in another summer barrack which fortunately burned down: the railroad, boat, and barges soon fell to ruins. Then those who had boarded at the hotels, or their children who had married bought land and built houses, large and small. The noise of the lawnmower was heard: Eagle Lake through pipe and hose watered the burnt plains, and the brilliant green of the lawn, with the more brilliant nasturtiums, gladioli, phlox, and roses sprang into life, bringing out the deep greens of the spruce and pine, and adding distance and dignity to the mountains behind.

What place is there, say the old residents, what place is there in the world, say travellers, which combines as does Mount Desert the glories, joys, and air of mountain and sea? — while physical comfort and art now have a part, for in the Hall of Arts, a Greek temple in the woods, are heard the musicians of the world.

With each succeeding change we have been told that Mount Desert was spoiled: the old days had gone. But neither clothes, pearls, nor automobiles can steal away the beauty of the mountains, the glory of sea and cliff, and the bracing air. Compensations, too, there have been, especially in the stimulating company. One of the richest contributions to my life has been the friendships gained at Bar Harbor and the companionship of able men.

Dr. Weir Mitchell, for instance, the pioneer and leader of nerve treatment, who gloried more in his novels and poems than in his professional leadership, was an unmitigated admirer of Mount Desert, and in his walks until over eighty covered the mountains, opened paths like the Cadillac, and talked most interestingly as he walked. He had been in Phillips Brooks's Philadelphia days, and through later life an intimate friend. He took pride in having suggested to Brooks the texts and subjects of some of his great sermons; and whenever I preached, would join me after service, and walking home would tell me more about my sermon than I knew myself, and insist on my trying out his subjects. I could fill a book with his absorbing talk and anecdotes.

John S. Kennedy was a canny Scotsman and a strong character. Beginning in a lowly position, he rose high in the railroad-building world, and as a friend and worker with James Hill amassed a great fortune, which he used, gave, and bequeathed in a generous and wise way. His avocation in the summer was the improvement of Bar

Harbor. Finding a meagre water supply in the hands of Rodick, he formed a rival company, obtained a charter from the Maine Legislature, and, opening the purchase of stock to others, saved Bar Harbor from conflagration and arid lawns and so created gardens. He saw to it that liquor saloons were kept out of sight and gambling-places driven out of town. One day he said to me, 'Bishop, there is a new gambling-hell here.' 'Strange, Mr. Kennedy,' I replied, 'that you are always the first man to know when a gambling-place opens. How is that?' He had a keen sense of humor, and, while reputed to be as keen as any Scotsman in a trade, was very kindly.

Morris K. Jesup was another citizen of great worth and public spirit, a near neighbor and warm friend. He did more than any one to finance Peary's expedition to the North Pole. We joined him one afternoon on his launch to see Peary off on the trip before that on which he discovered the Pole in his strange, double-ended ship, The Roosevelt, loaded as she was above the gunwales with every sort of preparation for the Arctic. It was a thrilling sight to watch her sail north in the light of the setting sun. The beautiful library perpetuates Mr. Jesup's memory.

Professor James B. Thayer, of the Harvard Law School, was there from the first; and later his son Ezra, Dean of the School. Was there ever a more delightful *raconteur* than Abram Hewitt, former Mayor of New York, unless one excepts General Horace Porter of Grant's staff, Ambassador to France and after-dinner speaker. President Harris of Amherst, Edward Coles, Charles Morrill, David Ogden, A. J. Cassatt, Butler Duncan, Robert Amory, John I. Kane, Montgomery Sears, George Bowdoin, Johnston Livingston, Charles Howe, A. Murray Young, and a host of names come to mind.

Captain Mahan, at the time almost unknown, walked the roads and hills in the afternoons, while in the mornings he wrote those volumes on 'Sea Power' as the secret of national dominance which aroused governments and peoples.

In 1881, President Eliot, who had before encamped on Calf Island in Frenchman's Bay, built a cottage on the Asticou Mountain side of North-East Harbor, and immediately gave distinction to the name of a harbor, which, although on the south side of the island, was in early days given its name because it was northeast of the older fishing village, South-West Harbor.

Bishop Doane of Albany built later a cottage in the centre of North-East Harbor, and there was soon a rustic chapel of timber and slabs, whose sides burst out into enlargements to meet the needs of a congregation, which, standing outside as well as within, took part in the service. For years before his death I was a devoted friend of the Bishop. I never knew him to fail in courtesy, courage, or faith. Although we were closely bound in many interests, the Board of Missions, the General Conventions, my memories of him at North-East Harbor are the freshest. His was a winning personality, and there gathered around him at North-East Harbor in cottage and hotel a circle of friends that was unique — Seth Low, President Gilman of Johns Hopkins, Professor Fisher of Yale, William Huntington of Grace Church, New York, Edward Perkins and Samuel Eliot of Boston, Bishop Greer, and a host of others. Saint Mary's Church was a spiritual centre whose influence spread throughout the country as the summer people went back to their winter homes.

In his early years he was bitten by a devotion to all things English in ecclesiastical and social standards. His enunciation was English: he adopted the apron and leggings as well as the shovel hat; at North-East he often wore a blue ribbon around the crown of his hat. At heart he was a true American. In later years I once said to him, 'Bishop, you have broadened and deepened so since you were consecrated, there is nothing left of you that was consecrated except your apron and leggings.' His answer was, 'Do you know, Lawrence, that I sometimes wish I had dropped them.'

In Saint Mary's gathered people of all denominations from over the country. To them he preached in simple, loving language; and together by his invitation all partook at the Lord's Table. The sunset services for the young people on the shore of Somes Sound, which still continue, dwell in the memories of hundreds of men and women as happy hours of their youth.

Seal Harbor, first settled by college professors and other teachers with small incomes, has grown apace, and deservedly, because of its picturesque cove, its glorious sunsets, its walks and nearness to that national, even international tea-house at Jordan's Pond. Here attractive cottages have been built, and men and women of culture have sojourned; here Lord and Lady Bryce passed two summers; and now the hilltops are crowned by the houses of the very rich, who enjoy scene and air as did we of other years, and who are doing much to prepare the island for the invasion of the American people. For in Mount Desert is the only National Park, Sieur de Monts, east of the Mississippi: and unlike most National Parks, it exists not by government purchase, but by the free gift of lovers of Mount Desert.

President Eliot with his usual foresight created with others a body of Trustees of Public Reservations, and a few of us were drawn into service. Working for several years under a charter, and adding to the original gifts other tracts, including most of the mountains of eastern Mount Desert, the trustees, represented by the indefatigable George Dorr, handed over this magnificent group of mountains, lakes, cliffs, and vales to the Government, which will, we trust, conserve their beauties for the benefit of coming generations.

In 1889 we built our house at Bar Harbor. Short holidays had permitted only short visits on my part. Julia with home responsibilities had never accompanied me, and, to speak the truth, was a bit jealous of the place, due to my laudation of scenes and people. Cambridge life permitted longer vacations, and one summer she accom-

THE FAMILY AT BAR HARBOR, 1924

panied me in a visit to my sister, Mary Amory, who had built a cottage perched on a hill in the midst of woods, and with an unbroken view of the mountains, the 'Eyrie.' Her prejudices vanished, and she was captivated.

The beauties of the shore never compensated in our minds for the chill and fogs. Hence we built our house on the eastern slope of School House Hill, on a small plateau with steep declivity overlooking without seeing the village. Here in a cottage of Austrian Tyrolese style, heavy-timbered, of rounded plank surface, we have lived, a grateful and happy family, for over thirty-six summers. Protected from intrusion by the estate of one of our good neighbors, the late General Morrell, and Mrs. Morrell, though within a stone's throw of hotels and cottages, we are undisturbed. From the piazza we look north under a great pine tree across Frenchman's Bay to Sorrento and the Gouldsboro Hills; then over Bar Island, the Porcupines, and Iron Bound to the mainland, Grindstone Neck and Schoodic Mountain; with vision sweeping east and south we see the open ocean, and Egg Rock Light, then Sol's Cliff, Newport, Dry, and Green Mountains, divided by the Gorge. Beneath the piazza is the tennis court where our seven children have played, and our little garden. Twice we have been driven by fire at night to the town for refuge, rushing the baby through the wooded avenue with large cinders and burning bits of wood falling on his blanket.

We have watched the sails of schooners, yachts, and dories driven by the east wind laden with fog, scurrying for the harbor. Great squadrons of the Navy, American and British, have come to anchor. Early one morning in the summer of 1914, at the opening of the war, as we looked out upon the Bay, there was the German ocean liner, the Kron-Prinzessin Cecilie, which with a full complement of passengers and ten million dollars in gold was turned back by order from Germany when only eight hundred miles from the other side, lest she be captured by the British. Running for the nearest neutral port, Bar

Harbor, she was piloted up the Bay by one of the passengers, a summer cottager who had sailed in her for Europe. This was our first vivid note of war.

Three years later we joined the people of the hamlet of Hull's Cove in dedicating the flagstaff and service flag; while as we drove through the lonely roads of Maine and passed the farmhouses, the starred flags in the windows, some of them golden stars, gave silent testimony to sacrifice; for from the fields and homesteads had gone the boys whom the parents had expected to carry on the farm as had their forbears.

CHAPTER XV

THE GENERAL CONVENTION IN BOSTON

1904

WHEN thinking over the coming of the General Convention to Boston, due in October, 1904, I felt that it would be of great advantage to the churches in England and this country if the Archbishop of Canterbury should be present. We could learn much from him, and in his consideration of the question of education then burning in England, and of the coming question of representative Church Government, he could learn something from us. Hence I took with me to Lambeth in 1903 an invitation from the Presiding Bishop, and had such talks with the Archbishop as to give me some hope that he might come. Archbishop Davidson has a very open mind; he took pleasure in the thought of being the first Archbishop of Canterbury to visit the United States and Canada; he fully appreciated what he might learn; but he is probably, year in and year out, the hardest-worked man in Great Britain: hence the obstacles to an absence were many.

In the spring of 1904, Mr. Pierpont Morgan, to whom I had spoken of the possibility of the Archbishop's coming, offered to do what he could when in London to prevail on him and Mrs. Davidson; and before sailing for home, he cabled his success.

Our family had increased so that during the winter we had enlarged our house at Bar Harbor to accommodate twenty-four persons — a large household for Mrs. Lawrence, who had kept house ever since our marriage, and who carried the responsibilities of children, guests, and servants with ability, working at times beyond her strength. It was a fortunate addition, for the Archbishop and Mrs. Davidson accepted our invitation to make a visit at Bar Harbor.

On the 26th of July, two months before the arrival of the party, I received a telegram from Mr. Morgan in New York, 'Expect me to-morrow morning to make arrangements for the Archbishop's visit.' At half-past seven I met him at the ferry. Bishop Doane from North-East Harbor joined us later; and, talking for two hours on the piazza, we completed the details of a visit memorable in many respects.

After I had dispatched the itinerary to the Associated Press, I said to Mr. Morgan, 'Is this all that you came down for, and how did you come?' 'Of course it is all,' he answered; 'I wanted to be sure that every detail was understood; so I decided to take the ten o'clock night train from Boston and wired you. But I had forgotten a United States Steel executive meeting in the afternoon; so I wired Tuttle [President of the Boston and Maine Railroad] that I was taking the five o'clock train from New York, due in Boston at ten, and asked him to look after me. We got to Boston at ten, drove across the city, and at ten-sixteen I was starting with a special engine and car to catch the train, which we did at Portland; and here I am.'

The next day the Corsair poked her nose around Sol's Cliff. Mr. Morgan boarded her, and ran back to New York — all to 'arrange the details of the Archbishop's visit.' It was characteristic of him.

The Archbishop had said very properly that he must make his first official appearance in Canada. His ship was several hours late in reaching New York. Hurrying the party into the special train, Mr. Morgan landed them at the door of the Cathedral in Quebec just an hour before the hour for service. From there they came to Mount Desert, and visited Bishop Doane at North-East Harbor.

On the 26th of September, they came to us, the Archbishop and Mrs. Davidson, two chaplains, the Reverend Messrs. Ellison and Holden, and for four days they had the freedom of the island. Dinners and receptions there were, of course; but they were so easy and natural that they seemed to belong in the house and hills. As they arrived,

I said, 'A rest, a drive, a walk, or what?' 'Oh, a walk,' was their answer. 'Mr. Morgan has carried us everywhere, and we have not felt the American soil.' As we were coming back across the golf links, I remember Ellison, who was playing, pointing up the Gorge to the mountains, and shouting to the Archbishop, Scotsman as he was, 'Scotland, Scotland.'

Just at that time the London 'Times' was full of letters about the necessity of making the workmen's cottages more secure against fire. What was their surprise at seeing our wooden houses and learning that death from fire in small cottages was very rare! Hence, whenever they saw such a house building, they jumped off the buckboard, studied the construction, and soon the 'Times' had their letters from American experience.

In the Church of Saint Saviour the Archbishop preached and celebrated the Holy Communion for the first time in this country.

On their departure Julia and I hurried back to Boston with the household, and for the next few days worked overtime in arranging for the coming of the Convention. We kept both our Cambridge and Boston houses open and ready for guests. Committees, too, had been at work during the summer, and so efficiently that by October 4th, on the arrival of the members of the Convention, everything was ready. There were eighty Bishops, who with the officers of the Convention were to be personally entertained, most of them in private houses: some four hundred Deputies, who with their wives and large contingent of Church people, members of societies and guilds, were to tax the hotel accommodations of the city. A special building was appropriated to give all members a daily luncheon. Trinity Church was devoted to the opening service and other great services, as well as to the daily Morning Prayer, where for the first time in the Convention's history there was a full choir every day. The House of Deputies met in Emmanuel Church, and the House of Bishops in its Chapel. The sessions lasted three weeks. To each Deputy was given a little volume, a short history of the Episcopal Church written for the occasion by Dean Hodges, an elaborate guidebook to the Metropolitan District, and a 'Church Militant,' with pictures of every church in the Diocese. I have always taken great satisfaction in recalling the perfect arrangements of the committee and the hospitality of the Boston people.

The courteous entertainment of one Bishop was much on my mind, that of the aged and saintly colored Bishop of Liberia; and I gave special injunctions to the office that he should be taken to my sister Hetty's house, our homestead in Longwood. To my surprise, word came to me that he was boarding elsewhere. I sought him out, and told him that my sister was expecting him; when he, with the humility and grace which belong to the best of the colored people, said, 'You are very kind, Bishop, and I thank you, but I have a very comfortable room and good board with a respectable colored woman; she is doing all that she can for me, and I would rather stay there; my Lord liked to live among the lowly.'

The Archbishop and his party came to us in Commonwealth Avenue the afternoon before the Convention, and were given a dinner by my brother Amory of forty representative citizens, ex-Secretaries Long and Olney, Senator Lodge, Charles F. Choate, Henry L. Higginson, Dr. Edward Everett Hale, and others. In introducing the Archbishop after the dinner, I called his attention to the thought that in all probability he had never before dined with forty men of such pure English blood as those at the table.

The fact that the Archbishop was the first Primate of the Mother Church to visit the United States and the daughter of the Church of England, raised or might have raised certain questions which interest sticklers for precedents, but which were settled in a moment by the wisdom and humility of the Presiding Bishop, Dr. Tuttle, and the Archbishop.

The Church in the United States is an independent

BISHOP LAWRENCE AND THE ARCHBISHOP OF CANTERBURY
1904

national Church, and the Presiding Bishop is its Metropolitan, as the Archbishop is the Primate of the Church of England. Hence in this country the Archbishop took the secondary place, and his crozier, which at the request of rectors he had used at Bar Harbor and other parish churches, lay throughout these days in its long, coffin-like box on the floor of our hall. Special duties in these arrangements fell to me as Bishop of the Diocese. As the opening service and the events of the day were of the highest significance to me and in my life, I quote from my diary.

Wed., Oct. 5. Beautiful weather. Eleventh anniversary of my consecration. A wonderful and surprising day.

A.M. 11: Trinity Church, Opening service of General Convention. Great crowd. All beautifully ordered. Bp. Tuttle presiding: he and Archbishop side by side. The latter had agreed decidedly with us that he had better not use his crozier. Bp. Tuttle entered the chancel first and took the service.

Bp. Doane preached a noble sermon. The Bishops were all in the sedilia and chairs in the apse. The music simple and fine: congregation sang. Bp. Tuttle administered to the Archbishop: and as I was serving Bp. Tuttle, they administered to me first, Tuttle the bread, the Archbishop the wine. I am the first to receive Communion at the hands of the American and English Churches as represented in their heads. The Archbishop wore his convocation robes as he did at Mt. Desert.

After the service I had 20 senior Bishops to lunch, and Bishop of Hereford and Archbishop. As they left, Bp. Brewer said to me, 'If some one nominates you as Chairman, don't decline to allow your name to be used.' I answered that the idea was so unexpected I had nothing to say: I had no idea anybody wanted to vote for me; but that if they and the House asked me to do anything, it was my duty to obey. The Bp. of Delaware a few minutes later said the same thing.

After House ready for business, Bp. Tuttle presiding, Dr. Hart elected Sec., nominations for Chairman were called for. Bp. Whitaker was nominated. He said his health would not allow him to serve. Then nominations being again asked for, I heard my name: several stood and seconded. To my amazement, no one else was nominated, and the Sec. was asked by a unanimous vote to cast a ballot for me. The most overwhelming and surprising thing that ever happened to me: most gratifying, yet I felt so helpless and incompetent. I entered the House of Bishops eleven years ago: ten years ago was my first meeting, and I was received coldly by some and suspected by others as a heretic. Now this comes: most creditable to the charity and broadmindedness of the high churchmen. Why they should have elected me, and so handsomely, I don't understand. I am bewildered by the action, delighted and humbled, and afraid of their disappointment at my incompetence.

Then began three of the busiest weeks of my life. My first duty was the appointment of committees, in which I had the great help of Bishop Doane, who had been Chairman a few years before. As Chairman, I presided morning and afternoon over the House of Bishops, was present and spoke at various meetings of organizations; and as host of the Convention and the Archbishop, was called on for all sorts of social and public occasions. In the midst of it, all Julia's jewelry was stolen while we were having a reception one evening; and so busy were we that we had no time to help the police towards the detection of the thief: we never had a clue.

The Archbishop was a constant attendant upon the Convention, studying the methods, listening to the debates, and with his wise and prophetic mind adapting them to conditions in the Church of England, which since then has created under his leadership the National Church Assembly and has taken other important steps towards legislative autonomy.

As the Archbishop is a representative and distinguished citizen of Great Britain, I felt that the citizens of Boston should meet him. Hence a Citizens' Committee, with Henry Higginson as Chairman, arranged for a noonday reception at Faneuil Hall at which Mr. Olney and President Eliot spoke. As we two walked over Beacon Hill down to the Hall, I said, 'I have no idea what will be the response to the call for this meeting; there may be only fifty there: there may be a crowd.' The situation at the main door answered the question. We had to get in by the back platform door, and found the Hall, with the floor cleared of chairs, packed with men; and what is always interesting at a Faneuil Hall meeting, a sprinkling of butchers in their white smocks.

President Eliot in his address referred to the fact that the Puritans had fled from England to escape Archbishop Laud, and hinted at the hospitality of the sons of the Puritans in welcoming one of Laud's successors. To which the Archbishop responded, 'Shortly before leaving England, I happened upon the last part of the diary of Archbishop Laud written in the Tower when waiting for his execution, running somewhat as follows: "Rumor hath it that I am about to be deported to the Colony of Massachusetts Bay. May the good Lord prevent me from such a fate." '

Dock Square was so crowded with citizens wishing to meet the Archbishop that a line was formed after the meeting whereby they were able to enter and circle around the Hall, bowing to the Archbishop standing on the front of the stage.

. In Sanders Theatre he spoke to a mass meeting of students; in Park Street Church to the ministers of Boston; and on other occasions. The Art Museum was opened for a great reception to him and Mrs. Davidson. They received the members of the Convention and their friends one beautiful afternoon at our Cambridge home, between the Theological School and the Longfellow House, both of which were open to guests: seventeen hundred and fifty persons by actual count passing through my study in two hours were received by Archbishop and Mrs. Davidson.

At the close of his visit and after the presentation to him by the Bishops of a silver vase for Lambeth Palace, he and Mrs. Davidson took leave of us, leaving with every one the happy memory of graciousness, tact, and wisdom, of humility and a spirit of brotherhood.

Meanwhile the work of the General Convention had gone steadily on. Although my only experience as a presiding officer had been in the Diocesan Conventions for ten years, I found the duties of Chairman of the House of Bishops comparatively easy; for the members were sympathetic and desirous on the whole of getting through business promptly. The essentials of a chairman are a spirit of fair play and an ability to convince the House that fairness is his purpose, clearness and promptness of decision, courtesy and patience. While every member of the House gave me cordial support, I was most fortunate during the six years in the Secretary and Presiding Bishop. The Reverend Doctor Hart, the Secretary, was the best of Connecticut products, a scholar and teacher, clear of thought and painstaking in action, with a keen sense of humor.

Of the Presiding Bishop, Daniel S. Tuttle, my chief, I cannot speak in too warm terms of admiration and affection. His career is too well known to require repetition. Consecrated at thirty, the earliest canonical age, to be the Missionary Bishop of Montana, Idaho, and Utah, when they were practically without railroads, leaving the railroad at its end near Omaha, he went by stage to Denver and Montana armed with rifles and ammunition against Indian attacks. He travelled with his rifle in his lap by day and his pistol under his pillow by night. During his first year he lived alone in his cabin with his cat. A man of refinement and a scholar, also of great physical strength and courage, of humility, humor, and consecration, he was revered on every stage-route in that vast country. Later Bishop of Utah, and at this time Bishop of Missouri, he was when in Boston, sixty-seven years old and very deaf, but with the alertness of mind and body of a young man. As he was unable to hear his own voice well, it would sometimes break forth into a roar and then drop almost to a whisper. How vividly every one who has been present at his consecration of bishops recalls his emphasis, his shout, and then his softened and tremulous appeal, 'Be to the flock of Christ a shepherd, not a wolf: feed them, devour them not. Hold up the weak, heal the sick, bind up the broken, bring again the outcasts, seek the lost.' As he always asked me when present to sing the 'Veni Creator' at the laying on of hands, I can testify, standing beside him again and again, to the reality and depth of his emotion. No slightest detail in the conduct of the office was too insignificant for his care. He always arrived the day before; went into the church, studied the chancel, and with his own hand wrote out the directions for each officiating bishop: I have many of them, and keep them with pride and affection. Here is one of the last handed me by him just before the consecration of Dr. Manning as Bishop of New York in the Cathedral of Saint John the Divine.

I will quote it, for it is alive with his sympathy, humility and affection: and note that these minute directions are the work of a man eighty-four years of age, in his own firm handwriting.

The Bishop of Massachusetts:

Read the Epistle, Acts 10:17.
Sit at left of Presiding Bishop.
Lay on both hands.
Please sing the Veni Creator for the Presiding Bishop.
Wait until the bishops have grouped themselves about the Bishop-elect, and until the Presiding Bp. nods to you. Then you nod to the organist, and he will give you the keynote.
It will be for you to see the organist before the service, that you may understand each other.
Please be ears for me.
In the Litany immediately after the Amen of 'We humbly beseech Thee, O Father,' I wish to take up the special prayer, 'Almighty God, giver of all good things, etc.,' and I may not hear when the Amen is said. I will look to you for that special prayer.
Also after the Trisagion I may not know when the choir finishes, so that I may go on to the prayer of Humble Access — I will look to you to nod.

Although I was thirteen years his junior, and he under no obligation to ask my advice in matters before him, he did so uniformly, and received what I wrote, humbly thanking me, and sometimes revising his decisions. Of jealousy there was never a note: of charity he was full. Upon his death at eighty-six years of age, I counted it a privilege to preach the memorial sermon in his Cathedral in the City of St. Louis, of which he was the leading and beloved citizen.

There was a fine missionary spirit throughout the Convention: and to my great gratification Logan Roots was made Missionary Bishop of Hankow. My first memory of him was when he, a rather unpromising-looking Freshman from Little Rock, Arkansas, called on me in Cambridge; his eye was alert, however, and his smile as pleasant as it is to-day. He was one of my boys in the Theological Seminary, and has been a source of pride to me ever since. Eight years before, when he was a candidate for Holy Orders, I had commended him to Bishop Graves in these words:

I have known Mr. Roots almost ever since he entered Harvard University. He has steadily developed in force of character and religious life. He has shown himself to be not only a faithful and capable student, but a man of exceptional parts in gaining the confidence of others and in rousing their enthusiasm. . . . The best men are needed for foreign missions, we all realize that, and Mr. Roots is one of the best. I feel, therefore, that you can have more than usual confidence in the wisdom of any plans or wishes in respect to his future work.

A month later he was consecrated in Emmanuel Church. Bishop Graves presided: I was a presenter and the preacher.

At the closing service of the General Convention, Bishop Potter, a leader of his time in Church and Nation, read the Pastoral Letter. After the Convention dissolved, I went downtown and bought a breastpin for Julia as a token of the whole occasion and to replace one of her stolen jewels.

Happy and quaint memories of the Bishops come to my mind as I write. I recall how the delightful Bishop Randolph of Southern Virginia, coming in during the session, stepped quietly up to my side and said, 'Bishop, what an awful waste of time it is for us to pass our days here tinkering Canons while there is the beautiful Public Library in Copley Square where we might be reading and learning something.'

Bishop Niles, who told me this himself, wandered out one day and sat on a bench in the Public Garden. He was of huge bulk and in his effort to rise from the bench he rolled a bit from one side to the other without success. Just then a little girl ran up saying, 'Let me help you get up, Mister.' 'Oh, no, my little girl, I am too heavy: you cannot help me up.' 'Oh, yes, I can,' she answered, 'I have helped Grandpa up lots of times when he was drunker than you are.'

One feature of the Convention days was unique. Bishop Boyd Carpenter of Ripon, England, had crossed the ocean to give the William Belden Noble Lectures at Harvard on the Evidences of Christianity — not a popular or drawing subject. Leaving his wife very ill in New York, he went over and back, being with us while in Boston. The number of people who wished to hear him was so great that the audience adjourned from the hall of Phillips Brooks House to that of the Fogg Art Museum; and before the course was ended, the audience had packed Sanders Theatre: an example of eloquent exposition of such a subject unknown in the history of the University.

CHAPTER XVI
HARVARD TEACHERS' ENDOWMENT
JUNE, 1904–1905

'HARVARD' has been a word familiar to me from the cradle. My father being for some years Treasurer and member of the Corporation, later an Overseer, had a part in almost every movement for the welfare of the College, often raising money and giving. 'My Harvard education costs me heavily every year,' he used to say.

From the time that I at twelve years of age walked over to Cambridge to see the dancing around the Tree on Class Day afternoon until now, I have been at almost every Class Day or Commencement — over sixty years. As I shall refer often to Harvard, it may be well for me once and for all to state my various connections.

Entering in 1867 and graduating in 1871, I was during the next year one of the few first 'resident graduates,' the beginnings of the Graduate School.

After eleven years in Andover, Philadelphia, and Lawrence, during which my interest in the college was active, I returned to Cambridge in January, 1884, having as one considerable part of my duties the pastoral care of students attending Saint John's Memorial Chapel as well as of many others. I preached in Appleton Chapel from time to time, and gave several baccalaureate sermons. The system of voluntary attendance at prayers and Sunday services having been adopted in 1886, I was appointed in 1888 a Preacher to the University, which involved the conduct of daily prayers for six weeks, besides weekday mornings in Wadsworth House for conferences with such students as called, and four sermons a year. While my work as preacher was probably helpful, I do not think that it was particularly effective. I was too familiar a person in Cambridge; and the students were naturally drawn by men of greater intellectual power and eloquence as well as of greater distinction. The service in the chapel, too, seemed to me, accustomed to the services of the Episcopal Church, rather cold, slow, and lacking in hearty response. Since those days these conditions have improved much. Hence the duty of preacher and adviser often weighed heavily on me. However, I served by annual appointment from 1888 to 1891, and from 1910 to 1913.

At the Commencement of 1893, immediately after my election as Bishop, I received the honorary degree of S.T.D. In 1896, at the twenty-fifth anniversary of the Class of '71, I served by the election of my class committee and appointment by the Corporation as Chief Marshal: a gratifying honor.

From June, 1899, to October, 1908, I was Vice-President of the Harvard Alumni and Chairman of the Executive Committee. By the initiative and industry of others rather than myself, the Alumni Association was reorganized, and Edgar Wells appointed as its first full-time secretary. Believing that younger men should take hold, I declined reëlection in 1908.

At the founding of the 'Harvard Graduates' Magazine' in 1892, I was made a member of the Council until 1898, serving as Vice-President from 1898 to 1913 and as President from 1913 to 1915. To William Roscoe Thayer and a few others was due the creation of this magazine whose numbers record the contemporary history of the University. Harvard has had no more loyal, industrious, and scholarly graduate than Thayer. In his modest home on Berkeley Street, a few yards from our house, were written many of his noble and illuminating interpretations of Italian history and modern leaders.

For several years I was a member of the committee of the Phi Beta Kappa to select the orator and poet and this year am President of the Chapter.

As to the two chief Governing Boards, I served as Overseer from 1894 to 1906; then according to law was ineligible for reëlection that year. In 1907 I was again Overseer, and served until, on the death of Dr. Arthur Cabot, I was elected in January, 1913, to take his place as a Fellow and member of the Corporation, where I now serve.

For labor given I have received manifold return in satisfaction and honors.

On March 20, 1904, President Eliot reached the age of seventy. A committee, headed, I think, by Henry Higginson, planned for its recognition by all alumni throughout the world. At their request I undertook the difficult task of preparing an address which also passed under the eye and criticism of Le Baron Briggs. Reverence for Dr. Eliot might tempt one to undue adulation; but those who knew him could say nothing but that which was honest. This address, mailed to every alumnus with a slip enclosed, brought nearly ten thousand signatures; and on the birthday, before a great company of officers, teachers, alumni, and students, Nelson Perkins read and presented the address to the President.

DEAR MR. PRESIDENT:

As with undiminished power you pass the age of seventy, we greet you.

Thirty-five years ago you were called to be President of Harvard College. At the age of thirty-five you became the head of an institution whose history was long, whose traditions were firm, and whose leading counsellors were of twice your age. With prophetic insight you anticipated the movements of thought and life; your face was toward the coming day. In your imagination the College was already the University. . . .

You have upheld the old studies and uplifted the new. You have given a new definition to a liberal education. The University has become the expression of the highest intellectual forces of the present as well as the past.

You have held firm from the first that teacher and student alike grow strong through freedom. Working eagerly with you and for you are men whose beliefs, whether in education or in religion, differ widely from your own, yet who know that in speaking out their beliefs they are not more loyal to themselves than to you. By your faith in a young man's use of intellectual and spiritual freedom you have given new dignity to the life of the college student.

The universities and the colleges throughout the land, though some are slow to accept your principles and adopt your methods, all feel your power and recognize with gratitude your stimulating influence and your leadership.

Through you the American people have begun to see that a university is not a cloister for the recluse, but an expression of all that is best in the Nation's thought and character. From Harvard University men go into every part of our national life. To Harvard University come from the common schools, through paths that have been broadened by your work, the youth who have the capacity and the will to profit by her teaching. Your influence is felt in the councils of the teachers and in the education of the youngest child.

As a son of New England you have sustained the traditions of her patriots and scholars. By precept and example you have taught that the first duty of every citizen is to his country. In public life you have been independent and outspoken; in private life you have stood for simplicity. In the great and bewildering conflict of economic and social questions you have with clear head and firm voice spoken for the fundamental principles of democracy and the liberties of the people.

More gracious to the sons of Harvard than your services as educator or citizen is your character. Your outward reserve has concealed a heart more tender than you have trusted yourself to reveal. Defeat of your cherished plans has disclosed your patience and magnanimity and your willingness to bide your time.

Fearless, just, and wise, of deep and simple faith, serene in affliction, self-restrained in success, unsuspected by any man of self-interest, you command the admiration of all men and the gratitude and loyalty of the sons of Harvard.

On April 11, 1904, Samuel Hoar died. He was a staunch representative of a staunch ancestry of New England and Concord, member of the Corporation and President of the Alumni Association. A few weeks before Commencement, I was notified that, as his place as President of the Alumni Association must be filled in anticipation of the Commencement dinner, I had been selected by the Executive Committee for nomination and election at noon of that day, and should be prepared for the duty.

My life in Cambridge and friendship with many college teachers, as well as my knowledge as Overseer of college conditions, led me to the decision that some action must be taken, and that soon, to place the teaching staff upon a better financial footing.

Annual deficits had been running for several years. Other universities, especially Chicago, were offering much larger salaries, which, however, several Harvard men had declined: other teachers were becoming restless. The Corporation had lately cut down the salary list by thirty thousand dollars; and the Overseers had resolved to call a halt. There was strong and reasonable pressure for the increase of the tuition fee, a step to be avoided, if possible, for State universities with free tuition were springing up over the country, and Harvard had a responsibility to the people of Massachusetts which had no State university.

While thinking over the strongest way of meeting this situation in my speech at the Alumni Dinner, I determined not to mention the subject to the President, but to let the challenge for action come from the alumni body as a spontaneous offer to help the President and Governing Boards out of the difficulty. Having, therefore, through Charles F. Adams and others gotten the figures and gauged the public sentiment, I gave the facts to the alumni and President Eliot in Memorial Hall, told them that if Harvard were to hold its primacy, at least one hundred thousand dollars additional income was needed, stated the possible ways out, and finally called on the alumni to come to the help of the University and raise and give at least two million, five hundred thousand dollars for the increase of the salaries of the teachers in the College of Liberal Arts.

Having said my say, I supposed my duty was done. What was my dismay, however, at receiving letters from Henry Higginson, the President, and others saying that it was my duty as President of the Alumni Association to form a committee and get to work. In vain I pleaded my inexperience in raising money, which at that time was a fact, the coming of the General Convention in the autumn, and my duties as Bishop. Frank Higginson positively refused to lead, but said that he would take the laboring oar in Boston, which he did finely.

In November, with the Convention out of my way and my desk and docket of back work cleared, I was able to take up the problem of raising two million, five hundred thousand dollars. This was over twenty years ago, long before campaigns for great sums were thought of or the word 'drive' invented. There had, of course, been money-raising campaigns by the Y.M.C.A. and other organizations, but this industry, which has thriven since, was in its infancy.

My experience had been limited to the Hasty Pudding Club and the raising of one or two sums of one hundred thousand dollars. We therefore had to feel our way. As the core of a committee of ten well-known alumni, three of us formed the working staff, and later experience has shown me that three is enough: Frank Higginson, Robert Bacon, and myself. Our only central office was under my hat. Our publicity consisted in a few syndicated articles on Harvard at a total cost of five hundred dollars, and such editorials and news as we could get into the papers. It fell to me to supply the material for these and frame the circular letter to the alumni and friends of Harvard (only ten thousand at that time), who were our only constituency. As a boy I loathed Latin composition; but in the composition of campaign literature, which demands an English style strong, direct, and suggestive, the handling of facts in a way to stimulate the imagination and the kindling of a generous sentiment, I delight. The hours and days are many which I have since given to this work. What a satisfaction it is so to frame an editorial for a Sunday paper, that, when you call upon a possible giver on Monday, he, having read the paper, tells you all about the subject as if he himself had just discovered the idea! And men are prone to give in behalf of their own discoveries.

We were agreed as to certain principles. The friends of the University were to be given an opportunity to strengthen the College by the increase of the salaries of the teachers in Liberal Arts; for we could not cover all teachers in the University. There was to be no crowding or jamming for subscriptions. It were better not to complete the full amount. As a matter of fact, the total gift fell short only about one hundred thousand dollars. We could doubtless have gotten the whole by pressure, but it was worth the amount to close with the good will and confidence of the alumni.

Our first duty was to get the facts into the heads of Harvard's friends, and in such a way as to give them a certain sense of chagrin at Harvard's parsimony, and a determination that they would do their part to increase the salaries of teachers who had loyally served them and the College.

Of the fifty-seven full professors at that time, thirteen received the maximum of $5000: the average salary was $3980. Of the thirty-eight assistant professors, nine received the maximum of $3000, the average being $2130; and of the eighty-eight instructors, one received $2000, twenty-nine from $1750 to $1100; the average being $990. The total salary list for 279 teachers was $437,821; with an average of $1570.

It also became clear to us that in the raising of such a great sum — for it was great for those days — we must first have some large gifts with which to stimulate the imagination of all and to give a thrust to later action. Hence in December, Frank Higginson and I started out in Boston on our quest for big money. I recall well one of our first defeats and first victories. One defeat was from a rich and prosperous alumnus from whom we looked for $50,000. 'While Mr. Eliot is President I will not give a dollar to the College. He treated some of our class in a shabby way, and that is enough.' By such prejudices do some men punish a university for a supposed personal slight or hurt. I note this in my diary: 'With Frank Higginson 2½ hrs. for $50,000 subscriptions: not a dollar.'

The victory was in the gift of Mr. George Parkman for

$10,000; for gifts from him were rare specimens. Upon his death he left five million dollars to the City of Boston for the improvement and upkeep of the Common and other City parks. 'Old George Parkman,' as he was usually called, was an interesting and pathetic figure. His father was murdered by Dr. Webster because it was supposed that Mr. Parkman was pressing the Doctor hard for the payment of a loan. On this account, probably, George Parkman lived in his house on Beacon Street alone and a recluse. Of slight figure and finely chiselled features, the old gentleman, very carefully dressed, walked from his house downtown as if he were a gentle duke stepping out of an old picture. On cold days he wrapped a shawl about his shoulders and held it there by his gloved hands over his chest. He spoke to no one: very few spoke to him. At our call he received us with great courtesy and some formality, expressed his interest in the cause, and promised $10,000. As I pass his house now, whereon is the tablet recording his bequest to the City, I seem to see standing at the window, the almost ghostly figure of the old man dreaming of how beautiful the Common will be some day by his beneficence, and hoarding every dollar for that one purpose.

The popular sentiment at that time was that people would give buildings which they could see, and would not give to the support of teachers: and there was good reason for this sentiment; for people had not then been educated to realize that the strength of a college or a church was not in the beauty of its fabric, but in the ability and character of the leaders. To educate the friends of the University in the value of what I have always called 'spiritual vitality' was one of our chief duties; and I am more and more clear that when this idea is rightly expressed, the response is more intelligent and generous than for buildings. Indeed, there has been great advance along this path; for men and women who are now giving buildings are doing so more and more, not for what the buildings are, or that they may be seen, but for what they may do as instruments for the expression of spiritual vitality, the upbuilding of intellectual and spiritual forces.

Colonel Henry Lee, that prince of beggars for Harvard fifty years ago, used to say that when the College needed money, she went down to State Street and got it, and that she could get it nowhere else. Up to this time the Harvard alumni outside of Massachusetts had with few exceptions never taken her needs seriously. New York had presented a boathouse, and made occasional gifts, but had done little to build up the College itself. And yet it was clear that we must strike out somewhere, and begin to reach a wider circle.

At the close of one of our committee meetings, Robert Bacon took me aside and asked if I knew Hamilton Twombly of New York. 'Certainly,' I said; 'he was a classmate and one of my most intimate friends in college, but since he has moved up into the billionaire class, I have seen little of him.' 'Well,' he replied, 'if you can enlist him, I believe that he and I together can raise one million dollars in New York in big figures!'

Of course I promised to try, and wrote Twombly immediately telling him something of what we had in hand, and saying that I was coming to see him. In half an hour after I arrived at the Albemarle Hotel, he came, and sitting down said, 'Bill, what do you want?' To which I answered, 'Ham, I want you, and have come to New York to get you: and that done, I am going home.' I then gave him the situation and told him of Robert Bacon's remark. He broke out in a stream of criticisms of the College and of President Eliot's experiments. 'I suppose you never try experiments on the New York Central,' I interjected. However, recalling college days, I realized that he had got first to blow off some steam. I therefore let him talk on for fifteen or twenty minutes, and then finally and seriously said, 'Ham, you are a graduate of Harvard: I am a graduate of Harvard: we are both of '71. Now this job has been laid on me: it is a heavy job and one that I don't want, but I have taken it. Isn't it up to you as a loyal son of Harvard to take hold too?' 'You are right, Bill,' he answered, and, falling back on his New York trading habit, he added, 'I'll take hold on one condition, and that is that Boston will raise half a million to meet New York's million.' Knowing that Frank Higginson had already close up to four hundred thousand, I said, 'Done: the bargain is closed. What do you want next?' 'Figures,' he replied. I took the train home, called on the President, Treasurer, and Bursar, and went back to New York loaded with figures.

It had seemed to me that some graduates might as a matter of sentiment prefer to specify a large gift for the endowment of a chair in the name of a beloved old professor, or perhaps a friend or relative who had died. With this in mind, I had with the help of President Eliot made out a full list of unendowed chairs, and of the names of distinguished teachers. The list included smaller sums for instructorships and fellowships. It was in my pocket during our talk; and as I mentioned the idea to Twombly, even suggesting that he might prefer to endow such a chair, he said in his bluff way, 'No, sir: we are not putting big doorplates on our houses and advertising who we are. We are merging in these days and sinking ourselves in big things and big enterprises. Stand by your big figure and forget the rest.' That list never came out again, but is on my table now as I am writing these chapters, and a very interesting array of names it is.

A few days later, Bacon, Twombly, and I met in Bacon's house on Park Avenue to get ready for Wall Street and wider fields. Then came another snag. Some of the leading New York men had said vigorously that President Eliot would use the gift to spread out and multiply courses; and they had insisted on a subscription heading more drastic than that in Boston. In vain I urged the danger of raising big money with two different forms of subscription, but it was of no use. After three hours of discussion, I said, 'Now that's done: let's get to work.' Twombly turned to Bacon with the challenge, 'We've got to start it, Bacon. I'll give what you do.' Bacon, generous fellow as he was, had already given and underwritten heavily toward his class twenty-five year fund of the next June. 'I'll give what you do, Twombly.' 'Fifty thousand it is,' was the response. So they signed their names to the figure. We lunched at Delmonico's, and they started downtown for the million. After they had gotten $800,000 in $50,000 bits from a few graduates and friends of Harvard, of whom three lived elsewhere, but had business in New York, Twombly went to Florida and left the faithful Bacon to worry, lie awake nights, and finally complete the subscription list; which also lies on my table.

Very few persons know the names; for in all campaigns for which I have been responsible I have never made public the name of a subscriber. I believe that if any one is asked to give a large sum, he has a right to know semi-confidentially who are investing largely, but that done, no publicity of names.

A few years ago, when inaugurating a million-dollar campaign, I had the editors of the Boston papers to luncheon, gave them the story, and asked their aid, which they cordially promised. One of them then said, 'We will publish the names of all your subscribers, Bishop.' 'Not a name,' I responded. 'But publicity leads others to give,' he answered. 'Perhaps so,' was my answer, 'but it is not my way. Men and women who are close-fisted and make a gift do not want their next week's mail loaded with appeals: generous men and women do not care to be advertised. The rightness of the cause is the most lasting appeal and the best publicity.'

Thus through the loyalty and generosity of these two men, Harvard got onto the list of public-spirited people in New York, as it has later throughout the country; and the harvest has been increasingly rich. I took to the road along the Gold Coast, Philadelphia, Baltimore, Washington, and elsewhere. Looking up Murray Crane in the Senate, I told him the story, and in his quaint way and nasal voice he said, 'Those Harvard people have been good to me: you can have twenty-five thousand dollars.' As the spring approached, the class secretaries and class committees entered the campaign and the pledges of the alumni, small and large, poured into the Treasurer's office.

The two differing subscription headings followed me, as I feared, up to the week of Commencement. I was worried as I seldom have been since, lest we lose the New York million or else the other subscriptions. Hours of talk and sleep it cost me; but in the end the combined wisdom of John C. Gray in Boston and Joseph Choate in New York framed a few lines which met the situation.

When Commencement Day of 1905 came, it was so mingled with other interests, the twenty-fifth anniversary of Roosevelt's and Robert Bacon's Class of '80, that I must go back and trace the history of several years.

CHAPTER XVII

THEODORE ROOSEVELT AT HARVARD

1900–1904

As I was dining with Roosevelt's sister Anna, Mrs.
Cowles, in Washington, sometime in February, 1900, she
said, 'You know that we are quite disturbed that Cabot
Lodge is urging Theodore for the Vice-Presidency.'

It so happened that Roosevelt and I were at Groton
School one night the following June. In the early morning
he burst into my room half-dressed, and, before I was
fully awake, said, 'Bishop, can you tell a bewildered Governor what time it is? My watch has stopped, and if I am
late to breakfast in this school, I may be disciplined.'

At breakfast I said to him, 'Why is Cabot pressing you
for nomination to the Vice-Presidency?' 'Well,' he answered, 'you know that Cabot is a very partial friend, and
he thinks that I am good presidential timber after McKinley's second term is over, and that, if I were Vice-President, I would be in line for the renomination.' 'What do
you think of it yourself?' I said. 'I don't think. What is the
use of thinking of what is going to happen in the kaleido-
scope of politics four or five years hence? What I know is
that I have a good job. I am Governor of New York, and
having a first-rate time of it. I am filling the offices with
good men: and they will last out for some time. Of
course, Platt wants to get rid of me, although we get along
pretty well together, and if he thinks that he can elect the
Republican Party without me, he will leave me out. But
I think he will discover that he cannot get the election
without me; so I am in. And as for the Vice-Presidency,
I should go wild rattling around in the chair of the President of the Senate with nothing to do. The people in
charge of the nominations at the Philadelphia Convention
have promised that I shall not be nominated: some of them

do not care to have me in Washington, so I am going to the convention easy in my mind. A lot of delegates from the Middle West and elsewhere will shout for me, but they won't get their wish, and I shall stay in New York.'

We all recall what happened in Philadelphia, and later the tragedy of President McKinley's death in September, 1901, Roosevelt's night drive down the mountain, and his taking the oath of office.

On the 1st of December, 1901, the Merchants' Association of Boston, of which my brother Amory was President, gave a dinner at the Vendôme, and my seat was between Senator Hanna, who managed the McKinley campaigns, and Mr. Watterson of the Louisville 'Courier-Journal.' When the dinner was well going, I said to Mr. Hanna, 'Senator, do you mind telling me the inside of Roosevelt's nomination to the Vice-Presidency?' 'Not at all,' he answered, 'I will do so gladly. Sometime before the convention, I was coming back from Europe, and as we entered New York Harbor, the pilot brought aboard some papers which were full of the question as to who should be nominated for Vice-President, for of course McKinley was booked for a second term as President. I noticed that ex-Governor Woodruff's name was prominent. On landing, I went directly to Washington to see the President at the White House. Early in the conversation I said, "Mr. President, who is to be the candidate for the Vice-Presidency?" "That is not for me to say," he replied; "it is for you people. I see that Governor Woodruff's name is mentioned." "I have seen that, too," I answered, "but if we must have a man from New York, let us have a real man and not Woodruff." The President then added, "Let me think it over a day or two, Hanna, and come again — I may have some one to suggest." In a few days I called, and the President said, "I have it, Hanna: Root is your man." "Good," I said, "Root it is," and I went off, told the rest, and got everything planned and the pipes laid for Root; when only a few days before the election I received a message to come to the White House. As I went into his office, the President said, "I have got to take it back, Senator." "You have got to take what back?" I asked. "I have got to take Root back: you cannot have him. He has the Army to reorganize and Cuba and the Philippines to settle, and I cannot let him go. He has got to stay." I protested that everybody was ready to support Root: that if we did not have him, it was too late to get any one; but the President was firm: so we had to go to Philadelphia with Long for our candidate — a kindly gentleman, but no one wanted him, and we knew it; and we had given our pledge to Roosevelt that he would not be nominated. Then when the convention opened and Mc-Kinley was nominated, the shouts and enthusiasm were all for Roosevelt. We did everything that we could to head off the stream, but we had no candidate to do it with, and of course Platt was quietly getting in his work. Finally, we had to throw up our hands, go to Roosevelt and tell him that we could not hold the crowd, and that we must go back on our pledge: and that is the whole story.'

When I told Senator Hanna's story to Douglas Robinson, Roosevelt's brother-in-law, a few years later, he said, 'That is all correct so far as I know the situation. But what do you think Theodore was doing? I was staying outside of Philadelphia, but received a message from him to come in immediately, that there was trouble. So in I drove as fast as possible, went up to the room where they all were, crowded with men talking, arguing, and shouting, and I finally found Theodore sitting quietly in a corner reading a volume of "Plutarch's Lives" which he had brought with him.'

At the Harvard Commencement of 1902, the honorary degree of LL.D. had been bestowed upon Roosevelt and Hay.

In 1904, Roosevelt was elected President by an overwhelming majority, and for several years had the eye of the whole country, usually for commendation and applause, sometimes the reverse: but he was always the centre.

As he was to receive the degree of LL.D. from Williams College in June, 1905, my cousins, Colonel and Mrs. Hopkins, gathered a little party, Joseph Choate, Morris K. Jesup, and myself, to stay with them for the Commencement. On the preceding evening, President Hopkins asked us to dinner to meet the President and Secretary Root, who was also to receive the same degree. Sitting beside Mr. Choate, I told him that it was Mr. Jesup's seventy-first birthday, and that I knew he would be pleased at some recognition. Mr. Choate immediately arose, and, turning to both Presidents, he said, 'Mr. President, I rise to propose a toast. This is the day on which our good friend Jesup, a public-spirited citizen and leader in all good works, passes threescore years and ten: and I ask you to drink his health.' After the health was drunk, Mr. Jesup addressed Roosevelt, saying, 'Mr. President, or Theodore, as I have always called you, a few days after you were born, your father, full of pride in his firstborn, asked me to come in to see you. We went up into the nursery, and you were in your bassinette, making a good deal of fuss and noise for a youngster of your age. Your father, however, lifted you out, and, asking me to hold you, placed you in my arms.' 'Was he hard to hold?' came from Mr. Root on the second. He was doubtless speaking from personal experience.

The crowd and enthusiasm at Williamstown warned me to anticipate greater crowds at Cambridge the next week; for this was to be the twenty-fifth anniversary of the Class of '80, with Roosevelt present. Secretary Taft and Chief Justice White were to receive honorary degrees. It was also the fiftieth anniversary of the class of Phillips Brooks, as the representative of which Alexander Agassiz, a great scientist as well as patron of the University, was to speak. And the Harvard Teachers' Endowment campaign had kindled a fresh loyalty among the alumni.

Up to this year it had been the custom of the Alumni Association to have a dinner, or an apology for a dinner, in Memorial Hall, after the Commencement exercises and the bestowal of degrees in Sanders Theatre. In expectation of an unprecedented attendance, the Executive Committee of the alumni arranged for luncheons in big tents in the Yard; and Jerome Greene, Secretary of the Corporation, and I, who had charge of the arrangements, saw that Memorial Hall was emptied of all tables and filled with chairs, leaving only the long table on the dais at the north side of the Hall, with a white tablecloth and a few flowers and pitchers of water as tokens of the ancient feast. Thus, instead of eight hundred alumni, almost twice that number were accommodated.

The President, Kermit, and Secretary Loeb were to stop with us: the secret service men in Lawrence Hall next us. Lieutenant-Governor Curtis Guild, acting in the illness of the Governor, had asked the President to take breakfast at the Algonquin Club with quite a company on his way out to Cambridge, which he had declined to do. A few days before his arrival, I received a letter from him saying that he wanted to breakfast quietly, adding, 'The people who think they ought to associate with me on occasions like this are politicians and contractors, whereas I have a rooted conviction that I would rather see Frank Lowell and Bob Grant. Do you know Dr. Samuel Crothers of 20 Oxford Street, Cambridge? I have been delighted with his book, "The Gentle Reader": if you would be willing to have him at breakfast, I should be delighted.' Governor Guild and President Eliot, of course, were invited also. The reference to Dr. Crothers is characteristic, for he was little known as a charming essayist at that time. Mrs. Roosevelt, however, had found him out and had read his essays aloud to the President.

Of course, I put them beside each other, and to the surprise of Crothers, Roosevelt in their discussion of 'The Gentle Reader' quoted pages to the author. After the Doctor had gone, I said, 'What do you think of our friend Crothers?' 'Well,' he said with his broad smile, 'when I first caught sight of him, I had my doubts; but he was really delightful.'

Meeting the President at the Back Bay Station on the morning of the day before Commencement at half-past six, I took him out to Cambridge in our open victoria, surrounded, to his disgust, by a dozen mounted policemen. He was often unreasonably restless at such protection. 'Any resolute man can shoot me at any time,' he used to protest. And in our drive later to Chestnut Hill to the Lees, the family of his first wife, he dismissed them and enjoyed his freedom.

As guests were coming, and we had ordered breakfast at eight, he had a half-hour to wait. Expressing my regret at this to Secretary Loeb, he said, 'Oh, the President is happy enough reading in his room.' Sure enough, he was reading Cohun's 'Turks and Mongols' in French.

In our drive and walk he was as usual full of talk and apt epithets. In speaking to him of our satisfaction at his transfer of George Meyer from Rome to St. Petersburg, he said, 'You and I know George, and we have always thought him a gentleman, but not markedly able. George, however, gets things done. And when I saw ahead the probability of negotiations for peace between Russia and Japan and the delicacy of the situation, I sent George there, and he is carrying things through finely.' He then went on to say how before Mukden he had sounded Japan and Russia as to the possibility of negotiations for peace, but Russia had refused: and again before the battle of the Sea of Japan, but Russia again refused. Then Japan asked him by letter to take it up of his own motion, which he did. He paid his respects to the Kaiser, 'that autocratic zigzag,' who, he said, was always trying to get his fist in and gain some credit. He added that peace was still uncertain, but a step had been gained.

'The Kaiser got a good speech out of you, however,' I said, 'at the reception of the statue of Frederick the Great.' 'Did you read it?' he replied. 'Of course I did: I read or try to read everything you say.' 'But did you read between the lines? The Kaiser thinks that he and I are after the manner of Frederick the Great. So he sent over that statue. I had it placed in the Navy Yard where no one will ever see it, and made the most democratic speech of my life, saying just what I knew the Kaiser did not want me to say.'

He went on, 'I am afraid that John Hay will never do any more work, and will have to retire. I hear from Europe that he is losing strength.' 'His retirement will be a great loss to your administration,' I said, 'for however much or little he may have done the past year or two, the people have confidence in his discretion, more than they have in yours.' 'Perhaps so,' he replied. 'He has of course been a great asset in the administration, but whatever has been done of late, I have had to do. Hay has been out of active work longer than people think.' 'Who next, then?' I asked. His answer was characteristic. Roosevelt was popularly supposed to act on the moment and without thought; whereas he had usually thought the matter out, and when his time came, acted quickly. 'Root, and if I cannot get Root, then Taft. Root's friends think that I cannot get him away from his practice, but I believe that Root's patriotism and conscience won't let him stay out when his country wants him.'

The Tuesday was given to the drive and talk, and especially to his class luncheon at Oakley Country Club, and the dinner at the Somerset where he talked to his classmates for over an hour about his work and problems, with the intimacy of a close friend. The Class of '79 had the year before given $100,000 towards the building of a Stadium. This year the Class of '80 gave at Commencement $100,000 for endowment, and thus started the annual gift of the twenty-five year classes, a gift which has lately risen to $150,000.

The next day Harvard received the President of the United States, one of her sons, and gave honorary degrees to the Chief Justice and the Secretary of War who later became President, an historic occasion.

It may be worth while, therefore, for me to quote from my diary:

Wed., June 28. One of the great days of my life. Perfect weather except two or three short dashes of rain.

Bob Bacon (Chief Marshal of the Class of '80 and of the Alumni) to breakfast with the President and ourselves: family prayers: all servants in as usual.

At 9.30 Lieut. Gov. Guild and Lancers arrived. He and President pass formal words at door: then drive off in first carriage to College Yard: secret service men next: Governor's staff: then Kermit and I: crowd cheering as the carriages passed. In Mass. Hall. Eliot not there: I ran over to University Hall to get him from Overseers Meeting.

Procession to Sanders Theatre. Commencement Exercises. Secretary Taft and Mr. Justice White got degrees.

At 12.30 I presided at Alumni meeting. Declined to serve another year, having presided at two dinners. Mr. Choate (who was President in '87–'88,) elected President of Alumni. To Chief Marshal's lunch. Roosevelt had meanwhile gone to Germanic Museum, Pres. Eliot's, Harvard Union and Porcellian. Then to Chief Marshal's lunch. Crowd of Alumni far greater than ever before. I had to arrange for open air overflow meeting for those unable to get tickets for Mem. Hall. Garceau and others took charge. I got Roosevelt, Taft and Bonaparte to speak at the out-of-door meeting which took place after we got into Mem. Hall.

Procession from Mass. 2.15: a short, sharp shower. Marshals, then I as Pres. of Alumni alone. Then Pres. Eliot and Roosevelt, The Corporation, etc. Lunch having been served in class rooms, Mass. Hall and elsewhere: no dinner or tables in Mem. Hall. So instead of 800, some 1500 got in, a larger number of Harvard Alumni than ever under one roof.

I called them to order at 2.50. After the usual hymn I spoke announcing the Teachers' Endowment Fund as 'rising' $2,400,000 (on Frank Higginson's authority) from about 2000 contributors. Speakers were Pres. Eliot; 'Fair Harvard' sung; Lieut. Gov. Guild; Chief Justice White; Sec. Taft; Mr. Choate; Pres. Angell; Agassiz for Class of '55; and Pres. Roosevelt, who spoke forty minutes. Through at about 5.30. We sang 'America' before Roosevelt spoke, and 'Auld Lang Syne' at end. The speaking fine, much enthusiasm. Pres. Eliot told me and said again next day at Phi Beta Kappa that it was the best Commencement he had ever known.

The Pres. went to Prof. Hart's to meet his class. Sec. Taft, Frank Lowell, and Beekman Winthrop (Gov. of Porto Rico) came to our house.

Soon the Pres. came and he and Taft worked hard for an hour in my study on Panama Canal question, Wallace's resignation and other things. At 7.05 we gave Taft and others dinner while Pres. sat with us. At 7.15 Taft off for Washington to go to Philippines. I escorted Pres. to Somerset Club to a dinner of twenty of the Class of '80. Lines of people all the way to the bridge: constant cheering. At the Club they urged me to come in and dine. So I did: Rob't Bacon, Richard Saltonstall, Henry Jackson, Minot Weld, Harry Chapin, William Hooper, Robert Winsor, W. Gaston and others. Stayed till 10.30, then bade Pres. goodbye and home. He went to his train for Oyster Bay.

A delightful visit from him: he kept the whole family, children and servants, alert: shook hands, 'Good-bye,' with Katy the nurse. Wonderful energy, spirits and enthusiasm. Talks about self in a way egotistic in others: but he so identified with his work, plans and national affairs that one doesn't think of it as egotism.

A few minutes after Secretary Taft had driven out of our avenue to catch the train and connect with his ship for the Philippines, which was to have a special party on board of Senators, Congressmen, and others, including Alice Roosevelt and Nicholas Longworth, he came back, and shouted, 'Where are those Panama papers?' He seized them off the mantelpiece, and rushed off, calling out, 'Bishop, telephone the station and hold the train.' I turned to the President saying, 'He is a first-rate fellow.' 'The best fellow in the world,' he added, 'the best man to work with: I would give anything to see him the next President.'

CHAPTER XVIII
LAMBETH PALACE AND ENGLISH CATHEDRALS
1906

It is the custom of the Archbishop of Canterbury to gather the English Bishops for a two or three days' conference at Lambeth Palace in May. He had to my dismay invited me months before to lead the Bishops on the first, the Quiet Day. I never felt so helpless, and yet it seemed as if I should be a coward, when such a privilege was granted to an American, to evade the duty. Hence, catching my note from the Archbishop's letter, I determined to speak in the simplest way as brother to brother.

No English home could be more domestic, informal, and sympathetic than Lambeth Palace has been during the Davidsons' residence. They took us all into the house and to their hearts: the children chased up and down the halls and through the garden.

The morning of May 22d opened and found me frightened and very humble. Some of the Bishops were staying in the Palace, the others arrived by half-past eight, when the Archbishop, assisted by the Archbishop of York, celebrated the Holy Communion. A short address was expected from me. As I stood at the chancel gate looking upon the Bishops, thoughts swept across my mind, almost enough to unman me.

The chapel is a beautiful example of Early English. The windows given by Archbishop Laud, destroyed in the Civil War, but later restored in their original design, looked down upon us. Here was the scene of the second trial of Wycliffe, and here on February 4, 1787, upon the very spot where I was standing, knelt Drs. White and Provoost for consecration by the Archbishops of Canterbury and York, assisted by the Bishop of Bath and Wells, and of

Peterborough, the first Americans to receive Episcopal orders at English hands.

Beside me were the two Archbishops; before me were the Bishops of London, Durham, Oxford, Winchester, Bath and Wells, Peterborough, with others whose titles ran back through the centuries. And I, a helpless young American, was appointed to lead them in prayer and counsel.

It was the fifth week after Easter, and as my first note for the day I drew from the Gospel the text, 'That in me ye might have peace.' In halting and it seemed to me almost broken voice, I spoke of the peace and serenity which can come to country, Church, and to each of us through complete consecration in Christ.

We went silently to breakfast in the noble Guard Room. There were perhaps fifty of us, and when each had helped himself from the side table, the Bishop of London began the reading of a devotional book, which to my amazement and gratification was Bunyan's 'Pilgrim's Progress.' Could spiritual history show a finer recompense than this? Looking down upon us from their frames were the faces of the Archbishops from earliest days — Laud by Vandyke, Warham by Holbein, Herring by Hogarth, Secker by Sir Joshua Reynolds — looking, and seeming almost to listen, while the Prelates of England turned to the Puritan, Baptist writer for spiritual refreshment. The Bishops of London, Winchester, and Oxford took turns in the reading.

Then back to the Chapel for prayer, meditation, and addresses. The Archbishop had given me courage with sympathy and appreciation, and I pulled myself together for the three longer addresses, 'The Worth of Spiritual Reserve Power,' 'Winning the Kingdom not by Evasion or by Force, but by the Truth,' 'The people heard him gladly.' In the late afternoon we dispersed to the garden for afternoon tea. The next day the conference on certain questions of policy and administration took place in the Archbishop's study; and as the Bishops took leave, I was given a taste of the hospitality of the best of the English. The invitations were so cordial that it seemed as if we

might be able to pass the rest of our lives sojourning in
bishops' palaces. We stayed on at Lambeth for a few
days, and in the intimacy of the family life gained a personal esteem and affection for every member of the household, the chaplains and secretaries. The butler, housekeeper, and other servants all joined in Morning and Evening Prayer in the Chapel. The humblest of the maids
was included in the family life.

A day or two later Dr. Wace, the Dean of Canterbury,
and Mrs. Wace came to London and to Lambeth, to be
presented in Buckingham Palace. As the Archbishop and
Mrs. Davidson entered the hall dressed for the presentation, she with ostrich feather and long train, they met
the Dean and Mrs. Wace, also in full dress. She was a
handsome, stately matron who was as excited as a girl;
and he, a vigorous, loyal, old Englishman, could not hide
under an assumed indifference his sense of the importance
of the occasion.

'You must practise your curtsey, Mrs. Wace, before
you start,' said Mrs. Davidson. 'We must have a re-
hearsal.' So the gong was sounded and all the servants of
the Palace assembled in the hall to represent the company.
Julia and I were placed against the wall to impersonate
Their Majesties. Mrs. Davidson stepped to the front of
us, turned, and with low-bended knee and one graceful
sweep of her train passed on. Then followed Mrs. Wace,
who of greater age and formal dignity did her best, but
was not allowed by Mrs. Davidson to pass on without
putting her muscles to heavy strain. The Archbishop
turned to the Dean and said, 'Mr. Dean, my man, Lamb,
asks me to tell you that your medals are hung in the
wrong order: you have the medal of Queen Victoria's
funeral after that of His Majesty's coronation.' 'What
does it matter?' growled Dean Wace, as he allowed
Lamb to make the change, 'who would notice it?'
'His Majesty would notice it,' answered the Archbishop.
'He is very precise about such formalities.' 'It is a very
meddlesome age,' punned the Dean in retort.

One day, as the children and I were sauntering along the Strand and by Temple Bar, a haberdasher with the courtesy of a London shopkeeper spoke from his door, 'You are Americans, sir: will not you and the little ones come upstairs and see the entrance of His Majesty into the City? He will be on his way to the dedication of the Chapel of Saint Michael and Saint George, in Saint Paul's.' We were no sooner seated at the window than the coach and retinue of the Lord Mayor with color and gold came up Fleet Street from the City. Brilliantly dressed lacqueys alighted and took from a carriage a rich scarlet carpet which they laid over the pavement. The Lord Mayor in red velvet cloak stepped from his coach, which moved aside. Then from the Strand appeared the coach and retinue of His Majesty King Edward, scarlet and gold conspicuous on servants and carriages. The coach stopped as it came to the Lord Mayor, who received from an attendant a pearl-studded sword, given for the purpose by Queen Elizabeth. This he offered to the King, who, sitting in his coach, took the hilt, released it, and bowed. He was now free to enter the City. Off went his coach and retinue, followed by that of the Lord Mayor, while the crowd which had gathered uttered that low roar which the English call a cheer. And we felt as if a window of history had opened and revealed to us 'London Town.'

Dorchester House was the residence of the American Ambassador, Mr. Whitelaw Reid, who with Mrs. Reid entertained with rich hospitality. A great event was the reception given by them to Alice Roosevelt Longworth with whose name the whole world had been just then made familiar. Her marriage in the White House in February had given opportunity for the press, not only of the United States, but of the world, to exploit her whose charm, adventures, harmless follies, and love of life put her father into the background for the season. The East Room of the White House was filled with officials, relatives, and personal friends. Dignity and reverence marked the service, which was read by Bishop Satterlee. The bride cut the

cake in the dining-room with Major McCauley's sword,
and we dispersed, conscious that we had witnessed one
of the most brilliant occasions of White House history.
When she came to stay with the Reids in London, all London pressed to meet her. The Fourth-of-July reception at
the Embassy was an American affair. Mr. Bryan, 'the
great Commoner,' was there: it was democratic and interesting. A small evening party at which His Majesty met
Mrs. Longworth, and where Caruso, Emma Eames, and
others sang, was given. Duchesses with diamond tiaras
were in the majority. King Edward was, as usual, gracious
and affable. But even the unique ability of Mrs. Reid as a
hostess, the beautiful house and rich supper in the tented
court, could make the occasion none other than formal and
somewhat solemn.

The spell of Westminster Abbey catches every one of
English stock. One Saturday afternoon in June, I went by
the invitation of my good friend, Dean Robinson, to the
Deanery. No matter how often I have been there, I cannot escape a sense of awe as I step into the cloister and ring
the bell. Entering the ample hall, one feels himself to be in
a monastery. A tall silk hat of American build is out of
place upon the table, black with age and London smoke,
and laden with shoe-stringed hats of varied shapes.

Walking up the broad staircase, from whose landings
doors opened into halls and rooms of various elevations, I
reached the beautiful drawing-room through whose windows the sun shone, lighting up ancient furniture, books,
pictures, and illuminated manuscripts. The Dean himself
was a part of the picture; no monk ever looked the part
better. In one corner he and his chaplain Rackman were
sitting talking over a pot of tea. This over, the Dean said,
'There is no one in the Abbey now, my Lord, but the
vergers and cleaners, preparing the Church for Sunday.
Go in there and have it to yourself.'

Entering the nave by the side door from the Deanery,
I wander alone up and down the aisles around back of the
altar, through the chapel of Henry VII with its delicate fan

tracery; then into the chapel of Edward the Confessor. The silence is oppressive, broken only by the echo of a verger's voice in the choir. The Kings and Queens of all England's history are here, each with touching story: Richard II and his Queen murdered on Saint Valentine's Day five hundred years ago. Near by is the Coronation Chair with the Stone of Scone under the seat, whereon for six centuries every King and Queen has sat at their coronation. Addison once wrote: 'The spaciousness and gloom of this vast edifice produce a profound and mysterious awe. We step cautiously and softly about, as if fearful of disturbing the hallowed silence of the tomb; while every footfall whispers along the walls, and chatters among the sepulchres, making us more sensible of the quiet we have interrupted.' As I walk through the aisles the sun's rays breaking through the clerestory windows no longer touch the pillars: they sweep almost horizontally up the nave, over the screen, and touch the carving above the altar. The vergers and cleaners have gone, and I am alone with the mysterious and awful company.

Darkness fell, and passing into the Deanery, I found the Dean and guests in the drawing-room, ready for dinner.

After Compline, I picked up my candlestick and walked through mysterious passages and up and down uncertain steps to my bedroom. It was very large, square, with high beds and higher posts. The flickering candle seemed almost to shed darkness. Here again associations set one's brain whirling. In this room, Dean Stanley and Lady Augusta lived and died. Across from the bed, I caught sight of a square of white in a frame. Taking the candle, I discovered that it was a large New Year's card, sent to Lady Augusta from Her Majesty Queen Victoria. At the bottom of the card was written in Dean Stanley's impossible handwriting something like this — 'Into this room, when Lady Augusta lay dying, Her Majesty the Queen came and bade her good-bye. My wish is that this card hang in this room always, as a token of their friendship.' As I fell asleep to the sound of the Westminster bells, the room seemed filled with the fine loyalty of that gentle courtier.

Canon Henson preached at the Morning Service the next day, which was Trinity Sunday. At luncheon I said to the Dean, 'Did you not break the law of the Church to-day in the Abbey? Should not the Athanasian Creed be recited on the great feast days?' 'Did you not hear it?' asked the Dean. 'I heard the Nicene Creed sung in the proper place for the Creed, and I heard a part of the Athanasian Creed sung as an anthem, but the damnatory clauses were omitted. Is not that contrary to the law?' 'Possibly, if you must have it so,' was his reply. 'The Abbey is responsible to no Bishop, only to His Majesty, and when His Majesty calls us to order, we will take notice.'

The English have their afternoon tea on lawns and mountain tops. Only the Dean and his guests can have tea upon the roof of Westminster Abbey. Here quite a party of us, the children included, gathered for sliced bread, loaf cake, tea, and talk.

That evening I preached in the nave. The glow of the sunset still filled the windows; the candles lighted the faces below. Through the half-light one could see the multitude only as a mass, rising at the west end and against the walls where men were standing. To me the most interesting gravestone in the Abbey is one which few see, that of Livingstone, set in the pavement in the centre of the nave. That he, a Scotch weaver, a missionary to the world's lowliest, should lie among the tombs of the mightiest is full of suggestion and romance. Now the body of the Unknown Soldier rests hard by.

Trollope is still fascinating, but the manners and customs of cathedrals and of those who dwelt under their shadows have passed. Twenty years ago, however, suggestions of Trollope repeatedly came to the surface. We shall never see the like of Bishop Wordsworth of Salisbury. He was simple as a child, learned beyond words. His chaplain told me that the Bishop wrote in Latin the celebrated letter to the Pope, upon the Validity of English Orders while he was waiting in a railroad station for a belated train. His hospitality was unbounded. He was obsessed with the idea that Americans came to see things; so while I would gladly have sat and talked with him, he insisted on showing me everything of interest, and much that was of no interest, every hour of my visit. Dean Farrar did the same years before, when I called on him at Canterbury, and the Rector of Bemerton would not let me enter George Herbert's church until he had shown me his own garden and every plant that he had brought from other lands. The relations of Dean and Bishop are always interesting, and never the same. A few days before I stayed with the Bishop, a terrible wreck of a boat train in the centre of Salisbury had killed twenty-seven Americans. As we were leaving the hospital where I had called on the wounded, the Bishop told me of the shock he felt when, leaving the cathedral after the early service, he had heard of the accident which had just then happened. He went directly to the station and did everything in his power for the sufferers. With American inquisitiveness, I asked, 'And when you took the eleven o'clock service and all the town was moved with sympathy, what form of service and special prayers did you have?' He replied with some hesitation, 'Since you ask me, I have to say that, as the Dean was away, I did not feel it to be quite right for me to change the usual order.'

One day at Lambeth, he called me aside and said, 'You know that I have accepted the invitation of your Church in the States to preach at their Synod a year hence. Is it necessary that I should take with me a top hat?' 'Bishop,' I answered, 'if an English Lord Bishop should come to the States without his shoestring top hat, as well as his apron and leggings, he would not be recognized or received.' 'Ah,' he murmured, 'that involves another article of luggage.' When we met in America, I observed him with interest. He had on his top hat, but carried his soft brim hat crushed under his arm. As occasion required, he wore the one or the other, but he had escaped 'another article of luggage.' After his sermon at the General Convention in Cincinnati, I called him aside and said, 'Bishop, you have done your full duty. Hand your top hat to your chaplain and let him box it and send it to the Cunard wharf in New York. Wear your soft hat and enjoy the States.'

The cathedral close at Hereford savored more of Trollope than any other that I remember. Bishop Percival, formerly Head Master of Rugby, was a man of distinct force, a radical liberal in politics, gentle in voice and manner, but capable of very emphatic language when thwarted. His wife was a thorough English lady. The Bishop was not on speaking terms with the minor canons across the lawn, but on cordial though somewhat formal relations with Dean Leigh, whose wife was a daughter of Fanny Kemble, the American actress. Henry James's 'An International Episode' was widely read at the time. In Hereford Cathedral we had an international marriage. The Bishop and the Dean officiated, while I gave the address to the bride and bridegroom, an ordeal which I dreaded and hope never to repeat. Owen Wister, the bride's cousin, led her up the aisle, and Henry James was a special guest.

To refer again to the relations of Bishop and Dean. When at Hereford a few years later with Mrs. Lawrence, I happened to mention that she had never seen the Cathedral, at which Mrs. Percival said to the Bishop, 'My dear, Mrs. Lawrence has never seen the Cathedral; will you take her across and show it to her?' After some hesitation he replied, 'Yes, my dear, the Dean is in Chester preaching to the Girls' Friendly Society; I will show her the Cathedral.' As we came to the west door, the Dean suddenly swept around the corner. 'Ah, Mr. Dean, I was about to show Mrs. Lawrence the Cathedral. I thought you were in Chester. You show her the Cathedral.' 'No, no, my Lord, I am on my way to the Deanery from the station. You show Mrs. Lawrence the Cathedral.' 'No, no, Mr.

Dean: it is your Cathedral: you escort her.' 'No, my dear Bishop, I have been away a night. You take Mrs. Lawrence.' So with due formality we entered the Cathedral.

English history and literature saturate every niche of the country. Stopping in the Palace at Ripon with our friend, Bishop Boyd Carpenter, and his family, we drove along a Roman road and across Marston Moor. We passed a morning basking in the beauty of Fountains Abbey. Walter Scott dominates Scotland: at Abbotsford one expects to meet him limping up the garden path. My experience on Loch Lomond was, I believe, unique. The boat was crowded with excursionists. The rain poured in sheets. The captain, seeing that I was an American, kindly gave me his key to his stateroom, where I passed the afternoon reading the back numbers of the 'Boston Weekly Transcript.'

We had intended to pass part of the summer on the French coast. One morning we asked ourselves if there is anything on the French coast better than the North Shore of Massachusetts Bay. So we changed our tickets and sailed for home, where families with young children belong.

CHAPTER XIX

THE GENERAL CONVENTION AT RICHMOND

1906–1907

ONE day when I was at the State Prison, Chaplain Barnes said to me, 'Bishop, we are trying to fit these men who are not lifers to take their places in society when they go out. We are keeping them in touch with their family life and the best in their past associations: we are teaching them trades: we ought to keep them in touch with their Church. Why cannot you ask a clergyman of your Church to come here and gather the men who claim to belong to the Episcopal Church, some sixty of them, hold a weekday service, be their friend, and create in them a loyalty to the Church of their childhood?'

I acted immediately, and from that day we have had a chaplain who has given himself to the work at the State Prison and other reformatory institutions: serving as friend and pastor and connecting the men with their families. I have made annual visitations to them, as to any other congregation. One day as I shook hands with them after service as usual, one of them said in a broken voice, 'My wife wrote me that she shook hands with you last week, and now I do. I thank you.' It is the personal touch that gains friendliness and confidence and saves souls as truly as do sermons. Here is the record of a service:

Ash Wednesday. 10 A.M. State Prison: Service for those connected with our Church. Fifty prisoners present. Penitential Service: confirmed eight: gave address: celebrated Holy Communion: twenty-eight partook. A touching Service, hearty singing and devotional spirit. Two of those confirmed are on life sentence for murder, one has been there thirty-five years.

For twenty-five and more years my interest in prisons, reformatories, and prison reforms has been keen and steady. The subject is too large for me to touch upon except to say that, though much improvement has been made in the last half-century, we are at the very beginning of our knowledge and treatment of the wayward and the criminal. The Massachusetts State Prison is, as I have said in public again and again, 'a mediæval dungeon,' in its form of construction. Although much is done to make it habitable and the inmates are on the whole healthy, the upbuilding of character, hope, and right ambitions there is almost hopeless. With the study and treatment of the feeble-minded and the handicapped from infancy up to adult years, with the adjustment of laws and court traditions to modern knowledge and social conditions, with the separation of reformatory institutions from politics, and the training of an adequate body of skilled, high-minded officers and helpers, we may hope to save the State thousands of souls and millions of dollars. Men and women of the best intelligence and finest citizenship have here great opportunities. Again and again I have felt that I would like to quit my job and take up the cause.

I know of nothing more tragic than an insane asylum managed by political favor, and no more moving scene than the inside of an insane asylum managed by devoted and skilled officers and nurses.

I recall talks to boys and girls in high schools and elsewhere. It is an invigorating audience, that of several hundred high-school boys and girls to whom one can talk on living subjects with certainty of response.

How well I recall talking to a hundred Boston débutantes and post-débutantes, sitting on the floor, chairs, and sofas of a drawing-room, on the 'Art of Spending Money,' and their delight as I said, 'If I had your father here, I would tell him to give you a larger allowance than you can reasonably spend,' a delight mitigated by my next remark, 'under the condition that you give away a certain proportion, save a certain proportion, and keep exact accounts.'

One spring morning in 1906, Appleton Chapel was

packed with officers and students of the University at the funeral of the friend of us all, Professor Shaler. I recall meeting him in the Yard the day after I had been appointed a University preacher, and as he shook hands he said in his usual dialect, 'I am glad that you are going to have a lick at the boys.' He was always at morning chapel. A few months before his death, he and I spoke one evening in New Bedford, and took the train home together. As we got out at the Back Bay Station he was telling me how he kept his health and vigor. 'The skin of a man's body should be as responsive to heat and cold as that of his face,' he said. 'When going to bed I undress completely, throw open the windows, no matter how cold the night, and put in a few minutes of violent exercise. The blood responds and my whole body blushes like a girl's cheek on a cold day.' I was wondering what the neighbors on Quincy Street thought of it, when he said, 'There goes the car on Boylston Street, let's sprint for it.' We did; I passed him, and he came up panting. I did not then know that hardening arteries were gripping him. He was virile, friendly, invigorating, fine, and deeply religious to the end. Exact scholars have their place in a university, of course; so do men like Shaler who value other things higher than exactitude.

My chief interest was, of course, in the Diocese itself. Almost every year I gathered the clergy at the Holy Communion; gave an address upon some phase of their work or personal life, then Mrs. Lawrence and I received them with their wives at our house to luncheon or tea. Much as I should like to have known all the clergy intimately, it was impossible, but I hope and believe that each and all have felt that I was at their service in time of need.

From time to time I have taken the candidates off for a quiet day or two before their ordination. During these years, too, I gave time and thought to the creation and development of a department of religious education. The weakening of a sense of responsibility on the part of parents for the religious education of their children and the haphazard and inadequate teaching in the Sunday Schools have compelled the Church to face the problem in a serious way. The Diocese of Massachusetts was, I am glad to say, early in the field. We are, however, only beginning to tackle the problem. With the enormous increase of subjects of study, the adjustments of knowledge, and the social and athletic interests, national religion and Christian faith must be expressed with fresh thought, enthusiasm, and confidence if the next generations are to remain Christian.

One problem upon which bishops and others are naturally silent, I must mention if I am really telling the story of my life, for it caused me many anxious days. I mean the treatment of clergy who have slipped or fallen. There is no use in concealing the fact that men who have consecrated themselves to the ministry are human and have the temptations common to men. There are certain special conditions, too, in a minister's life and work which make him susceptible to temptation. Hence there occur now and again downfalls of sad and tragic nature.

As to a few things I am clear. Men in the ministry who have so slipped or fallen must be treated by their Bishop, their Father in God, with the utmost sympathy. No time, sacrifice or pains are to be spared in bringing such a man to himself and in leading and lifting him.

At the same time the fact stands that the man is a priest of the Church, and that, while his penitence and reform may be gladly recognized, he must be dealt with in his official relations. I have been told again and again that, since such a man is penitent and determined to live a new life, he ought to be kept in the ministry or received back if he has been deposed. Each case must, of course, be decided upon its merits. But since our Church assumes that its ministers have free access to the homes of the people, every minister must be above suspicion. The continuance in the active ministry of a man who has fallen, even though he be reformed and a pure and humble Christian, is liable to cast suspicion on the standards of his brethren. Nevertheless, I have received back a clergyman deposed for drunkenness, who has stood years of testing.

I recall one sad and bad case of a clergyman who, persistently denying his guilt, insisted that if I should bring him to trial it would cause a public scandal, that the papers would headline every detail and the Church would suffer. I told him that no fear of public scandal would frighten me, that the greatest scandal to the Church was the continuance of a man in the ministry against whom such charges were made and who was unwilling to stand trial. Having come to a written agreement to abide by the result of an informal trial, we selected a master and counsel; and with witnesses testifying carried through a trial of two days. He protested his innocence to the end: when, however, the verdict of guilt was given, he confessed and was deposed. No matter how pure or Christian a life such a man may lead afterwards, he should in my opinion never be received back into the ministry. Fortunately, our canons have very stiff conditions about the reception of men deposed.

During three General Conventions I have pressed for such a change in the canons as will enable a clergyman, against whom there is no moral charge, but who for good reason wants to give up his ministry, to retire without the use of the ugly word 'deposition' in connection with his resignation. I am glad to say that at the last General Convention, with the help of Bishop Hall of the Committee on Canons, the canon was so amended.

When we went to England in the summer of 1906, we were pretty sure that the automobile was the coming vehicle. Having found an excellent position for our faithful coachman of years, Benjamin Rees, and having sold our three horses, we felt free to make our decision in the autumn.

In November I bought our first car. The relief from strain and exposure and the ability to add to my work were indescribable. Ownership of an automobile was, however, so associated in people's minds with plutocrats, that for a time I doubted the wisdom of my venture. For two or three years I never allowed the driver (the word 'chauffeur' was hardly in use then) to come up to the church door. I got out half a block away, for the novelty drew around the car the boys of the parish, and the noise of the engine disturbed the people already in church. Not that the noise was much greater than at present, but those were days of comparative quiet and Sundays were days of peace. Our ears had not then become accustomed to the ceaseless roar of these days.

As the year 1907 marked the three-hundredth anniversary of the landing at Jamestown, Virginia, Richmond had been selected for the place of meeting of the General Convention. The Churches in the Colonies in the eighteenth century had been under the care of the Bishop of London, and the Society for the Propagation of the Gospel had been chartered to preach the Gospel to the Indians and others in America; hence the Bishop of London, Dr. Ingram, and the Secretary of the Society, Bishop Montgomery, came across for the celebration.

On the Sunday preceding the Convention many of the bishops and other members of the Convention gathered at Washington to join with Bishop Satterlee in the laying of the foundation stone of the Cathedral, which occurred at noon on Sunday, September 29th. It was a perfect day for the open-air services. English, Canadian, and American bishops, clergy, and a multitude of people assembled; a massed choir supported by the Marine Band led the singing. The stone was laid; President Roosevelt, the Bishop of London, and Bishop Satterlee gave addresses. In the afternoon there was another open-air service with fifteen or twenty thousand people at which the Bishop of London preached. 'Two remarkable services,' my diary notes; 'well ordered, great crowds. Satterlee has a work of faith. Cathedral two miles from the solid city, a mile of woods to the nearest houses.'

The next day a party of us went out to Mount Vernon where 'Mr. Pierpont Morgan planted a mulberry tree, and

I an elm tree on the left of the lawn as you look from house to river.'

Mr. Morgan's party for the Convention was made up of himself, Bishop and Mrs. Doane, Bishop and Mrs. Greer, Mrs. John Markoe, Miss Townsend, and ourselves. We occupied the house of Mr. Rutherford on Grace Street, Richmond, and Mr. Sherry of New York, who was devoted to Mr. Morgan, was in charge and continually on duty.

The Commonwealth of Virginia had with great hospitality offered the Convention the use of the Capitol. At the opening meeting of the House of Bishops I was reëlected Chairman. As I took my seat in the chair of the President of the Senate, and looked through the open door of the beautiful building to Houdon's statue of Washington standing in the rotunda, I realized that we were really in the heart of the ancient Commonwealth, the home of the great Virginians, and the capital seat of the Confederacy. The glow of the early history of the country seemed to be about us during the whole session. The Bishop of London, too, with his winning personality made a vital centre for every incident.

For several years old Williamsburg, which was the capital of Virginia from 1699 to 1780, where are William and Mary College and the House of Burgesses, had been preparing for the event. Bruton Church had been restored; and King Edward VII had had a Bible especially printed and bound as a gift, in covers appropriately designed. When, therefore, the large company, representative of the General Convention, alighted at the station in Williamsburg, the whole countryside was out to receive us. Mr. Young, of the British Embassy, had in his arms the great royal Bible. In the confusion at the station, Mr. Morgan and I laid hold of a decrepit open carryall of pre-Civil War make, with horse apparently of like history. We helped Mr. and Mrs. Young in and placed the Bible on the front seat beside the pickaninny who drove. As he gathered up his rope reins and gave a starting lash to his horse, the carryall shook and moved, the side curtains flapped in the air, and the whole procession of barges, buses, carryalls, and men and women on horseback moved slowly through the town to the church. I doubt if ever a royal gift has been so escorted. It was a perfect day. As the congregation joined in the hymns, they were caught up by the crowd under the trees outside. A lectern from President Roosevelt and the Bible from King Edward were presented, and the Bishop of London made an address. History and memories of Washington and other Virginia worthies joined in making this a notable scene and day. A few days later, several hundred of us made a pilgrimage down the James River to Jamestown Island.

One Sunday afternoon a crowd so great that it seemed to be all Richmond gathered on the slope in the rear of the Capitol, where we had a short service and the Bishop of London spoke. During the last hymn I saw that they were pressing in to shake the Bishop's hand, the crowd being so great as practically to mob him. So the Bishop of Virginia, Dr. Gibson, at my suggestion, turned up the steps and pressed the crowd aside while I pushed the Bishop of London through and into the Capitol, and we bolted the door. There is that about the Bishop of London which arouses a London crowd to enthusiasm and loyalty, but I doubt if he had ever come so near being mobbed by a kindly crowd as on that Sunday afternoon.

One piece of legislation at that Convention made somewhat of a sensation, and marked a new step in the Church's life. It was Canon 19, which empowered a 'Bishop to give permission to Christian men who are not ministers of this Church, to make addresses in the Church, on special occasions.' This seems to us now quite innocuous; but at the time it sent something of a shudder through a part of the Church and caused a number of clergymen to renounce their ministry and enter the Roman Church.

It may be worth while for me to sketch one change which has come over the Church during the past half-century. I can remember when Bishop Horatio Potter forbade the Reverend John Cotton Smith, Rector of the Church of the

Ascension, New York, to invite the Reverend Doctor Adams, President of Union Theological Seminary, to preach in his church of a Sunday evening. In spite of Bishop Potter's inhibition of Dr. Adams, Dr. Smith persisted, and wrote a public letter justifying it. A generation later, Bishop Henry Potter, in his first appeal to New York for a cathedral, spoke of it as a church where the great preachers of the country would be heard. As a result, Mr. D. Willis James, a leading Presbyterian, sent him one hundred thousand dollars. I could not understand how the Bishop could consistently make such a statement, when it was generally assumed that only Episcopal clergymen could speak in the pulpits of the Church. I therefore took pains to ask him. His answer was, 'By the time the Cathedral is built, the Church will have reached a breadth of vision which will justify my statement.' Prophetic! — as is seen in the list of men who have spoken in the last few years in the Cathedral of Saint John the Divine.

Exchange of pulpits has been thought by many to be a test of the spirit of Christian unity. And yet Phillips Brooks, who stood for a large hospitality and for Christian unity, never exchanged pulpits. He preached in the pulpits of other churches, but he never invited a minister of another denomination to speak in the pulpit of Trinity Church. He thought it contrary to the law of the Church. To be sure, when the son of the great Presbyterian minister, Dr. John Hall, was married to a parishioner of Trinity Church, Dr. Brooks did allow his emotions to have such free play as to ask Dr. Hall to give the blessing to the young couple. For this he received a private reprimand from Bishop Paddock.

At the laying of the corner-stone of Saint Stephen's Church, Cohasset, in December, 1899, the Rector, the Reverend Milo H. Gates, had with my assent invited the pastor of the First Church in Cohasset to say a few words of welcome, which he did. I soon received a letter from twenty-six clergymen of the Diocese protesting against this as amounting to 'a compromise of Faith by our proper representatives, a recognition of Unitarian denials and an insult to God the Father and to his eternal Son Jesus Christ our Saviour.'

Answering them in a kindly way, I asked how 'any one could think that because a representative of the old religious life of Cohasset as well as of the citizens spoke a few words of welcome to the village, it could enter into his mind or the minds of the people or of any one that the Church was involved in sympathy with Unitarian doctrines.'

I added also, 'I trust that you will feel how happy it was that the Rector of Saint Stephen's Church, instead of affirming to the people of Cohasset that the Faith and Polity of the churches of Cohasset for nearly two centuries had been false or imperfect and that now the True Faith and Church had come there, should have offered the opportunity to the Pastor of the First Parish Church to give his gracious words of welcome.'

Fortunately, the widely published correspondence appealed to the right spirit and good sense of most people, and the 'Cohasset Incident' passed into New England's religious history.

Gradually, quietly, the temper of the Church has changed. No great principles have been yielded: loyalty to the standards of the Church is just as great. But we are coming to a clearer understanding of the relation of essentials to nonessentials; and the fresh, strong, and pervasive spirit of Christ is so sweeping through the churches as to lead us to recognize more fully the spiritual truths which we have in common, and trust to each man's loyalty to the creedal and institutional standards of his own Church.

I felt at the time and still feel that the adoption of Canon 19 did not have the importance that its advocates or opponents thought. I believe that the Church's law gave large liberty before, but that it was not realized or recognized. This canon was not the recognition of exchange of pulpits, but was a formal declaration of a more open pulpit.

Mr. Morgan had for years been a member of the General Convention. No matter how weighty his cares were in New York, he left his business for the Church's Council, was punctual and faithful at the sessions, sitting patiently through dull debates.

As the Richmond Convention drew to an end, telegrams were delivered to him more frequently than usual. If one came during a meal, he tore it open, read it; then putting the palms of both hands on the table, a habit of his, he looked straight ahead with fixed eyes and deep thought for a few minutes. One day a member of the party said, 'Mr. Morgan, you seem to have some bad news.' He shot his eyes across the table at the speaker and said nothing. No question of that sort was asked again. The fact was that we were so busy in our Convention work, we were not aware of the clouds gathering in New York and the country which were to break in the great financial panic of October, 1907.

The Convention was to adjourn Saturday afternoon the 19th, and we planned to leave Richmond Sunday evening. I now quote from my diary:

As I was going out of the door to the House of Bishops on Saturday morning, Mr. Morgan called me into his room and said, 'Bishop, I am going back to New York on the noon train.' I said, 'Why do you do that?' He answered, 'They are in trouble in New York: they do not know what to do, and I don't know what to do, but I am going back.' I replied, 'Why do you go back at noon? You will arrive in New York in the middle of the night. Why not get Mr. Sherry to have your two cars hitched onto the early evening train to-night: we will all pack up and go with you.' He said, 'I had not thought of that: I do not believe it can be done, but I will try.' It was done, and off we went by the evening train. Still, there was no suggestion of care or anxiety on his part, indeed rather the contrary: he was in the best of spirits. Held at Washington for an hour at midnight, he sat on the rear platform smoking until the train should start.

Sunday morning, as we ran into Jersey City, we went into Mr. Morgan's car for some bread and coffee before arrival, and found him sitting at the table with a tumbler turned upside down in each hand, singing lustily some tune which no one could recognize.

Arriving in New York, he put us into cabs. By that time we had begun to suspect that some big excitement was on. As we parted, we asked him if we should see him at Saint George's, and he called out, 'Perhaps so.' He went to his library, where through night and day during that week he was the centre and controller of the storm which the financial panic, reaching to the ends of the Nation, had sent whirling about New York.

This event, and his success in getting President Cleveland to issue bonds which stopped the flow of gold from the country and led to the resumption of specie payment, were, he always felt, the two great deeds of his life. The masterful way in which during that week he called upon the leaders in finance, the banks, and life insurance companies, to pledge enormous sums to check the panic and his success in so doing are unique in financial history.

CHAPTER XX

EIGHT WEEKS IN ENGLAND

1908

THE expansion of England from a Kingdom to an Empire during the last half of Queen Victoria's reign and the nine years' rule of King Edward, and the transformation in outlook and interests of the people, are beyond the imagination of the present generation. London became the centre of a world-wide administration. With the development of the Colonies and their increasing independence, the South African War, the Union of South Africa, and a growing consciousness of the mutual dependence of all parts of the Empire, came conferences of representatives from every part of the world, in order to reach better understandings and adjust their countries to new conditions.

It was natural, therefore, that the Church of England, the Colonial Churches, and the missionary representatives of the Church should assemble in London, and that they should invite representatives of their sister Church in the United States.

In the summer of 1908 were held in London two such conferences: one in June called the Pan-Anglican Conference, which brought from their fields hundreds, if not thousands, of missionaries and other Church workers; the other in July, the fifth Lambeth Conference, which was limited to the Bishops, of whom two hundred and forty met at Lambeth Palace by invitation of the Archbishop of Canterbury.

On the evening of June 7th, Mrs. Lawrence and I arrived in London, and were met at the station by Mr. J. P. Morgan, with whom we were to pass the summer. He took us to his house, 13 Prince's Gate, where a few close friends were already gathered for dinner. Our house-party were

Bishop Doane and his daughter, Mrs. Gardiner, and Bishop and Mrs. Greer. When we awoke the next morning, we found ourselves facing Hyde Park, where a few well-mounted men and women were taking their early morning ride in Rotten Row. There was no time to waste in watching them, however, as three busy weeks were before us; for being Chairman of the House of Bishops, I was thrust into duties and honors far beyond my deserts.

The next day Mr. Morgan saw us off on the train for Durham, where Professor Jevons of the University took us to his home, Hatfield Hall, Old Bailey: the very title smacks of Old England and ancient Durham. Late as it was, I took my seat at a dinner of the officers of the University to the candidates for Honorary Degrees, over which that delightful and courtly old gentleman, Dean Kitchen, presided.

As we separated for the night, I promised Archdeacon Watkins that I would celebrate the Holy Communion at the early service in the Cathedral. And then, too late, for he had gone, I had a panic; for while I, of course, knew the differences between the office in the English and American Prayer Books, I had never attempted the English service. The massive bells in the towers above, combined with my nervousness, gave me a restless night, and I am curious to this day to know how many mistakes I made; but I never dared to ask the Archdeacon. After we had seen the noble castle, the hill fortress of the Bishops, who were Earls of Northumberland, ten Archbishops and Bishops from various parts of the world, together with officers of the University in scarlet gowns, assembled for the conferring of honorary degrees. The Public Orator read his speech in English, to my surprise and comfort. The students at the other end of the hall interrupted him with facetious, rude, or witty remarks. Each of us stepped up to the Vice-Chancellor, was introduced, shook hands and sat down, henceforth a Doctor of Divinity by gift of the University of Durham, but with no visible token of that fact by way of parchment or hood. The

ceremony was in a noble hall, and, except for the students'
ribaldry, was conducted with simplicity and dignity.

Within a few hours we were in a beautiful country house,
close to Fountains Abbey, the home of Sir John Barran
and his wife Alice, whose childhood was passed in Boston
when her father, the Reverend Leighton Parks, was Rector of Emmanuel Church. The rhododendrons were in
their prime: only England can grow such. Sir John was
employed, as gentlemen of England often are, in cutting
out the blossoms that were degenerating into the wild pur-
ple, thereby sustaining the glorious crimson and scarlet of
the whole tree. When will American men love their gardens and work in them as the English do? One perfect
June morning in the grounds of Fountains Abbey, lying
on its lawns, dreaming of its history, and a perfect June
afternoon walking through the fields to the 'Fish Pond,'
taking tea in the 'hut,' and following the children home
along the path and between the hedges, is a day to remember.

Auckland Castle is the immense palace of the Bishop of
Durham, ten miles from the Cathedral. Here on the next
day we found as fellow guests twenty archbishops and
bishops, and passed a blustering, showery afternoon at a
garden-party; after dinner we had prayers in the chapel,
and, although it was after ten o'clock, the glory of the
setting sun threw the west window into brilliance. We
went to bed in one of the great wings called 'Scotland.'

The next day found us again in Durham, and with some
forty archbishops and bishops. The people were coming up
the hill from the town and surrounding country, and were
filling the Cathedral for a great missionary service; for
there had come back to their Durham home missionaries
from the ends of the earth, and they were all to praise God
together.

As I stood in the pulpit during the singing of the hymn
before the sermon, the scene and associations almost made
me dumb. Durham Cathedral, so stately without, is also
noble within; the Norman nave flanked by the massive

circular piers cut in zigzag and lattice-work patterns, the shrine of the Venerable Bede, and the graceful late Norman Galilee beyond, were almost oppressive in their glory. Outside the door was the very knocker which the malefactor of centuries ago, fleeing for his life, struck as he sought sanctuary in the House of God. Packed into the nave were men and women, miners, squires, clergy, innkeepers, bishops, city officers, missionaries, and university scholars: they were the living souls of to-day to whom it was my privilege to speak. Whatever I said, it was the occasion and the associations that spoke with stronger voice; and the spirit of the service went with the missionaries around the world. Reaching London at midnight, we found Mr. Morgan in his library waiting for us, playing 'Patience,' for solitaire or 'Patience' was his pastime every night of his life.

Yale had offered him an honorary degree of Doctor of Laws, and he was to cross the ocean for it and return to us. Two regrets beset him. In his loyalty to the White Star Line, he disliked to cross in a Cunarder, which happened to sail on a more convenient day; and in his ancestral loyalty to Hartford, he shrank from going to New Haven for the degree. 'Why cannot they bring the degree to a worthy city?' he exclaimed. However, the very next day we saw him off on the Cunard boat train. We then took train for Cambridge, where we stopped with our old friend, Dr. Donaldson, Master of Magdalen, who with Lady Albinia made us feel as if England's Cambridge were our home. Rowing down the Cam the next day to the races, we saw Magdalen make two bumps. From that time the College, which had lost prestige in past years, began to take its place towards the head of the river.

Why the University sermons should be preached at two in the afternoon of Sunday, the sleepiest hour in the week, I have never learned. Such was, however — perhaps is — the custom. The dons in scarlet gowns met in the Senate House, and with them I marched solemnly across to the Church of Saint Mary the Great. Besides the twenty or so dons and the choir, there must have been ten persons in the church. I gratefully recall the wife of a professor, an American lady, who cheered me through my sermon with her attentive look and wakeful eyes.

The next day we ran up to London, where at noon was the opening service of the Pan-Anglican Conference in Westminster Abbey, and a very real and beautiful service it was. Every English missionary looks from his distant post with eyes of affection to Westminster. After a quiet family lunch at Lambeth, I found myself at three o'clock in the great hall of the Mansion House beside the Lord Mayor, who was presiding at a meeting preparatory for Hospital Sunday. The President of the College of Physicians and Surgeons spoke, and I followed. It was a source of satisfaction that I could present to them an illustration of the connection between the hospital and the city in the social service work lately inaugurated in the Massachusetts General Hospital.

That evening at the dinner of the Pilgrim Society, at which Lord Curzon presided, Bishop Tuttle, following Mr. Asquith, spoke for the American Church; and whenever Bishop Tuttle spoke, he left no doubt that he was an Anglo-Saxon and an American.

Sitting beside a man who evidently knew London well, I asked him about Albert Hall, which has the reputation of having the worst acoustic properties of any hall in Christendom, as I was due to speak there the next day. He said, 'I can give you the secret of every hall in England, for I was for years secretary to Lord Salisbury. In Albert Hall speak to one o'clock.' Noting my surprise, he added, 'You know where twelve o'clock is on your watch, and one o'clock. Speak to one.' That was clear: my duty was to stand at the centre of the platform, and speak to the rear of the hall, at a slight angle to the centre aisle. I obeyed my orders, and, although the immense hall was filled with people, I was heard.

Persistence in building up my voice in my early ministry and in learning to direct and throw it directly to one person in the rear of the audience served me well on this trip. The common phrase, 'his voice filled the hall,' is a dangerous one. Of what use is it for a speaker with rotund and sonorous voice to fill the empty spaces up under the dome? No one is there to listen to him. His duty is so to speak as to make the people, each and all, hear him. If, therefore, he speaks to them, to one of them, well in the rear, simply, directly, and makes him hear, the rest of the audience have also heard. The warning to preachers in the choir of Westminster Abbey used to be, 'Speak to the Dean at the other end,' and in the nave of Saint Paul's Cathedral, 'Speak to the statue of Sir Joshua Reynolds — to be sure he is gospel-hardened, but the people will hear you.'

My duty at Albert Hall the following evening was to preside after the Archbishop had made an introductory address, and to speak on the topic, 'The Church and Human Society.' My diary records that 'I seemed to hold the audience.' My feeling at the time was that they were held because they could not get away. Scott Holland, a most effective speaker and preacher in his day, followed.

Plans for university convocations, pageants, meetings, and military reviews were suddenly broken into by the appointment by His Majesty the King of the afternoon of June 20th for a garden-party at Windsor Castle. When the King commands, all other engagements must yield. This was in one of the happiest years of King Edward's reign. England was prosperous and fully conscious of her imperial position. I doubt if Windsor Castle of glorious site and history has ever witnessed a more brilliant day and company. Description is beyond me. I simply copy my notes:

Sat., June 20. P.M.: Julia and I in motor went out to Windsor Castle Garden Party: a perfect afternoon.

Sir John Barran and Alice at the gate: several thousand guests on the great lawn back of the Castle: Ambassadors, Oriental Princes, the aristocracy, the Prime Minister and his associates, Generals and Admirals, leaders in Science, Art and Literature, hundreds of handsomely dressed women and well set up Englishmen.

Soon the crowd melted apart, leaving a broad aisle, down which walked the King and Queen, the Prince and Princess of Wales, and the members of the Royal Family, children and grandchildren to the number of forty to fifty, whom loyal Britons never tire of observing and greeting. All bowed or curtsied low, as they passed.

Then came afternoon tea. The scene perfect; the brilliant dresses of the women, the Orientals in many colored silks, and loaded with jewels: the distant landscape of the Thames Valley and hills beyond: the terrace with sunken garden: the music. Met a number of friends, English and American. It was a bit refreshing to see one unconventional democrat, Bishop Tuttle; for as he was led up to be presented to their Majesties in front of their marquee, he lifted with much dignity, a soft black felt hat such as might have been bought in a Salt Lake City shop. I have no doubt that King Edward took real pleasure in this note of reality.

Motored home by way of Hampton Court.

Worked in evening: Julia went to opera.

I needed to work, and I only wish that it had been put to better effect, for the next day was Hospital Sunday, which was at that time, and perhaps still is, a great occasion for the churches, when the whole people made their contributions for the hospitals. My diary runs:

Hospital Sunday. 10 A.M.: Westminster Abbey: preached. Lord Mayor and Sheriffs came in coaches: service in choir: full, many standing: preached without notes: Holy Communion, assisted.

The great service of Hospital Sunday was always at Saint Paul's Cathedral the same afternoon; for not only did the Lord Mayor attend, but His Majesty's Judges. The scarlet gowns and the wigs of the Lord Chief Justice and his associates gave a touch of color to the centre of the nave. As the procession of clergy moved into the nave, each of us was given a bunch of heather or twigs to carry in his hands; for ever since the London Plague whenever His Majesty's Judges have entered the Cathedral, the clergy of the Cathedral have carried bunches of preventive herbs to forfend their lordships from the pestilence. If these were effective centuries ago, why should they not be as effective now? The deep shame and remorse which follow me after attempting to preach on an important occasion received an added pang this day in that, in my terror, I forgot to take my bunch into the pulpit and lay it in its proper place.

The Pan-Anglican Conference came to an end with a noble service in Saint Paul's Cathedral, where a great thanksgiving offering was presented.

For a few days there was a respite of work, but not of interesting social functions. Ambassador and Mrs. Reid at Dorchester House were as ever hospitable, and entertained the American Bishops.

We were present at the marriage of Miss Jean Reid and the Honorable John Hubert Ward, equerry to the King, in the Chapel Royal before a small company including the royal family, a few statesmen and friends; it was a simple and beautiful ceremony.

I preached in Wren's noble church, Saint Mary-le-Bow, to a weekday congregation of men and thereby stood in the centre of London, for tradition has it that only those who live within the sound of the Bow bells are truly Londoners.

Rochester Cathedral had a wonderful missionary service, with some fifty bishops joining a large company of missionaries who had come back to their Diocese on furloughs. It is a larger and finer church than I had expected, and was packed with an earnest and sympathetic multitude. In order to enable those in the choir as well as the nave to hear my address, I had the audacity to avoid the pulpit and stand in the door of the heavy stone screen at the head of the steps. For once I felt that I had spoken with force and effect, and with a light step walked to the railroad station. The train was late, and, as I sat down on a bench, an English clergyman was beside me. He soon remarked, 'That Bishop who just spoke in the Cathedral was very dull, was he not? I could not understand what he was trying to say, and I doubt if he could.' Realizing that he had not recognized me, and fearing that he would, I mumbled a few incoherent remarks and looked straight ahead. There was a pause, and I could feel him studying my face: then, evidently enlightened, he rose and walked to one end of the platform and I to the other. We never met again; and I learned my lesson never to be confident of having said the right or effective word.

At Winchester the pageant of its history was enacted for several days. Here were the Saxons, the men of Wessex, Alfred the Great, Canute the Dane, William the Conqueror, William of Wykeham, and Henry VIII. To Winchester came Philip II, whose marriage to Queen Mary took place in the Cathedral. The walls of the old castle, the Saxon keep, were the background of the great stage, which was an ample and beautiful lawn. The Army had loaned men and mounts. The song of the Crusaders as they passed under the ancient walls still rings in my ears. The Deanery, where we enjoyed the hospitality of Dean Furneaux, is a part of the ancient monastery, and, as we wandered in the garden, we followed the banks of the little river Itchen, where Izaak Walton and Bishop Ken fished.

The next Sunday was 'Pageant Sunday,' when all Winchester sought the Cathedral; and here again, as I spoke of the worth of a great heritage, I could feel the sympathetic response of the people.

The next day we were in Lichfield, whose Cathedral is of 'exquisite symmetry, proportion and picturesqueness,' 'the queen of English minsters.' Its three great steeples command the town, wherein Dr. Johnson, whose house still stands, was born, and whose inhabitants he used to say were 'the most sober, decent people in England, the genteelest in proportion to their wealth, and spoke the purest English.'

The Cathedral had just been beautifully restored: rich glass and a new organ had been installed. My duty as preacher was to try to express the gratitude and sentiment of the people. The enthusiasm and devotion of the Dean and Chapter here and everywhere were touching, and their hospitality unbounded.

On July 3d, twenty days from the time he had sailed, Mr. Morgan came back via Paris, a Doctor of Laws of Yale. 'We will go out to Dover House to dinner,' were his first words. In vain Henry the butler expostulated that it was four o'clock, that the dinner was preparing, that it was impossible. 'Put the dinner into taxis and bring it out,' he said. So to Dover House beyond Roehampton and in the country we went. After tea under the magnificent copper beech, we walked over the grounds and through the greenhouses, saw the beautiful strawberries and wall fruit. Dinner over, we went back to Prince's Gate and by eleven o'clock Mr. Morgan was playing solitaire in his library, having left Paris that morning: and he was seventy-one years old!

At a dinner-party one evening an English lady said to me, 'What a wonderful and interesting collection of things Mr. Morgan has in this house!' 'My dear madam,' I replied, 'the most interesting thing in this house is the host.' Each day I had cause to marvel at some fresh characteristic. He was in some ways as simple as a child, most emotional, most bashful, masterful, courageous: a genius in his instinct for things beautiful; with a brain that drove him ceaselessly on in his search for beauty and his desire to acquire the best. His dominant characteristic was his intuition of truth: his eye and mind seemed to pierce and consume shams and lies. Hence the confidence which financial leaders placed in him.

Thirteen Prince's Gate, now by the gift of his son the residence of the American Ambassador, was two houses, his father's and his own, thrown into one. Here was gathered a large part of his art treasures, pictures, miniatures, the Fragonard panels, furniture, carvings, rugs, porcelains, ancient silver, priceless treasures. At the same time there was no suggestion of a museum or collection: it was a gentleman's home, and every part of it was in daily use.

His library door was open: life was informal, friendly, domestic, and simple, each day beginning with family prayers read by Bishop Doane in the library.

The Lambeth Conference absorbed us during July. A large committee upon the training of clergy, with the Bishop of London as chairman, was my chief interest, and I was surprised to find how far ahead the Church in this country is in the training of her candidates for the ministry. Our canons call for a college education, which is usually four years, and a theological education of three years. While the Church as a whole does not live up to this standard, the practical ratio is from sixty to eighty per cent. I had with me the figures of my Diocese, which was a full seven-year course for over eighty per cent. I found that the ambition of the best scholars of the Church of England was to bring up the standard to a residence of three years in a university, and one year of theological study. As any resolution along these lines would have lowered our standard, the American Bishops were released from voting, and I was asked to write a statement of the American standard as an appendix to the report.

The fact remains, however, that we look to the scholars of the Church of England for leadership. My interpretation of the situation is that the rank and file of our clergy are superior to those in England in education, but that the systems of education in the English schools and universities gave, and perhaps do give, a better foundation for scholarship. Added to this, their traditions as well as their stock of inheritance give a more thorough training and a broader outlook to men of real ability and industry.

Other subjects, such as 'The Moral Witness of the Church,' 'Revision of the Prayer Book,' 'Marriage Problems,' and 'Foreign Missions,' were discussed, studied by committees, and two weeks later reported upon and summarized in the Archbishop's final address. The fact that Archbishop Davidson had had an official part in every Lambeth Conference but the first, either as Archbishop Tait's Chaplain or as Secretary of the Conference, enabled him to carry the work through with dispatch, and of course with ability and a desire to do justice by every speaker and the various phases of the subject.

The Archbishop and Mrs. Davidson again showed themselves gracious, hospitable, and alert to the slightest comfort of their guests.

The University of Cambridge held a special Convocation at which, with other bishops, I received the degree of Doctor of Laws.

Weds. July 15. Took 10.20 train for Cambridge with Bishop Doane, Bishop and Mrs. Greer, Mrs. Gardiner, Mr. Morgan and Julia. Mr. M. and I went to a lunch of about 50 at Vice-Chancellor (Roberts) of Caius College. I spoke for a few minutes after luncheon for U.S. Bishops, and the Bishop of London spoke. Then scarlet gowns and velvet hats. We, the Archbishops and Bishops, the Vice-Chancellor, etc., marched to Senate House, which was quite full. Students did not guy but applauded, especially London and Liverpool. Those who got degrees were Calcutta, West Indies, London, Salisbury, Liverpool, Southwark, Tuttle, Uganda, Rupert's Land and myself. Degree LL.D.

On Saturday, July 18th, Julia and I went over to Lambeth to stay until Tuesday. A great garden-party at the Palace was a fixture for that afternoon, but a drenching rain drove the company indoors, where they pressed through the halls, drawing-room, guard room, and chapel, even to the top of Lollard's Tower. This was a heavy strain on the Archbishop and Mrs. Davidson at the close of three or four weeks of hospitality. But the Scotch are undaunted by rain. As we assembled in the drawing-room for dinner at eight o'clock, word came asking us not to wait for Mrs. Davidson and the Archbishop, for, after the guests had gone, they had been out on the back lawn playing golf, and were now dressing. Thus do the Scotch relax: we Americans had taken a nap.

Monday was a day of great interest, for in the afternoon the King and Queen received the Bishops at Buckingham Palace, and in the evening was the great debate and division in the House of Lords on the Old Age Pension Bill.

Mon., July 20. Mrs. D. came to breakfast after a horseback ride. A.M.: Commission on Ministry. Lunch at Palace. P.M.: With Archbishop to Buckingham Palace, where King and Queen received us at 3.30. It was like a King's levee: enter by Provinces: each bishop presented to King and Queen: he bows to King and Queen separately: they bow: later saw others presented: address by Archbishop: response read by King.

English ceremonials are prompt, short, dignified, and complete. What struck me especially was the German accent in the King's enunciation when he read — stronger than in conversation; also the fact that the Queen beside him was a Dane; and the Archbishop opposite was a Scotchman: truly the English are an absorbent race.

Then with Archbishop to House of Lords: there at steps of throne from 4.30 to 12 P.M., except 8.10: dinner at Lambeth. Very interesting debate on Old Age Pension Bill. First, a new Peer, radical, took oath of office: queer form: Lord Chancellor with three cornered hat on, herald: three bows at taking seat. Debate on Lord Wemyss's (aged 91) motion. Speeches by him, Archbishop, Lord Cromer, Lord Rosebery, Lord St. Aldwyn (Hicks Beach), Lord Avebury (Sir John Lubbock), Lansdowne, Crewe, etc. Division at midnight. Lansdowne and Crewe spoke with solemn, measured words. Walked back to Palace with Archbishop.

The steps to the Throne, which have a tread of some two or three feet, and height of three inches, come to the floor of the House of Lords, and one standing at the foot is practically on the floor of the House, separated by the members only by a silk cord. Here members of the House of Commons or Bishops introduced by a peer, may stand during debate or may sit on the steps, which in view of their dimension is neither easy nor graceful. At my side for an hour or so was the then most hated man in England, at least by the taxpayers, Lloyd George, who at the time was President of the Board of Trade.

When the division came, I had supposed that all those who had spoken against the bill would be counted: not so; they had said their say; it was clear that the country and the majority of the peers were against them; so only the redoubtable Lord Wemyss and three or four others passed through the minority door. Thus England took a long step towards social democracy.

It was half-past twelve when the Archbishop and I walked over Westminster Bridge. As we passed along the path between Saint Thomas's Hospital and the Thames, and then between the walls of the Palace and the river, where Archbishop Laud and the rest alighted from their barges, the bells of the Abbey struck; Parliament House and the Tower stood out clear in the moonlight. The ghosts of the past and the spirits of the future hovered in the air.

A few days later I preached in Saint Saviour's, Southwark, now the Cathedral. Here John Harvard was baptized, and hard by the Shakespeares lived and the Theatre stood. On the 6th of August in Saint Paul's Cathedral, the fifth Lambeth Conference ended with a celebration of the Holy Communion and touching addresses by Bishop Tuttle and the Archbishop. The 7th, Mr. Morgan devoted to showing us his art treasures at Kensington and elsewhere in the city. And on the 8th he saw us off on the ship train, having cancelled his own passage in order to meet Mrs. Morgan on her arrival in London.

In the early morning of the 16th, only eight days after we left London, our children and grandchildren were on the wharf at Bar Harbor to welcome us, and three hours later we were in Saint Saviour's Church giving thanks to God for His mercies.

CHAPTER XXI

THE PEABODY EDUCATION BOARD AND THE
TEACHERS' COLLEGE

1905–1910

MEMORIAL HALL at Harvard was dedicated on the 23d of June, 1873: eight years after Lee's surrender, but the 'bloody shirt' still waved, and sectional spirit was hot and bitter.

On the following day, Commencement, the alumni of Harvard, soldiers, sailors, and civilians, dined for the first time in the great Hall dedicated to the dead of the Civil War. The afternoon was hot, many speeches had been made, when General Frank Bartlett, the Chief Marshal of the day, was called upon. Gaunt, emaciated, full of spirit, hardly touching his crutches, he stood erect and strong on one leg, and threw into his sentences an even greater courage than he had shown in battle, challenging the Harvard men of the North, 'I firmly believe that when the gallant men of Lee's army surrendered at Appomattox (touched by the delicate generosity of Grant, who, obeying the dictates of his own honest heart, showed no less magnanimity than political sagacity), they followed the example of their heroic chief, and, with their arms, laid down forever their disloyalty to the Union. Take care, then, lest you repel, by injustice, or suspicion, or even by indifference, the returning love of men who now speak with pride of that flag as "our flag." And the Southern youth, in days to come, as he stands in these hallowed halls and reads those names, realizing the grandeur and power of a country which, thanks to them, is still his, will exclaim, "These men fought for my salvation as well as their own. They died to preserve not merely the unity of a Nation, but the destinies of a continent."'

That speech sounded through New England and the

whole country: and the people responded. As to myself, and I believe every alumnus there, I caught a new vision of patriotism.

This was in 1873. Seven years earlier, George Peabody, an American banker in London, who, born a poor boy in Danvers, Massachusetts, had won a unique position in England for his public spirit and his gift of model lodging-houses for the poor of London, had anticipated that speech by a deed which was a marvel of largeness of spirit and statesmanship.

During the Civil War for five years and more the children and youth of the South had had no education: indeed, the South had never had a public school system; the whites were largely dependent upon private schools; illiteracy was common; the negroes as a body received no education at all. While a few leaders realized the situation, and knew that an uneducated people could never rise and create a government or build up a new civilization, the mass of people and politicians had but little interest in the subject, and were hostile to the education of the negroes. Carpetbaggers and the reconstruction policy pressed on the South by the North destroyed the initiative, the self-respect, and the courage of the best of the Southern people. In May, 1866, Mr. Peabody laid before Mr. Robert C. Winthrop at his house in Brookline his plans for making a gift towards the education of the South, and on February 8, 1867, in Washington, he handed to a company of gentlemen from North and South one million dollars 'for the promotion and encouragement of intellectual, moral, or industrial education among the young of the more destitute portion of the Southern and Southeastern States of our Union.' In 1869, he added another million dollars.

There was in Mr. Peabody a touch of egotism and a satisfaction in publicity which worked to the advantage of his beneficences, especially of this fund; by the selection of men of national fame as trustees he called the attention of the whole country to the educational needs of the South and the common interest of North and South in building up a united Nation. General Grant and Admiral Farragut, William C. Rives of Virginia and William Aiken of South Carolina, William M. Evarts and Hamilton Fish were among the first board of sixteen trustees of which Mr. Winthrop was Chairman.

Dr. Barnas Sears, President of Brown University, resigned his office to become the first general agent; his creative genius charted the policy and directed the administration of the fund from the beginning. New-Englander as he was, he soon won the confidence and affection of the people of the South, becoming their leader in all their more important educational movements.

The Honorable J. L. M. Curry, a Colonel in the Confederate Army, and later United States Minister to Spain, was a worthy successor and brought the fund to a position of the highest influence and esteem. He, too, was recognized throughout the South as a leader. Appropriations were made, not as free charity to the needy, but as a stimulus to the enterprise and ambition of those States and institutions which were ready to meet the gifts by their own taxes, sacrifices, and contributions. The timeliness of the gift, the renown of the trustees, and the able administration of the fund enabled it to accomplish a work of educational and social redemption unique in the history of the country. As an object lesson to the country that North and South were socially as well as politically united, the trustees brought their wives to the annual meeting in New York, and in the evening met at the most sumptuous dinner that the great hostelry of those days, the Fifth Avenue Hotel, could provide; the report of which and of what they had to eat and drink was headlined in the press of the South and North. This annual event took place upon the suggestion of Mr. Peabody and at the expense of the fund; and in its social influence and publicity was well worth the cost.

Mr. Peabody in his original letter gave permission to the trustees to distribute the capital of the fund at any time after thirty years. By that time the trustees were beginning to feel that, as the pioneer work of education in the South was passing and other greater funds were entering the field, they would be wise to act upon this suggestion, and distribute the fund in such ways as would best promote Southern education and create a memorial to Mr. Peabody. Dr. Buttrick, later of the General Education Board, known then throughout the South wherever educational progress was undertaken, had with the help of Mr. Wickliffe Rose presented a plan to the trustees which had been adopted for the foundation of the George Peabody College for Teachers, so planned and situated as to make it a centre of Southern educational leadership. Nashville, Tennessee, was selected for the site. Acting on the basis of the report of Messrs. Buttrick and Rose, the trustees had appropriated for this purpose one million dollars, provided the State of Tennessee, the County of Davidson, the City of Nashville, and the University of Nashville (which had no real vitality, but some real estate and a small endowment), would meet this with a half million dollars, and provided also the new college should be placed in such close proximity to Vanderbilt University as to take advantage of its privileges. When at my first meeting, which was held in January, 1905, at the Arlington Hotel in Washington, I looked around the table, I saw at the head the Chairman of the Board, Chief Justice Fuller, and on his right President Roosevelt. There were also Joseph H. Choate, Richard Olney, Dr. Samuel A. Green, J. Pierpont Morgan, President Gilman, Morris K. Jesup, and a few others. Almost all of them happened to be my personal friends; but with the exception of President Roosevelt they were all much older than myself.

At this meeting the question, which had been under discussion for two or three years, as to whether the capital should be distributed or whether the Board should continue its work, came to a vote on the basis of the report of Messrs. Buttrick and Rose. To close the fund required a two-thirds vote. There were strong differences of opinion. The Chief Justice and Mr. Olney, for instance, were for continuance. As the roll was called, my name came last, and to my dismay it transpired that I had the deciding vote; and I was the only trustee who had but little knowledge of the merits of the case; and yet refusal to vote would be as decided an action as casting a vote. I have seldom been placed in such an awkward position. I knew well that public sentiment, as expressed by leading educators of the South and North, would regret the dissolution of the trust: as one leader had said to me, 'One dollar of the Peabody Fund is worth ten in any other name.' As, however, I realized the age of the trustees and their absorption in larger affairs, I made up my mind that, if the trust was really to continue doing effective work, it must either be filled with younger men or dissolve. The first was out of the question, for these men had been very loyal to their trust and could not be asked to resign. Hence I cast the vote for dissolution and the distribution of the capital.

The centre of interest was now transferred to Nashville, where the new Teachers' College was to be placed; and the Peabody Board soon found itself involved in a discussion and later a struggle of local politics, antagonistic interests, and personal ambitions lasting five years. Being the youngest member of the Board, I was made chairman of the committee to carry the action through, and in so doing I learned much of human nature and of the ability of a small group working through political influences to delay and jeopardize a great beneficence for the city and Nation.

I did not lack able support, for Chief Justice Fuller and Messrs. Choate, Olney, and Morgan were at my call for any service, and many hours and days they gave to the battle during the five years. At Nashville, Mr. Wickliffe Rose, a young graduate of the Peabody Normal School, was our agent, and throughout the struggle evinced the wisdom, tact, and courage which has brought him to his present high offices in the General Education Board and the Rockefeller Foundation.

As the fight was typical of many others in this democracy, wherein a forward-looking public enterprise opposed by local prejudices and vested interests wins its case by the creation of a more intelligent public spirit, I tell the story.

Nashville, Tennessee, was the railroad centre of the South, and because of this fact and the existence of Vanderbilt University and other institutions, gave promise of becoming the leading educational centre of the South. It was natural that those members of the Board who lived on the South Atlantic and Gulf States should be slow to accept this fact; and in the debate upon the distribution of the fund, that question had to be talked out. In the acceptance of the report of the committee, however, the decision was made for Nashville. As there were at the time only two real teachers' colleges in the country, those of Columbia and Chicago Universities, few persons realized the significance of such a college; that it was not a normal school, and that it must be in close relations with a university.

The trustees decided that the George Peabody College for Teachers must be in proximity to Vanderbilt University, whose site in the western part of the city amidst large spaces of open land gave opportunity for free development. On the south side of the city, approached through a negro district called 'Black Bottom,' stood the Peabody Normal College, a group of shaky buildings upon sixteen acres of land, enclosed with a new fence, which was the chief ornament. This had been the site of the defunct University of Nashville, which still held the title. Of this Normal College, which had been founded by the Peabody Board many years before, ex-Governor Porter, then eighty years old, was the President. The Governor was a typical representative of *ante-bellum* Southern chivalry, a man held in high respect by the whole city, possessing, however, a tenacity of conservatism and strength of will characteristic of some aged men, South and North, who have held high office.

He gave himself and his influence to the gaining from State, County, City, and the University of Nashville the half-million dollars to meet the million from the Peabody Board; and as a trustee of the Board he was supposed by the people of Nashville to represent the Board in all matters. He was sure in his own mind that the new Peabody College for Teachers (and he had no conception of what such a college should be) must be placed upon those sixteen acres where he had presided and where he hoped to preside. The Peabody Board were just as sure that the College should be placed in close proximity to Vanderbilt University. Hence, as the Board met year after year following its vote of 1905, it transpired that the action of one and another of the Nashville parties lacked something to complete the negotiations; and so this group of distinguished, able, and busy men composing the Board were held up by the political and local influences of Nashville, led by good old Governor Porter, who sat in the group and watched the struggle with the conditions.

Mr. Rose was, however, in Nashville guiding and educating public sentiment, winning the real leaders and organizations of the city. At the request of the Board and at Mr. Rose's urgent solicitations, I took an active hand, went to Nashville, studied the conditions, visited Vanderbilt, and met some of the leading citizens, Mr. Dickinson, Secretary of War under Roosevelt, a man of exceptional force and character, Mr. Vertrees, and others.

Upon reporting to the Board, I received from them support to fight the issue through. Dr. Pritchett and the Carnegie Pension Fund came to our help by retiring Governor Porter on a pension. Hence, at a meeting of the Board in Washington, January 31, 1910, just five years after the vote to place the College in Nashville, the committee reported that all obstacles had been overcome. The documents were signed; and George Peabody College for Teachers in Nashville in close proximity to Vanderbilt University was assured.

Soon after this the Board voted an additional half-million, which was met by gifts of over six hundred thousand dollars. Dr. Bruce Payne, the President, has by his indomitable courage and strong leadership wrought wonders. When I last visited Nashville, I found the College, endowed with over two and a half million dollars, standing upon a beautiful site valued at two and a half million more, and about to enter upon a campaign for twenty millions. With a strong faculty and a body of over one thousand regular students, increased by several thousand teachers and educational leaders in the summer school, the College is directly influencing every Southern State as well as a goodly proportion of Northern States.

The remainder of the capital of the Peabody Trust was distributed for educational endowments among the Southern State universities, and Hampton and Tuskegee Institutes. Upon our committee, also, with the advice of Mr. Rose and other experts, came the responsibility of creating the college organization and selecting the trustees. Mr. Choate stood strongly for the Harvard type of organization, others for the State university type. The result was a board of seventeen trustees selected from the South, a majority of them residents of Tennessee. We enlisted the best, and under the presidency of Judge Sanford, now Mr. Justice Sanford of the Supreme Court, the College has a future worthy of the name of its great founder.

As I recall those five years, the men and experiences, the characters and incidents, come clearly to mind.

Chief Justice Fuller was a quaint Yankee from Maine, with the dry humor and astute nature of his countrymen; of long body and short legs, with his snow-white hair falling over his collar, and an equally snow-white moustache covering but not concealing his pleasant smile, he wore even in summer a tall hat, which was rarely brushed, and a conventional black frock coat. His simplicity and democratic temper gave but little hint of his dignity of manner and vigorous temper when called for. He took pleasure in able debate and rather enjoyed a 'scrap.' I remember saying to him one afternoon before a trustee meeting, 'There is liable to be trouble to-morrow, Mr. Chief Justice: Governor Porter has on his war-paint; President Roosevelt will be there to talk. You will have to rule us with a rod of iron.' 'We'll see, Bishop,' he answered; 'I enjoy a little fun.' And on the next day I watched the alert face and keen eye as he listened to the indignant voice of Governor Porter, the impatient reply of Mr. Morgan, the lively speech of Roosevelt, and the effort of Mr. Choate to quiet the squall by his kindly wit.

In this particular issue, Mr. Choate and President Gilman were of a conciliatory temper: supporting the Board, lavish of time and thought in the cause, but holding back occasionally, lest there be a break which could not be repaired. Mr. Morgan listened, and, when he had the facts, gave his opinion and stood there. Mr. Olney, a friend and neighbor in Boston, was my closest counsellor. His habit of thought and expression was very simple, very clear and convincing. His record as Attorney-General and Secretary of State was that of a strong and determined man: many thought him a born fighter. My thought of him is that of a man who, when he was clear as to the right position, stood there, not stubbornly but reasonably, ready and glad to say why he stood there, but still standing. 'Why did you not say more at the meeting?' I used to ask him. 'You knew the facts and situation better than any one.' 'Well, Bishop,' was his answer, 'I have usually discovered that others like to talk more than I do, and when they are through, some one has usually said what was in my own mind.' In his modesty it did not occur to him that the fact that he said it was the important thing.

I have often wondered if a Southerner visiting New England feels the contrasts and the romance as I do in visiting the South. I do not mean the New South such as Florida and Atlanta, but those localities which suggest the South before the Civil War: what Mount Vernon and Monticello are in Virginia, the Hermitage is in Tennessee. The classic architecture, the baronial atmosphere, the beautiful proportion of house and rooms, the remains of the negro quarters, the furniture and the great bed in which 'Old Hickory,' Andrew Jackson, and his wife

Rachael slept, carry one back across the century to the Mexican War and the early days of the White House. One can almost hear the rattle of the wheels of his great carriage and the tramp of his four horses swinging around the Hermitage from the stable, and see the President and Mrs. Jackson step into it. Followed by a retinue of officers and black servants they start on the drive across the Appalachian Range to the Capitol.

As we were driving on the outskirts of Nashville, I witnessed a pathetic scene to which the North is a stranger. In a barren field set back from the dusty road stood a large gaunt frame building, a soldiers' home for Confederate veterans. Out through the gate, on either side of which hung a Union and Confederate flag, crawled an old horse with rope and leather harness driven by an ancient bearded soldier in gray, while behind him in the wagon lay a pine box containing the body of a comrade; then followed a creaking carryall in which sat four of the vanquished Army of the South. Turning in at the next field, they stopped at the open grave. It was a touching illustration of the Lost Cause. I went back to Nashville, grateful at the thought of a New South springing into a life rising in some degree from the College of George Peabody.

CHAPTER XXII

INCIDENTS, ANECDOTES, AND PERSONS

1909–1910

A MODEL autobiography ought, I suppose, to move along from chapter to chapter, revealing the developing character as a perfect tree grows to maturity. One difficulty in writing memories is that incidents, conversations, friendships, and even crises which cannot be thrust into the orderly life break in here and there.

This chapter will give a collection of unrelated facts and incidents, each having its place and influence in my memory and life, each standing out by itself. First, however, as a background I jot down samples of my daily routine during these years, drawn almost at random from my diary, for routine makes up the dominant interest, satisfaction, and usefulness of any worth-while life.

Mon. Oct. 5. Fifteen years Bishop to-day. Many blessings: far more than I deserve. Saw people and worked in morning: short ride in afternoon. Worked in evening.

Tues. June 11. A.M.: Wareham. Fine clear day. Called on Mrs. Tobey and prepared addr. Church of the Good Shepherd: Archdy. of New Bedford. Holy Communion and address. At 12 started in auto for Duxbury: lovely ride: lunched on road. P.M.: At Sisters of St. Margaret's Summer Home: blessed their chapel. Later: Church of St. John the Evangelist. Eveg Pr. and sermon. Called on sick man. Ran to Boston. St. Stephen's House: dined. Evening: St. Stephen's Church. Annual service of Guild of St. Barnabas: preached. Supper with nurses. To Cambridge in electric cars. To-day 116 miles auto and 4 services.

Weds. Nov. 20. No voice. In bed till noon. Wrote and read afternoon and evening.

Feb. 9. Ash Wednesday. Epis. Theol. School. St. John's Mem. Chapel. Conducted a Quiet Day for Students.

June 26. *Weds.* Harvard Commencement.

To Cambridge, about University Yard, to Class of '71 room in Holworthy, Chief Marshal's lunch, etc. Walked about with

Ambassador Jusserand: took him to Harvard Union. With honorary degree men to Mass. Hall; sat between Secretary Root and Cabot Lodge. Speeches good but a little long and heavy. Bonaparte presided. With Sec. Root to Harvard Union to see Sargent's portrait of Pres. Eliot. Packed the silver in evening.

Mon. June 7, A.M.: Symphony Hall, Boston. Inauguration of Dr. Maclaurin as President of Mass. Institute of Technology: made invocation: addresses by Mr. Fish, the Governor, Bryce, Pritchett, Lawrence Lowell and others. Long but excellent. Lunch at Brunswick Hotel.

Christmas Eve. At Sue's Christmas tree. Sat down 52 at dinner. A large, happy and good family party. Dancing afterwards. Home. Carol singers.

On Christmas Day I note, 'All at Holy Communion down to little Elsie.'

Tues. Oct. 20, 1908. New York. By midnight from Boston. Breakfasted at Grace Rectory with Huntington. 11. Grace Church. Funeral of Bishop Potter: beautiful and dignified, representative congregation of citizens: New York clergy: 18 bishops. Bishops Greer, Mackay-Smith, McVickar, Doane and I officiated. Went with Greer and Hare to Cathedral: his body laid before altar in crypt. Bishops Greer and Hare read committal sentences: I threw on earth.

As Bishop Hare, heroic missionary to the Indians, wonted to a life near Nature, and I were watching the men placing the body in the cold stone cavity, he said to me in an undertone, 'Lawrence, when my day comes, please see to it that my body is placed in Mother Earth.'

Bishop Potter once told me that he thought his father, Alonzo Potter, was the greatest bishop the Church had had. With the exception of Bishop White, I am inclined to think that he was right. Henry himself also held a unique position as bishop and citizen, and made distinct contributions to the life of the Church. The bishop of a great metropolis, he saw things in right proportion, and overlooked the unessential in ecclesiastical differences. His charm and his insight into human nature, his wit and

HARVARD COMMENCEMENT

From front to rear: Dr. Henry P. Walcott, Henry L. Higginson, T. Nelson
Perkins, Robert Bacon, William Lawrence, Francis L. Higginson,
Henry Cabot Lodge

courage, made him a most sought-for and effective speaker at public dinners and meetings. His speeches had a serious or religious note in the background, light as his touch might be; for, as I have said before, he had beneath his somewhat worldly manner the essence of evangelical piety.

He was the first bishop to recognize the responsibility of the Church in connection with industrial problems, and the relation of employers to their employees. By his speeches, writings, and reports to the General Convention, he compelled the attention of the Church and Nation. When he moved in the House of Bishops for a Commission on Capital and Labor, he asked me to join with him. Although the Commission met seldom, its triennial report, written by Potter, gained more publicity in the daily press than any other action of the Convention; for he was dealing with a living subject in a living way, and the Church did not then recognize it. I succeeded him as Chairman: the subject gained broader aspects, and the title was changed to the Commission on Social Service, which has since developed into the Social Service Department of the Church.

Believing as he did in the worth of public opinion, Bishop Potter was the first to urge the opening of the doors of the House of Bishops to the public. When there were only eight or ten bishops, they formed a friendly group who conversed and legislated in an informal way. As the number of bishops increased towards one hundred, talk, discussion, and legislation necessarily became more formal. The tradition was strong that the House of Bishops should shut the public out; there was a freedom and ease of talk which 'open doors' would check. I had no sooner entered the House than Bishop Potter took me aside, said that he had offered a motion for 'open doors' at a previous Convention, but had gained only two or three votes, and asked me to enlist in the cause. A few of us persisted, Convention after Convention, adding a few votes each time. When the General Convention met in New York in 1913, I was Chairman of a committee on the subject of 'open doors.' Mrs. Whitelaw Reid, with whom I was staying, invited to luncheon at my suggestion Mr. Melville E. Stone, General Manager of the Associated Press, to talk over the subject of 'open doors.' His first words were, 'Bishop, I assume that nothing is ever said or done in the House of Bishops of any interest to the public.' This remark from a master of public opinion gave me a jar. Had the House reached that level of dulness or social isolation that no one cared what was said or done? He continued, 'I assume this, because, if anything really interesting to the public does go on behind closed doors, the public will know it; for no company of one hundred men are keen enough to conceal their sentiments and actions behind closed doors against the inquisitiveness of groups of reporters, unless, as in the case of executive sessions of the Senate, reporters are in honor bound not to report what they have discovered. If anything of interest to the public goes on in the House of Bishops, the doors are practically open: and they open widest for the sensational features.' I reported this to the House. It took, however, until the Convention of 1919 in Detroit, some twenty-five years, to open the doors.

It is forty years since Bishop Potter called upon the people of the City of New York to build a cathedral. Soon after, the present commanding site, then occupied by a great orphans' asylum, standing isolate on a rocky hill, was bought. His vision was well in advance of his time. In this connection I quote from my diary:

April 19, 1911. *Weds. New York.* A.M.: Consecration, choir and chapels of Cathedral of St. John the Divine. Great body of clergy: about 20 bishops: long procession and service: too long: sermon by Greer: couldn't hear a word in the choir. I read Epistle. Procession started 10.30: service began 11.05: ended 2.50 P.M. Hotel Manhattan. Lunch with Greer and Bishops.

In administering the Diocese, I discovered that, while we were meeting our expenses and our fabric was growing, we were falling behind our real needs through lack of rectories and parish houses. I therefore undertook an enterprise which turned out most successfully. From about forty or fifty churchmen I collected one hundred thousand dollars, and named it 'The Reënforcement Fund.' I then notified parishes and missions in need of rectories and parish houses that, upon their raising a fund for construction, the Diocese would reënforce it by giving in the ratio of one to two, three, or four, as seemed wise. My committee, of which Bishop Babcock was the executive, after satisfying themselves of the soundness of each enterprise, added its share: sometimes the ratio was one to four or five. Thus parishes, stimulated by the interest of the Bishop and Diocese, raised sums which would have otherwise stayed in the people's pockets. They supplemented the cash by mortgages which they paid later. When the one hundred thousand dollars was gone, we raised fifty thousand more. I think that the replacement value of the property thus gained is now well towards a million and a half dollars. The comfort to rectors and their families and the added efficiency during these fifteen years have been of great worth also.

One day Mrs. Frank Shaw Stevens, of Swansea, called on me, and said, 'Bishop, I have sixty thousand dollars in the bank, which I do not know what to do with. I shall not invest, but give it away. I have come to you for advice. First, however, I want to give to some colored institutions in the South ten thousand dollars in memory of an old colored servant who has died.' This problem was quickly settled, for I advised giving it to 'The Church Institute for Negroes,' which Bishop Greer had organized and drawn me into as a holding trust to administer funds for Church negro schools and supervise the expenditure of the income. The ten thousand dollars is there and its income serving the schools.

'What next?' said Mrs. Stevens. A happy thought came to me. 'Mrs. Stevens,' I replied, 'I have just come from a rectory where the wife is simply worn out: two weeks' rest such as you and I would get at a winter resort would make a new woman of her. Now, why cannot you found a "Rest House" for the clergy, their wives, and for other tired Church people, teachers and others? What is wanted is a simple, attractive house in the country, built for the purpose.'

The result is 'Rest House, Swansea,' which has not closed its doors winter or summer since it was opened in June, 1911. It stands facing south upon a broad, gently sloping field, looking over the quiet village, and with vision unobstructed down Mount Hope Bay; accommodating from fifteen to twenty guests who in winter enjoy the open fires and sun room, and in summer the air drawing up from the Bay. Its atmosphere is that of a country home. There is sufficient endowment to assure its support with moderate rates. The good sense of the donor is recognized in her warning to me as to the furnishing of the house. 'Tired people ought to pass half their time at Rest House in bed. I want you to get the best box spring beds!' The next day came to me an extra check for the purpose. Some people began to ask for a chapel. 'No,' was my answer. 'A chapel will mean fixed hours and some moral compulsion to meet them. This is Liberty Hall. There is a lovely little church near by in the village, open to the guests at any time.' During several autumns, the Commission on the Revision of the Prayer Book has met here.

For two or three years, beginning in 1906, I was harassed by an outcropping of superstition in the form of a prayer chain, the source of which I have never discovered.

The prayer ran:

> O Lord Jesus Christ we implore Thee,
> O Eternal Lord, to have mercy on all mankind.
> Keep us from all sin by Thy precious blood,
> And take us to dwell with Thee eternally.

With it went this message:

This prayer was sent out by Bishop Lawrence asking the person receiving it to rewrite it and send it to nine others saying, 'He who will not rewrite will be affected by some misfortune or be eternally punished. He who rewrites this prayer for nine days will on the ninth day experience a great joy. Please do not break the chain; it must not be broken.'

Letters of inquiry, protest, and condemnation came to me from over the country, Europe, and beyond. The Associated Press and leading newspapers coöperated in an effort to stop the nuisance. Occasionally I had a nightmare that this persistent plague might follow me through life and into the next. It was like the perpetual dropping of water on a criminal's head, capable of breaking one's nerves. There was a pathetic side to it, the revelation of the number of people who would rather bother innumerable persons than run the risk of their own discomfort of mind. It finally died a natural death.

In December, 1908, the Tavern Club gave a dinner to Mr. Morgan in recognition of his great gift to the Harvard Medical School. He passed the night with us, and was so characteristic during those few hours that I am led to draw from my notes written some time later.

I met Mr. Morgan at the Back Bay Station at three o'clock. He arrived in good spirits. Knowing well his liking for his own cigars, I immediately went upstairs and got Phillips to give me a box. Mr. Morgan sat down in first-rate spirits to talk for an hour. A telephone from New York, however, called him two or three times. I then said, 'What next, Mr. Morgan?' He replied that he should like to go out to the Medical School, which he had not seen since it was dedicated; so out we went. With hardly a look at the School, he said, 'Where is that tablet in memory of my father?' We quickly found it; he walked up to it, read it, wet his thumb, rubbed it on the tablet, and said, 'I think that grain is fine enough,' walked off, and said, 'Now, let's go back.' Evidently there had been some question as to whether that particular stone was of the best and finest grain, and he was determined to test it himself.

On our return to the house a telephone call from New York was awaiting him. At the Tavern Club, Major Higginson presided, and Mr. Morgan had it understood that he was not to be called upon to speak. Speeches were made by Dr. Collins Warren, Dr. Councilman, and others, who dwelt on what Mr. Morgan's gift and the Medical School were going to do for science and humanity. Then Major Higginson called on me, having previously said that he wanted me to speak on Mr. Morgan personally. I plucked up courage to say, in Mr. Morgan's presence, what it was not easy to say, but which I felt was only just to him. After remarking that Mr. Morgan's face and look, which struck terror into many hearts, was a mask to conceal an unconquerable bashfulness and tenderness of heart, I added, 'You may think that the dominant thoughts in Mr. Morgan at all times are questions of finance and administration. So far from that, his chief interest is often as to how he can make some rich addition to his library or his art collection, or how he can do a kindness to some one who is forgotten.' Signor Ferrero, the Italian historian, had just read a delightful little paper, and I said, 'Signor Ferrero, Mr. Morgan's thoughts at this moment are probably on the problem as to how he can get that paper from you with your autograph for his library.'

As I sat down and Major Higginson was about to adjourn the dinner, Mr. Morgan surprised every one by saying that he would like to say a few words. After thanking the Club in a rather halting way for their kindness and telling them of his early associations as a boy in Boston, he added, 'I want to tell you this. My father used to say to me again and again, "Pierpont, have confidence in your country; never be on the bear side but on the bull side when the United States is in question."' He added, 'I have always remembered that, and have always acted upon it. We believe in our country and will do all that we can to uphold her,' and sat down.

We went home about midnight and found a telegram awaiting him. He tore it open and exclaimed, 'I have got them.' 'You have got what?' 'The Caxtons.' 'What Caxtons?' 'Why, you heard me telephone this afternoon?' 'Yes,' I said. He replied, 'The Amherst Library in England is to be sold: there are several Caxtons in the Library. I wanted them to add to my collection of Caxtons. Miss Greene went over some weeks ago quietly as my

representative. She has been negotiating with the auction-
eers and cabled to-day that I might be able to get them
before the sale. I cabled back from here through the telephone to New York naming a figure, provided I could have
them all, and here is a cable from her saying that I have
them.'

In the 'Life of Sir William Osler' (Vol. II, page 146), I
note a letter from him: 'I have been getting a few good
things, a first ed. of Avenbrugger wh. I have been after for
some years, & a Gilbert's Magnet; the first great scientific
book published in England. I got it at the Amherst sale
last week. Did you get a catalogue? Morgan bought the
Caxtons, 17 of them, 11 perfect!'

Mr. Morgan told me that he had no intention of speaking until Henry Higginson was about to close the dinner,
and that it was his first attempt. He made a very few
speeches after this which were, so far as I can learn, the
very speech of that evening. He could not so far overcome
his bashfulness before a company as to make a new one.

On the 4th of February, 1909, just a month before the
expiration of President Roosevelt's term of office, Mrs.
Lawrence and I passed the night at the White House. We
sat down to dinner at seven, but without the President, the
company being young James Roosevelt and wife, Mrs.
Dean Sage, Captain Butt, Mrs. Roosevelt, and Ethel,
Julia, and myself. My diary runs:

The President came in hurriedly a few minutes late and sat
down saying, 'I am mad. I have kept the wires to San Francisco
hot. Those Californians have with the lightest heart passed an
act which if we don't look out may lead to war with Japan. I
am glad that our fleet has left Japan and is on this side the world
by this time. The biggest fools in the country are the peace societies, who want to prevent the building of battleships, and without battleships Japan can press us.' He was much disturbed at
the situation, as the action of California in shutting Japanese out
of schools for whites will at least make Treaties difficult. After
dinner the President, James Roosevelt, and I went up to his library and sat down for three quarters of an hour's talk.

His three lectures which he is to give in Paris, Berlin, and
Oxford next year are already done, 'in his spare time.' Speaking
of the Race Question, he said, 'I made a mistake in saying that
this country welcomed people of all nations and races, Germans,
Italians, Japanese, etc. For the present, races have got to be
kept apart. We cannot welcome Japanese, for we cannot treat
them as inferiors: they must be treated as equals, and if they are
many, our people won't. We have got to arrange to receive only
Japanese who are students, travellers, etc. Japan wouldn't have
lots of Americans in her country.' He was full of his trip to Africa.

At 9: Congressional Reception. Aides came and took the
ladies down to the Blue Room. Then President and Mrs.
Roosevelt and the Cabinet and wives came down. Robert Bacon's first appearance as Secretary of State. George and Alice
Meyer, Bonapartes and we fell into line and made our bow to
them. Then came back to the Blue Room standing opposite
President and watched the line pass. Then we walked about,
talked with many friends. Bryces, Jusserands, Justices Holmes,
White, etc.

At about 11 the reception over, and 40 or so of us went upstairs to supper at small tables in the Hall. Julia sat at President's table with eight. I sat on Mrs. Roosevelt's left with
eight, Mrs. Scribner on my left, Gen. Magoon just from having
charge of Cuba next. He thinks that Cuba will now stand alone
all right. To bed at 12.30.

There are to me few more interesting rooms than that at
the east end of the White House, second story, which was
President Lincoln's office, and is now a guest room. Inscribed in a plate on the mantel is the record that in that
room Abraham Lincoln signed the Proclamation of Eman-
cipation, January 1, 1863. When bedtime came, I thought
of the gaunt, lonely man with divided Cabinet, gazing
from his desk through the window towards the south,
where across the marsh and the Potomac were the hills of
Virginia and its deep, heavy mud clods through which our
troops were wallowing. Beyond were the plantations and
the soldiers in gray: the slaves also with their hopes in
Father Abraham. I could almost see him bend to sign the
parchment. It was not easy to fall asleep.

Feb. 5. Breakfast downstairs at 9. President had breakfasted. Packed and left 'White House' at noon for the New Willard where Amory joined us in afternoon.

Evening: Jusserands gave us a dinner. Ambassador and Mrs. Bryce, Gen. and Mrs. Robert Oliver, Mr. and Mrs. Douglas Robinson, James Alsop, Miss Hopkins.

Julia too tired to go to the 'White House' dance. I went and stayed till 12.30, meeting many friends: was with Élise Jusserand mostly. President danced with her. Collation was only sandwiches, lemonade and a light punch. Many people, perhaps 400 there, Washington people, Army and Navy diplomats, etc.

Memorial Day in a village has a beauty and reality all its own: and I know of no more touching Memorial Days than those in Groton Village, where the boys of Groton School in their blue jackets and white pants accompany the veterans to the graves of those who have fallen.

In 1909, the 30th of May fell on a Sunday, which recognized the day by memorial services, postponing the procession and decoration until Monday:

Sun. May 30. At Groton. Memorial Day: my birthday: 59. Brilliant spring day after the rain. A.M.: Lovely ride in motor to St. Anne's, South Lincoln, to preach to the Old Concord Post and a company of militia. 24 Civil War veterans there by barge from Concord. After service shook hands with the veterans. Back to Groton: lunch at John Lawrence's with Mr. and Mrs. Choate. Talk with Mr. Choate about George Peabody College for Teachers.

Evening: Town Hall: townspeople, Groton schoolboys and their orchestra. Cottie took short service. I preached. Hall crowded: fine congregation and singing. Fine day.

Mon. May 31. Lovely day: holiday for all. To Groton Village. School and veterans marched to cemetery and decorated graves.

Among the graves was that of Farmer Samuel Lawrence who fought at Bunker Hill.

In June I received the high honor of a degree of Doctor of Divinity from Yale University.

At the dinner President Hadley announced the gifts. Ex-President Dwight said a few words. Speeches by Sec. of War Dickinson, myself and Pres. Taft. I spoke on endowed universities and State universities.

That afternoon we motored on to Lyme Inn; then in the morning to New London for the boat race.

6 P.M.: Observation train. Harvard-Yale race. Upstream: Yale got start: Harvard gradually drew away: for three miles anybody's race, though Harvard gaining: fourth mile gained 4 or 5 lengths and beat: beautiful race, perfect afternoon.

Got off train at finish, Red Top: onto motor ahead of everyone and ran to Narragansett Pier: people along the road shouting, 'Who won?' We first to announce 'Harvard.'

There is an exhilaration about that sort of thing which sends the blood rushing and gives one an undue sense of his own importance. I felt a little as if we were taking 'the good news from Ghent to Aix.'

A very different experience met me at West Point the following October, where I went to pass Saturday when the Harvard football team played against the Cadets, and to preach on Sunday. During the game a cadet fell badly hurt, and remained unconscious: the game was called off; the crowd silently melted away. That night his parents arrived and he died. Staying as I was with Chaplain Travers, I could feel the intense sympathy of the whole Academy. It was a moving service, that on Sunday morning: my words to the Cadets were halting, I know. The suddenness, the pathos, the hymns and prayers told the story; and those young men, some of whom were to pass through the awful carnage of war, were moved as seldom afterward.

After our return to Boston that autumn, as I was strolling across Beacon Street to the river, a new and great beauty unfolded itself, the Basin, Embankment, and Esplanade. The work had been going on for several years, and during the summer had been completed. The present generation cannot begin to realize the transformation or be grateful enough to those far-seeing citizens who in spite of opposition planned and carried through the great work of the construction of the Dam and the creation of a Basin unaffected by tides.

Up to that time, the river, responding to the tide pressure from the ocean at flood tide, crept up over the shining mud and onto the marshes, which bordered the Cambridge side as far up as Watertown. At ebb tide the river fell to a narrow stream, exposing the mud flats, while the sewage of Brighton, Cambridge, and the Back Bay fell from the pipes into the river, making it an open drain, the walls on the Beacon Street side reeking with filth. This description is not a pleasant one, but is true to fact, only twenty years ago. I had never expected to see the day when crowds would be skating on the Basin, but it came that winter, and I was among the skaters.

On the 22d of January, 1910, my diary runs:

P.M.: Unveiling of Phillips Brooks statue by Saint-Gaudens. Fine service in the Church: large choir: congregational singing. Excellent addresses by Henry Higginson and Dr. Mann. I read the prayers which I had composed. Church full of representative citizens: heavy rain: then out to unveiling.

As we moved out the Clarendon Street door and under the cloister, the wind blew the sheet covering the statue so as to bring one knee to view. I said to myself, 'That is not Phillips Brooks's knee.' Then, when the sheet fell from the whole monument, there was a feeling of dismay on the part of his friends, checked, however, by the thought that as the great master of sculpture, Saint-Gaudens, had designed and modelled the statue, our prejudice and first judgment must be held in suspense.

Years have gone by: I have passed and repassed the monument many times, and am still unreconciled to it as a statue and memorial of Phillips Brooks.

How vividly I recall a day when standing in the empty church he told me about the building of Trinity, and of La Farge and his men working upon the mural paintings!

'There was an attractive boy,' he said, 'running up and down the aisles, helping the painters and occasionally high up in the scaffolding, painting.' Brooks asked him his name and if he were going to be a painter. 'My name,' he replied, 'is Augustus Saint-Gaudens: my father says that I can never be an artist, so I am going to try to be a sculptor!'

I have no right to express an opinion upon the monument as a work of art. I assume, however, that a statue of a person should express the personality, the stature, as well as the spirit of the man. An exact likeness, though of some consideration in a public statue, is of secondary importance. While the features of the face and head of the statue are such a likeness as one who did not know Brooks might have gotten from a photograph, there is almost nothing in them that suggests the simplicity, the glow, and the spiritual feeling of Brooks's face and personality. As for the figure itself, its pose, attitude, action of arms, and the placing of his great weight upon his legs, Phillips Brooks is not there at all.

Assuming that the next and succeeding generations will not care whether or not the statue is a likeness of Brooks, they have a right to feel that it expresses him, his spirit and character. Here the failure is to me and to most of his intimate friends the greatest. He was simple: he shunned accessories of any kind; his inspiration was expressed in a touch, not from without, but by a spiritual presence within. The canopy and the veiled figure of Christ are alien to his whole temper and habit of life. The figure and pose of the statue are those of a conventional American orator making a speech. His own figure, gesture, and action were unique, often awkward, but natural to him — simple, real.

Saint-Gaudens was a great artist and sculptor. He declined in health for years; he died long before the statue was completed. What part he had in the first design or later work I do not know. But in my great admiration for him and his work done in the fulness of his strength, I cannot believe that he stands responsible for or should be judged by this statue.

It may be too late to hope for an adequate statue. Indeed, I doubt if Brooks's unique personality with its glow of the spirit can be adequately suggested in bronze. I have written with some decision, for it seems to me only just that these things should be on record as the expression of one who speaks advisedly for those who were closest to Phillips Brooks.

In June, 1910, the City of Edinburgh held hundreds of men and women of all Christian Churches, except the Roman and Eastern, from all parts of the world, to confer upon the work and methods of Christian Missions. The Church of England broke from her traditional reserve, and in the person of the Archbishop of Canterbury and others entered the Conference with keen sympathy. Appointed by the Board of Missions with Brent, Seth Low, and others, I went as a representative of our Church, and took the occasion to motor about England with Mrs. Lawrence and several of the children.

We crossed on the beautiful ship, Lusitania, and on Sunday morning the captain and I conducted a very impressive service in memory of King Edward, who had died a few days before. The great saloon was packed with the ship's company, passengers, officers, stewards, sailors, and stokers.

We arrived at Liverpool and motored from there over the Derbyshire Hills by Haddon Hall to Stratford-on-Avon, where we took tea with Sir George Trevelyan, who was anticipating with keenest interest a visit on the next Sunday from Roosevelt, with whom he had corresponded for many years, whom he had never met, and who was now on his way home from his hunting trip in Africa.

We found London stirred with excitement by Roosevelt's speech in the Town Hall upon the Egyptian situation. Statesmen and people knew that he told the truth: some were glad that he had done so; but the feeling was strong that an Englishman, not an American, should have said what he did. No Englishman, however, had dared to say it. He wrote me to come and see him at Sir Arthur Lee's. I went and found him in fine form and talking in the most decided way of his determination to keep out of politics on his return home. For a week we stayed, by Mr. Morgan's urgent invitation, at Dover House. We met again our friends at Lambeth, Westminster, and elsewhere. I preached in the nave of the Abbey. Then to Oxford, which was on tiptoe of expectation of Roosevelt and his Romanes Lecture. Here is my record of the day:

Tuesday, June 7. A.M.: To see colleges. As Roosevelt was seeing them, some were closed. Went into Christ Church Cathedral: Roosevelt was there. Showers. Crowds following Roosevelt. Took Ruth to several more colleges. At 12.30 went to a lunch in Masons Hall to Roosevelt. About 200 men and ladies there. Talked with Dr. Parkin, Sec. of the Rhodes Trust, also Pres. Wheeler, etc. Roosevelt, Mrs. Roosevelt, Alice, Kermit and Ethel all came. Ambassador Reid, W. Phillips, and others. A Rhodes scholar from California presided well. Short speeches by Ambassador Reid and Roosevelt and an American scholar.

Then to Sheldonian Theatre, packed with people, seldom such a demand for tickets. Stood on floor in crowd for two hours. First organ played, 'Marching through Georgia, etc.,' until three o'clock. Then Chancellor, Lord Curzon, Vice-Chancellor, Dr. Warren of Magdalen, and long line of doctors in scarlet robes entered. Then convocation. Chancellor asked if agreeable to give Degree of D.C.L. to Roosevelt. 'Placit.'

Then Roosevelt and orator entered. Audience rose, great applause and cheers. Oration. Excellent speech of introduction of Romanes Lecturer by Curzon. Then Roosevelt, Romanes Lecture on 'Some Analogies between Biographical Development and Racial and National Development.'

From Oxford through Banbury Cross and Peterborough we ran along the byroads and fields of our Pilgrim ancestors to Edinburgh. There for ten days we joined in the Conference, remarkable for its fine spirit, heroic characters, and enlightened discussion under the strong and dignified chairmanship of John R. Mott. We found Archbishop Davidson in his home at Muirhead where he was born — a bold rock on the Firth of Forth. From Edinburgh to the south we halted at the English Lakes, where Miss Arnold in her father's lovely house, Fox How, received us. Seventy-seven years old, alert, with the simplicity and charm of an English lady, she was a living link with Arnold and Wordsworth.

In London we stayed at Lambeth. One Sunday afternoon in the Chapel the Archbishop confirmed four of the maids of the Palace with a tenderness and simplicity as if they were his own children.

I like the frank way in which the English debate. At the Church Representative Council, an American would have thought by the way they met each other in debate that Gore and Henson were sworn enemies. In half an hour Henson at his own lunch-table was sitting with Gore and myself on either side, and one would have said that they were sworn friends. The debate was over and forgotten.

CHAPTER XXIII
HARVARD CHANGES PILOTS
1909–1910

In the spring of 1909, President Eliot, having reached the age of seventy-five, resigned the office which he had filled with great distinction for forty years.

Meeting him frequently in the College and as a neighbor, in several social clubs and in friendly talk, I had for him great reverence, high admiration, and an affection as warm as a man sixteen years his junior could sustain for such a stately character. To think of him, however, as only a stately character would do him injustice, for he was endowed with rare qualities of friendly interest, sympathy, affection and other homely virtues which supplemented and enriched his well-known characteristics revealed in educational and moral leadership.

I venture to jot down a few memories illustrating these friendly qualities. For the dignity of his manner often gave an emphasis and sometimes a diverting note to his familiar conversation.

One morning, soon after the election of Phillips Brooks, a friend meeting me, said, 'I have a story on you. I met the President yesterday, who in speaking of Brooks's election said that it was a great mistake, adding, "Brooks is a great man and a great preacher. They do not want either for a bishop. A man of good sense and administrative ability, not great, is what they ought to have. Dean Lawrence would do." '

Two years later, the morning after my election, as I was walking through Harvard Square, the President came across and congratulated me warmly, saying, 'You may not know it, but you were my candidate when Brooks was elected.'

The President then went on with characteristic advice, for he was a master of detail. This was the first conversa-

tion between the President of Harvard University and the
Bishop-elect of Massachusetts, both standing in the centre
of Harvard Square. 'Let me give you a word of advice,'
said the President. 'In your visitations you will be compelled to sleep in many cold spare rooms which have not
been occupied or aired for some time: the cold will have
permeated the bed. Buy as soon as you can a thin all-wool
blanket: always have it in your valise. Then, when, oc-
cupying such a room, you have undressed and have
put on your night clothing, wrap the thin all-wool blanket
about you and get into the bed: the chill will not strike
through to your body.'

He had, as every one knows, a habit of asking questions,
the answers to which he carefully tucked away in his retentive memory.

Sitting between the President and Mr. Bryce at a Phi
Beta Kappa dinner, I was called upon after they had both
spoken. I told the members that the dinner had been to
me a most interesting one; for ever since I had known Mr.
Bryce, I had been studying him and President Eliot in an
effort to discover which of them could ask the most questions in the same space of time: that an exceptional opportunity in sitting between them had convinced me that
Mr. Bryce was in the lead.

The President then rose and said, 'Bishop Lawrence has
referred to a habit of mine which has been noted by
others; for last summer Mrs. Eliot asked a neighbor of
ours at North-East Harbor, a farmer, to come into the
house and look at a recent portrait of me. The farmer
stood gazing at it for some time and finally drawled out,
"Yaas, that's him sure, but he ain't asking no questions."'

He had the patience of a true statesman. Just after
his retirement as President, he wrote me that at his last
meeting with the Corporation, favorable action was taken
upon a subject which he had had in mind at his first meeting, forty years before.

He was a deeply religious man; and was always at daily
chapel, not, as he insisted, as an example, but for his own

strength and comfort. I heard him once say, in speaking of Phillips Brooks's power of prayer, that prayer is the greatest achievement of the human soul.

At a great dinner given him at the time of his resignation, at the Somerset Hotel by the Harvard alumni, having been requested by the committee to speak of the President personally, I traced the development of his character as seen in the changing lines of his face for forty years: at the first austere and cold; then sad from personal sorrow; soon softening and mellowing as he felt the sympathy and growing appreciation of friends and alumni. Suggestions of isolation faded into the background, while friendly, social, and cheerful features, even a sense of humor, gained emphasis; the mellow, tender lines grew continually stronger, so that, as he reached threescore years and ten, his portrait revealed a man strong and serene, a lover of truth and of his fellows, full of hope and the spirit of optimism.

These features I illustrated with personal anecdotes. As I sat down, he turned to me, and remarked with much gravity, 'I recognize the truth of much that you have said.'

As Dr. Eliot grew older, he became solicitous for the health of his friends. At the funeral of Henry Higginson we walked together as pallbearers. As we were approaching the grave, he questioned me closely about my health, for I was recovering from a surgical operation. His solicitude was so evident that on my return home I wrote him a note saying how touched I had been at his kind thought.

His letter in response was so considerate and characteristic in its fulness of detail (he was eighty-four years old) that I cannot forbear quoting it.

My exhortation of last Monday was not based on any experience of my own, but proceeded from the intense desire on my part for your prolonged usefulness as church administrator and leader of public opinion through many coming years. So far as I know, I never worked unreasonably (my strength was unusually great) except for a period of about eight years from the time following May, 1869, when I became President of Harvard. Then I found incessant work my best support under the burden of a great sorrow. Even then I was careful to ride horseback vigorously every day. It seems to your friends that you have overworked seriously ever since you became Bishop.

In order that you may continue your good work for your church and your country ten years more, I suggest that you employ, first, some admirable person to make visitations for you; secondly, a private secretary who can write letters in first-rate form with only a few words from you to indicate their general purport, his letters to be read to you before you sign them, but not by you, and that only when they relate to important matters. The same secretary should handle all telephone work. Of course you should never go to a telephone yourself, or be called upon to decide anything on only telephonic notice. You should also have a thirty-minute nap somewhere in the middle of every day, go to bed early, get up late, sit at no long banquets, stay in the house in very cold weather, and in general avoid excitements and fatigues. It will be a safe practice for you to follow strictly the advice of your physician and of Mrs. Lawrence. I hope that you are employing the most sensible physician in Boston, and that he is not an old man. The bright young fellows have had a much better training than the old ones received.

All your friends wish for you long continued serviceableness, and therefore a prudent, protected mode of life under easy and happy conditions.

This confidence in youth was an unfailing characteristic and a beautiful one, increasing with his years. The youthfulness of his mentality, too, was a source of constant wonder: the keenness of his observation, his retentive memory, and his insatiable desire for information persisted even after his bodily strength had weakened in his ninety-third year.

On January 13, 1909, the Overseers, having gathered at the call of the Secretary to take action in regard to the election of a President, met in one room of the Treasurer's office. The Corporation, having in previous meetings discussed and informally decided upon the candidate, met in another room. My diary runs:

Weds. Jan. 13. 11 A.M.: Harvard Overseers, full meeting.

Pres. Eliot after asking in behalf of President and Fellows permission of Overseers to proceed to the election of a President, retired to other room where the Corporation waited. In a few minutes, he came back and reported the election of Abbott Lawrence Lowell: action to be taken by Overseers at next meeting. The election by Corporation well received, though evidently some New York, Chicago, and other alumni feel it to be a provincial Bostonese election; but they have no one better to suggest. He does represent the academic temper, and many want a 'personality' to arouse enthusiasm, etc.

A week later the Overseers met and confirmed the election of Professor Lowell as President.

Having been present as a student at the inauguration of President Eliot forty years before, and having been officially connected with Harvard during most of that period, I am tempted to pause a moment for a review.

Charles Eliot was thirty-five years old at the time of his inauguration: a chemist, a teacher who had caught the spirit of modern science. From boyhood he had been bashful, reserved, having very few intimates, self-reliant in thought and deed, one who had apparently never experienced the common passions and temptations of youth. He was distrusted by the conservative administrators and teachers and was at little pains to disarm their prejudices.

Such a young man was thrust into the office of the President of an old-fashioned New England College, of which his chief advisers and fellow workers were much his senior.

The influence of this strong personality was felt in the administration and teaching every day for forty years. Professional Schools and Graduate Departments came into being or were transformed from inchoate and rudimentary groups. The elective system, hardly existent in 1869, was developed into a freedom of choice which in the arts departments required the multiplication of courses and teachers to an extent which often bewildered many students of good intentions and gave great liberty to students of easy disposition. If boys coming from schools to the University found difficulty in adjusting themselves to the unwonted liberty of elective courses and social life, and if some fell by the way, the total result in intellectual development and self-reliance of character was in his judgment worth the risk. A university was not for immature boys, but for serious-minded young men. The education and development of Charles Eliot had been through testing to self-reliance and he administered the University on this principle. To those who have had the privilege of knowing him well, and among those I have the assurance to count myself, Charles Eliot was very human, very humble, very tender and full of charity. He was a great President, a great administrator, a great Educator, a great citizen. He was more than these — a great character.

Into the presidency of a university moulded by such a master character and leader of national education, Abbott Lawrence Lowell entered at the age of fifty-three. Like Dr. Eliot he was of strong and cultivated New England stock. Lowells and Eliots had for generations served the College, Commonwealth, and Nation in literature, statesmanship, and military duty. By inheritance and temperament, Lawrence Lowell was of a social nature. His mother entered society in London when her father, Abbott Lawrence, was Minister to the Court of Saint James's. Both parents were active in Boston society; both were of exceptional mental ability. His mother, gracious, of a somewhat nervous temperament, was of sweet and amiable disposition. His father was a man of excellent business ability, of definite views, cultivated, and with charm. Each of the five children showed marked ability through life. As a student, Lawrence, while holding high standards in character and study, was a member of the social groups; alert, conversational, sympathetic, democratic in convictions, though not always in manner. By training a lawyer with a love of literature and a sense of public duty, he gradually turned towards public service, especially in education, and in 1900 became Professor in 'The Science of Government.' He was a stimulating lecturer and skilful teacher. From 1900 he had been the sole Trustee of the Lowell Institute, a responsible office which he still holds. His intimate knowledge of the University, its administration, temper, and progress, led him to the conviction that the time had come for certain changes, and his election by the governing Boards was an expression that they felt the same. Great as had been the work of President Eliot, another generation with other methods and emphasis had come upon the scene.

The inauguration of President Lowell took place in October on a platform built in front of University Hall: the great audience in chairs set on the sod of the Yard, faced the Hall. A few quotations from his inaugural address strike the salient notes.

Every student ought to know in some subject what the ultimate sources of opinion are, and how they are handled by those who profess it.

The best type of liberal education in our complex modern world aims at producing men who know a little of everything and something well.

Education is not knowledge: it is an attitude of mind.

The change from the life of a school to that of a college is too abrupt at the present day. Taken gradually, liberty is a powerful stimulant, but taken suddenly in large doses, it is liable to act as an intoxicant or an opiate.

Our American Universities do not strive enough in the impressionable years of early manhood to stimulate intellectual appetites and ambitions, nor do they foster productive scholarship enough among those members of their staffs who are capable thereof.

All the activities of a University are more or less connected with, and most of them are based upon the College. It is there that character ought to be shaped, that aspiration ought to be formed, that citizens ought to be trained and scholarly tastes implanted.

The freshman dormitories, the restriction of electives

under the grouping system, and a more vital interest in true scholarship and in the individual student have been some of the logical results.

As I walked away from the inauguration to Phillips Brooks House, where we were to take off our gowns, the new President happened to come up beside me, and I said, 'Lawrence, your address is a pretty radical break with the past.' 'No,' he replied, 'the same old ship on the same course, only on another tack.'

CHAPTER XXIV

THE RESTORATION OF THE OLD NORTH CHURCH

1912

PAUL REVERE's ride and the lanterns aloft in the Old North Church kindled the patriotism and touched the sentiment of the youth of the country, even before Longfellow wrote his poem. The restoration of the church in 1912 gave me such satisfaction that I believe the story will interest others.

Apart from the 'lantern' episode, Christ Church has historic associations. It is the oldest church in Boston, and except the Old State House, the oldest public building. Built in 1723, its architecture is of the best Colonial type; its lines without and within are true, its proportions good; its exterior is of imported English brick, its walls two and one half feet thick. After 1740, when the spire was built by the bounty of Honduras merchants, it dominated the North End of the city and was 'a guide to the mariners.'

Major Pitcairn, of the Royal Marines, who led the redcoats out to Lexington, was to us schoolboys the embodiment of all that was brutal and cruel, shooting the farmers and insulting the women. In truth, he seems to have been a good soldier who did his duty in a soldierly way.

Two months later, he led his men at the battle of Bunker Hill. As he was scaling the redoubt, he fell mortally wounded into the arms of his son, who carried him on his back from the field to the boats, and then, kissing his father farewell, returned to his duty. Pitcairn bled to death, and his body was laid in a tomb in Christ Church, where, for any evidence to the contrary, it now rests.

I now come to modern history. Fifty or more years ago the native American population began to leave the North End; within a generation their houses, having become tenements, were occupied by recent immigrants. The people of

Christ Church moved to other parts of the city and the suburbs. Hence the affairs of the parish fell into the hands of a small group of men who were unable to support its services adequately or to keep it in repair. As it was visited by thousands of strangers every year, its condition became a source of scandal and its usefulness as a house of worship meagre.

Sometime in the eighties, Bishop Paddock, supported by a few public-spirited churchmen, tried to gain a hold on the parish, but those in power, suspicious that the control would go from them, refused all advances. Bishop Brooks in his day tried again, but without success.

The parish, being a corporation consisting of owners of pews, had full control of the property, and when I came on the scene there were eleven proprietors who were, of course, proud of the historic church and of their ownership of it. The senior warden, Mr. Thomas Hall, a worthy man, dominated the situation. He kept the valuable records under his bed in East Boston. The Communion Service, given by King George II, was stored in a dwelling-house and later in a jeweller's vault, and was carried on the first Sunday of each month to the church, where after Holy Communion the silver was shown to the congregation, which in expectation of the show was somewhat larger than at other times. The Bishop could visit the church, and hold confirmations, but was otherwise powerless.

After I became Bishop, I received letters from strangers in various parts of the country, who had visited the church, protesting against its condition, the charges of the sexton for entrance, and the fact that the breath of one vestryman passing the plate emitted fumes of whiskey. I determined to change the conditions and to put the Church under such authority as would ensure its safety, dignity, and usefulness. It took me eighteen years.

When, at my occasional request, Mr. Hall came to see me, I would state in strong language the disgrace to the Diocese in allowing an historic monument to be so neglected, but Mr. Hall was suspicious, saying, 'Bishop Pad-

dock and others tried that on, but they did not succeed.'
To which I replied, 'Why might I not enlist a few well-
to-do, public-spirited men to buy pews and coöperate with
you in carrying on the church?' 'We are not selling any
pews,' was his answer. 'Why should I not buy a pew myself and take part?' 'You cannot buy one, Bishop. We are
in possession and we are going to hold the fort.' And 'hold
the fort' they did, year after year.

Feeling some responsibility for the welfare of the neighborhood, the Diocese placed in a tenement near by one or
two social workers. My astonishment was great when in
May, 1911, I received word from one of them that the proprietors of Christ Church had plans for the construction of
a four-story tenement, close to the church, on the site of a
dwelling-house in the churchyard. There was no time to be
lost, for, if the tenement were once built, it would provide
income for the support of the church and for the unlimited
control of the present group.

I then discovered that an interested citizen had been
allowed to buy a pew, had been elected treasurer, and was
supplying the ingenuity which Mr. Hall lacked. He was
Mr. John D. Bryant, a lawyer in excellent standing, a man
of high character, and an acquaintance of mine. He had
been for many years a member of Trinity Church, Boston,
but when in Dr. Donald's rectorship the choir had been
moved from the rear gallery to the chancel, Mr. Bryant's
hatred of 'ritualism' prompted him to transfer his alle-
giance to old Christ Church, where the choir sang in the
rear gallery. It was he, I discovered, who invented the
tenement-house scheme, whereby Christ Church would
gain added income and remain under its present control.
I therefore called upon him immediately, told him of my
patient waiting, and of my efforts so to change conditions
that the church could be restored and supported; offering
at the same time to do anything in my power, but with the
understanding that I must have a part in the administration. He was courteous, but adamant. 'As soon as you
get control, Bishop, you will do what all the Episcopal

churches are doing, move the choir from the gallery down to the chancel.' In vain I protested that, while I had no power to promise for future generations, I felt that in a church of such Colonial architecture the choir belonged in the rear gallery. He was not satisfied. When he complained that his office as treasurer was irksome, I offered in vain to be the treasurer myself. I finally came to the real point.

'Mr. Bryant,' I said, 'I understand that you and the vestry are planning to tear down the dwelling-house next to the church and build a tenement there.' He acceded, saying that it was necessary in order to increase the income. 'You as a lawyer know,' I continued, 'that I have no legal power in this matter: I am, however, the Bishop of this Diocese and of Christ Church: I am also a citizen. I shall not allow the church to stand before the community responsible for covering one more foot of open land with a building. The people at the North End need all the open space and sunlight that can be given them; nor shall I allow the church for whose safety I stand in some way responsible to be endangered by fire from a near-by tenement. Your building will not go up.' To which he answered that it would, that they were arranging to borrow enough money on a mortgage to construct it. I closed the interview by saying, 'Mr. Bryant, if you allow this plan to go through, I will publish you and what you and the proprietors of Christ Church are doing over my own name, in every newspaper in the City of Boston.'

At my request a friend kept a sharp eye on the City Building Inspector's office, in order to report to me if any such plans came in for approval. Meanwhile, I tried to discover who was lending the money. This latter took some days, for Mr. Bryant was wary. One noon, when I was presiding at an Archdeaconry meeting in Winchester, word came to me giving the name of a bank in a neighboring city. I surrendered the chair to another, went to the telephone, called up the bank, and by good fortune found that I was talking to an old parishioner whom I had not heard of for years. In response to my question, he replied that the President had the loan in hand, and that the title was now being looked up. I then said, 'You may tell the President that I have no legal power in the matter, but that I am Bishop, and that if his bank lends that money, I will publish it in every paper in Boston'; and hung up the receiver. On inquiry a few days later, I learned that the bank had declined to make the loan. Thus far the church was safe; but we were in no better situation than we had been for years before. However, the summer was at hand, and Mr. Bryant had gone away. So I went to Bar Harbor. They still 'held the fort.'

On July 24, 1911, Mr. Hall died, and while his funeral service was being held in the church, Mr. Bryant died in his summer home in New Hampshire. Two worthy but stubborn men passed on. A cancelled bequest of ten thousand dollars to Christ Church in Mr. Bryant's will reveals an interesting cast of mind.

Article 55. . . . Half of the net income of such fund and of its accumulations, is to be applied through the Rector, Wardens and Vestry or otherwise as the trustees for the time being may think will best accomplish my purpose, to keep in repair the historic edifice known as Christ Church, on Salem Street, Boston. . . . So long and only so long as said Christ Church edifice remains under the control and management, as at present, of the corporation known as Christ Church, or as the Rector, Wardens and Vestry of Christ Church (I am at this writing not sure of the exact corporate name, but whatever name that is, I mean), and to improving the musical service of the said church, so long as and only so long as the present form of service in said church — musical and otherwise — is maintained, which form I understand has been in use in said church since its foundation, namely so long, and only so long as the choir is made up of male and female singers, not vested, and is located in the organ and choir gallery where the same now is, at the westerly end of the church, opposite the chancel and so long, and only so long, as the Divine Presence is recognized as pervading the church and encompassing the worshippers that it is not necessary to turn about, and look into any corner in order to find the Deity, or to acceptably declare belief, or to render homage, or to implore

benediction. Whenever a narrower belief of the Divine Presence
in His Church is taught, or is indicated by the habitual practice ('habitual,' as contra-distinguished from some sporadic or
exceptional use by a stranger), as by the habitual or customary
turning about of the clergy in reciting the creed, or in invoking
the benediction, or whenever the musical service in that church
shall be habitually conducted by a vested choir at the chancel
end of the church, or elsewhere therein, or whenever, if at all,
(quod Deus advertat) the church edifice shall pass out of the
control of the corporation and pew owners; then, and in either of
said cases, this trust as to Christ Church shall cease.... I
hope there will be no occasion for any diversion of this fund from
the purpose herein originally intended, and that others similarly
minded will similarly aid in the preservation of the Historic
Christ Church, and in maintaining the simplicity and dignity
of its worship.

In September, at the call of the clerk of the parish, the
proprietors, ten or twelve in all, met at my house. Some of
them were devoted members of the parish; others living at
a distance belonged to other parishes; one had just returned from a few weeks' sojourn at Deer Island in the
harbor. They did not want to carry on the fight, so after
conference it was agreed that they would exchange their
pew proprietorship for a life right in their pews; that they
would elect twelve persons whom I should name and who
would have equal rights in pews; thus enabling me to control the situation. In return, I pledged my best efforts to
raise such amount of money as would put the church and
other property in good condition and would give it my
support as a church and an historic monument.

These conditions were carried through: almost every
pew was taken by an interested supporter, and for the only
time in my life I solicited a public office, that of Rector of
Christ Church, to which I was elected in order that I
might carry on the work. The office of Rector of Christ
Church, by the way, includes this interesting responsibility: he as the pastor of one of the three churches of Boston
named in the will of Benjamin Franklin is one of the
trustees of the Franklin Fund.

At this point my labors really began. Upon my first visit of inspection, we found the flues of the four furnaces so riddled with rust that we immediately smashed them, so that no fires could be built. The tombs containing a thousand to twelve hundred bodies were many of them gaping open, while the coffins within were crumbling to pieces. Tons of ashes choked the passages. No burials had been permitted by the City for some years. It was an interesting fact, however, that there were no fresh air ducts to the furnaces: the worshippers for generations had been breathing air direct from the tombs. However, these things were expected in 'the good old days': but I do not understand how the custom of burial in tombs can be regarded as more reverent than that of cremation.

The tombs were, of course, carefully and permanently sealed, the cellar cleared, and the church closed until a new heating-plant was installed; after which worship continued through the winter. Expecting at first simply to clear up, repair, and renovate the church and other buildings, I started to gather ten thousand dollars; but as the work went on, my interest and that of friends and citizens in the complete restoration of the Old North Church was such that contributions poured in up to thirty-six thousand dollars, besides thirty-two thousand for endowment. R. Clipston Sturgis gave himself and his experience in architecture to a study of the reproduction of the church along its pristine lines; while Charles K. Bolton contributed his antiquarian knowledge. He also as senior warden has served the church with great devotion to this day.

In 1804, much that was beautiful about the church had been destroyed by so-called improvements. A rounded plaster wall of Pompeian red with a brilliantly frescoed ceiling had filled in the chancel. The nave, too, enjoyed Pompeian red, so popular at one time. Long slip pews stretched across the centre of the church, destroying the broad aisle; and modern furniture took the place of the old pulpit and clerk's desk. Fortunately the small-paned clear glass windows had not given way to colored glass.

Outside, the rich English brickwork had been painted a dusty gray.

The plans and construction of the ancient interior had first to be discovered, and then the lines followed.

When the slip pews were taken apart and the modern floor ripped up, the old floor revealed the lines of the square pews which with their paneling had gone into the slip pews of a century ago. The box pews were reconstructed in their exact proportions and by a study of the records the names of the original owners were placed on them. A hole in a roof timber showed where the chain of the ancient sounding-board had hung; under this the pulpit must have stood. The records said that the pulpit had been given to Saint Paul's Church, Otis, in Berkshire. At my request friends drove to Otis, took a photograph of the present pulpit, which, alas! turned out to be a modern affair. Christ Church pulpit had doubtless gone to kindling wood long ago. Hence the ancient pulpit in Trinity Church, Newport, with sounding-board, was taken for the model. The clerk's desk was reconstructed, the whole interior adapted to the original plans, and a chaste white paint covered all except the mahogany edges of the woodwork. No one had suspected the existence of the large east window, until the plaster mask had been removed and a piece of timber found in the brick wall. Then a study of the Burgis print of 1725 of the North End and Christ Church revealed this window, and a joint in the brickwork gave its size.

The peal of bells, the first imported into this country, was rehung, and the framework so repaired as to enable eight men to ring them, as originally intended. The two houses were made habitable, and the yard attractive. The Sunday School and side buildings of wood gave way to brick. A few years later the Dillaway House next the church, which had been a fire hazard, was bought by the Diocese, and by the generosity of a few friends of the Italians, the beautiful little Chapel of Saint Francis of Assisi, designed by Sturgis, was built.

Sunday, December 29, 1912, the one hundred and eighty-ninth anniversary of the opening of the church in 1753, when Dr. Timothy Cutler preached from the text, 'For mine House shall be called a House of Prayer for all people,' was a day of great satisfaction to the faithful group that had stood by the church in dark days, to myself, and to many of the citizens of Boston. For my sermon I took the same text.

My diary runs as follows:

Great crowds packed the Church, standing in aisles, interesting congregation. All sorts of people, from all parts of city and of the country. Theodore Roosevelt came in during the sermon and was put in the Senior Warden's pew, being the tenth person in a pew made for five. Fine, simple, hearty service; volunteer choir. After Service, told the congregation in ten minutes what we had done to restore the Church. Then they went over the Church, shaking hands with Roosevelt in pew and me in reading desk. Everyone keenly interested and much pleased.

In 1914 the Reverend W. H. Dewart became rector and has administered the church in harmony with its ancient traditions, as a spiritual home for citizens and strangers, and a priceless memorial of patriotism. Tens of thousands of people from over the country and beyond visit it every year, and as they read the tablets and history are reconsecrated to liberty and their country.

Each year on the evening before Patriots' Day a great company assembles for the services. Last year the two addresses were by Vice-President Dawes, great-grandson of William Dawes, who rode as messenger, 'an express by land,' to Hancock and Adams at Lexington by way of Boston Neck, while Paul Revere was riding from Charlestown; and by Mrs. Nathaniel Thayer (Pauline Revere), a great-granddaughter of Paul Revere. Then, as has been the custom, a descendant of Paul Revere hung the lanterns from the belfry tower.

CHAPTER XXV
FOUNDING THE CATHEDRAL
1902–1912

THE short and great Episcopate of Phillips Brooks gathered the Diocese into close spiritual unity through the power of his personality. My first duty and opportunity as Bishop seemed to me so to organize the Diocese as to make that spiritual unity a practical force and create a closer organic life.

Moving about the Diocese in trolley car, carriage, and railroad, with valise in hand, I soon found that each parish and mission was a unit in itself; and while the people recognized the Bishop as the head, they were, to a large degree, Congregationalists. My neighbor, Governor William E. Russell, used to pass my house on his political trips in Cambridge with his valise; but the chief part of his work was done at the State House which, through him officially and the Legislature, was a visible token of the organic life of the Commonwealth.

The question arose in my mind again and again as to whether in Massachusetts, with its strong Congregational traditions, the Church would not be the stronger for some visible expression of its organization as an Episcopal Church, a Church of people and clergy with a constitutional Episcopate. When, however, I came to think of a Cathedral and studied the relations of the cathedrals in England to the dioceses, I found but little to encourage me; for, standing, as most of them did, upon monastic foundations, they did not have the representative character of laity and clergy which bound them into the Diocese. They housed the Bishop's chair and were in the Diocese, but were not essentially of it. The experiments at cathedral-founding in this country were no more hopeful, for according to our usage a cathedral was either a church which a missionary bishop, who rightly felt the need of a visible centre, called a cathedral, or else a parish church with private pews and a rector and vestry who as a matter of courtesy invited the Bishop to place his official chair in it. There were one or two cathedrals which approached nearer to the representative ideal, but no one of these seemed to me adequate. Would it be possible to found in this country a real American cathedral?

While I was thinking this out and saying nothing of my air castle to any one, Mr. Lewis Dabney called at my house in the winter of 1898 and this conversation, taken from a memorandum written sometime later, followed:

Lewis Dabney called: asked for a client of his (no name given) if it would be agreeable to me if property were bequeathed for a Cathedral. He had consulted William Blake, Secretary of the Trustees of Donations, who said 'No.' I said, 'If it amounts to several hundred thousand dollars, Yes. If a small sum, No.' He said it would probably be as much as $700,000. I said 'Yes.' I then made a few suggestions: that it should be for endowment or support of building; that it should be so worded as to be available in case a Cathedral were already up at death of testator; that it should be as untrammelled by conditions as possible. A few days after, as I was walking with Mr. Olney, he said, 'Dabney saw you about Miss Walker and her Cathedral idea.' I said, 'Yes.' But I did not tell him that he had unwittingly given me the name. Since then I have heard and said nothing and could not, of course, say a word to Miss Walker.

Knowing Mr. Olney and his scrupulous feeling about keeping professional secrets, I never let him know that he had revealed to me the name of the donor.

Four years later, on the evening of February 16, 1902, I was called to the telephone by Mr. E. Rollins Morse, who said that he was the active executor of the will of Miss Walker, who had died the day before, and that in view of certain conditions I ought to be present at the funeral in her Boston house, 53 Beacon Street; and that I had better come, not to officiate, but informally. On arrival at the house, I was given a chair next to the body, apparently as chief mourner; her cousins and other relatives being next me.

When the will was opened and made public, it transpired that the two sisters, Harriet Sarah Walker and Maria Sophia Walker, had agreed that, upon the death of both, the residue of their property, after certain other bequests were paid, should, upon acceptance by the Diocese, be paid over 'to the Rt. Rev. William Lawrence, Bishop of the Protestant Episcopal Church in the Diocese of Massachusetts; the Rev. John S. Lindsay, Archdeacon of Boston; the said E. Rollins Morse, and the said Richard Olney, as trustees,' for the purpose of 'building, establishing, and maintaining a Cathedral or Bishop's Church of the Protestant Episcopal Church in the said City of Boston.' The will continued: 'I authorize and empower my trustees, after a convention of the Church for the Diocese of Massachusetts shall, within ten years next after a final decree admitting this will to probate, by vote have accepted the devises and gifts made by this will for the establishment of a Cathedral or Bishop's Church, if said trustees shall deem it expedient so to do, to cause to be incorporated and organized a church or religious corporation for the purpose of receiving, holding, and accumulating said trust property and any other property,' 'of buying a suitable site in said City of Boston, and of building thereon a Cathedral or Bishop's Church of the Protestant Episcopal Church and of holding and owning the same for the uses and purposes of such Cathedral.' The residue amounted to somewhat over one million dollars.

Immediately a vision of a great and beautiful Cathedral arose before the eyes of architectural enthusiasts and many loyal churchmen: even Dr. William Huntington, of Grace Church, New York, was so far carried away as to urge that a replica of Saint Botolph's Tower in Boston, England, be built upon the Cambridge side of the river where the Institute of Technology now stands.

How the Misses Walker came to make this unique bequest no one ever knew. They were very modest and retiring women of pure New England blood and type; their father was a Congregational minister; they had been led into the Episcopal Church through the ministrations of the old pastor of Christ Church, Waltham, where their home was, and of Phillips Brooks, for their winter months were passed in Boston. The property had come to them through their bachelor uncle with whom they had lived on the Governor Gore Estate at Waltham. This Governor Gore House is one of the beautiful Colonial houses of the country, built not so much after the model of Craigie House in Cambridge or of the mansions on the James River, Virginia, as that of Mount Vernon, Monticello, and the Hermitage. It stood in an estate of one hundred acres, its lawn sloping to the river on the south, while great beech and oak trees, gardens and a deer park surrounded it. In her will Miss Walker expressed a hope that the Cathedral might be built on this estate, or, if not, that it might become the Bishop's residence; and in case of this she left an endowment for its upkeep. Mrs. Lawrence, the children, and I drove out there several times from Cambridge and looked carefully over the house with a view of occupancy; but for various reasons it was out of the question. Had I been a follower of Anglican Episcopal traditions of pre-Trollope days, I might have driven in coach and four from the door of the Bishop's Palace in Waltham to the Cathedral of Saint Botolph, whose tower standing upon the Cambridge bank of the Charles was reflected from the calm surface of the river.

The duty laid upon me by the Misses Walker's gift of taking the first steps towards founding a Cathedral compelled me to think out the subject more fully, and at the Diocesan Convention in 1904 I gave an address upon 'The American Cathedral' which was afterwards published and had a rather wide circulation. In this address I said:

The Cathedral is not simply a great church — not only a Bishop's Church; it is the visible expression of the organic life and sentiment of the church of the whole Diocese. To understand the Cathedral idea, we must therefore first understand the organization of the Church. We are not Congregationalists: we are not a group of independent, self-governing parishes. The parish is not the Church unit; nor, on the other hand, are we a religious aristocracy. We are an organic body: the people, the clergy and the Bishop, who is the chief pastor. And we are bound together by spiritual ties, knit into our administration by constitutional bonds, traditions, and limitations, so that each order and individual is dependent upon the others and each does his best work through coöperation with the others.

The unit of the Church is the Diocese — the Bishop, clergy, and laity. The Cathedral is simply the expression in architectural form of the Diocese, its constituents and spiritual purpose. The Cathedral may be as noble as that of Durham or as humble as the chapel of a missionary Bishop. Its essential features are that it be the official seat of the Bishop and his spiritual home; that through its officers or chapter of clergy and laity it represent the whole Diocese; that it be recognized as the centre of diocesan worship, work, teaching, and preaching, as the church belonging, not to the Bishop, but to the whole Diocese; and that all the people, coming from the various parishes for counsel and mutual inspiration, find that here also is their spiritual home.

A cathedral in a great city may also be a house of prayer for all the people: and in these days when the majority of our city population has no regular parish or place of worship, the cathedral has a great opportunity for the spiritual service of all.

There has been in the last twenty years a great increase of interest in cathedrals and many foundations have been created. Beauty, bigness, and historic associations catch the popular imagination. My strong feeling is that in the construction of American cathedrals, the Church will do well to exert great self-restraint.

The real spiritual strength of the American Church is in the parishes and whatever tends to withdraw financial and spiritual resource from them weakens the Church. A great and attractive cathedral in a city of parishes offers to the people rich services and a beautiful church without cost or personal responsibility. We Bishops in the upbuilding of cathedrals will have to be careful lest we pull down the parishes and family religious life.

Again, it is comparatively easy in the excitement of a campaign to raise great sums of money and build great churches: the more difficult problem is in the meeting of the fixed charges generation after generation. If Christian people are to spread the Gospel throughout the world and sustain the Christian institutions of their own city, they must be cautious lest existent fixed charges hamper the great works which the coming generations must carry on.

True proportion is true art: bigness has no merit in itself. It may gratify some Americans to know that a cathedral is the biggest yet built, or that it can hold within it the Mormon Temple, but at bottom the American people gauge the relative worth of spiritual life and material fabric. The towns of great cathedrals have not always been associated with the most refined and sacrificial life. The millions of dollars that go into the structure of cathedrals lay upon the Church heavy responsibility so to use them as to give back returns in character, public spirit, and glad sacrifice. While we are constructing great fanes in our cities, are we looking to it that the lower parts of the city — the tens of thousands of poor and helpless, the anarchists, the Bolshevists, and radicals — have before them fruits which they have a right to expect from great churches in the pure and unselfish character of clergy and worshippers?

In planning for a cathedral in Boston, my dominant question was as to how, while the experiment was being tried out, the Walker Fund, with such other funds as might be added, could be used for the highest spiritual welfare of the Diocese and the whole people.

Saint Paul's Church on Tremont Street, which a few years before had, through the migration of homes and the lack of public transit, become a typical downtown church with privately owned pews, small congregations and Sunday School, and partial endowment, was through the development of the subway becoming a traffic centre. The proprietors were, however, strongly attached to the church and had some fear that if it should become the cathedral the Diocese might soon sell the valuable property and build a handsome church away from the centre of the city.

Hence, when the Bishop and a committee of the Diocese came to confer with representatives of the parish upon the question of Saint Paul's Parish giving up its property and identity for a cathedral of the Diocese, difficulties and objections were unfolded which called for patience and time.

The executors of Miss Walker's will, the four trustees under the will, and the Diocesan Convention worked together in mutual conference, with the results that on March 5, 1908, the Legislature passed an act of incorporation of the Cathedral Church of the Diocese of Massachusetts, and that at a meeting in my house on April 9, 1908, a constitution was adopted. Its first article ran:

The Cathedral is established for the glory of God and the good of men. It is the Diocesan Church of the Diocese of Massachusetts, belonging to the clergy and laity of the Diocese and for their use and also a house of prayer for all people who may resort there to worship God.

The Cathedral is the official seat and spiritual home of the Bishop and the centre of Diocesan work and worship. As the church of the whole Diocese, it shall represent the whole Diocese in the choice of its officers and the spirit of its administration, and the catholicity of its teachings. It shall set an example of constant and well-ordered worship, of effective preaching, of missionary zeal, and devotion to good works.

The Chapter is so organized as to be representative of Bishop, Diocesan Convention, clergy, laity, and congregation. By its election of the representatives in the Chapter of the Diocesan Convention in 1909, the Cathedral became existent on paper, but had not yet a House of Worship.

Divided and indefinite authority between the Bishop and Dean has checkered the history of many cathedrals: hence 'to the Bishop belongs the ordering of the services and work of the Cathedral.' 'The Dean shall have charge under the Bishop of the services and work of the Cathe-

dral.' He is a wise Bishop, however, who, after he has selected the Dean, gives him large liberty of action.

Meanwhile, after conference and negotiations between
the officers of Saint Paul's Parish and the Diocese were
coming to a happy conclusion, the Reverend Edmund S.
Rousmaniere, who in July, 1909, was called from Grace
Church, Providence, to the rectorship of the parish,
accepted under the condition that when he felt the right
time had come to advise the parish to transfer Saint
Paul's to the Diocese for the Cathedral, they would accede
under terms informally agreed upon. On April 8, 1912, the
Chapter voted to accept the proposal of Saint Paul's and
on May 4th formally accepted Saint Paul's, its site,
building, and other property, under conditions wherein
there was concession on both sides and in a spirit of mutual
confidence. The Cathedral was to be ever free and open to
all except that those proprietors who asked it could use
their pews during their life, surrendering them to the
Cathedral at their death. The Cathedral was to remain
on its present site for at least twenty-five years.

The church, to be sure, is small, seating only nine hundred worshippers: no such great functions as we associate
with historic cathedrals can be held there; there is but
little appeal to the artistic sense. For practical spiritual
purposes it has, I believe, been unique in the history of
cathedrals. It is in the very centre of the population of
eastern Massachusetts; is within an hour of the larger part
of the population and within two hours of practically
every member of the Diocese.

In order that the Diocese and City might know that the
parish church, which had stood back from the crowded
sidewalks and was owned by proprietors, was now a free
and open Cathedral, I had carpenters ready at the close of
the meeting to take off the doors from the pews and caused
that fact to be featured in the daily press.

Sunday, October 6, 1912, I inducted the Dean and on the
next day the Diocese, its clergy, and representative laity,
representatives also of the City and of other churches,

joined in the consecration of the Cathedral of Saint Paul. It was to all a happy day, and especially to myself, for it closed happily an anxious term of years. Personal associations also bound me to the church. My grandfather Appleton was one of the founders, and as long as he lived one of its chief supporters. My father, who was a vestryman and superintendent of the Sunday School, was with my mother confirmed there, and my older sisters and brothers as well as myself were baptized there.

The church, which was to be packed to the doors so many times in the coming years, was crowded with a body of men and women whose hearts were in the service. And while great functions in noble cathedrals have a glory all their own, there is to me in the service of such a church, limited in size as it may be, a fervor, devotion, and unity all its own.

One little incident after the close of the service has stood by me. As I came back into the church from which the congregation had gone, a man stepped up to me with a face full of satisfaction and said, 'Do you remember me?' I replied that his face was familiar, but that I could not place him. 'You have talked with me several times over there,' he added, pointing his thumb over his shoulder — 'over in the State Prison. I have been watching the papers and saw that our Cathedral was to be consecrated to-day — the day that I was to be released: and I came right over from the prison gate to have a part in the service.'

This was all that I wanted: I liked that pronoun 'our'; the people had caught on. Within a few weeks the traffic policeman asked what had come over Saint Paul's Church — the kind of people going in was so different and there were so many more of them.

It is an everyday church: four or five services each day. Though the church is small, some two hundred thousand worship there each year and thousands come for quiet rest and private devotion. Throughout the War it was a centre of praise, prayer, hope, and sacrifice — none who were at any of the services can forget them. On the great days of the Country and City, as well as on Sunday evenings in the summer, the crowd massed on the street and over into the Common joining with the choir upon the steps in singing familiar hymns, has now become a Boston institution.

In 1915, plans had been drawn for a beautiful reconstructed Cathedral upon that site, more ample and in closer touch with the people on the street; specifications were complete and the contractors' figures on the Chapter table, when the call went out to the whole Church for five million dollars with which to pension the clergy, their widows and orphans. The Diocese could not undertake both, and with a keen sense of disappointment, but great satisfaction, I put the motion that the plans be laid aside. Because of the increased cost of building and other conditions, they have never been taken up, although, in the creation of the Crypt Hall and other rooms and offices, some expansion for meetings and work has been accomplished, but the limited size of the church is as before. However, the Pension Fund is doing its work instead.

To Dean Rousmaniere, the Cathedral clergy and congregation, the larger part of this great work is due. The Dean's spiritual conferences have sent the people back to their parishes refreshed, and his weekly leaflets have gone around the world. Trusted by his Bishop with liberty of action, he has, while loyal to the stated services of the Church, tested out by experience various orders of service, some of which are in use in many churches throughout the country. By him the Cathedral has also become a centre for Diocesan organizations and charitable societies and has shown a hospitality to leaders of high purpose befitting an ancient and hospitable church.

To me the working-out of the American Cathedral along these modest but spiritual lines has been full of interest and hope for the happy relations of the Church and Community.

CHAPTER XXVI
EGYPT
1912

On January 10, 1912, Mrs. Lawrence and I sailed in the Adriatic for Egypt. We had expected to pass a few weeks in Rome, but Mr. Morgan, discovering our plan, urged us to give up Rome and go with him on the Nile. He had anticipated us in Europe by two weeks and met us as we touched at Villa Franca, whose harbor we entered in the early morning. No sooner had we dropped anchor than Mr. Morgan came up the companionway.

He had motored over from Monte Carlo that morning, hired a rowboat, and had come out to the ship to take us back to Monte Carlo for the day — an illustration of his courtesy to his guests.

Our party of six, Mr. Morgan and Mrs. Burns, his sister, Mr. Lythgoe, Curator of the Egyptian Department of the Metropolitan Museum, Mrs. Lythgoe, Mrs. Lawrence, and I, boarded the Adriatic that evening for Alexandria, whose harbor was impressive, but as a French-Turkish-Egyptian city was disappointing. It is hard to conceive of a city around which cling so many historic and romantic associations, ancient and modern, so meagre in its evidence of these associations.

Arriving at Cairo, we went to Shepheard's Hotel, where Mr. Morgan was given a large part of the first-floor front of the hotel, facing the street, with an ample piazza, which was the roof of the porch. Thus we were placed in the very centre of traveldom, a position open to ceaseless noise by day and night, smells, and great publicity, but Shepheard's had been Mr. Morgan's caravansary from his early days; Shepheard's, therefore, was the hotel to which he would go to the end of his life. The art collectors of all Egypt found it convenient, for on our arrival they were sitting outside the door of the drawing-room, and a succession of them continued to be there until we left.

As travellers have for many centuries described the Valley of the Nile, I shall do little more than depict a few scenes and incidents, and, since Mr. Morgan was our host and as always a dominant personality, I cannot escape bringing him into the scene continually. Indeed, the contrast of this Occidental, restless, art-loving enthusiast with the astute, deliberate Oriental was one of the chief interests of our four weeks in Egypt.

The dominant thought in Mr. Morgan's mind during the past few weeks had been his new dahabieh, the Khargeh. A year before, he had ordered it; complete plans had followed him to New York, where he gave thought to every detail; it was the latest and the best in the construction of dahabiehs that the Nile had seen. Hence his keen anticipation. Immediately after breakfast we all crossed the bridge, which throughout the day carries a more cosmopolitan and motley company than any bridge in the world, and boarded the Khargeh. Mr. Morgan eagerly inspected it from deck to engine. It was a beautiful boat, one hundred and thirty feet long, drawing about three feet, a glass room on the upper deck forward, the dining-room and open deck amidships; three large bedrooms, each with a bathroom; below were a number of staterooms with a large double stateroom in the stern, all beautifully equipped and comfortable; on a lower deck were quarters for the men. Forward on the lower deck was the wheel, where the captain, his steersman, and the sailors sat, where they ate their great thick wafers of Egyptian bread a foot in diameter, and where at intervals the captain spread out his cloak and knelt and prayed towards Mecca.

Throwing himself into a chair on the broad and shady deck which was covered with rugs and wicker-work furniture, Mr. Morgan lighted a cigar and sat for an hour in silence, with the consciousness that a hard winter was over and that he now had reached his point of freedom.

In a day or two we embarked on the dahabieh and

started up the river for Luxor. I remember well, as we passed under old Cairo, he said, 'There is the place where Moses was hidden in the bulrushes. It doesn't look it now; critics may say there never were any bulrushes or any Moses, but I know that there was a Moses and that he was hidden in the bulrushes, for there is the spot. It must be so.' It was in this somewhat humorous but serious way that his religious conservatism met the onslaughts of the critics.

The first vision of Egypt and the Nile can never be repeated. One may stand under the great pyramids at sunset and watch their shadows move across the plain of the valley, darkening the fields with green and bringing into more brilliant relief Cairo with its minarets and castle, throwing into a vivid pink the cliffs of limestone. However frequently one may go again, that first vision holds. Or, as one moves up the river and catches the first sight of a line of camels and donkeys, their riders silhouetted against the western sky, the mud villages half a mile inland, back in the fields, across which walk the graceful women and girls who have drawn into earthen jars the muddy water of the Nile for their domestic use, the great limestone cliffs whereon the midday sun pours its heat, and against this blaze of heated rock the Egyptian quarrymen at their work, standing or lying down as if glued to the cliff itself, one seems wafted back thousands of years. We were fortunate in starting at the time of the full moon. After the setting of the sun, the deep blue of the horizon shaded up through green to pink, the date palms stood with their outlines against the horizon; camels and donkeys, their riders picturesque at a distance, moved along the bank; upon the east rose hills and cliffs and from behind them appeared the moon, which threw a ghostly light upon the sails of the great boats with grain piled upon their decks, or the little feluccas drifting with the stream, while the drone of the incessant shadoofs, with the occasional song of the men at work upon them, echoed across the water.

Although the new boat had received only a short preliminary test, it was pushed with all speed up to Luxor, for at that point we were to meet the Memnon, whereon was the party of Mr. and Mrs. John Kane, including Mrs. Markoe, Miss Rhett, Miss Wharton, Dr. Kinnicutt, and Mr. John Cadwalader. We touched at Assiut for two or three hours, where three elaborate barouches with some eccentricity of livery met us to take us to the house of a rich native who had in his possession an ancient model of a funereal boat that Mr. Morgan coveted.

It was often said of him that he would pay anything for a work of art that he wanted. Here was an instance to the contrary. That boat he had wanted the year before. He had seen it and studied it; the price was exorbitant; he had returned to New York, had thought of it, and tried by correspondence for it with no result. Now he returned to the contest. Mr. Winlock, who was the resident representative of the Metropolitan Art Museum, and Mr. Lythgoe supported Mr. Morgan in his efforts to drive down the price, but with no result, and we started up the river again. The study of the Oriental and this most typical Occidental, as they met each other in the duel of a bargain for some treasure, was most interesting. At almost every place that we went objects were offered. At times treasures at a distance were offered through one of the experts of the party. If, through a personal visit of Mr. Lythgoe or Mr. Winlock, an inspection was worth while, Mr. Morgan halted at no difficulties to study the object for himself. When we arrived at such a house as that at Assiut, the Oriental, to whom time is of no consideration, received his guest as if it were a day's pleasure, offered coffee, and talked of matters of health and climate. Mr. Morgan pushed through these preliminaries as quickly as was courteous and came to the point. On inspecting some of the objects, he turned his back immediately. 'We do not want that.' 'We already have something better than that in the museum.' 'I bought one of those last year and it is in my collection; it is not necessary to have a second.' When, however, he saw something that he really wanted, he surprised the Oriental, unless that Oriental had had dealings with him before, by suddenly asking the price, which, of course, was double or several times its worth; and then with impatience Mr. Morgan either stood up to go, only to be called back again, or sat in silence. Gradually he drew in another treasure, and then another, and putting his hand on three, said, 'How much for the lot?' This enabled the Oriental to come down with dignity and to reduce his figure. The same might happen again with an added object, with the result that either Mr. Morgan left with determination, the Oriental following him to the boat, or struck the bargain. Certain unique treasures he was bound to have if he could get them by persistence; and before we had left Egypt, he had, through the agency of an Assiut banker and the members of our party, bought the boat that he first sought, another boat, a very rich mummy, and other valuable objects, thereby obtaining in one contract several objects which separately would have been gained at much greater cost.

While Mr. Morgan turned to experts for advice and as a rule followed their counsel before purchasing, he had educated himself to an exceptional knowledge of the genuineness and worth of Egyptian treasures. Moreover, a wise dealer would not undertake to cheat him, for it would be to his injury and loss of future business.

The morning after our arrival at Luxor, we started for a visit to the tombs and remains of ancient Thebes across the river. Taking boats, we landed on the other side, where donkeys, handcarts, and one or two victorias that had been ferried across awaited us. A drive of two or three miles, first through deep sand, then over dusty canal paths, passing filthy villages, and later the statues of Memnon, brought us to the base of the hills upon which the ancient city was built, and which now, covered with dust and sand, are honeycombed with ruins and untold wealth of antiquities.

At Deir-el Bahri the Metropolitan Museum of Art, of which Mr. Morgan was President, had received from the Egyptian Government the privilege of excavating a large tract and was at work opening up the hillside. The first signs of the excavation were great clouds of dust, in the midst of which were the black figures of some two hundred boys and men running to and fro carrying baskets from the excavation to the pile where the earth was deposited. One could hear the rather plaintive solo of a boy, followed by the refrain from the whole company of men and boys. In the midst of them stood the overseer armed with a heavy whip, which he used occasionally, the use of which caused a rather warm discussion in our party at evening. As we were leaving the spot, good fortune opened up a bit of Coptic work, and, at the suggestion of the overseer, Mr. Morgan crept up the slope, knelt down, brushed away the earth, put his hand beneath, and drew out a well-preserved Coptic bronze figured incense box. His delight was that of a child who has happened upon an unexpected toy. He kept it in his hand or near him on his table or in his room throughout the trip; and finally, on his arrival in Cairo, arranged with Maspero, Director-General of Antiquities, that he should be permitted to take it to New York, as one of the objects in the Metropolitan Museum's share of the season's results. The box was rather unique, and it required the turning-over of other valuable treasures to the Egyptian Museum to enable Mr. Morgan to carry this bit of bronze out of Egypt.

Mr. Winlock, acting for the Metropolitan Museum, had begun the construction of a house which was to be the best residence of an exploration family in Egypt. The interest of Mr. Morgan in the plans, the keenness with which he studied the situation, and the enthusiasm with which he planned for his own suite of rooms which in future years he was to occupy when visiting the excavations, suggested his feeling of perennial youth. To discover a place for the foundation had been the work of months, for the whole country was so honeycombed with ruins that it was only by deep excavation and by arching tombs that the foundation could be built. In order that the house might not be obtrusive as one approached from Luxor, and that it might catch the slight airs of the valley in the summer's heat, it was so placed as to face the hills and the desert rocks which blazed in the sunlight. From a knoll just behind, however, was a view of the rich valley of the Nile sweeping up and down for miles; and across the river was Luxor with the ruins of Karnak standing well up on the shore.

Although Mr. Morgan had visited once or several times every spot of interest along the Nile, he was ready to join the party each day and to take the lead in action. By an arrangement with Cook's, who had equipped, manned, and administered the dahabieh, donkeys met us at every point. On touching at the rude dock, we, like every other boat upon the Nile, were met by a mass of boys and men pushing, jostling, and shrieking, donkey boys pressing their donkeys upon the party, until the Arab policeman, well uniformed and well set-up upon a beautiful Arab horse, broke into the midst, and hitting the crowd here and there, scattered them for the moment, and gave Mohammed-Effendi, our big dragoman, a chance to help the party upon their donkeys. Then off we started, the mounted policeman in the lead, Mr. Morgan with his Panama hat, for he spurned helmets, spectacles, or other devices to fend off the heat and flies, Mohammed-Effendi, Mrs. Burns, and the rest of us. Riding quickly along the dusty paths which marked the top of embankments, we crossed the fields, mounted the slopes, and went sometimes well up into the hills where cliff tombs had been opened and so cleared as to bring out the form and color of four or five thousand years ago. One could not realize the age of Mr. Morgan as he enthusiastically led us from tomb to tomb, pointing out the characteristics of the scenes and carvings. Then back to the river we went, he still in the lead.

From Luxor we went up the river, landing at the interesting places, to Assuan. Passing through the canal of the great dam to the lake created by the dam, we landed at the lovely, half-submerged Temple of Philæ; we then entered Nubia, whose shores are a strong contrast to those of the lower river, for the ribbon of green fields between the river and the hills, sometimes reduced to a few yards, seemed capable of supplying with food only a small fraction of the negro population that lined the banks. At the great Temple of Abou-Simbel we passed a day and then started on our return down the river. One must say that in travelling with Mr. Morgan there was very little of the quiet and sometimes tedious days of which the travellers of an earlier generation write. Our movement was fast, really too fast to observe the beauties of the tranquil atmosphere of Egypt. In less than a month we had run up and down the Nile, two thousand miles, besides making many stops and excursions at various points.

Until we had gotten well up the river, I had not understood why Mr. Morgan had given to his dahabieh the name of the great oasis in the Desert of Sahara, Khargeh. I soon found that a visit to Khargeh was, in his mind, the climax of the trip. The Metropolitan Museum had been carrying on some excavations there. Mr. Cadwalader was a trustee of the Metropolitan Art Museum, and he must see Khargeh. We must all visit Khargeh. The whole trip, it seemed, was arranged with this date for Khargeh. Eighteen donkeys had been ordered up from Cairo to Khargeh. Unfortunately, Mr. and Mrs. Kane with Miss Wharton had been called to France by the illness of Mrs. Kane's sister. As we arrived at Naghamadi, where we disembarked for Khargeh, Mrs. Burns and Miss Rhett decided to remain by the Khargeh and Memnon. Our party, therefore, consisted of Mr. Morgan, Mr. Cadwalader, Dr. Kinnicutt, Mrs. Markoe, Mr. and Mrs. Lythgoe, Mr. Winlock, Mrs. Lawrence, and myself. After a few miles on the Nile Valley Railroad, we took a train which runs once every other day from that point one hundred and twenty-five miles straight into the desert. We moved across the green valley slowly, rising and winding through the hills, the ground becoming harder, hotter, and much more desolate, until, at about eight hundred feet, we reached the plateau of the desert. Across this we ran hour after hour, our eyes shielded from the glare by the blue glass of the windows. We stopped two or three times at galvanized iron sheds set down upon the desert; and in walking about realized how hard the surface is with loose sand blown off to the great hills at a distance. We saw the occasional mark of caravans and picked up here and there some bit of Roman pottery, the relic of ancient caravans. The silence and desolation were oppressive. There was no sign of life or vegetation, and yet we no sooner stood still than the persistent Egyptian fly appeared.

Approaching the oasis, we came upon great hills of pink and yellow sand that shift their position each year; then, through rocks and defiles, the oasis suddenly emerges, not as we have seen it in our geographies, a little island of rich green with date palms and fountains, but an expanse perhaps sixty miles long, part green with date palms, and part sand with here and there a well and sluggish brook. An English company, undertaking a system of irrigation and hoping to develop fertile lands, built the railroad, and, as we arrived at their headquarters on the edge of the oasis, there stood the inevitable Englishman with his equestrian equipment direct from Piccadilly, his pony and his dogcart. Entering the little house, we discovered that the Englishman had brought his home with him.

We moved across the oasis amidst sand and barren fields and rocky hills to our station, where donkeys carried us, with all our equipment, china, silver from the boat, food, Sherry's coffee, Poland water, about a half-mile up to a camp, where three mud-brick houses were open for our entertainment. Within comfort was not in evidence — a hard mud floor with rush mats, camp beds, small window openings, and a common room or dining-hall lighted by a clerestory. Mr. Morgan, who had been here before, was full of enthusiasm, and said, 'This is the place to live: first New York, then London, next Rome, and next Khargeh: that is my choice!' Going outside the houses, however, his enthusiasm became contagious, for we were standing upon the cliff looking towards the west; beneath were some wells, date palms, and green; beyond was the yellow plain of the desert, across which a caravan was moving, and beyond that were rocky hills of golden yellow, behind which the sun was sinking. The distances were so vast, the silence so complete, and the color so rich that one for the moment understood the attraction for some people of the desert.

Mr. Morgan was the first to lead us out on donkeys to the remains of the Coptic cemetery, of several thousand graves, which was being cleared of sand and débris. In one of the little Coptic tomb chapels he pointed out the quaint paintings of Adam and Eve, Noah, his ark, Jacob and Esau, and the rest. The place had a special interest for me, for no bishop, so far as we knew, had visited Khargeh since Nestorius the Heretic had been exiled there. Then we went down to a temple which the Metropolitan Museum had cleared and which the Egyptian Government was now restoring, and Mr. Morgan pointed to a line of color some twenty feet above on the pillars where he a year before had climbed up the débris and with his own hands dug away the sand from around the stone.

On the next day we made another visit to the temple and had lunch under the shade of its pillars and broken roof. Then, by invitation of the Omdeh of the town of Khargeh, we rode on our donkeys to an afternoon tea in his garden, for he is the mayor of a community of several thousand persons. His hospitality was generous, but, on account of flies, moist heat, and a certain amount of accumulated dirt, not altogether attractive. He then offered to show us the town. At his visit a year before, Mr. Morgan had presented him with a box of cigars which the Omdeh had evidently received as a precious treasure, for we had been told that he had informed his friends that each cigar was worth twenty-five dollars and had a band of gold about it. At all events, he had carefully preserved the box, for, on opening it, only five cigars, the same number that had been smoked the year before, were gone.

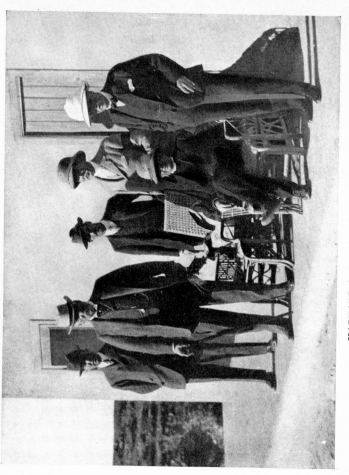

HARVARD CLUB OF KHARGEH, 1912

Left to right: Albert Morton Lythgoe, John Pierpont Morgan, Herbert Eustis Winlock, Dr. Francis Parker Kinnicutt, William Lawrence, John Lambert Cadwalader

Our procession started to inspect the village. Leading us was a boy holding high the box of cigars, then the Omdeh, Mr. Morgan, and the rest in single file, which was all that most of the alleys in the village allowed. Down we struck into the half-darkness of covered passageways cut through the sand and sometimes through the rock, on both sides of which were open doors into the only room of the family. Little children, blind and half blind with eyes covered with flies, slunk back; the women looked inquisitively out; occasionally we came out into the sunlight, and finally into the square, in the centre of which stood the one pump which supplied the village with water. In these subterranean homes the people have lived for centuries. They sleep on the roof, and in cooler weather no doubt live there, but in the lower rooms they are protected from the rays of the sun and in other days were defended from attack.

As we returned to our camp after dusk, I saw a camel standing silhouetted against the west; inquiring, I learned that it was a fast camel which had brought a cable message across the oasis from the Englishmen's telegraph station to Mr. Morgan. Cares followed him out into the Desert of Sahara.

As the party gathered in front of the hut to leave the oasis, Mr. Morgan said, 'Let us found the Harvard Club of Khargeh. We are all Harvard men by work or honor. Bishop, you are chairman: take the chair!'

Our week in Cairo was spent in seeing the sights, while Mr. Morgan oftener attended to the dealers. It was strange how things came to him. Some weeks before, he had happened to tell me of Napoleon's great publication upon Egypt, made by scientists and artists at the time of his expedition, a collection of plates and texts of many volumes and very difficult to purchase complete. One day the cards of an Egyptian gentleman and his wife were handed in. The gentleman said that he was about to leave Cairo, and added that he had in his possession the complete set of Napoleon's 'Egypt' which he would like to sell to Mr. Morgan. The bargain was struck in a moment, and within a few hours the great volumes were piled up in the drawing-room.

Mr. Peter A. Jay, then Consul-General in Cairo, and Mrs. Jay were old friends and most hospitable. At their house we met General Kitchener, who, usually described as rough, *gauche*, and grim, surprised me by his cordiality, rich voice, and ease of manner. After dinner he came around the table, sat down beside me, and talked of the modern Egyptians, of Gordon College at Khartum, and of his deep interest in the students. With his fine physical build and set-up, his strong face and quiet, deep voice, he was to me a winning personality.

We sailed from Alexandria on the Adriatic, passing on a perfect afternoon through the Strait of Messina and under Ætna, which was emitting a graceful stream of smoke, and arriving at Naples met my sister Hetty Cunningham and our daughter Elsie, who at Mr. Morgan's invitation had run down from Rome. After thirty-six hours at Pompeii and Sorrento, they all saw us off on the Adriatic and in a few days I was in the midst of Lenten visitations.

During the spring my brother Amory, who had been taken ill in our absence, steadily failed and died on July 5th. Two years older than I and stronger, he was the leader when we were together. Active and prominent in business as he was, we sustained close intimacy and our Boston houses were opposite each other.

Friendliness and common sense, transfused by religious faith and a strong sense of duty, were the elements of his character. To a host of people of all sorts the world was poorer when he fell asleep.

CHAPTER XXVII

TWENTY YEARS A BISHOP

1910–1915

In March, 1911, Mrs. Lawrence and I had the great satisfaction of entering the harbor of San Francisco through the Golden Gate. It happened in this way. Our thoughts had been on Southern California for years, and at last we struck West for four weeks by the Grand Canyon, through the California fruit country and Pasadena to Santa Barbara. Here the rain fell, the wind blew, and so beat upon mountainside and valley that every bridge was swept away and we were marooned. Food reached us by special boats, and finally, in order to reach home in time for Lenten visitations, we boarded the old ship, Santa Rosa, and ran up the coast made familiar by 'Two Years Before the Mast.' The Pacific was kind to us, and we slipped through the Golden Gate at the hour of sunset.

In the following June the New Haven Railroad was not so kind; for taking the midnight train to New York in order to receive an Honorary Degree from Columbia University, I awoke in the morning in the fields of Connecticut. A smashed freight train had sent us inland. Knowing well the rigid rule of universities that such degrees cannot be given 'in absentia,' I felt my honors slipping away. However, a kindly porter took my telegrams addressed to President Butler and the Dean, and, in his effort to send them, got left in a Connecticut village, and we crept on towards New York. Arriving at the Grand Central Station at half-past twelve, I seized a sandwich as I ran past a stall, shot into the subway, and reached the foot of the library steps as the academic procession, headed by the President, emerged through the door. Waving his hand, he shouted, 'All right: you did your best. You have it.' Dr. Butler, receiving my telegram during the exercises, conferred with the Trustees, and did me the high honor of bestowing the degree of S.T.D. 'in absentia.' I shall never forget his courtesy or my relief.

On the anniversary of the day at Khargeh, February 16, 1913, Mrs. Lawrence and I sent Mr. Morgan a message of good wishes. The next day came this response from Cairo. 'Thanks for telegram. Reciprocate pleasant memories Khargeh. Am not up to the mark myself, sorry to say. Dear love. Commodore.'

Five weeks later he gathered his last strength for his Easter Communion at Saint Paul's Church, Rome, for whose construction and welfare he had done so much in years past, and on March 31st he fell asleep. He had written in his will:

I commit my soul into the hands of my Saviour, in full confidence that having redeemed it and washed it in His most precious blood, He will present it faultless before the throne of my Heavenly Father; and I entreat my children to maintain and defend, at all hazard and at any cost of personal sacrifice, the blessed doctrine of the complete atonement for sin through the blood of Jesus Christ, once offered, and through that alone.

On the 14th of April, Saint George's Church, to which he, as senior warden, had given some of the best of his life, was packed with men. In simple, massive hymns we praised God. We accompanied his body to Hartford, where the whole city turned out, for they were proud of him as he had been proud of Hartford: and we laid him to rest with his fathers.

On New Year's Day, 1913, President Lowell called and asked me to become a member of the Corporation, a Fellow of Harvard University. It was a great honor, and would, I knew, involve much work, thought, and responsibility. Officers of the Diocese and friends advised me to accept, and on January 27th I took my seat at the table with the President, Charles Francis Adams, Treasurer, Dr. Henry P. Walcott, Henry L. Higginson, T. Nelson Perkins, and Robert Bacon. Of this, later.

The growth of the Diocese and the enlarging of my duties compelled me to consider the advisability of having assistance. Hence, upon receiving the approval of the Standing Committee, I took steps to prepare for the election of a Suffragan Bishop. Knowing that his salary would be a rather heavy lien on the income of the Diocese, and that, if an endowment were to be raised, it must be done before the election, I determined to ask individual gifts up to a total of $60,000, assuming that the Diocese could carry annually the remainder of the load. The response was so quick and generous that $109,436 poured in before the Convention met.

The Reverend Samuel G. Babcock, who had been for years the Archdeacon, was elected, and on June 17th was consecrated. He has been a most loyal and efficient assistant. Without him I could not have carried through the Church Pension Fund and other enterprises.

The summer of 1913 found us with three children in England and Holland. On the 4th of July we called upon our Ambassador, Mr. Page. This was, I think, his first public appearance in London. I had known him when he lived in Boston and was a fellow trustee with him on the Slater Fund. Coming as he did after the elaborate hospitality of Ambassador Reid, he found himself in a difficult position: his presence, too, was not impressive. His first remark to me was that he was looking for a modest house, and could not afford to entertain handsomely. This evidently weighed upon him. No one at that time dreamed of the position and influence that he was to gain later through his character, frank diplomacy, self-restraint, and patriotism.

Sun. July 6. A.M. Westminster Abbey: preached: choir, crossing, and transepts full: Holy Communion.

Fri. July 11. P.M.: To Lord's; Eton and Harrow cricket match: pretty sight: 20,000 in best clothes, top hats, etc.

Sun. July 13. A.M. St. George's, Hanover Sq.: heard Dean Inge preach. Took Drury to tea at Boyd Carpenters', then Canon Pierce's, then Dean Inge's at St. Paul's Deanery.

After giving the children a glimpse of Holland and its picture galleries, we returned to London; and in Lambeth Garden came upon a scene of typical, simple, English hospitality.

Sat. July 26. At 5 we went to Lambeth Palace for Sunday. Found Archbp. and Mrs. D. entertaining 500 people from Lambeth Parishes: eating in garden at long tables: sitting down. An entertainment for them in Guard Room. Then short service and short address by Archbp. in the Chapel: and the people went home. The Church of England at its best.

Motoring through the New Forest and into South Devonshire, we passed ten days with the Boyd Carpenters in their cottage, Riversea, hanging over the cliff at Kingswear, just across the river Dart from Dartmouth.

Wed. Aug. 6. Kingswear. Attractive house and terrace overlooking Dartmouth Harbor: hill and castle across: look thro entrance of harbor to ocean: from here Richard Cœur de Lion left on Crusade; the Pilgrims left for Plymouth, Eng.: just above on the river Sir Walter Raleigh lived: picturesque.

August 27th found us at home after sixty delightful days' absence. The next day the routine again began — 'Meeting of Com. on Cathedral, etc.'

The twentieth anniversary of my consecration came upon me almost unexpectedly, the years had flown so quickly. The people of the Diocese, however, made of it an opportunity to express their and my gratitude for these years of happy, united service. The New York children came on.

Mon. Oct. 6. A.M. Cathedral. 20th anniversary service by the Diocese. Clergy vested in Park St. Church: procession to Cathedral: clouds, no rain: prompt & dignified. Collects, Holy Com. Address by myself. Cath. full of clergy, delegates, guests & people. Lunch at Parker's by Rousmaniere to clergy: speeches. Later: Clergy and Laymen gave me a beautiful desk: they consulted my wishes as to its make in every way.

A simple & delightful day: spirit fine: people over appreciative.

A few weeks later, Julia and I were given great receptions in Lowell, Lawrence, New Bedford, and Fall River. In Boston the Art Museum was opened for the occasion: citizens, friends, and church people joining to greet us.

At the opening session of the General Convention in New York, October 8, 1913, in the Cathedral of Saint John the Divine, I was the preacher. I knew that the acoustics were very bad, but did not realize that no one in the choir or chancel where all the bishops and guests sat could hear a word spoken in the pulpit. Speaking slowly and distinctly, I held the close attention of the deputies and congregation in the crossing to the end of the sermon. I joined the recessional procession, confident that my sermon challenging the Church to organize and press home with fuller consecration the three issues, religious education, missions, and social service, had reached every one in the Cathedral. When, however, the Bishops met to take off their robes, the silence about me was oppressive. I soon learned to my amazement that, due to my slow enunciation, the sermon was an hour long, and that no bishop had heard a word. Fortunately, they did not put their feelings into language. However, friends had it printed and distributed immediately. Never again shall I preach an hour: never before had I approached that length.

The next evening I preached again in the Cathedral, this time, however, '16 minutes to show that I could preach a short sermon.'

While we enjoyed the hospitality of Mrs. Whitelaw Reid for two and a half weeks we worked hard at the Sessions and extra meetings. One happy event lingers in my memory. A number of those whom I had taught and other friends invited me to dinner at the University Club, at the end of which they gave me a beautiful loving-cup inscribed with their names each in his own handwriting. In its presentation Roland Smith said, 'We give you this, not because you taught us anything, or have accomplished anything in life, but because you are our friend and we love you.'

The Convention went through its usual routine for two and a half weeks. We made an unsuccessful effort to open the doors of the House of Bishops, which came about six years later at Detroit. And what was of much greater import, we obtained the hearty support of the Convention for the Church Pension Fund.

Two other subjects in which I had been deeply interested for several years took a strong step forward, Social Service and Army and Navy Chaplains.

With the deepening interest of the Church in social problems, the Joint Commission on Capital and Labor, which Bishop Henry Potter inaugurated, had broadened its studies, so that when I succeeded him as Chairman, the title of the Commission was in 1910 changed to that of Social Service, and in New York we made a report which prompted the Convention to make the Commission a permanent one. Bishop Brewster of Connecticut, Bishop Lines of Newark, and other clergy and laymen have brought this work to the dignity of a Department.

For several summers before the Spanish War, the Atlantic Squadron assembled at Bar Harbor, and manœuvred off Mount Desert. I met many officers; their wives also who were stopping at the hotels, but I met no wives of chaplains, they could not afford to come. I then discovered how in pay, allowances, rank, and in other respects, the chaplains were discriminated against by law. The chaplains, too, were few. Hence, when I went to Washington from time to time, I followed up the subject, talking with officers of the Government whom I knew, and officials in the two Departments. In 1842, the number of chaplains in the Navy was twenty-four; seventy-three years later, in 1915, although the Navy had fought three wars, increased tenfold in ships and men, the number of chaplains was still twenty-four. Appointments were to a large degree through political influence and usually without reference to the authorities of the Church of the applicants. Upon the request of a commission headed by Bishop Satterlee, who was a leader in the cause, President McKinley had corrected this last evil. Secretary Long presented to me a most flagrant case of forgery on the part of an applicant. These conditions militated against the desire of strong men to apply for the commission. The wonder is that the service held as many good men as it did. The fault was not so much with Congress and the authorities as with the indifference of the Churches. Successive Secretaries of the Navy, Long, Moody, Bonaparte, and Meyer, who were all my warm friends, were ready to support any reasonable action. Presidents McKinley and Roosevelt were actively sympathetic. Official recommendations were frequently made, but the lethargy of the people through the country and as represented in Congress could be overcome only by patient education, and finally by the exigencies of war. And when war came, much was done to raise the character and position of the chaplains.

It became clear to those of us who were active in the work that all Churches must combine in order to attract the attention of Congress and influence the people. Hence by the time that President Wilson was inaugurated and the war with Mexico loomed up, we were moving together, as is seen in my diary.

Tues. Jan. 20. 10.30 A.M.: Capitol. Hearing before House Naval Com. on Increase of Chaplains and putting them on fairer footing. Represent. of Federated Churches. Father O'Hearn with letters from Cardinal Gibbons and I as Chairmen of our Church Com. on Army and Navy Chaplains spoke: They kept me up some time: asked questions, pleasant and genial. Think that we made an impression.

12.30. To the House of Rep. Joint Session of House & Senate to hear Pres. Wilson's fourth address to them: this time on Limitation of Trusts. Very dignified and interesting. Pres. received with much applause from all & his points well applauded. Excellent literary style.

To Sec. of Navy: he very courteous, interested and sympathetic, but has no idea of Navy Methods or traditions: wants welfare secretaries for Chaplains.

Thurs. Jan. 22. 2.45. White House. To President's office: saw him five minutes, told him what we wanted: he very cordial.

Sat. Jan. 24. To Sec. of Navy for another talk on our Bill & discrimination against Chaplains. P.M. Wrote a careful letter to Chairman of House Navy Com.

Sun. Jan. 25. A.M. Washington, St. John's. Preached: Very full church.

On the 25th of April, 1915, I ordained to the priesthood my son Appleton in Grace Church, Lawrence. It was a happy coincidence that he should have begun his ministry in the same church that I did. After the service I baptized his son William.

In the summer of 1915, the Exhibition at San Francisco and the birth of a grandchild in Portland, Oregon, gave us an opportunity to be with our daughter Elinor, her husband, Lewis Mills, and child. Later in the month I took office as President of the New England Province at the Synod in Concord, New Hampshire.

On Christmas Day of that year we had a unique family party at the home of my sister Susan, wife of Mr. Justice Loring. Susan from childhood until her death in 1923 was a radiant spirit, of social grace, and deep religious faith, beloved by young people and every one. Having no children of her own, she was the centre of the family, especially at Christmas and other festivals, and on this occasion invited us all to the centennial commemoration of the marriage of our grandfather and grandmother Appleton. One hundred and two descendants were asked: photographs, snuffboxes, and other mementoes were exhibited. Sixty-nine were at the luncheon and twenty-five more, mostly youngsters, came later to the Christmas tree. Our host and brother-in-law, Caleb, who was then a Justice of the Supreme Court, disguised as Santa Claus, entered by the second-story window, to the delight of the whole crowd.

Our Cambridge home, between Craigie House and Lawrence Hall of the Episcopal Theological School, was endeared to us by happy associations: here in the sun-flooded house, with its terraced lawn, we had lived with our children since 1888. Old Cambridge was, however, becoming noisy: children had married; the house was large; and,

HOUSE AT LONGWOOD

HOUSE AT BAR HARBOR

HOUSE AT READVILLE

although we shrank from leaving Cambridge friends and associations, we felt the need of a smaller, quieter house in spring and autumn. Hence in 1911 we sold the estate and a year later bought six acres of pasture at Readville in the thirty-acre estate of my boyhood friend,George Minot, who, after marrying Agnes Olney and building there, had died in the prime of life.

Here in 1913 we built our small and simple house with possibilities of an overflow to the guest rooms over the garage. About us are old family friends, Wolcotts, Cunninghams, Hallowells, and others. To the east is the Blue Hill Reservation; on the south is our lawn built from bequests of my sister Sallie and brother Amory; beyond, a path leads under the noble oaks and pines of the estate of my sister Harriet and her husband, Augustus Hemenway, to their house; to the west is the Neponset River Meadow Reservation over which the setting sun falls behind the Westwood hills. Pheasants cross the lawn and partridges whirr from the underbrush, owls hoot by night, woodpeckers awake us in the morning, the birds splash in the garden bath and sing in the lilac and rose bushes. The shadows of the clouds move across field, meadow, and hill, while the tiny fenced-in garden sends out brilliancy and sweet odors. Here we work and rest; and here our children and children's children come to stay and play. At times our blessings seem too abundant. The only relief to our consciences is to try to do a little to bless others.

Fifty and seventy-five years ago architects, contractors, and patrons seem at this distance of time to have conspired in building schools, colleges, and hotels in the form of stupendous fire-traps. It was natural, therefore, that when Mr. Durant planned the construction of Wellesley College, he should have followed the example of Vassar and have concentrated the whole college, lecture rooms, laboratories, library, chapel, refectory, kitchens, and dormitories, which at one time held nearly four hundred girls, in an immense five-story brick building with a mansard roof of wood, well constructed for those times. The authorities of later years, realizing the risk, had provided fire escapes and instituted fire drills, an innovation in those days.

It was in this hall that Alice Freeman, barely more than a girl in years, began her constructive work as the second President of the College.

I became a trustee in 1893 and was President of the Board from 1902 until 1905, when at my request another President, Dr. Capen, was elected and I took the place of Vice-President.

Upon the death of Dr. Capen, President Pendleton and a committee urged me again to take the Presidency, but I declined, saying to Miss Pendleton, 'If I should accept and anything should happen to you or the College, I should be bound in honor to see the emergency through.' However, that was improbable and I finally consented to accept the office for a short time, and wrote President Pendleton to that effect. Before the letter had been delivered to her a great disaster had befallen the College.

On the morning of March 17th, 1914, upon coming home from a night at Groton School, I received word that the great building of Wellesley College had burned to the ground, and that all were safe. I immediately motored out, some twenty miles from Boston, and arriving there found the college grounds almost as deserted and silent as in the holidays. Only the outside walls of the building were standing. The mansard roof and the whole interior had gone up in flame and the brick dividing walls had fallen in. So rapid and hot had been the fire that the walls left standing were almost totally unmarred by smoke either inside or outside. On the lawn there was hardly a scrap of paper or bit of furniture; everything was licked up by the fire or had been cleared away.

The story was this. At about half-past four in the morning, while it was still dark, a student noticing smoke and flame rang in the alarm through the halls. Each of the two hundred girls jumped out of bed, put on slippers and wrapper, closed her window, and without waiting a moment to rescue her valuables walked into the hall, leaving her door open. Forming in line they walked downstairs and, standing in ranks in the great central hall while the ashes fell from the roof upon their heads and shoulders, responded to their names, and were dismissed. There was no scream or cry as they went out of the building to other halls. Having borrowed clothing from others, they and their fellow students went back to the hall and, forming a fire line, passed along the books of a special Browning Library to another hall. At the usual hour of prayers they assembled in the chapel and joined in thanksgiving. The President told them that the Easter holiday would be anticipated by a few days. Suitcases were packed, the trains notified to stop, and by eleven o'clock the grounds were deserted by the students on their holiday.

The report of this cool, brave, and intelligent deed on the part of American college women went through the country and was the best possible form of publicity for a financial campaign.

Two problems were before the Executive Committee the next morning. One, that of supplying living-quarters and administrative and lecture halls upon the return of the students, and, second, that of reconstruction. As to the first, although these were pre-war times and hut construction hardly known, the executive officers, led by President Pendleton and the Treasurer, Mr. Lewis Kennedy Morse, contracted for the construction of a hut of twenty thousand feet of floor space and fifty-nine rooms and lecture halls. Within fifteen working days of the time that the workmen were on the ground, the returning students found the building complete in every way, heated and lighted. The 'Hen Coop' as they irreverently called it, is now, twelve years later, still a hive of industry.

Several months before the fire, a quiet effort had been made to gather one million dollars for endowment, wherein Professor Palmer of Harvard, who had married Alice Freeman, was active. Four hundred and thirty thousand dollars of this had been subscribed, of which two hundred thousand dollars had been conditionally promised by the General Education Board. The insurance upon the old hall was also an asset, five hundred and ninety-three thousand, five hundred dollars. One million, eight hundred thousand dollars was the additional figure set to raise.

Dodging between Lenten visitations, I went to New York with Mr. Morse, saw Dr. Buttrick, who pledged the coöperation of the General Education Board, and went across Broadway to Mr. John D. Rockefeller, Jr., who took up the enterprise with keen sympathy, advised the setting of our figure at two million dollars, and two days later telegraphed me that, acting under the conditions informally made, he promised, for the Rockefeller Foundation, seven hundred and fifty thousand dollars, the campaign to end with the year. For two days I haunted, with Mr. Morse, the offices of New York, little thinking how familiar they would be to me within two years. My diary of March 30th runs: 'Presided at Trustee Meeting. Wish I were out of it, but can't shirk now they are in trouble; a big job.'

The alumnæ organized and with fine leadership worked through the spring and autumn. I did little but obey orders when told to see individuals here or there. It was a very heavy bit of work. The national character of the College had distributed its alumnæ throughout the whole country, and many of them were teachers or were otherwise self-supporting. The quiet growth of forty years had not brought Wellesley to the attention of the business men of New York or even of Boston. Other and more immediate duties were pressing me. However, Mr. Morse and I went boldly to Minneapolis and St. Paul, Chicago, and Detroit. My most interesting remembrance is that of an hour's talk with Mr. James J. Hill, the genius of railroad-building. He talked much of that of which he knew everything, and gave us with equal decision his views on education, of which he knew almost nothing. He began by frankly telling us that he would not give anything and he kept his word. We were, however, rewarded by his courtesy and talk on railroads.

Our trip through the West brought us experience and little else, but we took satisfaction in feeling that we were sowing seed for Wellesley's next campaign. Feeling that these people in the West had heavy responsibilities of their own, I could not make a full-hearted plea for this New England college.

At Detroit I slipped off to a meeting of the Provincial Synod and a drive around Belle Isle, and then took the train for home; recording: 'Glad to get away; begging for Wellesley from those who have no interest a burden; have done it to satisfy Mr. Morse that I am "game."'

The fact was that the Church Pension Fund was looming up before me, for at about this time I was resigning from the Board of Missions, and my diary runs: 'New York; organized the Church Pension Fund under New York Charter: filled up Trustees and made up Exec. Com. I made Chairman of Trustees: a tremendous job.'

However, the fine spirit, skilful organization, and generosity of the alumnæ, officers, and patrons of Wellesley brought the campaign to a successful conclusion, and on January 1, 1915, Mr. Morse was able to report to the Trustees that the completion of the two million dollars brought with it also the four hundred and thirty thousand dollars conditionally subscribed before the fire.

This stiff experience was worth much to me in the Church Pension Fund Campaign, as was the dogged perseverance and optimism of the Wellesley campaigners. The resolutions of the Trustees at my resignation in June, expressive of their gratitude for my twenty years of service to the College, are treasured by me, for I know that they were as sincere as they were generous.

CHAPTER XXVIII

THE CHURCH PENSION FUND — BEFORE THE CAMPAIGN

1914–1915

A CONVERSATION with a railroad president, who was a friend and neighbor in Cambridge, sometime in the eighties, has stuck in my memory. In telling me how a freight brakeman had been knocked off the top of the car by a bridge and killed, he added, with some satisfaction at the generosity of the road, that they had made a gift of several hundred dollars to the widow. This action was an illustration of the habit and temper of those days. A corporation or individual hired men or women and, when they dropped out through age or disability, definite responsibility for them stopped. The common sentiment was that they ought to have saved enough out of their salaries and wages for 'rainy days' or their old age, and if they did not it was their own fault.

The town and State, of course, provided poor-houses and doles: humane persons left bequests for old peoples' homes and widows' associations. The attitude of society to those who were disabled by accident, health, or old age was that of charity, and there was much that was beautiful in the personal relations of the helper and the beneficiary.

The Church naturally held the same attitude towards her servants, the men of the ministry. To be sure, their salaries were small, still the sentiment of the vestries was that the clergy ought to lay up something, and, when the old parson resigned his parish, somebody would probably be kind to him. There were societies, too, for the aid of aged clergy, the widows and orphans.

This was my frame of mind when I became Bishop. Having had always a liberal income and knowing almost nothing of the personal family life of clergymen, I had given but little thought to the subject.

My first step in education came at the General Convention of 1901 in San Francisco when Bishop Morris of Oregon, who, in the years of his strength had built up a noble missionary work, preached the Convention Sermon, which was that of a man in feeble old age; and on inquiry I learned that his Oregon work was crumbling under him.

At the Convention six years later, my seat happened to be just behind Bishop Kendrick of New Mexico, and, noting the thin neck and rough skin of that dauntless missionary, I asked his age. He was seventy-three. His job at that time of life was crossing the deserts and ministering in mining camps and small hamlets.

In the freshness of my youth I offered a resolution in the House of Bishops that every bishop should be compelled to resign at seventy. Immediately the old bishops arose and protested; they cited Gladstone, Prime Minister at beyond eighty; they protested their own youthfulness and ability to do their work. Whether they wanted to stay in active service or not, most of them had to, for they had no income to retire on.

The inefficiency and stupidity of the system so gripped me that one morning in November, 1909, I called on Mr. Morgan in his library, told him of these men, of others, and of the wasteful conditions, and said, 'Mr. Morgan, I have come to you to support me in a plan for the endowment of a pension system for missionary bishops. That is all that the Church can do at present; their posts should be filled by younger men.' 'How much would it cost?' he asked. 'Let us call it a million dollars,' I answered almost offhand. 'Of course I do not ask for any pledge on your part, simply your encouragement to make a study and report to you.' 'I would like to pension some of them,' he said, 'but I do not want to give a dollar for others.' 'You cannot do business in that way,' was my answer. 'It is all or none.' 'You may go ahead,' was his reply.

After I had consulted with Dr. Pritchett, of the then lately organized Carnegie Teachers' Pension Fund, and received suggestions from him, Mr. F. Lynde Stetson drew up a deed of trust: and I worked out the figures of the age, number of missionary bishops, and other conditions. Just then the question of the creation of suffragan bishops arose which would involve an increase of bishops and endowments. Without going any further, I saw that the problem of an endowed pension system for even a small group was too intricate for such offhand action, and that any endowment system for an increasing constituency was unsound.

Knowing that it was useless to bring a proposition which was not essentially sound and fully worked out to Mr. Morgan, I put the papers in my files where they now rest and I never mentioned the subject to him again.

Meanwhile the Church continued under the charity system for its aged clergy, widows and orphans. Pathetic stories of poverty and almost starvation were told in pulpit and press: indeed the Church press found that the harrowing tales were good 'copy.' The richer dioceses had endowed societies for the relief of 'aged, infirm, destitute clergy,' and for widows and orphans. The General Church had its General Clergy Relief Fund, founded in 1855, which appealed to all parishes for annual collections. A later study showed that in about 1910 there were about fifty separate societies, national, state, and diocesan, with discordant rules or no rules at all, often overlapping each other in their gifts and bewildering the laity with their variety of appeals. About two hundred and thirty thousand dollars a year was spent in aid; giving from fifty to four hundred dollars to beneficiaries according to their supposed need, though no one could judge the relative merits of the cases. How was it possible for a few trustees of the General Clergy Relief Fund, meeting in New York, to decide with the help of a secretary the relative conditions of a widow in Texas and one in Michigan. With all the care that could be given by conscientious men, abuses sprang up which must exist when there are many funds for the same purpose and no system. I found that the aged clergy of a rich Diocese were receiving aid from the General

Fund, while the Trustees of the Diocesan Fund were tucking away surplus income for the increase of its principal. There was, of course, no intentional wrong, merely thoughtlessness through lack of system.

Moved by sympathy at the suffering and poverty of the aged servants of the Church, bishops, clergy, laymen, and women bemoaned the conditions, declaimed at the [injustice, and made their appeals more and more pathetic. No body of persons dependent upon charity can long retain their self-respect. Men and women working in the fulness of their strength find ambition and efficiency weakened at the anticipation of falling into the charity class in their old age. As a member of the Board of Missions, I became more and more uneasy at the steadily mounting total of pensions voted for the retired missionaries or their families: a burden placed upon the future Church for work already done. But how could one protest at or criticise the gifts to these pathetic people or the system until he had something better to offer?

When somewhat later I was elected a trustee of the General Clergy Relief Fund, I accepted in order that I might make a study of the charity system from the inside as well as take my part in the work until a better system came. I find, in my diary, that at my first meeting, 'I said rather strongly that certain reforms were needed.' The trustees who were of course accustomed to the old system, were open-minded and later became strong supporters of the proposed pension system, voting at the proper time to merge the Fund into the Church Pension Fund. The more I thought and studied the situation, the clearer I became that the whole system of charity for the clergy and their families must go by the board if the ministry would hold its own self-respect and the respect of the people.

There were doubtless many persons throughout the Church thinking along the same lines, but, not knowing who they were, I worked on alone. Except for a study of Massachusetts salaries, made by me in 1906, no one seemed to have made an effort to obtain or classify facts as to salaries, life insurance, charities, or pensions. To be sure, the General Clergy Relief Fund, and a special committee, responding to the rising tide of interest in pensions, had received authority from the General Convention to raise an endowment of five million dollars, whose income would, it was hoped, provide an automatic pension of six hundred dollars for every clergyman who had reached the age of sixty-four; a scheme which an hour's study of facts would have shown to be hopeless, but in those days the payments of pensions seemed so easy that States, cities, and industrial concerns were cheerfully creating pension systems, most of which have gone bankrupt, or have been amended at heavy cost. The publicity of this movement was, however, preparing the Church for the systematic pension idea.

Without any conception of the size of the task that I was undertaking, with an ignorance as stupendous as it was innocent, I offered in the General Convention of 1910 this motion:

With a view of increasing the support of the active clergy, and the pensioning as well as the relief of the retired clergy,

Resolved, that a Commission of five Bishops, five Presbyters, five laymen, be appointed to consider the whole question of the support of the clergy, including salaries, sustentation, insurance, annuities, and pensions.

The resolution passed unanimously, the commission was appointed, excellent men, but so scattered through the country as to make coöperation impossible except on the part of three or four. I was made Chairman, and soon found that, if work was to be done, I was expected to do it.

Hence I went again to Dr. Pritchett, who helped me to draw up a questionnaire to be sent to the fifty-five hundred clergy whose answers would give me roughly the vital statistics for a preliminary study. These papers I sent out myself. Upon receipt of the answers I, with the help of my secretary, began to classify them and soon found myself in deep waters. I then went back to Dr. Pritchett, who introduced me to a young man in his office, a communicant of the Church, Monell Sayre, who, to quote Dr. Pritchett, 'knew more about pensions than perhaps any man in the country,' under whose advice the work then began to take shape.

Supported by four or five men, Bishop Greer, Samuel Mather, W. Fellowes Morgan and others, I gathered a few thousand dollars and with Mr. Sayre gave myself to the study of the problems. Of the subjects given to the Commission, that of pensions was clearly the first to be tackled. A new and more complete questionnaire was sent out to the clergy, ninety-eight and one half per cent of whom responded. With these vital statistics in hand, Mr. Sayre made a study of the leading pension systems of the world, drew up a tentative plan adapted to the conditions of our Church, and gave it with the vital statistics to one of the leading actuaries of the country, who reported to us. The result was a pamphlet of one hundred and twenty pages, which was recognized as the most thorough statement of pension systems yet published. This I presented to the Commission for their approval, and it became the basis of the report of the Commission to the General Convention of 1913, from which I quote a few paragraphs (General Convention Journal of 1913):

If the Church is to undertake in any adequate way a system either for the increase of support, the pensioning or more effective aid of the clergy, it must first have a knowledge of the conditions and a statement of the facts.

The subject has never been laid before the laity in such a way as to make it clear to a business man that there is any method or plan so well worth his serious consideration as to prompt him to invest a large sum.

This distinction must also be kept clear. A pension is not charity and charity is not pension. A pension is something which when once the contract is made, the pensioner may claim as a right, and there is no charity involved in receiving it. The indiscriminate use of the words pension and charity has caused misunderstanding and is liable to cause legal complications.

The Church has reached the parting of the ways in this large and difficult subject.

The Commission has felt it, therefore, its duty to place before the Church a scheme which may be called impractical or ideal, but which we believe the Church must in its general principles move towards and finally adopt if it is to place the calling of the ministry on an efficient basis and stop the pathetic appeals, and to place the whole body of the ministry of our Church in a position where young men looking towards the ministry may be measurably confident that if he does his work faithfully, he will be enabled without unreasonable anxiety to put his best strength and thought in the work of his calling.

Those expressions were at the time very radical; only patient reiteration and education of the people could make them acceptable. As I had sent a copy of the pamphlet to every member of the Convention with a personal letter from myself asking its reading, the Bishops and Deputies took up the discussion with vigor. Indeed, I doubt if any one subject before the Church has been discussed with keener interest during two Conventions than this. Mr. Sayre and I were called before both Houses in 1916 to explain the proposed system, justify its various measures, and clear up misunderstandings. It was, I think, the first time in the history of our Church that an expert had testified before the two Houses or that a Bishop had stood before the House of Deputies in business session to be questioned and to speak. For the Convention had now come to realize that this phase of the support of the clergy was a matter vital to the whole Church and that something must supersede the charity system. Finally the resolution was passed 'that the Church should work towards the adoption of one pension system covering the whole Church.'

At the end of the Convention my diary runs: 'Put through the Pension System: a tremendous work ahead to get it on its feet for some one.' I had not yet realized that the job was in store for me. It was now the plain duty of the Commission to press forward the work, and I again found ·that, with a body of men so widely scattered, one man must lead and take responsibilities, trusting to the later approval of the others. Hence, on December 11, 1913, two months after the Convention, I find: 'Engage Sayre to set up the Pension System. A stupendous work: wish I were out of it, but can't get out decently.'

From time to time I called to my aid men best fitted for certain lines of action, who gave wise and strong support, but as chairman, with Mr. Sayre as secretary and expert adviser, I laid out the programme of action, which was, first, to construct on the basis of 'The Preliminary Report' a sound pension system. Second, so to prepare and educate, not only the Bishops and other legislators and officers, but the whole body of the people that they would give intelligent as well as cordial support to the system. Third, to raise such a sum as our actuaries might decide necessary. These three processes were of course interlinked, but I state them that we may the more clearly follow the process of construction.

That we may not be confused with detail, I shall consider the pension plan as it was finally adopted and written into the canons three years later.

When I first went to see Dr. Pritchett he said, 'Bishop, no voluntary system of pensions has ever succeeded, it must be compulsory.' My immediate answer was, 'Then the Episcopal Church can never have a pension system. You cannot compel a dollar out of any Diocese, parish, or individual.' Mr. Sayre's problem, therefore, was to invent such a voluntary system as would have in it the elements of the strongest moral compulsion under the circumstances: one which it would clearly pay every parish to enter, one which made such an appeal to the loyalty of the Church as to hold all elements together and to crystallize that loyalty in canonical legislation. That he was successful is seen in the fact that to-day, after almost ten years of action, practically one hundred per cent of the five thousand active clergy, with their nearly eight thousand parishes and missions, are in the system, and that it has been at the basis or has deeply influenced the consideration or construction of the systems of the Church in Canada, the Presbyterian, Methodist and Disciples Churches, the Church of England, and other great organizations.

Its basic principles technically expressed were:

(1) It must be the only Pension System of the whole Church.

(2) The assessments and continuing liabilities must be actuarily calculated so as to balance: and the assessments to support the continuing liabilities must be adjusted upon the principle of an actuarial relation between the liabilities and the benefits.

(3) Before the system goes into operation an amount necessary to meet the accrued liabilities must be raised and in the Treasury.

These technical terms were incomprehensible to me at the first, for upon the subject of pensions my mind was a blank. What I know now is due to study and hard experience. I will now try to translate these three technical principles for those persons who are as ignorant as I was twelve years ago.

1. Calculations of averages in order to be safe must be based upon large numbers, a broad spread of vital statistics. Averages based on five hundred cases would be unreliable. Averages based on five thousand cases are reasonably safe. Hence, the whole body of the clergy and all the parishes must be included.

2. We all know that in our family accounting our expected income for the year must be as large as our expected expenses or we will move towards bankruptcy. As, however, the clergymen's ages are from twenty-four to over ninety, our calculations of income by assessments and outgo for pensions must be made, not for a period of one year, but of many years, unless we are ready to have the pension system move towards bankruptcy. The assessments, that is, the income, and the continuing liabilities, that is, the outgo, must be so calculated by actuaries as to balance, and both must, if necessary, be changed or adjusted to meet the relations between the two.

3. Here was the crucial principle which drove me into the campaign. A sum to meet the accrued liabilities must first be raised. At the beginning I had no idea of what 'accrued liabilities' meant. Later, however, I had to explain it, hundreds of times in business offices, drawing-rooms, mass meetings, lunches, and churches, and I did it in this way. A clergyman who was ordained at twenty-eight happens to be fifty-eight when the Pension Fund starts: he wants to retire at sixty-eight, and does so. Stepping up to the office for his pension, he receives only a fraction of what he had expected. In response to his protest that his parish had paid its assessment since the Fund started, ten years in all, the officer asks him who paid for his assessment from the time he was twenty-eight to fifty-eight. 'No one,' is the answer, 'there was no pension system in those years.' 'How, then,' responds the officer, 'can we pay you a full pension as if assessments had been paid for forty years, when they have been paid for only ten? During those first thirty years you have been piling up heavy accrued liabilities. You or your friends or the Church must contribute an amount which will enable us to pay you the full pension, or we go into bankruptcy.'

Because pension funds have not at the start secured or raised the amount of the accrued liabilities of all future pensioners, many, many pension funds have gone into bankruptcy, and have not only been unable to pay the pension to those who had faithfully paid their assessments, but have caused anxiety and distrust in the whole body of the young and middle-aged who are in active work. When I was in the campaign, almost every pension system of the City and State of New York was running towards danger or disaster. Cities and States can, however, save their systems by extra taxes on the people. The Church has no power of taxation, and is dependent upon the good will of the people; hence the necessity of having the full sum of what accrued liabilities it was planned to assume at the start. No pension system had ever undertaken to do this.

The process of raising the Fund included also the equally

difficult work of educating the people to the necessity of doing what had never been done before: at the same time, the kindling of the imagination of the people in the effort to raise a big sum of money is one of the greatest stimulants in their education as to what the money is to be used for.

In this process of education we pressed, and pressed hard and persistently, two or three points which ran counter to the common and traditional habits of the thought of the people of the Church. While some persons stubbornly opposed these points as interfering with certain charity rights or vested interests or parochial integrity, the great body of the people were ready to be convinced.

We had to make it clear that if a clergyman worked hard for many long years, and then had several years of retirement in old age, or perhaps total and permanent disability, or dying left a widow and minor children, some one had got to see him and his widow through to the grave. Who was to do it, and how was it to be done? Only by so creating the system that every parish which paid him a salary, whether for one or for twenty or thirty years, should pay its fair share of his support for his non-earning years. Hence, every parish should year by year pay as assessments a certain added percentage of their rector's salary, which, forwarded to the Church Pension Fund, would be put at interest, and on the basis of our actuarial tables be sufficient to see him and his widow through to the end of their lives: in other words, it was part of his life salary; but a deferred salary, held for later years, when it would be paid out to him in proportion to the salaries of his life: those who had received larger salaries would have larger pensions.

Educated as the Church had been in the theory of a uniform or flat pension, the thought that rectors of rich city parishes would on retirement have larger pensions than the rectors of weak parishes and missionaries who had borne the burden and heat of the day seemed unjust. In

vain we pressed the point that, so long as salaries were unequal, pensions must be unequal; that only thus would the
system commend itself to the strong parishes, only thus
could it be founded upon safe foundations. The answer
was reiterated that it was uncharitable and unjust. At
one General Convention in the House of Deputies this
point was argued out for and against until it seemed almost
doomed to defeat. We pressed the words, 'deferred salary,'
to show how, so long as salaries differed in amounts,
pensions must differ. During the discussion, two rectors
of two of the richest parishes in the Church arose one after
the other, and in eloquent tones of justice proclaimed that
all pensions should be equal, that it was unfair and unkind
that they, who were receiving large salaries during their
active service, should have larger pensions than their
brethren who had served in poor and barren fields. When
a clear-headed layman arose and said, 'Will the reverend
rectors who have just spoken begin now to divide their
salaries evenly with their brethren and not wait until retirement?' the House burst into a roar of laughter, and the
system was saved.

Again, it was difficult, and still is difficult, to persuade
many people that there can be in a loving Christian
Church an organization, which, however exceptional or
harrowing the case, stands rigidly by its rules; for on full
obedience to wise rules the safety of the system and confidence in it depend. The Pension Fund is the first instance
in our Church where there has been a sharp edge set in
contact with the personal, kindly sentiment. There were
times in the campaign when I felt that on the setting-up of
the system I should have to get out of the country for two
or three years; and there have been times when the criticisms, protests, and complaints of injustice on the part of
some clergy and some Church papers have almost driven
me out. But realizing that during these ten years we have
been carrying on a process of education, we have tried to
meet every protest with patience, courtesy, and reasonable
discussion. Many have been the letters of bewildered

widows and aged clergy; one's heart is wrung in replying that, though the hearts of the Trustees are full of sympathy, they must stand by their trust and refuse the request; and the answer is usually that of acquiescence and gratitude for even the small pension.

The system drafted by Mr. Sayre and completed by the actuaries which could go into full effect only years later, when the assessments paid in full for each clergyman had earned it, gave, speaking roughly, one half the average salary of a clergyman who had served the usual full amount of years, forty, from twenty-eight to sixty-eight; and in smaller proportion for shorter service; the widow to have half that amount; proportionate pensions were provided for those totally and permanently disabled, and minor orphans. The rate of assessment was equal to seven and one half per cent of the salary, paid into the Fund treasury. The system would go into full effect only when the amount paid in assessments for each clergyman had earned for him a full pension. Meanwhile a temporary pension system, giving six hundred dollars pension for full service, with recognition also of widows and permanently disabled, could be undertaken upon the raising of the sum, five million and sixty thousand dollars, to meet the indispensable portion of the accrued liabilities.

For some two years this system was our talking point; our duty was to present it to the Church and to assure ourselves whether the parishes, dioceses, and the whole people were willing to enter it. From October, 1913, when the General Convention resolved to move towards a pension system, for two years I shot about the country, not to raise money, but to talk, to teach, and then to discover whether the Church as represented in the various dioceses was really determined to enter upon this great work. From Boston to San Francisco, through the Middle West and down to Washington, I went talking at lunches, dinners, in offices, and at mass meetings, discussing the system in synods and Diocesan Conventions. No care was too great to convince the delegates, for upon the vote, and an intelligent vote too, of these conventions depended the decision as to whether there would be a pension system. I believe in personal touch and personal letters: thousands on thousands of letters composed and signed by myself accompanied the preparatory literature. Then, when I spoke at a Convention, the delegates knew who I was and what I was after. Thus Convention after Convention fell into line. I was still actively responsible for my Diocese, aided by the recently consecrated Suffragan Bishop. I ran back to Boston for visitations and the biweekly meetings of the Harvard Corporation. The Peabody Education Board was closing. I was during the first year a member of the Executive Committee of the Board of Missions; and just then came the fire of Wellesley College and my part as President of the Trustees in that campaign. As Trustee of the General Clergy Relief Fund, it fell to me to raise money for the publication of the New Hymnal. We had also the Pension Fund Budget to meet.

Meanwhile, we were organizing the Fund, filling up the body of Trustees, and conferring about the form of the charter. Here Francis Huntington gave his most valuable services both in drafting the charter and seeing it through the New York Assembly. His death soon after was a heavy loss. Mr. J. P. Morgan became Treasurer, and has ever since given freely of his time and ability.

Throughout the campaign I stood again and again at the elevator gate of some tall building, hesitating and with palpitating heart, saying to myself, 'I would give a thousand dollars not to go up,' then, shooting up with a dizzy, bewildered feeling, I entered the office of some stranger to whom I described the system.

We had set as our goal of education the day when Diocesan Conventions representing a majority of the strength of the whole Church had come into line. The custom was for a Convention of 1914 to take up the subject, appoint a committee, which was usually of influential men, whom we educated in the system during the year.

Upon that committee's report, which was always favorable, the Convention of 1915 acted always favorably and usually with unanimity. The action of the Convention of the Diocese of New York in November, 1915, would, if favorable, pass the majority line and commit the Church. My diary runs:

Wed. Nov. 10. New York at Greer's. Convention in Synod Hall. Sayre and I there to watch pensions. Com. on Pensions reported in favor of the Diocese entering the system: passed without debate, unanimously and with applause. I had before the Convention written every delegate and clergyman, sending also a pamphlet: have done the same for every Dio. Convention that has had the subject up. Lunched with the Convention.

P.M. The Com. on Canons reported favorably the Canon on Pensions which passed unanimously and with applause. The Diocese enters the system only on condition that $5,000,000 be raised for accrued liabilities: that is a challenge to the Church and to me: a very heavy load.

Thurs. Nov. 11. At Convention all morning, thinking questions might be asked on Pensions. Before lunch, at Greer's request spoke to Convention, said that Commission and I consecrated ourselves to effort to raise the five million: from now on so far as possible in justice to my Diocese give myself to that.

With exhilaration but with awful dread and humility, I found myself pledged to lead in the raising of the largest sum of money that, so far as we could learn, had ever been raised by a church by voluntary contribution, five million and sixty thousand dollars. Since then the War and its enormous figures have changed the whole aspect and perspective of financial campaigns.

In order to test the judgment of the type of churchmen, who, if the movement was to be a success, would have to give strong, financial support, I invited eighteen such men to meet me at luncheon at the Down Town Club, and when the oyster course was over I said: 'Gentlemen, I want your advice. Here is the proposed pension system and the requirement of five million dollars. If you say that there is reasonable chance of success, I will go home this afternoon, cut my wires in Boston, come back to New York, and give myself to the work until it is done. If you say "No," I shall go home with intense relief and take up my routine in the Diocese.' One of them said, 'It is a fine thing, Bishop.' 'I know it is a fine thing,' I answered, 'or I would not have asked you here. What I want is your honest judgment as to whether with the utmost strain it will go through.' After talk they all said, 'Yes,' and Mr. Newcomb Carlton, President of the Western Union Telegraph Company, whom I had never met before, added: 'Bishop, you have said that one of your chief motives is to promote efficiency in the Church. That is in my line. If you undertake this campaign, I will give you the free service of the Western Union Telegraph wires until you are through. If you want to send out five hundred night letters at a time, send them.' He fulfilled his promise, and with others' help was instrumental in giving us the free use of the long-distance telephone every day for two afternoon hours. Such a gift in those days of less frequent use of the wires was of untold service.

From the luncheon I took the train home to cut connections with the Diocese. Calling the Standing Committee together, I read them a letter from which I quote:

The responsibility laid upon me is a very heavy one. I shrink from it all, and yet as I think of thousands of Clergy, their widows and orphans, thrown upon charity for generations yet to come, as I see the tragedy of old Rectors clinging to their posts while the work of their active years crumbles, as I realize the enormous waste which comes from the fact that because old men hold their posts young men cannot enter in their prime upon their best work, above all as I know the strain under which strong men work who are subject to the pettiest economies and the dread of illness or poverty, as I come into close comradeship with men of high ability and consummate devotion who are working to-day with courage and apparent cheer and who now and again feel the sudden pang, 'If I drop out disabled or dead, what will become of my wife and children?' — I am impelled to undertake the duty.

I believe that if the laymen and women of the Church can be made to know the facts, the enormous economic waste, the lack of efficiency, the pathos and the tragedy of our present conditions, they will rise to the opportunity and by a mighty effort correct them.

If I should undertake this work, it would mean that I would have to make it for a time my first interest, the Diocese my second. I should hope to remain as the Ecclesiastical Authority and return at intervals to keep in touch with the work and hold a few confirmations. To our Suffragan Bishop, who is always ready to take any load laid upon him and carry it well, I should hand the practical administration of the Diocese and much of its visitations. I had hoped to organize the Diocesan resources for the reconstruction of the Cathedral: many plans and enterprises will have to stand still. More than all, as it affects me, I shall be cut off to a degree from the personal associations with Clergy, people, and home.

I believe, however, that if Massachusetts, her Bishop and people are ready to make a sacrifice for this cause, the Church will feel that it is a real cause, a great one and worthy of her sacrifice, and give it the right of way. I do not minimize the difficulties or the discouragements. I do not dread the failure, if failure it is. Success or failure is of no consequence to a man if the cause is worth the venture. The Church commands. It is for her servants to make sure that it is her command, and when sure to obey.

I ask your counsel. Shall I, your Bishop, also Chairman of a Commission of the Church, undertake this duty?

The Committee told me to go, and gave me Godspeed.

One of the fondest hopes of my Episcopate had been so to enlarge and enrich the Cathedral as to make it a more worthy and beautiful House of Worship. Plans had been made, specifications and contracts drawn, and the contractors' bids were on the table at the meeting of the Chapter which I called. It was clear that the Diocese could not undertake this construction and give her fair share towards the Pension Fund. The welfare of the whole Church came first. We knew that the sacrifice of our hopes would make us stronger for the larger work. So the plans were laid aside; the War followed, and the Cathedral, still under cramped conditions, carries on its spiritual work.

The Campaign Committee of Massachusetts, of which Mr. J. Grafton Minot was Chairman, told me to go to New York and they would raise and send on five hundred thousand dollars, which later overran six hundred thousand dollars.

Bishop Babcock took on and carried through the extra duty, and my friend Charles E. Mason arranged to leave home and family to accompany me as my secretary.

Of course, I ran back to Boston at intervals, usually twice a month for visitations and the Harvard Corporation, but for two winters New York and the eastern part of the country were my home. The pressure to raise an average of twenty to thirty thousand dollars a day prevented long journeys, and I went no farther west than Minneapolis and St. Paul or south than Richmond.

Under Mr. Sayre's able leadership the office force was organized for campaign work. Messrs. Guy Emerson, George W. Burleigh, and others came to our aid, and the connections were made between the office, the Bishops, the Diocesan Committees, and through them with the parishes, for we had in hand a work in which every member of the Church was to take part. We determined to carry through everything from our own office.

My trip from Boston back to New York was suggestive of the obstacles which faced me the first few weeks. A storm of sleet broke down wires, signals, and all connections, so that as our engine, the electric system being out of commission, crept slowly on, she had only her headlights with which to search the switches and fallen telegraph poles. Instead of arriving in the evening, we reached the 125th Street Station at seven in the morning, where I found my faithful but loquacious chauffeur and car. 'Spencer,' I said, 'you have done well to wait for me through the night in this storm.' 'Oh,' he said, 'I have had a fine time. The police officer and I have had a good talk.' Arriving at Greer's house I found tied to the gate a card reading, 'Keep on ringing and some one will come.' In five minutes Greer in pajamas and dressing-gown let me in. And to his hospitality during the campaign, to his kindness and readiness to sacrifice anything for the Fund, I owe much.

CHAPTER XXIX

THE CHURCH PENSION FUND CAMPAIGN

1916-1917

On the fourth day of January, 1916, I shot up to the twenty-eighth floor of the Bankers' Trust Building and took charge of the campaign. 'An Exhilarating Avocation,' I called the raising of money for good causes in an article in the 'Atlantic Monthly' of September, 1923, which, specially printed later by campaigners, tells something of what I would otherwise say here. I shall not repeat, however, but tell the story of this particular campaign in a more personal way.

The consciousness that one has a big and ennobling job ahead, and that upon him depends the success, is stimulating: the unexpected successes make one leap, and the failures call up a determination and courage even finer and more buoyant. From a distance I hated the job and shrank from it with dread. Every morning I had to lash myself to go downtown. There I found Mr. Sayre and Mr. Mason with their list of persons whom I must call on during the day, if they would see me. One by one they or their secretaries were rung up. When the office or house was connected, I usually took the receiver and did the talking; for the personal equation over the telephone is a big one. Conscious that if I were to get pledges I must see the people, I heard with sighs of relief that one and another and another could not see me: if the morning's list was cancelled, I felt like a free man, and with cheer took up the office work, knowing well that I was only postponing the evil day. 'Pressed to get out and beg,' is the record of day after day. When, however, one is really in the midst of the game and meeting some success, the exhilaration is very real.

I will describe the situation more fully. Up to this time, before the War, there had been no campaign like it.

Young Men's Christian Associations and other organizations had, of course, carried through many drives for smaller amounts. There were no professional campaign firms, and but little skilled publicity. There were no precedents for the organization of our work, which covered the Church throughout the country and in the mission fields. To Mr. Sayre and the office fell the duty of creating the organization which, entering every diocese and parish, was in the course of a few months to gather such a united support and enthusiasm as to roll in contributions, far, very far, beyond our highest hopes. In spite of the fact that the whole Church was behind the system by its votes, there was a latent but pervasive scepticism about the raising of five million dollars; for within three years the Church had failed in a like effort. The form of pledge, simple as it might seem, cost us much care, and two or three lawyers much time and thought; our conditions were, it must be legally binding on the pledger's property in case of death; it must be clear; it must be in duplicate; and it must be so worded that the plain man can understand it and not shy at legal phrases. The wording of that pledge, amended to other conditions, went through the war campaigns and survives to-day. Our paper, 'The Progress,' and our form of pamphlets, especially 'The Plan,' are still copied. We had to blaze paths in many directions.

My duty, besides that of general oversight and suggestion, was that of starting organizations in the leading cities, and especially of reaching those who might give in substantial sums. In this last line of duty came the exhilaration, sometimes the depression of a good sportsman.

Vigorous health is an essential in one whose business it is to gain the confidence and command the attention of busy men and women. Again and again I knocked off work for a day or a week with poor voice, or exhausted went to bed and stayed there until I was in buoyant health: no weak voice or half health can persuade strong men to sacrifice. I was sixty-six years old, ten years too old for such a job. At first I thought the work might kill me. What if it did?

— the cause was more than worth it. As the months passed, my dread was that I might break before March 1, 1917. After that I didn't care.

This may sound somewhat exalted. The fact is, the War was on in Europe; men and women were going over as volunteers. On February 8, 1916, I find the record, 'At the Belmont Hotel, met Misses Curtis and Homans just off to the war as nurses: also met Dr. Strong.' Later, Helen Homans gave her life to the work in France and breathed her last as a Croix de Guerre was pinned on her breast. A few days later, I spoke at the annual dinner of the New York Harvard Club, 'on preparing young men to defend the country,' for the Mexican trouble was acute. In May, eighty thousand men marched through Boston in a preparedness parade, and the next day I sat at a dinner in Cambridge next General Wood who had, while on inspection duty in France, been wounded. I had been out to the Harvard Medical School for a cup of tea with Dr. Strong, who with his staff of doctors and nurses was starting for Serbia to stay the plague of typhus. At the time their life risks were not worth fifty per cent. Chivalry and consecration were in the air. The widows and orphans of God's ministers and the ministers themselves in their old age and disability were an equally worthy cause. I did not think much of these things, but I know that without that full consecration of service I should have wilted at times; with it there was continual buoyancy and high spirit.

Even a mascot helps. When I went down Wall Street on the campaign for Wellesley, I wore a long frock coat and a beaver hat, as became a Bishop and President of the Trustees of a college. My dress made me a marked man on the street. Informality in dress was increasing fast, and when I realized that two winters must be passed downtown, I decided not to appear in the dress which was worn only by members of the House of Lords and advance agents of a circus. Hence, I had made a cutaway suit and bought a derby hat: the clerical vest gave me enough distinction from the brokers and clerks. That suit and that same hat, dingy and cracked as it was, I wore every day to the very end. Without that hat my luck would have gone. Queer people we rational beings are!

The first few weeks were like wandering through a bog under the mountain before one catches his breath above the trees. We pressed this way and that, experimenting, laying out a line of action, and dropping it for another; counselling, often nervous and anxious.

The publicity was a great problem; for there were no precedents. We tried two or three excellent young men, and were driven wild by their inabilities. I took train for Philadelphia to ask Mr. Bok's advice. He was most kind. After listening to our plan of pension and of action, he said, 'You are all right, Bishop. Go on as you are: only visualize your individuals; depict, describe your pathetic cases. Money for Belgium stopped flowing in last summer; then I happened to see in the paper that Belgian babies wanted milk. We plastered the city with "Belgian babies want milk," and the flow began again. People give when their sympathies are touched.'

I went back to the office elated. We now had a clear line for publicity, and, calling in Ivy Lee, I repeated Mr. Bok's advice. 'Mr. Bok is on the wrong track this time,' he said. 'The sympathies of the American people are bruised and raw with the cry of Belgium: you cannot depict an old parson or his widow and orphan to-day in such a way as to move people to give. Moreover, in the long run emotional appeals lose their force. The American people, intelligent, just, and generous to a cause that appeals to them, want facts and figures: they must be assured that the cause is sound and the cure lasting. What have you in hand?' 'Only this pamphlet,' I answered, 'a study of the pensions systems of the world, and reliable facts about the salaries and conditions of the clergy of the Episcopal Church.' He put the pamphlet in his pocket; the next morning, coming into the office, he patted his breast-pocket and said, 'You have it: all you want: facts.'

Our first job was to give the people a few hard facts. We

organized for this, and on a given Monday morning a majority of the daily papers throughout the country featured the statement that each bishop in his own diocese, North, South, East, and West, had said on Sunday morning that the average salary of a clergyman of the Episcopal Church was only twelve hundred dollars. Simultaneous publicity was then in its infancy: by the courtesy of the New York papers we saturated the city with a few more facts, and attached to them the words, 'Church Pension Fund.' The 'Wall Street Journal' headlined, 'A Bishop in Wall Street.' There was sincerity and dignity in the columns. Hence, instead of wasting time introducing myself and my subject at every call, I was already introduced and well received.

Mr. F. Lynde Stetson, one of New York's leading lawyers, a warm friend to whom I had first gone for advice on pensions, was an influential member of the General Convention which had approved the system and its proposed call for five million dollars. One Sunday afternoon, in the morning of which I had preached in Princeton University Chapel, I called at his house by appointment on my way through New York to Boston, and told him that I was now definitely pledged to raise five million dollars. Expecting an enthusiastic support, I was dumbfounded to hear him say that I was on a Quixotic enterprise. In vain I protested that he had voted for the Fund: his answer was that he believed in the system, but that to try and raise five million dollars was foolhardy, and that I had better stop then and there. Dazed and broken in spirit, I fell into my seat in the train, and for two hours was almost numb: my heart seemed to stop, I could not think, and never came so near a collapse. Gradually, however, light came. I found myself, and gained a true perspective and courage. On reaching home I wrote Mr. Stetson telling of the blow that he had given me, and thanking him that he had brought me down to hard realities. Immediately he came in to the support of the work, and saw the vote through the New York Convention.

It is a part of the excitement that no one can tell what results may come from untoward facts. A few days later, my sister Sarah, Mrs. Peter C. Brooks, heard indirectly that I had a heavy work ahead and had gotten a hard knock at the start. Lying on her couch, from which she never again arose in health, she sent me a letter of cheer and a check for twenty-five thousand for a start. Such a gift, coming from one who died before the campaign began, fixed my determination: after this nothing but death would turn me back.

The Wellesley College campaign had put me through severe training. I felt the worth of it, and decided to tackle the man who was said to be the toughest problem in New York, an elderly, autocratic, rich man, 'a devout Churchman.' On the minute named by him just after his breakfast, I entered his dining-room and stated the case. It was a new idea to him, bred as he had been on the principles of charity and patronage of the clergy. His response was vigorous, and, as he went on, more and more heated. 'The clergy have no business to marry: their wives are a nuisance to their husbands and the parishes. I am a Catholic: I believe in the celibacy of the clergy: none other than celibates.' A bright idea struck me, and I suggested with patent innocence that he give half a million dollars to be used exclusively for the pensions of aged or permanently disabled celibates. He scorned the thought. I turned the subject: we had a short, pleasant chat about his pictures. Then, with the utmost ease and cheer, I bade him a pleasant day. Going out the door, I felt deep pity for the old man who knew not one of the greatest joys in life.

Soon after, at Dean Grosvenor's suggestion, and with his card, I called upon Mr. James McLean, a name unknown to me until that afternoon. As he was out, I left the card and my address. In an hour he was on the telephone saying that he would send me something. My answer was presuming, but clear, 'Mr. McLean, I have no ordinary job. I am not a Missionary Bishop — I am after deep interest and big gifts.' He told me to call again in three weeks. Before the time was up, a gentle, unassuming man came into my office and said that he had called to see what we were doing, and what our system was. I told him in a few minutes, and as he rose to go he said, 'I want to give something, and will write the figure on my card in case anything should happen to me, and leave it on your desk.' He bade me good-morning, and slipped quietly out. The card read, 'James McLean, $50,000.' This was the first of many surprises. Can any sportsman tell a better story?

For weeks, however, the campaign would not move. As I talked in offices and at downtown lunches, then as I went uptown day after day, I felt as if my shoulder were against a heavy motor truck that would not budge. I recall with gratitude a response of a friend, 'Keep at it, Bishop; some day the old thing will move and begin to run.' Sure enough, it did.

My chief effort had been to gain a thrust of one million dollars in four quarter of a million dollars. As I entered the office one morning, I picked up a letter, opened it, and therein was the first pledge of two hundred and fifty thousand dollars. Another came later; both were from two generous women who, with their business advisers, had been studying the system and watching me for months.

I decided to take an hour off that afternoon and enjoy a cup of tea with a friend on Fifth Avenue. As we sat before the kettle, she said, 'Bishop, can people give pledges for five years to the Pension Fund? I ask because that is the only way I can give at present.' 'My dear madam,' I answered, 'I have come here for a cup of tea, and I am not going to talk business.' 'Very well,' she said, 'I am going to talk business, and you cannot stop me. I have been thinking, and have decided that, if I can pledge for five years, I can promise ten thousand dollars a year.'

Here is the story of a day:

Wed. Feb. 16. Rather late downtown. Voice too poor to beg: at work in office: home rather early. Greer gave me a dinner. Joe Choate, Root, Wickersham, Pres. Butler, Mr. Kingsbury of N.Y. Life Insurance, Robert Brewster, Edmund Baylies, August Belmont, Stephen Baker, Fellowes Morgan & others. At Mr. Choate's suggestion, I talked 20–25 minutes on Ch. Pension Fund: they seemed interested, even applauded.

No one knows what a dinner may bring forth. The next morning one of these men, whom I had never met before, came up to the office, and dropped a pledge on my desk for twenty-five thousand dollars, saying that he wanted to get it in quickly. Mr. Belmont, as he bade me good-night at Bishop Greer's, had remarked,' I am going to do something.' Two or three weeks later, as I dropped into his office, he turned in his chair and said, 'Bishop, you ought not to come down here to my office; I have intended to go up to yours.' 'Here I am, however,' was my answer; 'you were kind enough to say at Bishop Greer's that you were going to give something.' 'Oh, yes, of course; I will give one hundred thousand dollars anyway.' I thanked him and bade him good-morning. As the colored doorkeeper helped me on with my coat, he said, 'You did not stay long, did you, Mister?' 'No,' I said, 'but long enough.'

Pledges of $5,060,000 payable during five years were not, of course, the equivalent of that amount in immediate payment, and, as we had to have that amount on March 1, 1917, we required an added sum equal to the interest on the delayed payments. I told Dr. Pritchett of our awkward situation and asked if the Carnegie Corporation would contribute an amount equal to the interest, on the ground of Mr. Carnegie's support of pensions and because ours was, as Dr. Pritchett knew, the best system for the purpose up to date. He was, of course, sympathetic and advised me to talk with Mr. Root, the Chairman, who, when I called on him, said, 'When I heard you tell the story at Bishop Greer's, I was much interested.' At their request we figured out the probable amount needed, which was $324,744.87. In a short time a pledge for that amount was on my desk with a very handsome letter. Every man at Greer's dinner joined scores of other generous men and women in making gifts up in the thousands.

A Philadelphia dinner was no less fruitful. I had been to the Quaker City several times, had been handsomely received, and had given my message at two dinners. But the movement was slow to start. They were thinking.

An invitation from Bishop Rhinelander to a small dinner of men whom he had carefully selected brought me to Philadelphia again. As we talked over the system, the plan and methods of campaign, Mr. E. Walter Clark said, 'Bishop, how much are you expecting from this town?' 'That is for you to say,' was my answer. 'Will one million dollars be enough?' said Mr. Clark. I assented. He then said, 'I propose that we start at twenty-five-thousand-dollar subscriptions.' 'I am afraid, Mr. Clark,' I added, 'that you cannot get one million dollars in this town with that start.' 'Then let us make it fifty thousand,' was his reply. Within a few days I heard that he had headed the paper and was standing on Chestnut Street and would speak to no one who would not pledge fifty thousand dollars. Mr. Charlton Yarnall became the Chairman, and threw himself into the work with such ability and devotion that, with the support of others, Philadelphia subscriptions ran well beyond the million.

Our first public note of progress went through the press in the announcement from the large committee meeting in Mr. Morgan's library on March 9th, that the first million had been pledged. On May 8th I ran down to Philadelphia again to announce from there through the Associated Press the second million; and soon after in Cleveland I announced one half million more.

Of Samuel Mather, of Cleveland, I must write a few lines. Several years before this he had supported and financed the other five-million-dollar campaign. With an open mind he studied this system, found it sound, and transferred his support to the Fund. Cleveland is in the habit of turning to him for leadership. He carried through the campaign, gave in large figures for overhead expenses and towards the five million, and also endowed the pension assessments of Kenyon College. The gift of his time and thought to the Fund to this day have been unique.

One afternoon I called up Pittsburgh and, getting the Chairman, Dr. McIlwain, I said, 'Doctor, where is Pittsburgh? Every large city is on the map but Pittsburgh.' Somewhat bewildered by the suddenness of the question, he promised to go to work, and within a few days announced that one man had given him ten thousand dollars. Going to Pittsburgh soon after, I learned from the Doctor that the man had fallen to his request so easily that he had gone to him again asking for fifty thousand. Naturally I was alarmed, for that generous and indignant layman might easily spoil the Pittsburgh temper: however, I made peace with him. I was taken by a friend to the office of an elderly citizen, rich and often generous. He opened the conversation with the remark, 'Bishop, I am afraid that you have come to the wrong place. We have learned to make money in Pittsburgh, but we have not learned to "loosen up."' Assuring him that my purpose in coming to Pittsburgh was to try and educate them to loosen up, I said, 'I suppose that Wilkes-Barre is something like Pittsburgh: they have made money and have not learned to loosen up.' 'Yes,' was his answer, 'much alike.' To which I replied, 'A few weeks ago I wrote to a citizen of Wilkes-Barre telling about the fund and received back a pledge signed for fifty thousand dollars. That was from Wilkes-Barre; how about Pittsburgh?' 'Well,' he said in a dazed way, 'I suppose so. Yes! I suppose so.' I bade him a cheerful good-morning. Whether he ever gave a dollar or thousands, I never inquired, but I knew that he would tell the Lunch Club how a strange bishop who was raising five million dollars, talked of fifty-thousand-dollar bits and said 'good-bye' in a pleasant way without asking for a dollar. It was good publicity for Pittsburgh.

By May and June the pressure of work and the strain relaxed. With the exception of occasional calls and many letters, the campaign was dormant while we rested at Bar Harbor where the family gather. In September I note, 'We have had ten grandchildren born in less than three years.' We rejoiced in two sons, each over six feet, and in four sons-in-law, to use Julia's phrase, 'twenty-five feet of sons-in-law.' The last line of my September diary runs: 'A happy, grateful family.'

March 1, 1917, was the date set for the end of the campaign and for the start of the Church Pension Fund, provided we had in hand $5,060,000. Hence my work for the next five months was clearly cut out.

We had so far gained the confidence of the Church as expressed in the favorable action of the Diocesan Conventions and the support of the campaign that the General Convention which met in October at St. Louis organized a Joint Session of both Houses for the Pension Fund, to hear addresses upon its various features. In business sessions both Houses adopted with only one dissenting vote the canons proposed and then set up the system as a part of the Church's administration. The House of Bishops presented me with a handsome resolution of grateful appreciation. Thus fortified, we at the office and the increasing body of devoted men and women who throughout the Church had enlisted for the campaign put thought, nerve, and life into the issue. My life was much as it was the months before. I could fill pages with surprising incidents of generosity and of contrasts. 'Received from a little girl a card in which she had cut a hole and placed one cent: four brothers gave $100,000.'

No name of a donor was given to the press, but those who had large gifts in mind had a right to know who else were making them. Hence I carried with me on one or two sheets of paper, typewritten, a list: at the head was a list of the six donors to pay the expenses, amounting to $125,000. In this list my sister Sallie's name stood for $25,000 and mine for the same amount, that those who saw it might know that I was in the cause. Then the two $250,000 gifts — one anonymous; followed by the names of those who pledged $100,000, $50,000, $25,000. Sometimes lists of one or two lower figures were added. On entering an office, I told my story in five or ten minutes, left a copy of our little pamphlet 'The Plan,' a list of largest givers, and a blank pledge in duplicate. I then said 'good-morning,' trusting the man or woman to think it out.

That list was effective. As I walked down a city street with the local chairman he said, 'Bishop, do you mind coming with me to Mr. Blank's office? He is very rich; we have tried him several times and cannot move him.' The gentleman received us courteously and I said, 'There is no need of my taking your time; you know what I am here for.' 'Yes,' he answered, 'but you people talk in such large figures.' 'We must,' I replied, 'if we are to get a large figure,' and I laid the typewritten page on his desk. He glanced at the names and said immediately, 'Oh, I will give you $25,000, of course.' And we bade him 'good-morning.' Perhaps his motive was that of sympathy, a devotion to the clergy and their dependents, perhaps it was that he saw three of his near relatives' names who had only a fraction of his wealth on that $25,000 list. How could he do less?

It became clear that we were going to run over the five millions before our date. Now that over five million dollars were in sight, were we under moral obligations to publish the fact? When we had reached one and two million figures and other critical points, we had published it through the Associated Press. We had made no promise to the public or the committees throughout the country to keep them informed; we might well go on and say nothing until March 1st. Moreover, our advisers in other parts of the country, especially in the South, telegraphed that the campaign was just beginning to move at many points, and that the publication of the completion of the five million was not fair to those workers and would cost the Church hundreds of thousands of dollars: I believed at the time that they were right. On the other hand, we had been frank at every point, had never concealed or held subscriptions to be thrown in at a critical time. We had trusted our constituency, and they had a right to trust us.

My diary of Friday, February 2d, runs:

Downtown all day. Talked out problem of announcement of totals to press and at the dinner: don't want to stop work thro' country yet must make announcement at dinner on Monday. Decided what to do: give stuff to press for issue Monday night: will put in press general condition and give more in detail at dinner.

Monday evening, February 4th, was for me a great event; I simply quote:

7.30 P.M. Waldorf Astoria. Dinner given me by the laymen of N.Y. and elsewhere. Mr. Burleigh managed it extremely well. 464 plates. W. Fellowes Morgan presided. Greer asked blessing. Very good dinner. Then toast to President and Flag: country apparently on edge of war. Sang America. Two excellent speeches by Darwin P. Kingsley, Pres. N.Y. Life Ins. Co. and Geo. W. Pepper. When Fellowes Morgan introduced me they all rose and gave three cheers. I spoke 50 minutes giving personal account of the Campaign: they all seemed keenly interested: closed at 11.10: they gave me three cheers again. An exceptionally good set of men and women present, every one said, for a public dinner. 12 Bishops, Charles Fairchild, J. P. Morgan, Belmont and others on dais: Ex-senator Wetmore, Ex-Atty. Gen. Wickersham and a large number of well known lawyers and business men; about 30 from Boston. Randall and Keyser from Baltimore: a table full from Philadelphia. The balcony filled with ladies in full dress. Julia had 18 in her two boxes: Julia, and Ruth each had a box of eight. Six of our children were there, only Elsie absent, Sue, Hart. and Laura came on. Hetty in California: also Kitty Hopkins. Certainly a gratifying tribute. I should not have encouraged it except that it was arranged to raise money at the end of the Campaign: that reason unnecessary for I announced $4,800,000 in solid pledges besides a good amount scattered thro' the country: indeed we shall have a large overflow. I tell Julia that we have struck our climax and will now run down. Have had what I thought a climax several times in my happy life, but this is doubtless the last.

Winston Churchill's story, 'The Faith of Frances Crawford,' written for the Fund, was distributed as a souvenir.

My chief gratification in the dinner was the fact that all were my friends, and that, while a large proportion of the company were strangers to me two years before, our friendship had been made in a common work and gifts for a great Cause. Throughout the campaign no man, woman, or child had been so pressed for contributions as to take offense: all were happy givers. The flood of pledges and contributions swept into the office until September, when the total reached eight and three quarter millions.

On March 1st, the Fund started its work. For nine years, supported by Mr. Sayre and an able and faithful Executive Committee, I have served as President, by no means a sinecure. The road has been rough at times: pathetic people have not understood and officious persons have broken in; but the Church as a whole has been loyal, patient, and strong in support of the system. Every day brings some duty. For five years I signed every check, thousands of them, that left the office, that beneficiaries might be assured that I was active in interest. Upon the death of a married clergyman in active service, a check for one thousand dollars is sent the widow immediately. All pensions are paid monthly. Through the faithfulness of diocesan committees, vestries, and people we receive practically one hundred per cent of assessments. By the wisdom of our Investment Committee, the values of our securities have increased and the rate of interest is larger than that on which we based our calculations; we have been able systematically to begin the increase of the pensions, and on the very day in which I close this chapter I have received from the auditor the report that on January 1st we had in our reserve twenty million dollars which with compound interest will in time go back to the Church in pensions.

CHAPTER XXX
THE WAR: I
1914–1917

THE first visible token of the War to me was, as I have already written, the Kron-Prinzessin Cecilie at anchor in Frenchman's Bay, Mount Desert, its nearest neutral port of refuge.

A few weeks later I received this letter from Archbishop Davidson, which, coming from a friend and a man who knew, impressed me with the awful solemnity of the times:

> LAMBETH PALACE, S.E.
> *30th October,* 1914

The War runs its terrible course. The carnage has, as you know, been fearful. No such battle-fields has the world ever seen. I have from the first endeavored to the utmost of my power to look fairly and reasonably upon the conflict, the history of its origin, the immediate causes of the declaration of war, the character of our alliances, and so on, and have asked myself again and again whether we could have done otherwise than we did. And I am firmly persuaded that we could not. . . .

I honestly believe that if we were at this moment standing outside the conflict and watching what would I suppose have been the ruin of France following upon the devastation of Belgium, we should have felt ourselves disgraced both in our own eyes and in the eyes of the world for disgraceful breach of our promises and betrayal of those who trusted us, and the time for vengeance to fall upon us would then be rapidly approaching and we should not have deserved either sympathy or support. Terrible as the present position is, we have at least the satisfaction of a clean conscience. . . .

I am trying myself to maintain friendship with German friends notwithstanding all that is happening, for I do not believe that they are constantly acting in defiance of what is true and right. But in the first place it is difficult to get any communications into their hands, and in the next place they are of course unpersuadable as to what seemed to us the rights and wrongs of the matter. We may have terrible times ahead of us before peace can be restored, and the process of reaching such peace is fraught with difficulties which look insurmountable, for Germany like England is unable now to give way unless she be brought to humiliation. It is all dark and difficult, but with the sense that what we are fighting for is righteous and true and that the wholesome intercourse of international life depends upon our maintaining faith and justice is, I think, beyond dispute. . . .

We boiled with anger at the German atrocities in Belgium, and some of us would have had the President and Congress protest. We were loyal to the President in being officially neutral as a Nation, but it was impossible to be neutral at heart; our blood, our love of liberty, our sense of justice rebelled. The self-restraint of the country was wonderful. We were again and again disappointed that, in the machinations of German representatives in this country, the President did not stand more firmly for what we believed to be national honor. Perhaps the country as a whole was not of our mind; we waited patiently and loyally, supporting the President even in his postponement of preparation for national defense or possible entrance into the War. On the 8th of May, 1915, as I was taking the Reverend William Temple, son of the late Archbishop of Canterbury, and now Bishop of Manchester, to see Groton and Saint Mark's Schools and Wellesley College, we heard the appalling news of the torpedoing of the Lusitania. A feeling of horror ran through the country that men could be so ruthless, and then rose a wave of deep anger. The next Sunday morning, being in Trinity Church, Boston, for an ordination, I read as Bishop of the Diocese a protest against the cruel methods of war by the Germans.

After President Wilson's reëlection in November, 1916, events moved so fast that one week before the day of his inauguration he asked Congress for armed neutrality. On Saturday, the day before his inauguration, Congress had adjourned without granting the President authority to arm our merchant ships.

Thursday morning, March 1st, found me at my desk in

Boston; the Church Pension Fund starting its wheels moving at the same hour in New York.

On Saturday we went out to Readville for a few days' complete rest and with the intention on my part to pass all Sunday in bed. At about eleven o'clock, as I was dozing, the thought suddenly struck me — this is the fourth of March, in an hour the President will quietly take his oath of office; for to-morrow is the ceremonial and the message: Monday's papers will lack news: here is a chance for a voice from Massachusetts to press and support the President towards leadership and action. I dressed and, having walked half an hour through the woods beautiful in falling snow, went to my desk and wrote off quickly a message in behalf of the people of Massachusetts. In the afternoon I went to Boston and through my friend the Reverend Doctor Sullivan, favorably known to all newspaper offices, the message was featured on Monday morning on the front page of every Boston paper.

Now that Congress has failed the President and the country, and at the moment when the President is laying his right hand on the Bible and taking his oath of office, I venture to place on record what I believe are the feelings and convictions of the great body of the people of Massachusetts. . . .

We have gradually turned our gaze from ideals of peace and international comity to hard and cruel facts. Some of us have begun to think that those who ten years ago worked and argued for a big Navy and a strong Army were wise in their day.

We have been compelled to revise many of our judgments in the light of facts. We have, however, the satisfaction of feeling that if we have erred it has been on the side of self-restraint and a longing to keep the peace and sustain ideals of international comity.

On this 4th of March, 1917, our thoughts have become firmer, our convictions have crystallized. We look no longer backward, but forward. Our President has spoken strong words in behalf of humanity, of the rights of Nations and of this Nation; rights to life, to trade, to succor others; the right as a Nation to be. To these he has pledged for us our lives and fortunes. We believe that he will stand to this pledge.

We citizens of the Commonwealth now demand that he stand to it; and we call upon him in this juncture to use to the full the powers with which the Constitution invests him to protect the citizens of this country on sea and land; to prepare the Nation to meet every emergency which may endanger its liberties; and to lead the people to defend at all costs the integrity of the Nation.

The people of this country are not wedded to ease and wealth. We are not lovers of safety, nor of peace at any price. We love peace and we do not want war. When, however, the country is in danger, when liberty, justice and the rights of humanity are at stake, the lives and wealth of the citizens of this Commonwealth are at the Nation's service.

WILLIAM LAWRENCE

A few days later there went to the President a telegram signed by Professor L. B. R. Briggs:

More than two hundred officers and professors of Harvard University, ninety-five per cent of those who could be reached, are sending you their endorsement of Bishop Lawrence's statement in Monday's newspapers supporting your strong words in behalf of humanity, and your pledge to maintain national principles and international right. Letter from President Lowell accompanies.

To whom this action was due I never knew, but such support was gratifying.

By the end of March, war seemed to be near. I therefore had at luncheon the seven Massachusetts chaplains who had served on the Mexican Border, and asked how the churches could help them. Upon their making up a list of the equipment needed for each; a large tent, motor truck, motion-picture machine, and incidentals for worship, I pledged them all in behalf of the Boston churches. Ready as were the churches of all denominations to help, I soon found, what was impressed upon me again and again, that a war cannot be fought by committees and conferences. So on the next Sunday, Palm Sunday, as I had visitations at Trinity, Emmanuel, and the Cathedral in Boston, I told the congregations the story and by evening had in hand pledges for the equipment of all the chaplains.

My diary tells the movement of that week:

Mon. Apr. 2. At desk: busy over Chaplain's Equipment. Congress meets: suppressed excitement as to President's position: no one knows it.

Eveg: Went to Harvard Club and listened to ticker working off President's address to Congress.

Tues. Apr. 3. President's strong position a surprise and gratification to all: the country behind him. Awful, but must be.

Wed. Apr. 4. A.M. At Diocesan House, talk with John Mott on Army and Navy Y.M.C.A. in relation to chaplains.

Thurs. Apr. 5. P.M. Preparing War Prayers: Senate voted for War last night.

Tues. Apr. 10. 12.30: At his apartment on Fenway officiated at funeral of Richard Olney. As Attorney General and Sec. of State of U.S. very strong: had elements of a great man: very friendly to me.

Mr. Choate's death, following that of Mr. Olney in a few weeks, severed two strong bonds with the past: a new era was coming on.

Wed. Apr. 11. 10 A.M. Clergy of the Diocese at Cathedral. Celebration of Holy Communion: gave short address on our work as Pastors in War. Then we had conference in Cath. rooms upon what we as clergy should do to help in War conditions. I am to appoint Committees. They endorsed a statement by me — 'Military efficiency demands total abstinence on the part of the whole people.'

Tues. Apr. 17. 11.30 A.M. To Cotton Waste Assoc. to speak on raising money for ambulances. Gen. Wood, Adm. Fletcher, the Mayor and I spoke.

May 3. Eveg.: To Pres. Lowell's reception to the six French officers.

This recalls President Lowell's brilliant thought and enterprise whereby Major Azan and his comrades, who had served at the front in this War, were permitted by the French Government to train Harvard students and later army officers in modern warfare.

After our entrance into the War, orders came for the United States Base Hospital No. 5, the Harvard Unit, to embark for France. Dr. Harvey Cushing, who was the Director, fell in heartily with my suggestion that they all join in a service at the Cathedral before starting. Malcolm Peabody was the chaplain. It was the first real evidence to Boston that War was calling men across.

Sun. May 6. 10 A.M. Cathedral: Special Patriotic Service for Hospital Base Unit No. 5. The Cath. packed. Governor, Mayor, Gen. Edwards, Dr. Cushing and 35 surgeons, 100 nurses in their uniforms: 200 enlisted men: their friends and others: great congregational singing of patriotic hymns. I dedicated the flag; the color sergeant and two men coming forward. Probably the first flag of the War to enter France (as the Cleveland Unit took ship first it was the second flag) Malcolm Peabody and I made addresses, Cottie P. in Chancel, also the Dean.

On the 12th of May, Boston received General Joffre with enthusiasm and Harvard gave him an honorary degree in Sanders Theatre. Then Joffre and a few officers of the University went up into the gallery of Memorial Hall while below were the students of the University in their R.O.T.C. uniforms: massed in solid ranks. Here, in the Hall dedicated to the memory of the Sons of Harvard who fell in the war to save the Nation, the students of Harvard, preparing to go overseas in the name of Liberty, gave in a mighty cheer their welcome to him who had held and driven back the Germans and saved his country and the cause. Joffre looked the man that we had expected, in carriage and speech a soldier, modest, strong, and kindly. We understood why the *poilus* called him 'Papa' Joffre.

During these months Belgian relief was making its moving call upon every one for money and help. As the spring opened, ploughs and spades cut through the lawns and smallest back yards for the planting of potatoes and other vegetables, for the country had other people to feed besides her own.

June 1. Eveg. Kingsley Hall: talked to First Active Corps: young women, about 300. Nora Saltonstall presided. Later in Ford Hall talked to body of girls: both on war; spirit of work.

June 4. A.M. War Committee Meeting. *Eveg.* Tremont Temple; presided at Meeting for War Y.M.C.A.: Governor and others spoke.

June 6. A.M. State House: Constitutional Convention: opened it with prayer. Governor presided: first Constit. Conv. for 65 years: 320 members.

June 13. *Eveg.* Copley Plaza, made speech at dinner of Mass. Medical Society on opportunity of surgeons in War to protect men against drink and women, on basis not only of physical results but of injury to efficiency and character.

June 19. To see Geo. Lyman and Mr. Endicott of Com. of Public Safety on question of camps and surroundings.

Eveg. Dined at Harvard Club with ex-Pres. Taft and others of Com. on Red Cross Meeting. Grand Opera House: Mass meeting to start great Campaign of Red Cross for one hundred million dollars. Henry Higginson presided. Taft spoke finely for almost 1½ hours. I closed with short speech.

June 22. 9 A.M. Washington. At Fed. Chs. office: Com. meeting; 12–1 as Chairman of Com. had interviews with Sec. of War (Baker) and Sec. of Navy (Daniels) on several Chaplain questions.

June 24. Gloucester, City Hall, Mass meeting for Red Cross one hundred million: made speech.

July 18. Washington. A.M. at Hoover Bldg. in response to Hoover's request to organize Chs. for Food Conservation Campaign: a very thorough and elaborate program for all Churches: will take enormous work to carry it on.

The most imperative call upon me seemed to be the religious conditions in the officers' training camps. Under the leadership of General Wood and others, Plattsburg had started a year before, and now in August sixty thousand young men had suddenly left home, gone into camps throughout the country, and in the whole outfit there were not more than a score of chaplains. When Dr. Thayer of Saint Mark's School called these facts to my attention and mentioned Plattsburg as an instance, I asked him to go immediately, which he did. On his return we kept a clergyman there, helping the very few commissioned chaplains and the workers in the Y.M.C.A. huts, holding services and meeting emergencies as they came along.

Drury, Appleton, and I motored from Bar Harbor through the White Mountains and Vermont to visit the Plattsburg Camp. As a boy in the Civil War, I had seen the camps and drill of the recruits. The training for modern warfare bore little resemblance, except that there were men, tents, and buglers.

Sat. Aug. 4. Plattsburg: At Murray Young's: breakfast on piazza. To the camps: saw trenches, wire entanglements, barracks, Hostess House, Y.M.C.A. Dined with Drury, Ap and Lawrence Hemenway at hotel, many friends among the 'rookies,' their parents, etc. A perfect eveg. from Hotel terrace, full moon over lake: Green Mts. in distance: music and dancing of soldiers and girls in hotel.

Sun. Aug. 5. 7.30 A.M. at Y.M.C.A. hut, I celeb. Holy Com. with Drury assisting: about 75 Communicants. 9 A.M. in Y.M.C.A. Hut. Farewell of a company as its last Sunday in Camp: I took service: Captain Moretti, Drury, and I gave addresses: about 300 there. 10.30 A.M. Trinity Ch. Plattsburg Conf. 2 soldiers and a boy: preached, full Ch. about 100 'rookies.' Drury celeb. Holy Com. Lunch at Young's: they had several reserve officers, etc., DeLancy Jay, Barney, John Dix, Jack Prentice and others. Supper with Col. of 1st New York Artillery, Col. Smith and Chaplain Shipman. Later spoke to men in Y.M.C.A. Tent: crowded and attentive.

Plattsburg was a sample of what was going on all over the country. As Chairman of the Chaplains' Commission, I stretched my authority, and wrote to every bishop, calling his attention to the facts, to the creation of officers' camps, to the danger of conditions about the camps, to the opportunities of the people by way of hospitality to the men, and to the necessity of placing strong clergymen in camps so far as the Commandants would allow it. Of course, some of the bishops had anticipated this, and the various denominations were doing their part.

By the middle of the summer every business concern, profession, and church was organizing for war work, but there was neither organized movement nor a call for one in the Episcopal Church. No one had the authority to move: the

Church had never had an executive, but was a congeries of dioceses with the senior Bishop as Presiding Bishop. As Chairman of the Commission on Chaplains, appointed only for peace routine, I had perhaps as much reason to lead as any one. At all events, late in July I wrote the Presiding Bishop, giving him a few facts, also telling him that, although he had no authority to do so, he ought to assume the authority, appoint a War Commission and get the Church moving. In response I received this proclamation to the Church from Bishop Tuttle, the fine old man writing in his quaint way:

BISHOP TUTTLE'S COTTAGE
WEQUETONSING, MICH., *Aug.* 4, 1917

I am asked to appoint a War Commission. In turn I ask myself what right I have to appoint such. Then the thought comes up — these are days in which grave responsibilities devolve themselves of a sudden upon leaders in State and Church. Under their impact procrastination cannot plead that it is prudence nor can inactivity name itself modesty.

Therefore, exigent duty seeming to call for a stretch of authority, I venture as Presiding Bishop to appoint the War Commission asked for, and to assign for its charge the watchful care and direction of Church work in connection with camps and cantonments, battle-fields and hospitals, Army and Navy Chaplains, and such like matters.

I beg to name for the members of such War Commission the Bishop of Massachusetts, the Bishop of Washington, the Bishop of Rhode Island, the Bishop of Western Michigan, and the Bishop Coadjutor of Southern Ohio; the Reverend W. R. Bowie, D.D., Mr. George Wharton Pepper, and Mr. Bayard Cutting. I am writing to these several gentlemen notifying them of this appointment.

I beg forgiveness from the sovereign authority, the House of Bishops, for this usurping action; and I beg forgiveness from the Chairman of the House, whose function it is to appoint all committees.   DAN'L S. TUTTLE,
Presiding Bishop

In the early autumn came the tidal wave of recruits. When at Groton in June, I had driven through a thicket of woods and waste country where soil was just being broken for a camp. In four months, when I was there again, the woods were gone and the land graded; huts had been built; also remounting station for horses from the West; everything equipped and forty thousand men moving in. It was now Camp Devens.

The first batch of recruits from Boston and vicinity assembled in this way. The orders were that they should assemble on Sunday afternoon, September 23d, at the Boston Theatre. As I went down West Street, the crowd was so great that the theatre was clearly out of the question, and upon an order to assemble at the bandstand on the Common the crowd faced about and the squads of recruits, each under a leader, gathered about the stand, some two thousand of them, with an enormous crowd of friends and citizens pressing in. The band played, the crowd cheered, the Governor, Mayor, and two or three of us made short speeches. Then came the order to fall into line and march to the North Station and entrain for Camp Devens. The men and boys around the bandstand this Sunday afternoon looked like a body of recently arrived immigrants; for while the majority were native-born, they were of every national stock, Anglo-Saxon, Irish, Italian, Greek, Scandinavian. Dressed in their everyday clothes, carrying suitcases, or with a bag of clothing swung over their backs, they fell into line, the band struck up, the Governor, Mayor, and a small group of us joined in, and we all marched along Tremont Street to the North Station. As we passed through the North End, the farewell shouts of the people in every language gave us the thrilling thought that with no distinction of stock or race the whole country would fight in her defense. An epochal event came a year later, on September 12, 1918, when, in registration week, the Nation laid its hand upon the shoulder of every man of from eighteen to twenty and from thirty-five to forty-five, some fifteen millions, and said in its peremptory way, 'You are now called and at the service of your country for whatever duty she may command.'

One of the great feats of the War, due to the leadership of those in authority in Nation and State, was, in my judgment, the way in which moral protection was thrown around the recruits, camps, and civilians. The disastrous experiences among some of our troops two years before on the Mexican Border had given the people a shudder as to what this war might bring forth. How vividly I recall the remark of Mr. Baker, Secretary of War, 'Bishop, we must throw protection about our camps and give the men all the social and moral influences possible, building them up in character and self-respect, so that when they cross to France they may stand on their own feet.' Indeed, the same protection followed the men to France.

The way in which the Camp Recreations Activities of the War Department organized the social and moral forces about the camp, the Y.M.C.A., the Knights of Columbus, the Hostess Houses, and a thousand other instrumentalities, was a marvel. Because my duties led me along the lines of these organizations, I mention them.

The whole people knew well that in the long run intoxicating drink weakens efficiency; hence, when citizen and soldier were called to work with the highest efficiency, war prohibition was observed. The citizens as a whole enforced the law themselves.

There was, however, another source of danger to which the people seemed determined to shut their eyes. Some of us had been, in days of peace, trying to get from the Legislature better protective laws against venereal diseases, but with meagre results. The newspapers would not mention the subject because their readers did not like it. Surgeons, physicians, and some social workers were, of course, alert to the dangers. I felt that some civilian whose general interests were in other lines must speak out, and, disagreeable as was the duty, I studied up the subject with the help of surgeons and physicians, read a paper upon 'Venereal Diseases in the Army, Navy, and Community' one Sunday afternoon in the Harvard Medical School, challenging the newspapers to report the authoritative facts. Surgeon-

General Gorgas wrote me, 'I think the medical-social aspects of the prevention of venereal diseases have never been stated more clearly, and such a statement from you has the added influence of placing the clergy squarely behind the whole programme of recreation, education, law enforcement, and medical measures'; at his request the address was printed and widely circulated by the American Social Hygiene Association.

The problem of the chaplains, their quality, number, rank, and efficiency was, of course, the problem of all the Churches and other religious organizations, and in meeting this and all other questions in the War the Churches worked in mutual confidence and coöperation. As the War progressed, it became more and more clear that great departments and organizations must absorb the smaller ones, creating simplicity of organization. I had hoped that a group of fifty or one hundred outstanding leaders from Protestant, Roman Catholic, Jewish, and all other religious organizations might be given large powers by their Churches, so that, when the religious forces of the Nation wanted to present a cause to the Secretary of War, he would have only one group to deal with. But that was not found possible; hence the religious interests were forwarded by conferences, commissions, the War-Time Commission, and other bodies, representative, to be sure, but not as effective as a more authoritative body. Efficiency in war suspends democracy in executive functions. Again and again, however, we all stood together in representing the cause of religion and character in Army, Navy, and Country. At the opening of the War, chaplains were by law discriminated against in rank and pay; veterinary surgeons had better recognition. There was in peace one chaplain to every regiment of twelve hundred men, later twenty-two hundred; when the quota of a regiment was raised to thirty-six hundred, with equivalent officers, the chaplains were again omitted. Hence the Churches pressed Congress and the War Department for an adjustment.

Thurs. Sept. 26. Washington 11 A.M. Before Com. of Senate
on Military affairs with Dr. McFarland of the Federal Council
of Churches, Father Egan and others to press the Chamberlain
Bill for one Chaplain for every 1200 men. I had charge of case at
hearing: Com. very sympathetic; Sen. Weeks interested. At
request of Chaplain of Senate went to Vice Pres. Marshall's
office. Then opened the Senate with Prayer. From there to
Mr. Fosdick, Chairman of Camp Recrea. Activities, had good
talk with him about relation of Chaplains to Y.M.C.A. Saw
Mr. Hoover on Ch. Conservation Campaign. Told him I thought
it an unwise plan but would back it out of loyalty to him. He
said he questioned wisdom of it.

Then to White House with representatives of all Churches,
Bp. McDowell of Methodist, Bishop Corrigan of Rom. Cath.,
Father O'Hearn, Dr. McFarland and about 20 Prot. ministers
and 20 Priests; Pres. Wilson received us. 3 or 4 of us presented
the case for the Chaplain Bill. He said he was interested and
would do all that he could for it. Then to Sec. of War; we waited
there an hour. We presented the case of bill to him: he favorable:
I also had a talk with Gen. Bliss, Chief of Staff; Then to Frank
Polk's, First Assist. Sec. of State, about protection of camps and
morals of soldiers in France & of Cottie's going to France. Then
to Red Cross to see Ivy Lee, also saw Mr. Davison. Dined at
Station and took Federal at 7.30 for home.

The contrast between the speed of administration in
Washington and in France seemed marked. Here there
was a military organization with conservative traditions
and red tape, and a War Department dependent upon the
Executive, the General Staff, Congress, and political conditions. In France there were authoritative leaders and a
war machine. Hence, while General Pershing, with his
chaplain staff headed by Bishop Brent, was cabling for
chaplains and more chaplains, there were picked men of all
denominations, accepted by the War Department, who
were eating their hearts out for lack of orders. This was
true, of course, in many lines of the service, but none the
less rather trying for those at both ends of the line.

We pressed the Department and Staff for a school for
chaplains; for the best civilian minister or priest might

fail as a chaplain for lack of military training as might the best civilian fail as a captain for the same cause. The answer of the Adjutant General was, 'a good chaplain is a good chaplain and a bad one is a bad one. A school is of no use.' And this decision was given in Washington after a well-ordered Chaplain School was working in France. So rigidly do soldiers, as well as ecclesiastics, stand by traditions until some cataclysm shakes them up. However, with all said the development of organizations and their efficiency were remarkable.

The exigencies of the situation compelled the War Department to recognize the appointment by the Churches of voluntary chaplains or camp pastors, who with the permission of the Commandants worked throughout cantonments and in Y.M.C.A. Huts, helping where needed and holding services. Without them the thousands in the great hospitals would often have been without spiritual care or cheer. It was an unmilitary procedure, but was due to the past neglect of the Churches, of Congress, and the Army, in not building up a strong body of chaplains with the privileges and training of the other officers.

The War-Time Commission represented practically the whole body of Protestant Churches, the Reverend Doctor Speer being President and I Vice-President. Most of the duties to which I have referred came upon me as an officer of this War-Time Commission. There was, however, the very important and more intensive work of our Church's War Commission, of which Bishop Tuttle had appointed me Chairman. For if the scores of thousands of the men and boys of our Church were to do their best work for their country, they must be made conscious of the fact that their Church was behind them in sympathy and moral and spiritual support. Our slogan was, 'The Church must stand back of its men who are fighting.'

Upon Bishops Perry, McCormick, Reese of Southern Ohio, and Harding, supported by Mr. Arthur Newbold, the Treasurer, and a few other clergymen and laymen, fell the chief responsibility for this work. Through the kindness of the bankers, Messrs. Hodenpyle, Hardy and Company, the larger part of whose clerical staff was in the service, the Commission had ample quarters in the Bankers' Trust Building, a few floors under those of the Church Pension Fund. From the windows the camouflaged troop ships could be seen passing the Statue of Liberty, while from the steps of the Treasury Building floated up the bugle calls, speeches, songs, and cheers in the Liberty Loan Campaigns. In these offices these men did most effective work in organizing, in correspondence, and in giving moral support to our men and boys on both sides of the water. It fell to me to lead in raising the half-million dollars needed, and to have general oversight, while these others did the real work.

Chaplains, both commissioned and voluntary, who were clergymen of our Church, needed equipment of various kinds, service books which had been specially prepared, portable altars, typewriters, and cash for all sorts of emergencies; parishes near cantonments required help to meet calls for hospitality to soldiers.

Bishop McCormick and later Bishop Perry went to France, and from Paris extended the work of the Commission to the front trenches. We thereby supplemented for the men of our Church, and for others who turned to us, the work of the greater general organizations.

The raising of the half-million dollars brought me back to the familiar methods of two years before. I first reached those who could give in large figures, while the officers, aided by the experience of Mr. Sayre, organized the work throughout the country; then I travelled through Eastern cities, speaking in churches; and finally on Sunday, January 27, 1918, came a general collection resulting in an overflow of one hundred thousand dollars — six hundred thousand dollars in all.

As Bishop Perry had made an inspection of our work throughout the South and Middle West, I undertook in May, 1918, to visit the camps and naval stations of the Pacific Coast. Sixteen miles from Tacoma was Camp

Lewis, the finest in site and lay-out that I saw: a plain of from two to three miles across gave a magnificent parade ground and ample room for quarters and huts, while up in the hills were ranges for gun practice and trenches for the training in the hideous warfare of gassing. Down the coast we went, passing a Sunday with the Naval Reserves on Goat Island in the harbor of San Francisco, and a day here and there in camp and naval station, to San Diego with its great Camp Kearny, the beautiful naval station in the exhibition grounds of Park Bilboa, and the aeroplane station at Coronado.

This journey impressed me with the unifying force of the war. There was no West, nor East; no North nor South; Eastern friends were in camp and station on the Pacific Coast as were Western soldiers and Southern sailors at our homes in Boston.

The routine work in the Diocese was more important than ever, for with the loss of clergy who were chaplains, the departure or engrossment of parish officers in war work and the war calls upon the women, the Diocese needed personal leadership.

Thousands of young men from all parts of the country were stationed in and around Boston: several thousand Naval Reserve boys were in Cambridge, where the Common was covered with barracks, and the College Yard and surroundings had the appearance of a camp. Besides the Y.M.C.A. and Y.M.C.U., various organizations created hostelries and social centres for the men. Our Sailors' Haven was strained to the breaking point. Hence, at my suggestion, and under the leadership of Mr. F. Nathaniel Perkins, four Boston parishes joined in the creation and support of the 'Naval Service Club,' for which we took two empty buildings at the corner of Beacon and Somerset Streets; broke down partitions, set up sleeping-space, showers, lunch-counters, billiard-tables, and common rooms, where many scores of thousands of sterling young Americans, homeless and strangers, passed their time when off duty. This was a most satisfying, happy bit of work.

PREACHING TO SOLDIERS AT CAMP BARTLETT, WESTFIELD

WILLIAM LAWRENCE AND HIS TWO SONS
William Appleton Lawrence and Frederic Cunningham Lawrence
(About 1920)

A typical confirmation service at Camp Devens merits description. The Y.M.C.A. Hut, with its counter of cigarettes, stationery, and candy at one end and platform at the other, gives space between for an audience hall, with benches and tables for writing. While the voluntary chaplain, the Reverend Howard K. Bartow, is cleaning up the platform and setting the altar service in order to give an ecclesiastical tone to the platform end, fifty to seventy-five privates with their hats on and cigarettes pouring smoke are writing or talking. Vested in my robes I walk onto the platform and, as I begin to call the company to order, a football from the game outside bounces against the back wall, and the shouts of the players enter the windows. In a few words I tell the men what is going to happen, and invite them to come forward as witnesses: about twenty respond; a class of fifteen privates with perhaps a non-commissioned or commissioned officer step onto the platform. We sing a hymn. Meanwhile the other men, with hats on, continue writing, or stop to gaze, but all as a matter of respect stop smoking. The confirmation service over, I say a few words to the class, then to all the men, who look up and listen attentively; then follow a hymn and the blessing.

There was to me in such a service more significance, reverence, and reality than I have felt in many a great orderly parish church.

Here is a sample record:

Sun. Sept. 9, 1917. Westfield, Camp Bartlett: New U.S. Camp: New Engl. Regiments 15000. 9 A.M. Brigade Service at Headquarters: Chaplains took part: used Rom. Cath. altar and tent chancel. I preached to about 400 men in open air: they from 2nd Mass. and other regiments. Had a talk with Gen. Cole: with Col. Ballantyne, went thru' Camp of Maine Heavy Artillery. Chaplain Danker with me: looked about the Camp, into the stockade, jail, etc. Back to Springfield. P.M. Motored home.

Danker, who entered the ministry under me, and who had seen service as chaplain on the Mexican Border, sailed with the 104th Infantry of the 26th Division ten days after my visit. He was awarded a Croix de Guerre with silver star for gallantry in action at Seicheprey, France, and soon after was mortally wounded in action in front of the church at Royaumeix, the first American chaplain to fall.

CHAPTER XXXI
THE WAR: II
1917–1918

I AM one of the fast vanishing company which has vivid memories of the Civil War. Hence, before telling several incidents in my experience during the last few months of the World War, I jot down a few of my impressions of the contrasts between the two wars.

In 1862 to 1864, we, boys and citizens, rushed into the streets or onto the Common to see the outgoing regiments pass, and to cheer them off at the railroad station or the dock. Within a few days the men had written home from the South, and their families knew approximately where they were, what they were doing, and in case of battle heard quickly the result to the cause and themselves. Later, wounded young men would be about the streets, and soldiers' funerals with muffled drums passed through towns and villages throughout the country. I can remember, as if it were yesterday, when my father, on coming home from business, said that Charles Lowell had been killed: and his funeral is vividly before me.

Contrast these conditions with those of 1917 and 1918, when the regiments slipped down the harbor shrouded in darkness and secrecy: the soldier's wife knew not where or when her husband was starting upon the torpedo-haunted Atlantic; and though she may have received word of his landing in France later, weeks and months would pass without any clear idea of his whereabouts or condition. No doubt censorship was necessary, but it weakened immensely the support of enthusiasm kindled by personal sight and knowledge. It added greatly to the anxiety of the people at home.

On the other hand, the very secrecy and mystery perhaps gave a seriousness to the temper of the people. They were not distracted by the trappings of war: uniforms, huts, and guns were dull of color and made for war business. People's minds were concentrated on the great things and the great cause.

Here is another contrast — the solidarity of the whole people. In the Civil War we had right among us, friends and neighbors who were 'copperheads,' obstructers of the Northern cause or indifferent to its success. Union Clubs and Union League Clubs were organized in large cities to offset the indifference of many social clubs. Riots arose against recruiting or the draft. There were profiteers, makers of shoddy uniforms, and great numbers of men and women who did nothing to help.

In this War, millions of men and women were enlisted in Liberty Loan, Red Cross, Y.M.C.A., and other campaigns, whose organization and enthusiasm extended to the smallest hamlet in the plain or the lonely mining camp. Can any of us who walked across the Common ever forget the village of huts and model gardens, the bands and shoutings on the Tremont Street Mall; and the mass meetings in halls and theatres with the community songs and the 'Long, Long Trail' of soldier choruses? Two hundred soldiers detailed from Camp Devens would crowd the platform of Symphony Hall, and their voices would meet the song of the people thrown from floor and galleries. There has been no singing like it. How vividly I remember the response to a chance remark that I made in Symphony Hall in telling of the boys leaving home for Ayer and Camp Devens! 'Do you people know Ayer Junction?' I said. 'I have known it sixty years, and have waited long, long hours there for belated trains. It is the dullest spot on this Continent — dull enough to drive a man to drink.' To my surprise there was a roar of laughter from behind. I turned about. I had forgotten: two hundred men from Camp Devens knew how dull Ayer was and how dry!

The World War was massive: as contrasted with the Civil War, everything was massive; and before the mass movement, the personal element was inconspicuous. Grant, Sherman, and Sheridan rode, mounted on their chargers, from Headquarters to point and point, and the soldiers cheered. Pershing rode in a limousine, hardly recognized by the men: tanks plunged to the front.

While there were, of course, inefficiency, slackness, dishonesty, political treachery, and traitors in the World War, the whole spirit, leadership, and management were, so far as a layman like myself views it, unspeakably superior to those of the Civil War. This was, I hope — indeed believe — because the character and intelligence of the Nation are superior and in the awful emergency, finer results followed.

At the close of the Civil War General Grant said, 'Let us have peace'; and Sherman echoed, 'War is hell.' The World War was to us so short that we as a people did not have the hungry craving for peace which comes from exhaustion, nor did we respond immediately to the expression of Sherman. Our reaction was different. From the first moment that we watched in some encampment, intelligent, high-minded American boys absorbed in the grim duty of bayonet practice, or learning the technique of gassing, we revolted at the whole business. War was stupid, sickening, squalid, beastly. In spite of its noble incidents and personalities, it was debasing, foul, and a libel on civilization. We would fight it through and never again get caught in such an idiotic way of settling national disputes.

Throwing my memory back, I recall times of deep depression. I felt it when I went to some college to preach, and, instead of seeing before me a body of young men preparing for the constructive work of civilization, I found a body of boys and men haled in from over the country learning how to handle the business of destroying the works of civilization.

The red stars hanging in the windows of the homes told of those who were in the service, and the gold stars of those who had fallen. We could glory in the stars in the city where there were lots of people; but in driving through the country roads, when we saw the lone red star in the little farmhouse window, we knew that the working force and the hope of the old people had marched away: and the gold star found the old people stunned. Who would work the farm now? The lowing of the cows in the barn was a requiem, and the weeping willows bent over the sloping roof.

A different emotion was aroused as we sat down in the dining-room of a great New York hotel, wherein a few months before, guests had ordered what they would of meats, game, relishes, sweets, and wine, to see these same guests selecting from a short menu and contentedly accepting what was put before them, one pat of butter, one lump of sugar, no meat on meatless days; no bacon; no sweets.

These things seem trivial: and they were trivial compared with the tragic sacrifices of many. But they suggest the fact that, when a whole people have resolved to carry a certain business forward, they adjust themselves to it and are content. There were sharper tests, however, and every man, woman, and child felt them. Ships, allies, camps must have coal: hence the rationing of coal, the impossibility at times of getting coal. Then there fell upon us the bitterly cold January of 1918.

Sun. Dec. 30. N.Y.: 13° below zero: coldest on record. A.M.: Preached in Grace Church: almost full to my surprise: some came in from Calvary where church was only 40°. Spoke on War Commission. Bitterly cold all day: fear of coal famine.

If this was the record in New York City, its bitterness was multiplied in village and farm. Then came the heatless days.

Fri. Jan. 18. Train for New York. Country excited because on account of fuel shortage, Garfield has ordered all industries closed for five days beginning to-day; and every Monday for 10 weeks. R. Roads congested with freight & ships waiting in harbor for coal, held by the congestion.

Mon. Jan. 28. N.Y. Heatless Monday: all shops and offices closed to save coal. 11. Com. meeting with Chaplains Com.: Drs. Speer, Brown, McFarland, etc. Sat in heavy overcoats.

Ambassador Page was anxious that men should go from this country, and move among the English people to allay misunderstandings and especially to hearten them and assure them that we were with them in the fight for liberty and constitutional government. One day Dr. Wallace Buttrick, having telegraphed ahead, called upon me and said that I had been selected as one of the group to go, including Mr. Taft and others. I also received a warm invitation from the Archbishop of Canterbury to make Lambeth my headquarters. Soon the message came that President Wilson disapproved the plan, and would allow no one to go.

Having received intimation through the Reverend Doctor Manning that the Archbishop of York would come to this country on such a mission if invited by a national organization, I asked him in behalf of the War Commission, to be the guest of the Commission. Upon his acceptance we made out an itinerary which would enable him to speak during six weeks in the great halls and churches of the country east of the Mississippi and in Canada: and Mr. Sayre undertook to carry this through.

Landing early in March, the Archbishop went directly to Washington, paid his respects to the President, and then started upon his task. Dr. Lang is a man of great intellectual ability, an orator of the best English type of this century, refined, restrained, sympathetic, clear in style; rising at times to heights of eloquence and heat of passion, but always in command of himself; leaving upon his audience the confidence which comes from understatement where the facts would have warranted an appeal to revenge. It was a delicate piece of work, that of describing the spirit of Great Britain and the Allies to a people who had watched, waited, and finally entered the battle. Any appeal for sympathy and help had to be so concealed as to sustain England's pride and self-respect; while the slightest note of declamation as to what England had done and was then doing would have alienated sympathy. Each day I watched anxiously the reports in the papers, lest a slip be made or a phrase misunderstood, but the Archbishop went through to the end with increasing power and influence.

Spring opened, and as the Germans made their desperate drive towards the Channel, our hearts sank: the British line held. Patriots' Day, April 19th, came, and I sent off to every Massachusetts boy and man of our Church who was in the service this letter in my own hand with the Old North Church in the corner:

MY DEAR FRIEND,

This is Patriots' Day. From this Belfry Tower of the Old North Church hung the lanterns that sent Paul Revere galloping to Lexington and Concord. The old spirit is in the air of the Old Commonwealth to-day.... We are thinking of you this morning. You stand to us as the men who stood their ground at Concord Bridge, while we are like those who were left to till the farms. You are at the front, we in the rear: all of us bound together in our common cause.

As your Bishop and friend I could not let this day pass without sending to every Massachusetts man and boy belonging to the Episcopal Church who is serving in the Army or Navy this letter of Godspeed. The chances are that I confirmed you. At all events I follow you with deep interest....

You know better than I do that the man who serves his country best is the man who does his military duty right up to the hilt. You know also that the test is not only in detail but in character, the man behind the gun.....

We all of us in our homes and our churches are thinking of you and praying for you. We are proud of you. We will do anything we can for you. You will do everything you can for us: true to duty, true to your Master Christ. God bless you.

Count me sure as faithfully

Your friend and Bishop

WILLIAM LAWRENCE

On the 15th of August there met in Harvard University some one hundred and fifty representatives from fifty-three theological seminaries of fifteen denominations in the United States and Canada for conference upon moral and spiritual problems aroused by the War. My diary runs:

Fri. Aug. 15, 9.30 A.M.: Harvard Univ. A remarkable service in Appleton Chapel. The strongest men as a rule of the seminaries present at the conference; no such gathering since the Reformation: they met to discuss questions of ministry and theology & the Churches arising from the War. Their Com. asked me to administer the Lord's Supper & I accepted believing it a time for Christians to gather at the Lord's Table, putting in background differences due to the past, to inherited traditions, to misuse of technical words. We are glad to have soldiers in camp of various Churches meet to partake of the Lord's Supper: why not theologians also?

I officiated in robes: had the Com. Service of Prayer Book: had distributed 100 Pr. Books: gave out page, etc. All took hearty part in the service: some 76 received, kneeling or sitting and leaning over in the front pews using the bench in front for rail: everything as natural, reverent and hearty as possible. Dean Fenn of Harv. Divinity School, Dr. McGiffert of the Union Sem., Dr. McKenzie of Hartford Sem., Dean Hodges of Cambridge, also a Baptist. Most gracious of them to unite on our service. And so far as I could learn, all much impressed with beauty and sincerity of the service.

It seems strange that it should take a war to bring √ Christian theologians together at the Lord's Supper: so far have we wandered from the Master.

One day the request from Washington went throughout the country that, on five successive Sundays, beginning September 29th, no motor car leave its garage except in case of necessity. Of the millions of people who took their families and friends each Sunday to drive, not one should go. No one went. Boulevards, roads and city streets were empty and silent. Those Sundays were Sabbaths, indeed: quieter than any since the days of the Pilgrims.

Just then came the tragedy of the influenza.

Sun. Sept. 29. All churches closed on account of influenza and pneumonia. Probably 50,000 cases in Mass.: deaths by hundreds. Sallie at work trying to get doctors and nurses all day. My two engagements at Swampscott and Cathedral off.

Sat. Oct. 5. Twenty-fifth anniversary of my consecration. Twenty-five happy years and many blessings. Diocese wanted some kind of a celebration: I felt that these are not times for personal recognition. However, the Standing Com. arranged for Diocesan service at Trinity, and a lunch for men, another for women: informal: no speeches. On account of epidemic of influenza the service and everything called off: schools, theatres, and every assembly of people stopped: churches will be closed Sunday, and bar-rooms after Monday. Many thousands of people ill, influenza and pneumonia: many deaths: over 2000 soldiers in camps died this week. Nurses cannot be had and school teachers volunteering as nurses.

The risk of contagion through the use of the common cup in the Holy Communion led me to commend to the Diocese the method of intinction, that is, the dipping of the bread in the wine. This use proved to be so reverent and safe, relieving the fear of many communicants, that I commended it later as an alternative custom. As this was the first instance of a Bishop commending intinction for general use in his Diocese, it was challenged in some quarters as irreverent, unlawful and contrary to the tradition of the Church. At the last General Convention the use was placed among the proposed changes in the Prayer Book.

In the autumn of 1918, when we were thrilled with as much of the story of the valor of our men in France as seeped through the press; with suggestions also of discontent in Germany and the crumbling of her power; when visions of men returning home floated before us — a thought seized hold of me which I could not shake off, something like this:

The men and boys across the sea and at home in the service have stood for and fought for an ideal; in spite of grim and squalid conditions, they must have been ennobled; they have been under discipline; are accustomed to vigorous action, promptness, and concentration. What are they going to think of us when they get home? We have had no such discipline: our parishes, their parishes, are running comparatively slack; slack in organization, sense of duty, and devotion. We must meet them on their own ground. We must go into spiritual training.

Unwilling to have a marked celebration of the twenty-fifth anniversary of my consecration on October 5th, when our men were going to hospital, death, or victory, I jumped at the opportunity after Armistice Day to make a later celebration the starting-point of a spiritual revival of the churches in the Diocese. If I had had any experience in organization for money-raising, why should not that be put to service in arousing the moral and spiritual life of the people committed to my charge? Hence, calling together representative clergymen and laymen, I told them that as our Liberty Loans and Church contributions had been gathered by the personal work of men and women through the whole community, I wanted the leading men and women of the church, who were little known to the rank and file of their parishes, to take up the cause of a more Christian life and a finer Church loyalty by going themselves into every home, tenement, or room where a Church man, woman, or 'child lived, not to preach or talk, but [to carry to them a message from their Bishop: the chief purpose being not the message, but the personal contact.

Hence arose the 'Twenty Weeks' Campaign' in the Diocese, running from December 1st to Holy Week. The purpose was 'To mobilize the spiritual forces of the Church in this Diocese.' I fell to the work of organizing the campaign, using every device of financial campaigns, simultaneousness of action, groups of representative bodies, suppers, local meetings, and literature. Every move and word was on a plane of earnestness and consecration.

The three little books, framed exactly on the plan, paging, and attractiveness of the literature of our financial campaigns, I wrote myself. Nothing cheap or unattractive would do. Five thousand dollars went into a dollarless campaign. In bold type on the outside stood, 'A Message from the Bishop,' 'Twenty Weeks.' The Church was going into camp and training. Hence the three successive titles were: (1) 'Enlistment and Preparation'; (2) 'Service and Expansion'; (3) 'Consecration and Victory.'

Within each pamphlet were definite suggestions for

each day, with appropriate text: everything practical. A page in red ink for the children.

On certain Sunday afternoons from a score to one hundred men and women carried the Bishop's Message into every home in each parish, placing it in the hands of the parishioners. It was well done. I am confident that the campaign deepened the moral and spiritual life of the whole Diocese.

In November came the thrilling days.

Thurs. Nov. 7. 2 P.M. Com. on '20 weeks.' 3.30 Naval Service Club. 5 P.M. Took train with Julia for New York. New York in an uproar: the whole city has been out all day: Boston too has been out on' the streets: a false report of the signing of the Armistice. The German army suddenly broken down and offer of Germany for armistice: great surprise. The false report sent people wild: downtown knee deep in paper which, torn in small bits, was thrown from the windows of offices and houses.

Mon. Nov. 11. At 4.30 A.M. Whistles of all factories announced signing of armistice. They sounded steadily for 2 and 3 hours. By 10 A.M. the city filled with people: motors in lines coming in from towns about. I had a 'Twenty Weeks' Com. and writing, but city outside excited, horns, cannons, cheers, people marching through the streets. 1 P.M. Cathedral: full: gave address: it had been packed to doors at 12, when trumpeters had led singing from porch: 12 services in the Cath. to-day, one every hour. Tremont Street and all streets jammed with people, processions, etc.: drummers marching thro' the shops, etc.

At desk: to Common, stood with Mayor as procession passed. Then to the Cathedral: trumpeters at 4.30, great crowd in Cath. yard, Tremont St. and back into Common: thousands singing patriotic songs and hymns. Then service at 5. Dr. Mann spoke.

Eveg. Symphony Hall: Mass meeting. Mayor, Gen. Crozier, Admr. Wood, Dr. van Dyke and I spoke: great enthusiasm. Symphony Orchestra: cheers and songs. Beautiful autumn day.

Tues. Nov. 12. 10.30. Great service at Trinity Church. Governor, Mayor, Gen. Crozier, Adm. Wood, etc. Patriotic service of thanksgiving. I gave address. 12. Cathedral: solid mass of people. Sullivan and I gave addresses. Same as yesterday: streets crowded with people celebrating.

To lunch at Robert Grant's to meet Lord Charnwood.

Cabot Lodge, Rhodes, Thayer, Barrett Wendell. Cabot in the change by election will be Chairman of Com. on Foreign Relations.

Downtown: procession over, but I walked and squeezed through the cosmopolitan crowd to feel the spirit of the people: all celebrating in fine and cheerful way.

Eveg: Symphony Hall. Great mass meeting: enthusiasm: Governor, Mayor, Gen. Crozier and others. I gave benediction.

Eveg. Great Britain's Day: tribute of America to Great Britain. Two great mass meetings in Symphony Hall and Opera House to hear Capt. Carpenter the hero of Zeebrugge, Captain of Vindictive, give account of the closing of the harbor. I spoke at Symphony Hall first: fine audience: many British Societies: officers and crew of H.M.S. Devonshire and much enthusiasm. I then went over to Opera House, where Capt. Carpenter was speaking with pictures. When he was done, he went over to Symph. Hall and at Opera House I spoke. Another crowded house. I then went back to Symphony and heard him finish. His was a wonderful exploit.

Ten days later I ran on to New York for a War Commission meeting; adjusted the budget for the immediate future, and on my return tumbled into bed, knocked out. In the next few days while still in bed I finished up odd jobs and completed to the last detail the Twenty Weeks' Campaign, organization, and messages. The Christmas family party went by and I was still useless. My diary written from Julia's notes and my memory six weeks later, tell the story:

Mon. Jan. 6. Dr. Crockett came at 9.30 A.M., said that my mastoid was affected and advised the operation. So they went to work fixing up my study as operating-room. At 2 P.M., Dr. Freeman Allen came and gave me subcutaneous injections: soon Dr. Crockett led me into the study all hung in white, the nurses and doctors except Dr. Richardson in white, and immediately laid me on the operating table, my first experience: a very narrow shelf it was to stay on. The same Psalm came to mind that I had in mind all the time of my typhoid fever forty odd years ago, 'Bless the Lord, O my Soul.' Then the Virgin Mary and child Jesus over my mantelpiece looked down, and

408   MEMORIES OF A HAPPY LIFE

just as Dr. Allen started to give me the anæsthetic the photo of Theo. Roosevelt hanging on the opposite wall seemed to look straight at me, and I said, 'There is my old friend Roosevelt; no one can wince while he is looking on,' and I went off unconscious. I did not know that early that very morning he had died quietly in his sleep.

CHAPTER XXXII

AFTER THE WAR

1919–1926

On Monday morning, February 24, 1919, President Wilson, crossing from France in the steamship George Washington, landed in Boston bringing with him the draft of the Covenant of the League of Nations. Weak from my operation and about to take the one o'clock train for Aiken, South Carolina, I sat limply at my window, watched the crowds beneath, and heard the cheers as he came up Commonwealth Avenue. I can see him now, standing erect in an open motor, dressed in a fur-lined coat, waving his tall hat, and bowing to the people right and left as they cheered. Helped out the back door and through the back alley, I caught the train.

As soon as I read the Covenant of the League in the paper at Aiken, I sat down and wrote Cabot Lodge, before he had spoken on the subject, that I did not see how any loyal citizen could support the Covenant so long as Article 10 and other conditions were in it. Article 10 still stands: so does my opinion. I believe that this Nation should take every wise step to come into close and sympathetic relations with other nations, and on occasions at some risk. I believe also that with others she should build up traditions of international comity and a system of international judicature. The nation will, in my judgment, do her greatest work for other nations and civilization by preserving her independence of political action: making such treaties, connections and adjustments from time to time as may seem wise.

Illness and absence for several weeks, with the Diocesan Convention ahead, pressed me hard on my return. For I now had in anticipation another and more serious operation, which took place in Phillips House on May 13th.

Successful as it was and skilful as were the surgeons, an infection gripped my system which was to me as a chain and ball to a prisoner, for three years.

Throughout my ministry I have been grateful for an attack of typhoid fever at the start. I have often said that a part of the training of a young man for the ministry should be a personal experience in illness or surgical operation. He thus gains a first-hand knowledge for his pastoral work. In six years I had four severe surgical operations and a number of minor cuts; and am grateful for the experiences. With modern surgery, nursing, and hospitals one rests confident. In flowers, messages, and prayers friends gather in support: pains, though terrific at times, give one an inkling of what chronic suffering may be. One of the happy memories of my life is of a birthday cake with candles made in the hospital kitchen and presented by the nurses.

A determination to be present enabled me to sit with the President and Fellows for one half-hour at the interesting Commencement of 1919. Besides the presentation of honorary degrees to General Crowder, Admiral Sims, and Henry P. Davison, eight honorary degrees of Master of Arts were given with appropriate commendation by the President to eight graduates of Harvard who had in some special way distinguished themselves in the War. Then the whole audience arose and in deep silence heard the President announce that an honorary degree of Doctor of Laws had been voted, and except for his death would have been presented, to Robert Bacon.

Our kind nephew and niece, Augustus and Alice Thorndike, have a lovely lodge nestling in the trees near their gate at Bar Harbor. Here, at their invitation, Mrs. Lawrence and I passed the summer, basking in the sun and enjoying sweet scents from the gardens and the voices of the lawn-tennis players. A third of a mile across the hills were four families of our children and grandchildren; who one by one came to see us while we occasionally watched their play. It was a quiet, happy summer.

By October I was able to go to the General Convention at Detroit, but took an inactive part. Upon the motion of Bishop Gailor the doors of the House of Bishops were finally opened. Although I could not approve of the policy of the Church in making larger appropriations of money than there was reasonable expectation of receiving, I felt bound in loyalty to accept an election to the Council, but was continually uneasy: three years later I dropped out. The General Convention at New Orleans in 1925 voted to stand for a sound financial policy, and it was a source of satisfaction to me to become again a member of the National Council.

In the winter of 1920, Julia and I began a succession of winters wherein we have passed a few weeks as guests of the Jekyl Island Club. The island off Brunswick, Georgia, some fifteen miles long, was Governor Oglethorpe's plantation. A fine forest of palmetto, live-oak, pine, and other heavy timber, intersected by shell roads and paths, fringes the beautiful beach running the length of the island. The members are our warm friends. Dr. Walter B. James presides, and makes of the group of from eighty to a hundred one congenial family, while Mr. George F. Baker is the beloved and recognized patriarch.

Outside the little chapel sets a heavy iron trough, whose inscription suggests other days:

> This kettle from Slave Yacht Wanderer,
> Captain Corry
> used for feeding the slaves landed
> on Jekyl Island, November 28, 1858.
> Yacht owned by Charles A. L. Lamar, of
> Savannah, Georgia.

In this chapel the choir and I practise together on Saturday evenings for the service on Sunday, when members of the Club come to worship.

On May 30, 1920, I reached the venerable age of threescore years and ten, but, except for an occasional pull of my ball and chain, felt no older than at fifty. My birthday was on a Sunday, when I consecrated Saint Paul's Church,

Brockton. A bit of ritual took place which was, I think, unique in Christian history and which pleased me immensely. The service was ended and I had given the benediction, when the Rector, Dr. Matthews, stepped to the chancel gate and told the congregation, which packed the church, that in recognition of my seventy years the parish wished to make me a present. Then from the rear of the church two boys came up the broad aisle, weighed down with a great frosted birthday cake upon which was inscribed in frosting, 'Our Bishop, 1920,' and presented it to me. Placing the cake upon the chancel rail, I spoke a few words of thanks; then a warden stepped forward, lifted the cake, and bore it before me in the recessional procession.

The Lambeth Conference, which had been postponed by the War, was called for July, 1920, by the Archbishop of Canterbury: an act which showed courage and faith in view of the post-war conditions in England. Mrs. Lawrence and I went, taking my sister, Hetty Cunningham, and Fred, who was to pass the next winter at Corpus Christi College, Cambridge. The Archbishop of York showed great leadership in uniting the Conference upon the message in behalf of Unity, which was a long step forward on the part of the Anglican Church.

Although I was knocked out occasionally, I went through the routine of the Conference.

The unveiling of the replica of Saint-Gaudens's Lincoln in Parliament Square was a significant event. After a short address in a near-by hall by Lord Bryce, Mr. Root spoke more fully of Lincoln. He was eloquent in his simplicity and directness. Then Lloyd George, the Prime Minister, kindled the audience by the vitality of his personality, his beautiful voice, and his effective diction. As the company moved out to unveil the statue, the clouds emptied themselves, and I took a taxi to cover at Lambeth. The next Sunday, preaching at Saint Margaret's, Westminster, which stands opposite the statue, I took for my text, 'There was a man sent from God.'

We caught a glimpse at Oxford of our friend of many

years, Lady Osler, and found there Dr. Harvey Cushing hard at work on 'The Life' of Sir William.

The happiest part of our visit was the renewal of our friendship with Archbishop and Mrs. Davidson. I can hear her voice as she sought me out among the two hundred bishops after every luncheon, 'You must come with me and I will tuck you up on the sofa for a rest.' The Archbishop has had the longest primacy since that of Archbishop Wareham who died in 1532. Dr. Davidson's statesmanship in leading the Church of England during these twenty-three critical years of history is universally recognized. More than an archbishop he has been a great statesman of the Empire. Of deep and simple Christian faith, he has won the regard of Christians of every name and citizens of all faiths by his transparent sincerity, his unselfish devotion and his great wisdom. The closer one approaches him, the more conscious one becomes of the Archbishop's friendliness and saintly character. As we left the Garden of Lambeth Palace on an August Sunday afternoon where tea was spread and a few friends gathered, we felt as if we were leaving a second home.

I used to think that when a college class passed its fiftieth anniversary, the time had come for the members to repeat their '*morituri salutamus.*' When, however, on the afternoon before Commencement, the Class of '71 marched around the baseball field to the plaudits and cheers of the multitude, we felt ourselves to be as of the graduating class. There is a conceit of youth and love of applause which warms the hearts of the old boys. Preceded by the great banner of '71 carried by Barnes and Eustis of our college nine, Cabot Lodge and I led the class in circling around the field. Since then the ranks have thinned fast, and among the fallen is Cabot.

After his death in the autumn of 1924, the Legislature asked me to give an address before them in his memory. He had been a great Senator, an orator, and a statesman. A leader of the Republican Party, he had received the highest honors from them; but in the last few weeks of his career, he had conscientiously voted for two measures which brought upon him — unjustly to my mind — the hostility of those who formerly applauded him. He had limitations of manner and temperament. I could not therefore write a mere eulogy. I should have been false to his tradition of honesty. Hence I wrote a short 'Life,' revealing him clearly and frankly, bringing out also the beautiful friendship of himself and Roosevelt. From this I prepared the address for the Legislature, and later published the 'Life.' [1]

Cabot's last great piece of work was as a representative of the Nation at the Washington Conference on the Limitation of Armaments, for it was in the meeting of problems of statesmanship associated with history that he was very strong: and in this Conference his leadership was recognized.

When I was Dean of the Cambridge School, it was clear to me that until the School had larger endowment, it could not move forward. With the election of Henry B. Washburn as Dean in 1921, an increase in endowment became imperative. For several years I had evaded the hints and requests from officers and alumni to lead in a campaign, but in the summer of 1922, I became convinced that it was my duty.

The number of people interested in theological education is small, the alumni live on meagre salaries, and the title of the School, 'The Episcopal Theological School,' was calculated to throw a drabness of atmosphere over the movement.

Each campaign has its special interest and demands fresh methods. Hence we evolved this thought. Every one is interested in spiritual leadership and agrees upon its need to-day. Fortunately, the Cambridge School has sent out spiritual leaders. Our slogan, instead of being 'Episcopal Theological School,' was 'spiritual leadership': our salient fact was that of every thirty living graduates

[1] *Life of Henry Cabot Lodge*, published by Houghton Mifflin Company.

one was a bishop. Then, instead of starting our campaign in Cambridge, where the headquarters were, or in the East, we opened it on the Pacific Coast. Taking advantage of the meeting of the General Convention at Portland, Oregon, we set up a big dinner there: we had a photograph taken of the fifteen graduate bishops, and did our utmost to throw publicity back across the country to the Atlantic. This was not easy, for the object of the campaign was comparatively insignificant. I worked hard in getting up the dinner, corralling the bishops for a photograph, and sending out just the right publicity. We succeeded thereby in making a small dent upon that part of the Church which we wanted to reach. Then, coming East, we organized: others carried through the broader campaign, while I sought for individual gifts with personal calls and personal letters.

The large gifts came as usual, in response to intelligent education of individuals and the pressure of an atmosphere of general interest created through organization, dinners, conferences, and meetings. The loyal friends of the School responded finely, the alumni also; new friends were made and by the first of March, five months from our Portland dinner, the million dollars was given or pledged.

On the Commencement Day of the School, the alumni at their dinner presented Mrs. Lawrence and myself with a handsome silver bowl and plate. Boston University as well as the Cambridge School gave me during that year the degree of S.T.D.

The day of the thirtieth anniversary of my consecration, October 5, 1923, seemed to be an opportunity to tell those who had worked and worshipped with me something of my own spiritual experience.

The Diocese had invited the clergy, members of the Diocesan Convention, and some of my friends, to the service in the Cathedral, wherein was gathered a large congregation. To the preparation of the address I gave much thought, for I was well aware that parts of it touched upon sensitive subjects. I was determined, however, to be frank in telling my story, and to present my position with such clearness that I could not be misunderstood.

A day had not passed before I learned through letters and messages that the address had elements in it which would arouse opposition on the one side and gather commendation upon the other. Hence Messrs. Houghton Mifflin Company asked that they might publish it under the title of 'Fifty Years,'[1] with the result that its circulation was very large. It was also published in England.

The readers of the little book were doubtless multiplied by the advertisement given it through the sending out of a Pastoral Letter by the House of Bishops, meeting in Dallas, Texas, which controverted in strong terms some of the opinions expressed by me. The public interest in 'Fifty Years' was a great surprise to me. As I have thought over the incident, the conviction has been borne in on me that there is a real, though often unconscious, yearning on the part of the present generation for the frank and helpful expression of their elders upon subjects connected with religion and life. The younger people do not care so much for theories, principles and homilies, as for real experiences. They want to know how this or that older man or woman, whose character and intelligence they respect, really thinks and lives. And they respond quickly to such frank and real experiences. Within the last two years I have, at the request of Harvard students, not the University authorities, spoken to a number of them upon 'Real Life in the Ministry' and upon 'Personal Religion.' In each case I have talked from my own personal experience, and in each case I know from many sources that I have been helpful.

Since 1913 I have been a member of the Corporation of Harvard University, a responsible, interesting, and engrossing office. The duties are those, not of an executive, but of counsellor to the President, who is the executive.

[1] *Fifty Years*, published by Houghton Mifflin Company.

The questions coming before the meetings relate to every subject connected with the University, from the purchase or sale of a piece of real estate to the appointment of a Professor of Philosophy. Every appointment to scholarship, fellowship, or teaching office, every item of the budget, passes through the Corporation. And to the Fellows the President gives in advance his plans for future development which may not come in practical working or before the public for years; or which may call for decision then and there.

President Lowell has held consistently to the path of advance, first projected in his inaugural address. While the various Departments and Graduate Schools have increased in strength, the College of Arts has been strengthened in greater ratio. The endowment has grown from twenty-two to seventy-six millions, while the cause of true scholarship and devotion to culture and pure research have made even more rapid advances. Harvard's closest friends do not realize the amount of reserve power that is accumulating in the teaching, the enthusiasm for learning and in the prophetic outlook of the University. Until the past three years, the attention of the President and Governing Boards has been concentrated upon the spiritual and intellectual rather than the material side of development. By 1923, the University was clearly suffering for lack of material construction: every room and bit of space was overcrowded; the chemical laboratories were in lamentable condition. The freshman dormitories were almost the only evidence of recent construction: and another hall was needed there.

At the end of the summer of 1923, I came back from Bar Harbor for a winter of quiet routine. My days for high pressure and quick execution had passed. I was being released from diocesan activities.

To my dismay Dean Donham, of the Harvard Graduate School of Business Administration, asked and pressed me in rather strong terms to be the Chairman (he called it the Honorary Chairman) of a campaign for five million

dollars for the School. Loyalty to the business traditions
of my family and a conviction that this was a real missionary enterprise for the welfare of the country made me
consider his appeal. Then conditions transpired which led
the Corporation, I think for the first time in its history, to
give support to a financial campaign; for in it were now
involved the Chemical and the Art Departments to the
figures of three and two million dollars respectively. I acceded and took hold of the campaign for ten million dollars.

As has been the case before, others did the heavy work,
and there was much heavy work done. It fell to me to
have the general oversight, to advise, and speak when and
where I was told to, and present the facts to individuals
here and there who might give in large sums.

Here again the campaign had unique features. The
three objects, Business, Chemistry, and Art, had no relation to each other except that all needed buildings and
endowment. They were liable to blanket each other's
appeal; hence we united them in one larger purpose, and
created the slogan, 'An Opportunity for National Service.'
The title was an honest one, for Harvard is in many respects a national university. Its Business School, the only
graduate Business School in the country, was of national
significance; its chemical staff and research likewise; and
its Art Department in training teachers and curators was
distributing them throughout national art schools and
museums.

Our appeal, therefore, was not to the alumni, who had
within a few years given over fourteen million dollars for
endowment, but to citizens as citizens; and our campaign
methods and education were adjusted to the search for
large gifts. Indeed, the leaders in these three departments
had been carrying on a quiet process of education of a
strong constituency for several years.

In taking the chairmanship, I was entering upon the
labors of these men and gathering in the fruits of their
work. New Year's Day was on us before we could move.
We therefore made a standing start, and were in the thick

of it as soon as we began. Ignorant as I was of chemistry, art, and even business, I found myself broadcasting and speaking upon these subjects with the utmost confidence. The truth is that if one can cram under the right coaches, learn the salient points, and set them forth in clear and untechnical language, he may speak more effectively than an expert. He has the enthusiasm of a recent convert, and is not hampered by the exactness of expression and the conditions and exceptions which often clog the flow of an expert's exposition.

I soon discovered that the Committee hoped that Mr. George F. Baker, the dean of the business of this country, would give the first million, and that I was selected to see him. In spite of strong and sincere protests on my part at so treating a friend, I yielded. And again I had the oft-repeated experience that when two men meet, be they friends or strangers, who have public spirit and a large outlook, they will become more closely bound together than before, even though the one be the presenter of a cause and the other a potential giver. This experience with Mr. Baker was to me a source of real pleasure, and has been to him, I am confident, a cause for real gratification.

Early in January I suggested to him the thought of a million-dollar gift. Later he kindly talked over the subject and took the matter under consideration. Weeks passed, three months, indeed; but we had full confidence in him, knowing that whatever answer he might give, whether 'Yes' or 'No,' it would have been after careful thought.

Meanwhile, on March 20th, the interesting celebration of President Eliot's ninetieth birthday took place in Sanders Theatre, and, in behalf of the Committee, I announced $1,250,000, a large sum, but a rather small fraction of the whole ten million.

On the 21st of April, as I was on the way to New York to talk on the three subjects at a drawing-room meeting at Mrs. Harold Pratt's, a telegram was handed me at New Haven saying that Mr. Baker would call on me at my daughter Ruth's house at six o'clock. Promptly at six, Mr. Baker appeared, alone. We sat down, passed a friendly word or two, and then he said, 'Bishop, I have been thinking over the matter of the Business School. I have lost interest in your suggestion that I should give the first million. I am not going to give it or half a million either.' He paused, and then told an anecdote, while I sat tight, for he evidently had something more to say. He went on, 'If, however, by giving five million dollars I could have the privilege of building the whole School, I should like to do it. If it were one of several such schools or an old story, I should not care to do it, but my life has been given to business, and I should like to found the first Graduate School, and give a new start to better business standards. I want to do it alone. Do you think Harvard will let me?'

Mr. Baker's vision was greater than our dreams. After he had gone, Messrs. Donham and Sachs, who were within telephone call, came in, also Mr. James Byrne, and we were a cheerful group.

Early in June, Professor Sachs and I passed three days of heavy campaign work in New York. I came home well worn. Then followed several hard-pressed days in Boston, speaking at Saint Paul's School, Concord, preaching the Technology baccalaureate sermon, with confirmations and campaign meetings; and I fell out of the ranks and slipped into bed, much disappointed at losing the Commencement of the Cambridge Theological School and my boy Fred's graduation, when I was to be the preacher, Groton and St. Mark's Prize Days, the Harvard-Yale baseball game, and my class dinner.

Determined, however, to present the Campaign Committee's report at the alumni meeting on Commencement afternoon, I swung the doctor and nurse into line, and went and told the great company of the almost completed campaign and of Mr. Baker's gift. For two weeks I lingered in bed; then motored slowly to Bar Harbor, where, on the second day after our arrival, my physician determined on a mastoid operation. A telephone from Mrs.

Lawrence to Boston fortunately caught our skilful and devoted nurse, Miss Maud MacDonald, who has carried me through successive operations. She arrived Sunday morning, the surgeon from Portland at noon. By three o'clock I was on the operating table in the quiet Bar Harbor Hospital: the refrain 'Bless the Lord, O my Soul,' again came to my support. For three weeks I watched the sun swing over Newport and Green Mountains. Then followed a very happy summer on the piazza, surrounded by children and grandchildren. Friends called; President Eliot, only a few days after Mrs. Eliot's death, drove over from North-East Harbor and passed an hour. With no impulse to walk, drive, or rush about the island, one really absorbs the beauty of Frenchman's Bay, the islands, the mountains, and changing lights and clouds. I mention these things again as evidence of the compensation of illness, and the happy memories therefrom.

True to my principle that bishops should retire from their executive functions before old age creeps upon them, and thus give way to the younger generation, I began when seventy years of age to plan for the change. Bishop Babcock had been, was then, and still is, an efficient and loyal Suffragan. It was time that the Diocese elect a coadjutor who would have certain independent responsibilities and prepare to succeed me.

At the Convention of the Diocese in April, 1922, I made the canonical request for a coadjutor, relinquishing my salary, and the Reverend Doctor Charles L. Slattery, Rector of Grace Church, New York, was elected to that office. On October 31st he was consecrated in Trinity Church, Boston. It was a natural and happy selection, for Bishop Slattery had been to a good degree led to Harvard College and to the ministry by Phillips Brooks; he had been a student at Cambridge when I was Dean, and, having had pastoral experience in Minnesota as well as in the East, would bring to the Diocese wide experience as well as great native ability.

Two years and a few months sufficed for him to become familiar with the Diocese and gain the confidence of clergy and laity. Hence, after notification to the Convention of 1925, I transferred to him the full administration of the Diocese and drew out from all official relations with diocesan organizations, keeping only those which by election or by charter conditions could not be cancelled. On my birthday, the 30th of May, therefore, when I was seventy-five years old, I made the transfer.

It was a sharp wrench to me to be thus officially cut off, especially from the Cathedral and other enterprises which I had begun and nurtured, and which I had hoped to lead on to larger opportunities. I am sure, however, that when a man undertakes to retire, he should definitely leave the field free and open to others. The vigorous condition of the Diocese to-day justifies the action.

Duties and opportunities enough await me. As President of the Church Pension Fund, the Church Hymnal Corporation, and the Church Life Insurance Company; as Chairman of the Trustees of Saint Mark's and Groton Schools, of the Board of Visitors of the Episcopal Theological School, and of the Church Board of Finance, and also as a member of the Corporation of Harvard University, I have interesting work ahead, and earnestly trust that I shall have the grace to retire from these offices before inefficiency creeps on. I am keeping in a friendly and informal way my personal associations with clergy and people. There are many paths opening in Church and public service into which I should like to enter with the younger generation, to each of which I would gladly give my whole time and thought. All men, even old men, have their limitations, however. But there is one path of happy opportunity open to those who have passed their active years. Towards this I look forward. Herein may be some of the happiest and most helpful associations of my life: I mean comradeship, and sympathy and friendship with the younger generation.

Two years ago, May 19, 1924, my dear wife and I cele-

MRS. WILLIAM LAWRENCE
Portrait by Miss Putnam

brated our golden wedding day. When we were married
she was twenty-one years old, admired and beloved by all
who knew her for her grace, beauty, and strength of
character. The responsibilities of a mother of seven children, of the wife of a Rector, then Dean and Bishop,
are many and heavy, as are those of a housekeeper of a
large household and of a centre of a wide social circle.
During these fifty years she has met every event of joy and
sorrow with quiet confidence and has given me unfailing
support in my public duties, illnesses, and the general
stress of life. To my great advantage she has filled
wonderfully well an office in which many parsons' wives
fail, that of a keen and constructive critic of her husband's
sermons and writings.

To their mother the children now turn in their maturity
for guidance as intimately as in their earliest youth.

Sunday, the 18th, brought a happy prelude. In Saint
John's Memorial Chapel, Cambridge, where I was ordained
in the same month forty-nine years before, we gathered, a
grateful company, for the ordination by myself to the
diaconate of our youngest boy, Frederic: his brother
Appleton presented him, and his brother-in-law, Bishop
Slattery, preached the sermon. A year later, fifty years
after my ordination to the diaconate, we met again in All
Saints', Worcester, where Fred was curate, and ordained
him to the priesthood, Appleton again presenting him, I
preaching the sermon and ordaining.

To return, however, to the Golden Wedding. It has been
our habit on great occasions to give presents to our children and grandchildren: hence for several evenings before
the day, I had with polish and chamois been shining up
twenty-dollar gold-pieces, while Julia made little bags of
cloth of gold, tied with golden string. Spring rains and sun
had done their best for our lovely home at Readville: the
lawn was of the greenest, the gardens and shrubs in full
flower. Brothers and sisters, children and grandchildren,
nephews and nieces, great and great-great (we have one
hundred and forty-eight of them altogether), friends of

our youth and of later years, trooped through the house and onto the terrace. A box of gold on a gold plate presented by them was later transformed into a portrait of me by de Laszlo. It was the close of half a century of blessings; and the opening of another, with what a vista we know not; whether happy and serene depends upon ourselves even more than upon events.

Our great gathering-place is Bar Harbor, as was Nahant in my boyhood days. Four large cottages within a quarter of a mile hold us: and I hasten to say, lest extravagance be charged, that they were bought in times of real estate depression. Our oldest daughter, Marian, with her husband, Harold Peabody, and Gertrude, live on Eagle Lake Road. Julia and Morton Fearey with their four boys, and Appleton and Hannah with their six boys and girls, talk to each other from their near-by piazzas. Ruth and Lansing Reed with their four girls, or Elsie from Portland, Oregon, with Lewis Mills and their two boys and two girls, or Sallie and her husband, Charles Slattery, and Fred come under our roof. On Sunday mornings we all fill half the transept of the church. In the afternoon at about five o'clock, after the majority have climbed a mountain or walked the Cadillac path, we all gather at our house and sing hymns until ginger ale and cookies appear; and then, after a little wrestle and byplay, the children call 'goodnight,' and a quiet evening settles in. The full moon rises behind Schoodic across the Bay and casts its silver path from over Egg Rock Light to our open door.

THE END

INDEX

INDEX

Throughout the Index, *L.* stands for the author's name.

church in, 46, 47; raising funds for parish house, 52, 53; personal work of rector in, 53 ff.; the Sunday School, 55, 56; successive rectors of, 60.

Church of Our Saviour, Longwood, built by Amos A. and William Lawrence, 27.

Church of St. Bartholomew, London, 68, 69.

Church of St. Mary-le-Bow, London, L. speaks in, 260.

Church of Saint Saviour's, London, L. preaches at, 266.

Saint Paul's Church, Boston, its adoption as the Cathedral, 316 ff.; conditions of its acceptance, 318. And see Cathedral of Saint Paul.

Saint Paul's Church, Brockton, Mass., consecration of, on L.'s 70th birthday, 411, 412.

Saint Paul's Church, Brookline, 27.

Saint Stephen's Church, Cohasset, laying of corner stone of. See 'Cohasset Incident.'

Churchill, Julius, Bishop of Christ Church (New Zealand), 119.

Churchill, Lord Randolph, 68.

Churchill, Winston, *The Faith of Frances Crawford*, 377.

Civil War, the, boyish memories of, 7 ff.; contrast between, and the World War, 397 ff.

Clark, E. Walter, 373.

Clark, Robert, 130.

Clark, Thomas M., 61, 84, 85.

Class of 1871 at Harvard, scholarship of, 21; end of its course, 25; L. chief marshal at 25th commencement of, 211; 50th Commencement of, 413.

Class of 1880, 25th Commencement of, 225 ff.

Class-Day Tree at Harvard, 17, 18, 25.

Clergy (Episcopal), alleged socialistic tendency of, explained, 49, 50; where do they come from, 174; salaries of, 175; pensions for, 175, 176, 346, 347; proper treatment of those who have fallen, 244, 245; voluntary retirement of, now permitted, 245; former

attitude of Church toward, in relation to their financial condition, 346 ff.; General Convention of 1910 passes L.'s resolution for a commission to investigate question of their support, 350. And see Church Pension Fund.

Clerical half-fares, 44, 45.

Cleveland, Grover, and the bond issue of 1893, 252.

Coal strike of 1902, 156, 157.

Codman, Charles R., 79.

'Cohasset Incident, The,' 249, 250.

Coleridge, S. T., 62, 75.

Coles, Edward, 194.

Columbia University, gives L. degree of S.T.D. *in absentia*, 333, 334.

Connaught, Arthur, Duke of, 160.

Coolidge, Calvin, 16, 105, 384, 385, 388, 406.

Coolidge, Mrs. Calvin, 105.

Corrigan, Bishop, 391.

Cottage Farm. See Longwood.

Councilman, W. T., 283.

Courtney, Frederick, Bishop of Nova Scotia, 84, 85.

Cowles, Anna (Roosevelt), 222.

Crane, W. Murray, his character, 155, 156; at Commencement, 156; and the coal strike of 1902, 156, 157; mentioned, 220, 221.

Creighton, Mandell, at the Lambeth Conference of 1897, 126; mentioned, 123, 164.

Creighton, Mrs. Mandell, 123.

Crewe-Milnes, Robert O. A., Earl (later, Marquis) of Crewe, 265.

Crockett, Eugene A., 407.

Cromer. See Baring.

Croswell, James G., and the Brearley School, 22; his character, 22.

Crothers, Samuel M., 226.

Crowder, Enoch H., 410.

Crowninshield, Caspar, 10, 20.

Crozier, General, 406.

Cuba, in 1869, 23, 24; rehabilitation of, 154.

Cubitt, Baron Ashbourne, 120.

Cunningham, Frederic, senior, Mrs. L.'s father, 109.

Cunningham, Frederic, Jr., 109, 143.

LAWRENCE, WILLIAM.

The Lawrences and Appletons, 1, 2; the home in Longwood, 4, 5; first schooling, 5, 6; memories of the Civil War, 8 ff.; first hears Phillips Brooks preach, 11; at Mr. Dixwell's school, 12; sports and neighbors at Nahant, 12–15; family visit to Europe, 15, 16; enters Harvard, 16; his studies and teachers, 18, 19; reminiscences of Dr. Peabody, 19, 20; Hasty Pudding plays, 20, 21; tutors with Brearley, 22; beginning of Brooks's influence, 22, 23; visits Cuba, 23, 24; travels with General Sherman, 24; in Washington, 24, 25; end of his college course, 25; memories of his mother, 25, 26, and of his father, 26; the family routine, 27; his parents' wise method of dealing with their children, 27, 28, 29; his opinion of smoking, 28; his father's financial dealings with, 28, 29.

His thoughts first turned to the ministry by the life and preaching of P. Brooks, 30; interested in history, 30; the line of thought that led him to the ministry, 30, 31; goes to Andover through Brooks's advice, 32; Mark Hopkins's counsel, 33; on the religious system taught at Andover,

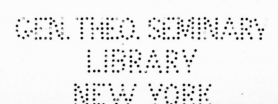